7/

Economic Theory for the Environment

NEW HORIZONS IN ENVIRONMENTAL ECONOMICS

General Editors: Wallace E. Oates, *Professor of Economics, University of Maryland, USA* and Henk Folmer, *Professor of General Economics, Wageningen University and Professor of Environmental Economics, Tilburg University, The Netherlands*

This important series is designed to make a significant contribution to the development of the principles and practices of environmental economics. It includes both theoretical and empirical work. International in scope, it addresses issues of current and future concern in both East and West and in developed and developing countries.

The main purpose of the series is to create a forum for the publication of high quality work and to show how economic analysis can make a contribution to understanding and resolving the environmental problems confronting the world in the twenty-first century.

Recent titles in the series include:

Global Emissions Trading
Key Issues for Industrialized Countries
Edited by Suzi Kerr

The Choice Modelling Approach to Environmental Valuation
Edited by Jeff Bennett and Russell Blamey

Uncertainty and the Environment
Implications for Decision Making and Environmental Policy
Richard A. Young

Global Warming and the American Economy
A Regional Assessment of Climate Change Impacts
Edited by Robert Mendelsohn

The International Yearbook of Environmental and Resource Economics 2001/2002
A Survey of Current Issues
Edited by Henk Folmer and Tom Tietenberg

Sustainable Farm Forestry in the Tropics
Social and Economic Analysis and Policy
Edited by S.R. Harrison and J.L. Herbohn

The Economic Value of Water Quality
Edited by John C. Bergstrom, Kevin J. Boyle and Gregory L. Poe

Implementing European Environmental Policy
The Impacts of Directives in the Member States
Edited by Matthieu Glachant

Economic Theory for the Environment
Essays in Honour of Karl-Göran Mäler
Edited by Bengt Kriström, Partha Dasgupta and Karl-Gustaf Löfgren

Instruments for Climate Policy
Limited versus Unlimited Flexibility
Edited by Johan Albrecht

Economic Theory for the Environment

Essays in Honour of Karl-Göran Mäler

Edited by

Bengt Kriström

Professor of Resource Economics, SLU-Umeå, Sweden

Partha Dasgupta

Frank Ramsey Professor of Economics, University of Cambridge, UK

Karl-Gustaf Löfgren

Professor of Economics, University of Umeå, Sweden

NEW HORIZONS IN ENVIRONMENTAL ECONOMICS

Edward Elgar
Cheltenham, UK • Northampton, MA, USA

Published by
Edward Elgar Publishing Limited
Glensanda House
Montpellier Parade
Cheltenham
Glos GL50 1UA
UK

Edward Elgar Publishing, Inc.
136 West Street
Suite 202
Northampton
Massachusetts 01060
USA

A catalogue record for this book
is available from the British Library

Library of Congress Cataloguing in Publication Data

Economic theory for the environment: essays in honour of Karl-Göran Mäler/edited by Bengt Kriström, Partha Dasgupta, Karl-Gustaf Löfgren.
    p. cm.—(New horizons in environmental economics)
  Includes bibliographical references and index.
    1. Environmental economics. 2. Mèler, Karl-Gèran. I. Mäler, Karl-Göran. II. Kriström, Bengt. III. Dasgupta, Partha. IV. Löfgren, Karl-Gustaf. V. Series.

HD75.6.E2956 2002
333.7—dc21   2001054306

ISBN 1 84064 887 2

Typeset by Cambrian Typesetters, Frimley, Surrey
Printed and bound in Great Britain by MPG Books Ltd, Bodmin, Cornwall

Contents

Figures

Tables

Contributors

Thomas Aronsson Department of Economics, Umeå University, Sweden.

Kenneth J. Arrow Department of Economics, Stanford University, CA, USA.

Scott Barrett Paul H. Nitze School of Advanced International Studies, Johns Hopkins University, Baltimore, MD, USA.

Lars Bergman Stockholm School of Economics, Sweden.

William Brock Department of Economics, University of Wisconsin, Madison, WI, USA.

Parkash Chander Indian Statistical Institute, New Delhi, India.

Partha Dasgupta Faculty of Economics and Politics, University of Cambridge, UK.

Aart de Zeeuw Department of Economics and CentER, Tilburg University, The Netherlands.

Anthony C. Fisher Department of Agricultural and Resource Economics, University of California at Berkeley, CA, USA.

Henk Folmer Wageningen University, The Netherlands.

Ing-Marie Gren Department of Economics, Swedish University of Agricultural Sciences, Uppsala, Sweden and Beijer International Institute of Ecological Economics, Royal Swedish Academy of Sciences, Stockholm, Sweden.

W. Michael Hanemann Department of Agricultural and Resource Economics, University of California at Berkeley, CA, USA.

Geoffrey Heal Columbia Business School, Columbia University, New York, USA.

Per-Olov Johansson Department of Economics, Stockholm School of Economics, Sweden.

Bengt Kriström Department of Forest Economics, SLU-Umeå, Sweden.

Chuan-Zhong Li Department of Economics, University of Dalarna, Borlänge, Sweden.

Karl-Gustaf Löfgren Department of Economics, Umeå University, Sweden.

Charles Perrings Environmental Department, University of York, UK.

Clifford S. Russell Vanderbilt Institute for Public Policy Studies, Vanderbilt University, Nashville, TN, USA.

Domenico Siniscalco University of Torino and Fondazione ENI Enrico Mattei, Milan, Italy.

Tore Söderqvist Beijer International Institute of Ecological Economics, Royal Swedish Academy of Sciences, Stockholm, Sweden.

Robert M. Solow Department of Economics, Massachusetts Institute of Technology, Cambridge, MA, USA.

David A. Starrett Department of Economics, Stanford University, CA, USA.

Henry Tulkens CORE, Université Catholique de Louvain, Louvain-la-Neuve, Belgium.

Hirofumo Uzawa Research Center on Global Warming, RICF, Japan Development Bank, Tokyo, Japan.

Jean-Pascal van Ypersele ASTR and Department of Physics, Université Catholique de Louvain, Louvain-la-Neuve, Belgium.

Pierre von Mouche Wageningen University, The Netherlands.

Stephane Willems Organization for Economic Cooperation and Development (OECD), Paris, France.

Anastasios Xepapadeas Department of Economics, University of Crete, Greece.

Jinhua Zhao Department of Economics, Iowa State University, Ames, IA, USA.

Introduction*

Bengt Kriström

I should like to begin by noting that the compilation of this book has been an easy task. Everyone we contacted in this matter was truly enthusiastic about the whole idea and vigorously supported it. It is quite common that a Festschrift is compiled by the students of the professor in question, and this is, to some extent, also true here. In one way or another, we are all Karl-Göran Mäler's students. His contributions have in many ways served to define the shoulders of knowledge on which we stand when exploring our subjects further. Paul Samuelson once said that the only coin worth having was the appreciation of one's peers. With Samuelson's currency, Mäler is a very rich man, indeed, not only because the coins come, so to speak, from social scientists but also, for example, from natural scientists.

Mäler's work has been a mainstay of the frontiers of environmental economics for more than three decades, in both a stock and a flow sense. This is a remarkable achievement in itself. I certainly wish I knew the secret behind this, besides the usual formula: to work hard and to have exceptional powers. But I think we need more than this. Richard Feynman, one of the outstanding scientists of the last century, once said:

> 'With more knowledge comes a deeper, more wonderful mystery, luring one on to penetrate deeper still. Never concerned that the answer may prove disappointing, with pleasure and confidence we turn over each new stone to find unimagined strangeness leading on to more wonderful questions and mysteries – certainly a great adventure!' (Feynman, 1988)

This kind of passion for exploring the unknown is, to me, a hallmark of the exceptional scientist.

---

* Many of the chapters in this Festschrift were presented at the Karl-Göran Mäler Symposium, held in conjunction with the Environmental and Development Economics (EDE)-conference at the Royal Swedish Academy of Sciences, 6–8 September 2000. What follows are essentially the introductory remarks used to provide the setting for the book chapters. I acknowledge useful input from V. Kerry Smith and my co-editors. Because I did not include all their suggestions for changes, any remaining errors are my own.

BACKGROUND

It is useful here to provide a brief summary of Mäler's background. His academic career began in 1958 with the study of mathematics at Stockholm University, and he obtained a BSc degree in 1962 (subjects studied included statistics, economics and political science). He did his military service in 1963, and subsequently he was appointed junior lecturer at the Stockholm School of Economics in 1964. His Licentiate thesis on optimal growth was defended in 1968 (the Licentiate is a Swedish degree, somewhere between a Master's and a Doctorate. At that time, the requirements for a Licentiate thesis were probably more stringent than for a PhD today). In 1969, Erik Dahmén, in some ways the father of environmental economics in Sweden, and Assar Lindbeck, obtained a grant from the Riksbank foundation to do research in resource economics. This period also marked the beginning of Mäler's entry into environmental economics. A couple of years of intensive international activity followed. A Ford Foundation Grant enabled Mäler to visit the Massachusetts Institute of Technology and Stanford in 1969–70. A successful visit to Resources for the Future, Washington, DC, in 1971, included the completion of his thesis that autumn. The thesis was defended in 1973 and published in 1974 by Johns Hopkins University Press. It has long been out of print, but remains one of the classics of environmental economics. That same year, Mäler was promoted to associate professor at the Stockholm School of Economics, and to full professor the following year. In 1975 he was also a guest professor at the University of New Mexico. In 1989 he was a World Bank guest professor, and since 1991 he has been director at the Beijer Institute of Ecological Economics. Much more could be said about his background than has been included in this brief sketch, but a more detailed biography must be left to others. Here, we shall discuss some of his contributions.

CONTRIBUTIONS

The General Equilibrium Perspective

The general equilibrium perspective is one of the salient feature of Mäler's work. The thesis opens by putting the environment in the general equilibrium context, thereby providing a badly needed structure for the analysis of environment–economy interactions. Prior to Mäler's work, general equilibrium concerned the multiple interconnections between markets. His framework recognized that economic agents' activities generate impacts on the environment and there are feedback loops. That is, general equilibrium includes market and non-market interactions. Moreover, these non-market interactions prevent a competitive equilibrium from providing an efficient allocation of resources.

While the early work on general equilibrium theory was theoretical, the interest in applying it came early. His PhD student Lars Bergman presented an early application of computable general equilibrium modelling with environmental perspectives in 1977. Several later contributions have clear connections with the general equilibrium perspective. The pioneering work on resource accounting is obviously relevant here. Mäler's 1991 paper lays out an accounting system based on an intertemporal general equilibrium model.

The works on game theory, in particular the acid rain game, are also relevant here, since they are in some ways related to the ideas underlying equilibrium theory. In addition, interdisciplinary work with ecologists has always been motivated by exploring links between the economy and the environment; the pivotal idea which Mäler introduced in his 1974 book.

The Weak Complementarity Idea

In the autumn of 1969, watching a long-forgotten television programme somewhere in the United States, Mäler was contemplating an idea on valuation, put forward by Joe Stephens, concerning water quality and lake recreation (1966). The paper by Stephens was empirical. Mäler wanted to know under what conditions one could usefully infer something about the value of environmental quality, by looking at a related market for a private good, say travel expenditures. The conditions turn out to be a special form of complementarity between the private and the environmental good. Because it was not the standard strong sort of complementarity that was needed, the conditions were called 'weak complementarity'. The basis for this idea came from the duality methods that Peter Diamond was teaching, in 1969, in a now classic course on public finance. Franklin M. Fisher and Karl Shell use the same concept in discussing price indexes for quality change but miss the full significance of its revelation principles. The idea of weak complementarity is of extraordinary importance for empirical work. Hardly a day passes without some application of weak complementarity being made.

Cooperation

Mäler's attitude towards cooperation within and across sciences seems to have been borrowed from John Stuart Mill, who said that it was hardly possible to overrate the value of placing human beings in contact with persons dissimilar to themselves, or with modes of thought and action unlike those with which they were familiar and that such communication had always been one of the primary sources of progress.

It is no surprise that the Beijer Institute of Ecological Economics is Mäler's brainchild, and that the continuing success of the institute is in no small measure a product of his belief in the value of cooperation in science.

Teaching

Mäler is an excellent teacher, perhaps with a more flexible attitude towards the role of schedules than most of us. In recent years, he has been deeply involved in capacity building in developing countries, by giving a series of short courses in various, invariably rather pleasant locations, around the developing world. This is an investment in human capital with potentially very high returns.

CONCLUSION

Most of us came to environmental economics because of a deep appreciation for environmental amenities. Nature in all its varied dimensions enriches our lives. When Mäler began his research in environmental economics, few would have believed that such amenities could have a place in the 'dismal science'. Within economics, beauty was found in the skill of the analyst in capturing the essential insights that stem from how choices respond to incentives. The honour of a Festschrift has, to this point, been limited to the finest of conventional economists – scholars such as Paul Samuelson. Indeed, at the Brown–Solow Festschrift party in honour of Samuelson it is reported that 'Franco Modigliani rose, pointed his finger towards Samuelson and said: "you . . . have enriched our lives" '. Karl-Göran Mäler has shown how the beauty that enriches our everyday lives is an integral part of Samuelson's traditional economic analysis. Surely we are 'doubly enriched'.

REFERENCES

Feynman, Richard P. (1988), 'The Value of Science', in *What do You Care What Other People Think: Further Adventures of a Curious Character*, Ralph Leighton (ed.), New York: W.W. Norton & Company, pp. 240–48.
Stevens, Joe (1966), 'Recreation benefits from water pollution control', *Water Resources Research*, **2**, pp. 167–82.

1. An example of dynamic control of negative stock externalities

Kenneth J. Arrow

1   INTRODUCTION

In this chapter, I want to carry through a rigorous analysis of the dynamic control of a simple case of negative externalities arising from stocks. As Starrett showed in his classic paper (1972), negative externalities imply non-concavity of the benefit function. Non-concavity in turn implies that the first-order conditions for an optimum are not sufficient. In a dynamic context, where the policy in each period leads to accumulation of stocks, the first-order conditions are those of the Pontryagin (Pontryagin et al. 1962) principle. Just as in a static optimization problem, there will in general be several solutions, all of which satisfy the Pontryagin conditions but only one of which will correspond to the global maximum.

This fact has two important implications. One is that the optimal solution will involve specialization in some sense. Concretely, with negative externalities, it may be best to abandon one area to the negative externality, say pollution, rather than try to spread the externality over all areas in some balanced way, as we would expect from analysis of the concave case.

The second is methodological; the existence of a supporting price system, which is what the Pontryagin principle supplies, is not at all sufficient for an optimum. It may support even the worst possible outcome. This probably has implications for the foundation of the principle of net national product (where 'net' includes allowance for the depletion of environmental stocks), which is based on the Pontryagin principle (see Dasgupta and Mäler (2000) and the references to earlier work found there).

2   THE MODEL

I assume an activity which yields benefits and which can be carried out in either of two locales. In either locale, it creates a waste product in proportion to the activity there. The waste products accumulate without decay. Each stock produces a negative externality which increases with the stock but is, however, bounded. As Starrett showed, this function cannot be convex. It may be assumed concave everywhere. The aim is to optimize the net benefits over time, that is, the discounted sum of net benefits. The variables are the activity levels at the two locales.

To state the model more formally, there are two activities with levels x and y. The activities are perfect substitutes in direct benefits and in production. They are constrained by some scarce resource, so that their sum has an upper bound. Without loss of generality, it can be assumed that the feasible set of activities is given by,

$$x \geq 0,\ y \geq 0,\ x + y \leq 1. \tag{1.1}$$

By the previous assumptions, the benefit derived from the activities is a function of the sum of the two activity levels, $x + y$. For simplicity, I assume this function is linear, so without loss of generality the direct benefit from the activities is, $x + y$.

The two activities generate stocks of wastes, denoted by X and Y, respectively. By suitable choice of units, we can say,

$$dX/dt = x,\ dY/dt = y. \tag{1.2}$$

Each stock generates a (negative) benefit, a function of the stock level. For simplicity, I assume the function, f, is the same in both locales. From the considerations above, we have,

$$f' < 0,\ f'' > 0,\ f \text{ bounded from below.} \tag{1.3}$$

That is, stocks are damaging at the margin, but the marginal damage is decreasing, so much so that the total damage is bounded. We may think of dumping wastes into two streams; if the damage is to fish, then the worst that can happen is their complete elimination.

In this model, then, the felicity at any moment of time is,

$$U = x + y + f(X) + f(Y). \tag{1.4}$$

The control problem is to maximize the infinite integral of discounted felicities.

$$W\,[x(t),\ y(t)] = \int_0^\infty e^{-\rho t} U(t)\ dt, \tag{1.5}$$

subject to the dynamic constraints (1.2) and the flow constraints (1.1).

Remark The choice of strategies is confined to piecewise continuous functions.

The current-value Hamiltonian is,

$$H = x + y + f(X) + f(Y) + p_X x + p_Y y, \tag{1.6}$$

where p_x and p_y are the accounting prices for the stocks, X, Y, respectively. (They are, of course, negative in this example.)

3 PRELIMINARY ANALYSIS

In this section, a few basic implications of the model for its control-theoretic analysis will be derived for use in the later sections.

The Pontryagin principle tells us that the choice of x and y should maximize (1.6) subject to the feasibility constraints (1.1). The following inferences are obvious:

$$p_X > p_Y \text{ implies } y = 0, \ p_Y > p_X \text{ implies } x = 0, \tag{1.7a}$$

$$\max (p_X, p_Y) > -1 \text{ implies } x + y = 1, \tag{1.7b}$$

$$\max (p_X, p_Y) < -1 \text{ implies } x = 0 \text{ and } y = 0, \tag{1.7c}$$

with the obvious ranges of indeterminacy when equalities hold in the above. I am mostly interested in the cases where $x + y = 1$ and will occasionally specify conditions under which, correspondingly, $\max (p_x, p_y) > -1$.

The accounting prices evolve according the differential equations,

$$dp_X/dt = \rho \, p_X - (\partial H/\partial X) = \rho \, p_X - f'(X), \tag{1.8a}$$

and,

$$dp_Y/dt = \rho \, p_Y - f'(Y). \tag{1.8b}$$

If we take the transversality condition into account, we see that,

$$p_X(t) = \int_0^\infty e^{-\rho u} f'[X(t + u)] \, du. \tag{1.9}$$

To simplify notation, it will be convenient to multiply (1.9) and similar formulae below by ρ. The function, $\rho \exp (-\rho u)$ is everywhere positive and integrates out to 1, so that it is a weighting function. For any function, $g(t)$, define,

$$M_\rho[g(t)] = \rho \int_0^\infty e^{-\rho t} g(t)\, dt, \tag{1.10}$$

which is then an average of the function, $g(t)$, with exponentially declining weights. Then, (1.9) can be written,

$$\rho\, p_X(t) = M_\rho\{f'[X(t + u)]\}, \tag{1.11}$$

and correspondingly,

$$\rho\, p_Y(t) = M_\rho\{f'[Y(t + u)]\}. \tag{1.12}$$

Since f' is increasing, it follows from (1.11) and (1.12) that,

$$\begin{array}{l} p_X(t) \text{ and } p_Y(t) \text{ are non-decreasing and increasing} \\ \text{when } x > 0 \text{ (respectively, } y > 0). \end{array} \tag{1.13}$$

As can be seen from (1.7a), it will be convenient at some points to consider the difference between the two accounting prices,

$$q = p_X - p_Y. \tag{1.14}$$

By subtracting (1.8b) from (1.8a), it can be seen that,

$$dq/dt = \rho\, q - \{f'[X(t)] - f'[Y(t)]\}, \tag{1.15}$$

and therefore,

$$\rho\, q(t) = M_\rho\{f'[X(t + u)] - f'[Y(t + u)]\}. \tag{1.16}$$

We assume, of course, that there might have been some activity before the optimization begins, so that $X(0)$ and $Y(0)$ are given.

4   OPTIMAL PATHS WITH SPECIALIZATION: DIRECT ANALYSIS

Intuitively, the optimal path under non-convexity is one in which there is only one activity carried on. Further, we would expect that the activity chosen is that in which the marginal stock-induced damage is the least, which is that in which the initial stock is the greater. This intuition is correct, but it seems to take some argument.

First, take as given the total amount of activity at any time, that is, $x(t) + y(t) = z(t)$, $z(t)$ given. Let $Z(t)$ be the cumulative integral of $z(t)$. Then, from (1.2),

$$X(t) + Y(t) = X(0) + Y(0) + Z(t), \quad X(t) \geq X(0), \quad Y(t) \geq Y(0). \qquad (1.17)$$

From (1.4) and (1.5), we wish to maximize,

$$\int_0^\infty e^{-\rho t} z(t) \, dt + \int_0^\infty e^{-\rho t} \{f[X(t)] + f[Y(t)]\} \, dt, \qquad (1.18)$$

subject to (1.2). The first term is taken as given for the time being. Since (1.2) implies (1.17), the maximum of (1.18) subject to (1.2) cannot be larger than the maximum subject to (1.17). But the maximum of (1.18) subject to (1.17) can be obtained by maximizing the integrand subject to (1.17) for each t. Since the function f is convex, the maximum is obtained at an extreme. That is, at the maximum, either $X(t) = X(0)$. $Y(t) = Y(0) + Z(t)$, or $X(t) = X(0) + Z(t)$, $Y(t) = Y(0)$. As can easily be seen, the second yields the higher value of the integrand if,

$$f[X(0) + Z(t)] - f[X(0)] > f[Y(0) + Z(t)] - f[Y(0)],$$

or,

$$\int_0^{Z(t)} f'[X(0) + u] \, du > \int_0^{Z(t)} f'[Y(0) + u] \, du.$$

Since f' is increasing, by (1.3), the last holds if $X(0) > Y(0)$.

If $X(0) > Y(0)$, then the policy $X(t) = X(0) + Z(t)$, $Y(t) = Y(0)$ optimizes (1.18) subject to (1.17). But it is easy to see that this policy can be implemented by a choice of the instruments, $x(t)$, $y(t)$; simply let $x(t) = z(t)$, $y(t) = 0$, for all t.

If $X(0) > Y(0)$, then the policy, $x(t) = z(t)$, $y(t) = 0$ is optimal (for the original problem), given that

$$x(t) + y(t) = z(t) \text{ for all } t. \qquad (1.19)$$

Remark A careful review of the argument leading to (1.19) shows that the conclusion remains valid if $X(0) = Y(0)$. I return to this point later.

It is now necessary to show that the optimal policy is extreme, that is, $x(t) = z(t)$ is either 1 for all t or 0 for all t. First, it will be shown that $z(t)$ must be 0 or 1 for each t. If (1.19) is substituted into (1.18), the optimal policy is that path, $z(t)$, which maximizes.

$$\int_0^\infty e^{-\rho t} \{z(t) + f[X(0) + Z(t)]\} \, dt + \int_0^\infty e^{-\rho t} f[Y(0)] \, dt. \qquad (1.20)$$

The last term is a constant and may be ignored. Suppose that $0 < z(t) < 1$ for some t. Since we are considering only piecewise continuous policies, there is an interval, $< a, b >$, in which $0 < z(t) < 1$. Consider now an alternative policy, $z(t, h)$, which changes the activity level in $< a, b >$ by a constant, h. For all $|h|$ sufficiently small, $z(t, h)$ is a feasible policy, satisfying (1.1):

$$z(t, h) = z(t), \text{ for } t < a \text{ or } t > b,$$
$$= z(t) + h, \text{ for } a \leq t \leq b.$$

If $Z(t, h)$ is the integral of $z(t, h)$ with respect to t, where $Z(0, h) = 0$, then,

$$Z(t, h) = Z(t), \, t < a,$$
$$= Z(t) + h \, (t - a), \, a \leq t \leq b,$$
$$= Z(t) + h \, (b - a), \, t > b.$$

Replace $z(t)$ by $z(t, h)$ in the maximand, (1.20), and delete the last, constant, term:

$$F(h) = \int_0^a e^{-\rho t} \{z(t) + f[X(0) + Z(t)]\} \, dt$$
$$+ \int_a^b e^{-\rho t} \{z(t) + h + f[X(0) + Z(t) + h \, (t - a)]\} \, dt$$
$$+ \int_b^\infty e^{-\rho t} \{z(t) + f[X(0) + Z(t) + h \, (b - a)]\} \, dt.$$

If $z(t)$ is optimal, then $F(h)$ must be maximized at $h = 0$, and therefore $F''(0) \leq 0$. But if the above expression is differentiated twice, it is seen that,

$$F''(0) = \int_a^b e^{-\rho t} f''[X(0) + Z(t)] \, (t - a)^2 \, dt$$
$$+ \int_a^\infty e^{-\rho t} f''[X(0) + Z(t)] \, (b - a)^2 \, dt > 0,$$

a contradiction. Therefore, it cannot be that $0 < z(t) < 1$ anywhere.

Suppose that the optimal policy, $z(t) = 0$, over some interval. Then $X(t)$ and $Y(t)$ have the same values at the end of the interval as at the beginning. Since the optimal policy depends only on initial conditions, it must be optimal to continue the policy, $z(t) = 0$, for a further interval. Hence, if $z(t') = 0$ for some t', $z(t) = 0$ for all $t \geq t'$. Therefore, the optimal policy must have the form, $z(t) = 1, 0 \leq t \leq T, z(t) = 0$ for $t > T$, for some T, which may, of course, be 0 or infinity. The maximand for such a policy is,

$$G(T) = \int_0^T e^{-\rho t} \{1 + f[X(0) + t]\} \, dt + \int_T^\infty e^{-\rho t} f[X(0) + T] \, dt.$$

Then,

$$G'(T) = e^{-\rho T} \{1 + \rho^{-1} f'[X(0) + T]\},$$

$$G''(T) = e^{-\rho T} \{-\rho - f'[X(0) + T] + \rho^{-1} f''[X(0) + T]\}.$$

If the function $G(T)$ has a maximum for any finite $T > 0$, then it is necessary that $G'(T) = 0$, $G''(T) \geq 0$. But if $G'(T) = 0$, it must be that,

$$1 + \rho^{-1} f'[X(0) + T] = 0,$$

and then it would follow that $G''(T) > 0$. Hence, $G(T)$ is maximized at either 0 or infinity. Therefore, from (1.19), the optimum policy must be either

$$x(t) = y(t) = 0, \text{ for all } t, \text{ or } x(t) = 1, y(t) = 0, \text{ for all } t. \tag{1.21}$$

Which is optimal can, of course, be determined by calculating the maximand, W, as given in (1.5), for each of the two policies. Then, the condition that the policy, $x(t) = 1$, $y(t) = 0$, for all t, is optimal is easily to be seen that,

$$1 + M_\rho \{f[X(0) + t]\} - f[X(0)] > 0. \tag{1.22}$$

Theorem 1 If $X(0) > Y(0)$, then the optimal policy is, $x(t) = 1$, $y(t) = 0$, for all t, if (1.22) holds; if the inequality in (1.22) is reversed, then the optimal policy is, $x(t) = y(t) = 0$ for all t.

Remark In accordance with the Remark following (1.19), it is clear that the characterization of optimal policies in Theorem 1 remains true if $X(0) = Y(0)$. Suppose (1.22) holds. Then clearly, by symmetry, the policy, $x(t) = 0$, $y(t) = 1$, is optimal, so that there are two optimal policies, though intermediate policies are not optimal.

5   PONTRYAGIN PATHS WITH SPECIALIZATION

From the Pontryagin analysis, the optimal path of the last section must be supported by costate variables (accounting prices). For either of the paths described in Theorem 1, $Y(t) = Y(0)$, for all t. Since $X(0) > Y(0)$, by hypothesis, $X(t) > Y(0)$ for all t, and therefore $f'[X(t)] > f'[Y(t)]$, for all t, so that, $M_\rho \{f'[X(t) + u)] - f'[Y(t + u)]\} > 0$. From (1.16), $\rho \, q(t) > 0$, so that, $q(t) > 0$, for all t. From (1.7a), it follows that $y(t) = 0$, for all t.

To support a policy in which $x(t) = 1$, for all t, it suffices that $p_X(t) > -1$, for all

t, by (1.7b). From (1.13), this holds if and only if, $p_X(0) > -1$. From (1.11), this is equivalent to the statement, $M_\rho\{f'[X(0) + t]\} > -\rho$, since, $X(t) = X(0) + t$, under the policy, $x(t) = 1$, for all t. From the definition of M_ρ and integration by parts,

$$M_\rho\{f'[X(0) + t]\} = \rho \int_0^\infty e^{-\rho t} f'[X(0) + t]\, dt$$

$$= \rho\{e^{-\rho t} f[X(0) + t] \,|_0^{\text{infinity}} + \rho \int_0^\infty e^{-\rho t} f[X(0) + t]\, dt\}$$

$$= -\rho\, f[X(0)] + \rho\, M_\rho\{f[X(0) + t]\},$$

and therefore, for an x-specialized policy,

$$p_X(0) > -1 \text{ if and only if, } 1 + M_\rho\{f[X(0) + t]\} > f[X(0)], \qquad (1.23)$$

that is, if and only if (1.22) holds.

Theorem 2 If $X(0) > Y(0)$, then the optimal path is a Pontryagin path and is supported by the corresponding accounting prices.

So far, there are no problems. Consider, however the case, $X(0) = Y(0)$. Clearly, all the above arguments apply, as may be easily checked. Thus, if (1.22) holds, then the policy of complete specialization in the x-activity is optimal and is supported on a Pontryagin path. But because of the symmetry between the two activities, it is equally true that complete specialization in the y-activity is also optimal and is supported by a Pontryagin path. However, the supporting paths are different. Indeed, the accounting price of the stock generated by the unused activity is constant, whichever one it is. (The accounting price of the stock generated by the activity in use is increasing.) Thus the accounting value of a given stock depends on its future use.

There is no contradiction in this two-valuedness, but it shows that there are difficulties in the non-concave case. (If all payoffs were concave, the accounting prices would have unique values.) Now, suppose that (1.22) holds, and consider the policy of complete x-specialization. As has been seen, this policy is supported by a Pontryagin path so long as, $X(0) \geq Y(0)$. Even when equality holds, it is still true that, $q(0)$ is strictly greater than 0. Indeed, from (1.16), with $t = 0$,

$$\rho\, q(0) = M_\rho\{f'[X(0) + t] - f'[Y(0)].$$

Consider this expression as a function of $X(0)$. Since f' is increasing, $\rho q(0)$ is positive for $X(0) = Y(0)$, and it must still be positive, by continuity, for $X(0) < Y(0)$ but sufficiently close. Similarly, the condition (1.22), if it holds strictly, remains valid for some range of $X(0) < Y(0)$, and therefore, by (1.23), it remains true that $p_x(0) > -1$ for that range.

What this argument shows is that x-specialization is a Pontryagin path for a range of value $X(0) < Y(0)$. But Theorem 1 (with x and y interchanged) implies that y-specialization is optimal.

Theorem 3   If (1.22) holds with $X(0)$ replaced by $Y(0)$, then for $X(0)$ in some range below $Y(0)$, x-specialization is supported by a Pontryagin path although y-specialization is optimal.

This illustrates the limitation of the Pontryagin principle under conditions of non-concavity.

6   PONTRYAGIN PATHS WITH COMPLETE NON-SPECIALIZATION

It has been seen that non-concavity of the problem studied in this chapter implies that the optimal policy is necessarily completely specialized (unless it is optimal to retrain from all activity). Can a non-specialized path be supported as a Pontryagin path?

Suppose that both activities are engaged in at some point of time. Since attention has been restricted to piecewise continuous paths, there must be some interval $< a, b >$ in which both $x(t) > 0$ and $y(t) > 0$. Then, from (1.7a) and (1.14), it must be that $q(t) = 0$ over $< a, b >$. Then of course $dq/dt = 0$ over the interval. From (1.15), it follows that $f'[X(t)] = f'[Y(t)]$, and therefore, $X(t) = Y(t)$, over $< a, b >$. Then, $X(a) = Y(a)$, $X(b) = Y(b)$, and, by differentiation, $x(t) = y(t) > 0$, $a \leq t \leq b$.

Since $x(a) > 0$, $y(a) > 0$, it must be that $p_X(a) \geq -1$, $p_Y(a) \geq -1$, by (1.7c) (recall that $p_X(a) = p_Y(a)$, since $q(a) = 0$). Then from (1.13), it must be that $p_X(t) = p_Y(t) > -1$, for $a < t \leq b$, and therefore, $x(t) + y(t) = 1$, by (1.7b). Hence, along this Pontryagin path, $x(t) = y(t) = 1/2$, $a < t \leq b$.

It will now be shown that if non-specialization holds in some interval, it must hold for the entire path. Suppose $< a, b >$ is a maximal interval in which both activities are carried out at positive levels. Since $p_X(b) = p_Y(b) > -1$, it must be that $x(t) + y(t) = 1$ in some right-hand interval of b and therefore, by assumption, either $x(t) = 1$ in some right-hand interval of b or $y(t) = 1$ in some right-hand interval of b. I show that the first assumption leads to a contradiction; the argument for the second is similar.

As already seen, $q(b) = 0$, and $dq/dt \big|_b = 0$. Under the assumption that $x(t) = 1$ to the right of b, $X(t) = X(b) + (t - b)$ and $Y(t) = Y(b)$ for t slightly greater than b. Substitute into (1.15), the equation governing the evolution of q:

$$dq/dt = \rho \, q + f'[Y(b)] - f'[X(b) + t - b].$$

Since the right-hand side is right-differentiable, differentiate the above with respect to t, and evaluate at $t = b$.

$$d^2q/dt^2 \,|_b = -f''[X(b)] < 0.$$

Therefore, $q(t) < 0$ in a right-hand neighborhood of b, and so $x(t) = 0$ there, a contradiction.

The assumption that there is an upper bound to the non-specialization interval leads to a contradiction. By a similar argument, the lower bound to that interval cannot be positive.

Theorem 4   If $X(0) = Y(0)$, then the path of complete non-specialization, $x(t) = y(t) = 1/2$ for all t is supported as a Pontryagin path. No other non-specialization path is possible, not even for some interval.

In a way, this result is reassuring. The path of Theorem 4 is clearly about as bad a path as is possible. But it can be supported only for very special initial conditions, and only a very special path can be so supported.

7   PONTRYAGIN PATHS WITH SPECIALIZATION IN ALTERNATIVE ACTIVITIES

As a last example of the variety of possible Pontryagin paths in the problem being studied, it is shown that it is possible to support a path in which specialization takes place in one activity for a while, then in the other. Assume that $X(0) > Y(0)$.

The proposed policy is to specialize in the y-activity for an interval then in the x-activity forever after, that is, for some $T > 0$, $x(t) = 0$, $y(t) = 1$, for $t < T$, and $x(t) = 1$, $y(t) = 0$, for $t > T$. We need to have, $q(t) < 0$ for $t < T$, $q(t) > 0$ for $t > T$, and, of course, $q(T) = 0$. For the proposed policy, $X(t) = X(0)$, for $0 \le t \le T$, $= X(0) + t - T$ for $t > T$, and $Y(t) = Y(0) + t$ for $0 \le t \le T$, $= Y(0) + T$ for $t > T$. Substitute in (1.16), the closed-form expression for $\rho q(t)$.

$$\rho\, q(T) = M_\rho\{f'[X(0) + t - T] - f'[Y(0) + T]\} \\ = M_\rho\{f'[X(0) + u]\} - f'[Y(0) + T]\} = 0, \tag{1.24}$$

which determines T. For $t > T$,

$$\rho\, q(t) = M_\rho\{f'[X(0) + t - T + u]\} - f'[Y(0) + T].$$

Since f' is increasing, the first term on the right-hand side is increasing in t, so that, from (1.24), $q(t) > 0$ for $t > T$.

To show that $q(t) < 0$ for $t < T$ is slightly more complicated, and I abbreviate the details. I introduce a new concept and corresponding notation, the ρ-*mean for a bounded interval*,

$$M_\rho\{g(t) \mid a\} = \gamma(\rho, a) \int_0^a e^{-\rho t} g(t) \, dt.$$

where,

$$\gamma(\rho, a) = \rho/[1 - e^{-\rho a}].$$

(This constant ensures that the weights integrate to 1 over the interval $< 0. a >$.) Then, for $t < T$, it works out, with the aid of (1.24), that,

$$\gamma(\rho, T - t) \, q(t) = f'[X(0)] - M_\rho\{f'[Y(0) + t + u] \mid T - t\}. \tag{1.25}$$

From the differential equation governing $q(t)$, (1.15), it is seen that,

$$d\,[e^{-\rho t} q(t)]/dt = [e^{-\rho t}]\,\{f'[Y(0)] + t] - f'[X(0)]\} \text{ for } t < T.$$

Since $Y(0) < X(0)$, while $Y(0) + T > X(0)$, it must be that $e^{-\rho t} q(t)$ decreases as t increases from 0 and then increases to its value at $t = T$, which is 0. Therefore, $q(t) < 0$, for all $t < T$, if and only if $q(0) < 0$. From (1.25), that is equivalent to the statement,

$$f'[X(0)] < M_\rho\{f'[Y(0) + u] \mid T\}. \tag{1.26}$$

Now, the right-hand side is an exponentially weighted average of the values of f' $[Y(0) + t]$, as t varies from 0 to T. Note that, from (1.24), $Y(0) + T$ is determined by $X(0)$ and also is greater than $X(0)$. Therefore, (1.26) is sure to hold if $Y(0)$ is not too much smaller than $X(0)$, since f' is increasing.

Thus a path in which the activity with the smaller stock value is specialized in for a while, with a subsequent switch to the other activity, can be supported by a path of accounting prices. Although the analysis gets messier, the argument can be extended to find cases where there are several alternations.

To complete the analysis, it would be necessary to show that a positive value for at least one activity can be supported at all times, that is, that $p_y(t) > -1$ for $t < T$, $p_x(t) > -1$ for $t > T$. I omit the tedious details but simply remark that the condition, $f'[Y(0)] > -\rho$, is sufficient though stronger than needed.

8 CONCLUDING REMARKS

This chapter has had two themes. One is policy relevant and is based on the results contained in Section 4. Under a common kind of stock externality, non-concavities occur. In those cases, it is best to specialize, to concentrate the adverse consequences to achieve whatever benefits accrue.

The other theme is methodological. Since the Pontryagin principle (or parallel methods) is so basic both to determining dynamic controls for individual environmental problems and to the national income accounting framework for judging the macro consequences of economic behavior, it will, I hope, contribute something to understanding the misleading possibilities of this method in the frequently occurring non-concave situations.

REFERENCES

Dasgupta, P. and K.-G. Mäler (2000), 'Net national product, wealth, and social well-being', *Environmental and Development Economics*, **5**: 69–93.
Pontryagin, L.S. and V.G. Boltyanskii, R.V. Gamkrelidze and E.F. Mischenko (1962), *The Mathematical Theory of Optimal Processes*, New York: Interscience.
Starrett, D. (1972), 'Fundamental nonconvexities in the theory of externalities', *Journal of Economic Theory*, **4**: 180–99.

2. On optimal R&D for a patent race with uncertain duration

Thomas Aronsson, Per-Olov Johansson and Karl-Gustaf Löfgren

1 INTRODUCTION

In this chapter we consider a patent race where independent firms (or research laboratories) compete in order to develop a 'winner takes all' innovation. We look at the optimal strategy for the individual firm, the non-cooperative Nash equilibrium, and how to design policy instruments such that the Nash equilibrium replicates the socially optimal resource allocation.

There are several distinct features that distinguish this chapter from the patent races considered by Bhattacharya and Mookherjee (1986), Dasgupta and Stiglitz (1980), Gilbert and Shapiro (1990), Grossman and Shapiro (1986), Gruver (1991), Klette and de Meza (1986), Loury (1979), Scherer (1967) and Tirole (1988). First, previous authors typically consider research and development (R&D) costs as instantaneous, whereas, in our model, a firm builds up a stock of R&D capital. Instead, a research intensity parameter, which captures research intensity at each instant, plays the same role as the constant R&D cost in previous studies. We use the necessary conditions for an optimal control to highlight the difference between flow expenditures on R&D and changes in the stock of R&D capital. Second, in our model the hazard is a function of (among other things) the stock of R&D capital.[1] This is an important generalization, since the magnitude of a firm's R&D capital is central for its chances to win a patent race. Building up competence is not a short-run business, which implies that it may be misleading to assume that a firm can buy competence in the spot market. Third, we use the (dynamic) envelope theorem in order to derive the effects on the value of a firm arising from parametric changes in the research intensity.

2 THE MODEL

In order to focus on the patent race issue, we assume that the firm's instantaneous costs at time s, $c(s)$, are a function of the firm's R&D stock and its investment in such capital. In other words, we suppress the use of inputs other than R&D expenditures. We define the instantaneous costs as follows:

$$c(s) = c[h(s), h_I(s)] + I(\alpha) \qquad (2.1)$$

where $c[\cdot]$ is a strictly convex C^2 cost function, which is increasing in both its arguments, and both inputs are necessary. The variable $h(s)$ denotes the firm's stock of R&D capital at time s, $h_I(s)$ denotes the flow of R&D research activities, and $I(\alpha)$ is a strictly convex C^2 cost function, which is increasing in the control parameter α. We assume that, by spending on R&D, the firm becomes more efficient in the sense that it increases its probability of winning the patent race. The stock of R&D capital, that is, human capital or knowledge, accumulated over time also has an effect on the success probability. One can think of h and h_I in terms of a state variable and a control variable, respectively, while α is viewed as representing parametric attempts to increase the likelihood of the firm's success, for example, through brand names, goodwill and/or political channels. We shall also use the research intensity parameter to mimic the results derived by previous authors, for example, Gruver (1991). These authors typically assume time-independent variable costs and benefits.

The accumulation of R&D capital follows the accumulation equation:[2]

$$\dot{h}(t) = h_I(t) - \gamma h(t); \, h(0) = h_0 \qquad (2.2)$$

where γ is a strictly positive parameter reflecting the depreciation of R&D capital (human capital). Depreciation does not mean that knowledge is forgotten. It only means that the knowledge becomes obsolete and loses part of its value.

The present value of the costs accumulated up to point t is:

$$C^0(t) = \int_0^t c(s)e^{-rs} \, ds. \qquad (2.3)$$

If the innovation is made at time t, the present value of profits (from time t and onwards), at time zero, associated with the innovation is:

$$B^0(t) = \int_t^\infty b(s)e^{-rs} \, ds. \qquad (2.4)$$

In what follows we shall, for simplicity, treat $b(s)$ as a constant for all s.[3]

There are n competitors acting in the market under consideration. The probability of making the innovation in the short interval $(t, t + dt)$, conditional on not having made the innovation before time t, that is, the 'market' hazard function, is defined as follows:

$$\frac{F^{M'}(t)}{1 - F^M(t)} = \delta^M(t) = \delta[h(t), \alpha, t] + \sum_{j=2}^{n} \delta^j[h^j(t), \alpha^j, t] \qquad (2.5)$$

where $F^M(t)$ is the probability that the innovation is made by either the firm under consideration or its competitors (denoted j) before t, and $F^{M'}(t)$ is the probability density, that is, that the innovation is made at t. The market hazard is, hence, a function of all the firms' R&D stocks, which we can use as an indicator of R&D experience, the parameters α, and time. We assume that each individual hazard function, $\delta^j(\cdot)$, is non-negative, bounded away from zero, and increasing in h^j, and α. The derivative of the hazard with respect to time is perhaps best put equal to zero, since we are looking at an innovation of a particular product. At an aggregate level, when a continuum of successive patent races have been studied, Romer (1990) assumes that R&D workers become more productive over time. Grossman and Helpman (1991) assume that R&D productivity does not change over time, while Segerstrom (1999), pointing out that the most obvious ideas are discovered first, assumes that it decreases over time.

Integrating we get:

$$1 - F^M(t) = e^{-\int_0^t [\delta(s) + \sum_j \delta^j(s)]ds} = e^{-\Delta^M(t)} \qquad (2.6)$$

where $1 - F^M(t)$ is the probability that the innovation has not been made before time t, and we have suppressed the dependency of the hazard on the stock of R&D capital and α.

Note that $\Delta^M(t)$ is given by the differential equation:

$$\dot{\Delta}^M(t) = \delta^M(t); \; \Delta^M(0) = 0. \qquad (2.7)$$

This equation will play an important role for the formulation of the optimal control problem, as will be explained below.

The expected present value of the firm, conditional on the actions taken by its competitors, can now be defined as follows:

$$V^E = \int_0^\infty \{-C^0(t)F^{M'}(t) + B^0(t)F'(t) \prod_{j=1}^n [1 - F^j(t)]\}dt =$$

$$-\int_0^\infty C^0(t)\delta^m(t)e^{-\Delta^M(t)}dt + \int_0^\infty B^0(t)\delta(t)e^{-\Delta^M(t)}dt = \qquad (2.8)$$

$$-\int_0^\infty c(t)e^{-[rt+\Delta^M(t)]}dt + \int_0^\infty B^0(t)\delta(t)e^{rt}e^{-[rt+\Delta^M(t)]}dt$$

where $1 - F^j(t)$ is the probability that the jth competitor makes the innovation *after* time t. The firm will invest in R&D until one of the firms is successful; it would be a waste of resources to continue if a rival competitor wins the race. The benefit side is adjusted so as to reflect the fact that the winner takes all.

Our problem can be viewed as an open-loop differential game; see Kamien and Schwartz (1991, section 23), Seirstad and Sydsaeter (1987) or Başar and Olsder (1982). Each firm maximizes the value of its V^E function with respect to $h_I(t)$, subject to the relevant state equations, treating the actions of its competitors as fixed.[4] However, our problem is not quite a standard optimal control problem, that is, to maximize V^E with respect to $h_I(t)$ subject to equations (2.2). The reason is that $\Delta^M(t)$ is a function of a state variable, the stock of R&D capital. It is turned into a standard control problem by maximizing V^E subject to (2.2) and (2.7). Throughout, we assume that the profit-maximizing V^E is positive at the Nash equilibrium.

The expected present-value Hamiltonian corresponding to this case is:

$$H(t) = \{\delta[h(t), \alpha, t]B(t) - c[h(t), h_I(t)] - I(\alpha)\}e^{-[rt + \Delta^M(t)]} \quad (2.9)$$
$$+ \lambda(t)[h_I(t) - \gamma h(t)] + \mu(t)\{\delta[h(t), \alpha, t] + \textstyle\sum_j \delta^j[h^j(t), \alpha^j, t]\}$$

where $B(t) = B^0(t)^{rt}$, with $\lambda(t)$ and $\mu(t)$ as the expected present-value co-state variables associated with equations (2.2) and (2.7), respectively. The necessary conditions for an ('interior') optimal control read:

$$\frac{\partial H}{\partial h_I} = -c_{h_I}(t)e^{-[rt + \Delta^M(t)]} + \lambda(t) = 0 \quad (2.10a)$$

$$\dot{\lambda}(t) = -\delta_h(t)\{B(t)e^{-[rt + \Delta^M(t)]} + \mu(t)\} + c_h(t)e^{-[rt + \Delta^M(t)]} + \lambda(t)\gamma \quad (2.10b)$$

$$\dot{\mu}(t) = [\delta(t)B(t) - c(t)]e^{-[rt + \Delta^M(t)]} \quad (2.10c)$$

$$\dot{h}(t) = h_I - \gamma h(t), \; h(0) = h_0 \quad (2.10d)$$

$$\dot{\Delta}^M(t) = \delta^M(t), \; \Delta^M(0) = 0 \quad (2.10e)$$

$$\lim_{t \to \infty} \lambda(t) = \lim_{t \to \infty} \mu(t) = 0 \quad (2.10f)$$

where $c(t) = c[h(t), h_I(t)] + I(\alpha)$.

The transversality condition (2.10f) presupposes certain growth conditions in terms of the state variables. The reader is referred to Theorems 3.16 and 3.17 in Seierstad and Sydsaeter (1987, pp. 234–5). They also provide necessary and sufficient conditions for a unique solution to infinite time optimal control problems. The more complicated problem, the existence of a (unique) solution to a Nash differential game is discussed in Başar and Olsder (1982), and more recently by Jensen and Lockwood (1998). In what follows, we shall simply assume that there exists an optimal and unique solution to the differential game under consideration. This concludes the presentation of the model.

3 OPTIMAL INVESTMENT IN R&D AND THE PROPERTIES OF THE NASH EQUILIBRIUM

Let us now turn to the incentives to invest in R&D capital facing the firm. The co-state variable $\lambda(t)$ measures the present value to the firm of an additional unit of R&D capital. By solving equation (2.10b) subject to the transversality condition (2.10f), we obtain:

$$\lambda^*(t) = \int_t^\infty \{\delta_h^*(s)[B(s)e^{-[rs+\Delta^{M^*}(s)]} + \mu^*(s)] - c_h^*(s)e^{-[rs+\Delta^{M^*}(s)]}\}e^{-\gamma(s-t)}ds \quad (2.11)$$

where the super-index * is used to denote the non-cooperative equilibrium path. It is instructive to rewrite the shadow price of R&D capital in terms of the value increase arising from a successful patent race. The value function at any time, s, during the patent race can be written:

$$V^*(s) = \int_s^\infty [\delta^*(\tau)B(\tau) - c^*(\tau)]e^{-[r\tau+\Delta^{M^*}(\tau)]}e^{[rs+\Delta^{M^*}(s)]}d\tau. \quad (2.12)$$

By solving equation (2.10c) we find that:[5]

$$\mu^*(s) = -V^*(s)e^{-[rs+\Delta^{M^*}(s)]} \quad (2.13)$$

Equation (2.11) can now be rewritten as:

$$\lambda^*(t) = \int_t^\infty \{\delta_h^*(s)[B(s) - V^*(s)] - c_h^*(s)\}e^{-[rs+\Delta^{M^*}(s)]}e^{-\gamma(s-t)}ds. \quad (2.14)$$

The term $B(s) - V^*(s)$ measures the difference between the post-discovery and pre-discovery values, if the firm wins the patent race, while $\delta_h^*(s)$ measures how additional R&D capital changes the conditional probability of winning. The first part of the integral on the right-hand side of (2.14) is the expected marginal benefit of additional R&D capital at time t discounted to time zero. The second part of the integral represents the marginal cost of holding additional R&D capital. Note that the depreciation rate of R&D capital shows up in equation (2.14) as an additional discount rate. In other words, the higher the rate of depreciation (*ceteris paribus*) the lower the future value of an additional unit of R&D capital. Finally, with equation (2.14) at our disposal, the rule for the optimal investment in equation (2.10a) is easy to interpret. The firm chooses investments at each instant of time such that the expected present value of future net benefits of additional R&D capital will be equalized with the instantaneous marginal costs associated with this investment.

Previous authors have concentrated on the impacts of parametric changes in costs. In order to introduce such changes, we start by defining the optimal performance function. For fixed α, n and r, this function is defined as follows:

$$V(0, \omega) = \max \left\{ \int_0^\infty - c(t)e^{-[rt+\Delta^M(t)]} \, dt + \int_0^\infty B^0(t)e^{rt}e^{-[rt+\Delta^M(t)]}dt \right\}, \quad (2.15)$$

where $\omega = (d, n, r)$ is a parameter vector, and the maximization is performed subject to equation (2.2) and (2.7).

In order to use equation (2.15) for comparative dynamics, we employ the results on the properties of the value function in dynamics optimization, which are known from the work of among others, Seierstad (1981), Caputo (1990), LaFrance and Barney (1991), and Johansson and Löfgren (1994). Roughly speaking, the dynamic envelope theorem says that the total effect on the objective function of an infinitesimally small change in a parameter is obtained by taking the partial derivative of the maximized present-value Hamiltonian (or more generally the Lagrangian) with respect to the parameter and integrating along the optimal path over the planning horizon. This result greatly simplifies the analysis of patent races and other R&D activities in an intertemporal setting, and enables us to derive some new results on the workings of markets where innovations play a central role.

If $V(0, \omega)$ is continuously differentiable,[6] the effects of small changes in the parameter α can be evaluated as follows:

$$\frac{\partial V^*}{\partial \alpha} = \int_0^\infty \frac{\partial H^*(t)}{\partial \alpha} \, dt = \int_0^\infty \{ \delta_\alpha^*(t)\{B(t) + \mu^*(t)e^{[rt+\Delta^{M^*}(t)]}\} - \Delta_\alpha^{M^*}[\delta^*(t)B(t) - c^*(t)] - I_\alpha(\alpha)\}e^{-[rt+\Delta^{M^*}(t)]}dt. \quad (2.16)$$

If α is optimally chosen, equation (2.16) equals zero. Note the similarity between equation (2.11) and (2.16). The intuitive explanation is the fact that α, just like $h(t)$, can be treated as a state variable with $\dot{\alpha} \equiv 0$. Treating α as a state variable in the maximization problem would mean that the Hamiltonian in (2.9) is augmented with the term $\Lambda(t)\dot{\alpha}$, where $\Lambda(t)$ is an expected value co-state variable equal to (2.16).

It is important to stress the fact that we view α as a part of the firm's maximization problem, that is, we evaluate (2.16) conditional on the actions taken by the competitors in the Nash equilibrium.

In order to provide a simple interpretation of equation (2.16), let us consider the case analysed by Gruver (1991), that is $h = h_I = 0$ for all t, and $\dot{\Delta}^M = (\alpha + \sum_j \alpha^j) = \delta^M$. It is easily verified that:

$$V^*(0, \omega) = [\alpha^* B^0(0) - I(\alpha^*)][r + \delta^M]^{-1} \qquad (2.17)$$

which is a variation of equation (5) in Gruver (1991). It follows that the optimal value of the parameter is such that:

$$B^0(0) - V^*(0, \omega) = I_\alpha(\alpha^*). \qquad (2.18)$$

The left-hand side of (2.18) is the present value of immediate success less the present value of the game. The right-hand side of the expression is the marginal cost of increasing the parameter. Optimally, α is chosen in such a way that the difference between the post- and pre-discovery values equals the marginal cost of increasing α.

To go further, assume a steady-state solution in which the stock of R&D capital $h(t)$ is constant and equal to h for all $t > 0$. Then it is easily verified that a more general model, in which $\Delta^M = [\alpha + \beta h + \sum_j (\alpha^j + \beta^j h^j)]t = \delta^M t$, where β and β^j are strictly positive constants, produces a performance function that is a straightforward generalization of the function in equation (2.17). This is so because the steady-state assumption ensures that $\delta^M(t)$, $h(t)$, $h_I(t)$ and $c(t)$ are constant over time. However, as is shown by Kamien and Schwartz (1991, pp. 281–5), the optimal policy in such a model is not, in general, to set the control variable, h_I, constant over time so as to maintain a constant R&D stock. The reader is referred to Kamien and Schwartz (1991) for details.

4   THE SOCIALLY OPTIMAL PATENT RACE

Let us now turn to the socially optimal R&D strategy when there are n identical firms. Assume for the sake of simplicity that the private and social present-value benefits coincide, that is, $B^s(t) = B^0(t)$, where a superscript s refers to society. The social maximization problem (for a fixed α) can be stated as follows:

$$\max_{h_I} V^s = \max_{h_I} \{ \int_0^\infty -nc(t)e^{-[rt+\Delta^M(t)]}dt + \int_0^\infty B^0(t)n\delta(t)e^{rt}e^{-[rt+\Delta^M(t)]}dt \} \qquad (2.19)$$

subject to n times equation (2.2) and:

$$\dot{\Delta}^M(t) = n\delta[h(t), \alpha, t] = \delta^M(t)$$
$$\Delta^M(0) = 0. \qquad (2.20)$$

Note that the social benefits of an innovation made in a short interval $(t, t + dt)$ are $n\delta(t)B^0(t)$, as it does not matter to society which firm makes the innovation (while the benefit is equal to $\delta(t)B^0(t)$ for the individual firm). The reason is not that there are n firms that share the benefits from the innovation; only that the relevant hazard increases by a factor n.

The expected present-value Hamiltonian for the social case is written:

$$H^s(t) = \{n\delta[h(t), \alpha, t]B(t) - nc[h(t), h_I(t)] - nI(\alpha)\}e^{-[rt+\Delta^M(t)]}$$
$$+ \lambda^s(t)n[h_I(t) - \gamma h(t)] + \mu^s(t)n\delta[h(t), \alpha, t] \quad (2.21)$$

and the necessary conditions are written as:

$$-c_{h_I}(t)e^{-[rt+\Delta^M(t)]} + \lambda^s(t) = 0 \quad (2.22a)$$

$$\dot{\lambda}^s(t) = -n\delta_h(t)\{B(t)e^{-[rt+\Delta^M(t)]} + \mu^s(t)\} + nc_h(t)e^{-[rt+\Delta^M(t)]} + \lambda^s(t)n\gamma \quad (2.22b)$$

$$\dot{\mu}^s(t) = n[\delta(t)B(t) - c(t)]e^{-[rt+\Delta^M(t)]} \quad (2.22c)$$

$$\lim_{t \to \infty} \lambda^s(t) = \lim_{t \to \infty} \mu^s(t) = 0. \quad (2.22d)$$

Equation (2.22a) has the same interpretation as in the non-cooperative equilibrium, and means that the expected present value of the net benefits of additional R&D capital is equal to the instantaneous marginal cost of investments in R&D capital. However, the expected present value of the net benefits from additional R&D capital is measured from society's point of view, and not from the point of view of the individual firm. To highlight the difference, let us use equations (2.22b) and (2.22d) to derive an expression analogous to equation (2.14) above. We obtain:

$$\lambda^{s**}(t) = \int_t^\infty n\{\delta_h^{**}(s)[B(s) - V^{**}(s)] - c_h^{**}(s)\}e^{-[rs+\Delta^{M**}(s)]}e^{-n\gamma(s-t)}ds \quad (2.23)$$

where:

$$V^{**}(s) = \int_s^\infty n[\delta^{**}(\tau)B(\tau) - c^{**}(\tau)]e^{-[r\tau+\Delta^{M**}(\tau)]}e^{[rs+\Delta^{M**}(s)]}d\tau. \quad (2.24)$$

The super-index '**' is used to denote the first-best equilibrium.

The key difference between the socially optimal shadow price in (2.23) and the Nash equilibrium shadow price in equation (2.14) is the fact that the difference between the post- and pre-discovery values are scaled by the number of firms. In addition, the pre-discovery value function is, itself, scaled by n as is the rate of depreciation.

Moreover we can solve for the shadow price of the accumulated hazard to obtain:

$$\mu^{s**}(t) = - V^{**}(t)e^{-[rt+\Delta^{M**}(t)]}. \qquad (2.25)$$

A similar result holds true with respect to the optimal choice of the parameter α. In order to arrive at this result, we differentiate the social performance function resulting from the above maximization problem with respect to the parameter α to obtain:

$$\frac{\partial V^{s**}}{\partial \alpha} = \int_0^\infty \frac{\partial H^{s**}(t)}{\partial \alpha} dt = \int_0^\infty n\{\delta_\alpha^{**}(t)[B(t) + \mu^{**}(t)e^{[rt+\Delta^{M**}(t)]}] \\ - n\Delta_\alpha^{M**}[\delta^{**}(t)B(t) - c^{**}(t)] - I_\alpha(\alpha^{**})\}e^{-[rt+\Delta^{M**}(t)]}dt. \qquad (2.26)$$

The question now arises as to how we should design policy instruments such that the market economy (the free-entry symmetric Nash equilibrium) replicates the social optimum.[7] Intuitively, there is a tendency for the firm to overinvest in R&D capital, since winning the race means that it takes all, while losing means that it gets nothing. From society's point of view it does not matter who makes the innovation, only that it is made. A natural way to induce the firm to invest less in R&D would be to tax such investments. In this particular problem, however, it is not the incentives to invest that are fundamentally wrong, it is the shadow price of a unit of R&D capital. It is not crystal clear whether the value is too high or too low, since the hazard function of the individual firm does not reflect society's chances of making the innovation in the correct manner. In other words, the shadow price of the artificial state variable, which reflects the integral of the hazard function, is also distorted. The firms, in a market equilibrium, underestimate the conditional probability that the innovation is made. This means that the measures needed to correct the market failure are more complicated than usual.

Consider the following proposition:

Proposition 1 Hamiltonians of the following form induce a fixed number of identical firms to replicate the socially optimal solution:

$$H(t) = \{\delta[h(t)]B(t) - c(t) + P_E^{**}(t) - t_h^{**}h(t) + T^{**}(t)\}e^{-[rt+\Delta^M(t)]} \\ + \lambda(t)[h_I(t) - \gamma h(t)] + \mu(t)\{\delta[h(t)] + \sum_j \delta^j[h^j(t)]\}$$

where:

$$P_E^{**}(t) = (n-1)\{\delta[h^{**}(t)]B(t) - c^{**}(t)\}$$

$$t_h^{**}(t) = (n-1)\{-\delta_h[h^{**}(t)]B(t) + \mu^{**}(t)e^{[rt+\Delta^{M^{**}}(t)]}]$$
$$+ c_h[h^{**}(t),\, h_I^{**}(t),\, t] + \gamma\lambda^{**}(t)e^{[rt+\Delta^{M^{**}}(t)]}\}$$

$$T^{**}(t) = t_h^{**}(t)h^{**}(t)$$

The super-index denotes that the entities are measured along the socially optimal path.

To see why the above 'tax subsidy system' works, we derive the first-order conditions for an optimal control for an individual firm:

$$\lambda(t) - c_{h_I}[h(t),\, h_I(t)] = 0 \tag{2.27a}$$

$$\dot{\lambda}(t) = -\delta_h[h(t)][B(t)e^{-[rt+\Delta^M(t)]} + \mu(t)] + c_h[h(t),\, h_I(t)]e^{-[rt+\Delta^M(t)]}$$
$$+ \gamma\lambda(t) + t_h^{**}(t)e^{-[rt+\Delta^M(t)]} \tag{2.27b}$$

$$\dot{\mu}(t) = \{\delta[h(t)]B(t) - c(t) + P_E^{**}(t) - t_h^{**}(t)h(t) + T^{**}(t)\}e^{-[rt+\Delta^M(t)]} \tag{2.27c}$$

Inserting the expressions for t_h^{**}, P_E^{**} and T^{**} yields the first-order conditions in (2.22). Condition (2.27a) shows that the incentives to invest in R&D capital are not fundamentally distorted. Given that λ is correctly set, the incentives to invest are correct. Condition (2.27b) contains the necessary corrections for getting λ right. It contains a tax or subsidy depending upon whether the firm overinvests or underinvests in R&D capital in the market solution. Note that t_h^{**} can change sign over time, and that it is the stock of R&D capital that is taxed or subsidized.[8] Since it is far from clear how R&D capital can be measured in practice, this complicates the implementation of the optimal policy beyond the fact that it requires that the social optimization problem has been solved. The lump-sum subsidy $P_E^{**}(t)$ corrects the shadow price of the accumulated hazard, which measures (the negative of) the logarithm of the survival probability, that is, the logarithm of the probability that the innovation is made at a point of time $s > t$. The lump-sum tax or subsidy T^{**} nets out the net revenues of the tax or subsidy on the shadow price of the 'survival probability'. The latter can be financed consecutively within the R&D sector, while P_E^{**}, will have to be financed in a non-distortionary manner in other sectors of the economy.

5   CONCLUDING COMMENTS

The patent race that is studied in this chapter is very general, and yields fewer clear-cut results than most earlier studies. There are, however, a couple of new aspects that are worth mentioning. A comparison between the non-cooperative Nash equilibrium and the social optimum shows that the implementation of the latter requires that the stock of R&D capital, rather than the investment in R&D capital, should be taxed or subsidized. The particular regime (tax or subsidy) depends, in a complicated manner, on the two shadow prices involved, the shadow price of the stock of R&D capital, and the shadow price of the accumulated hazard. Intuitively, the switch from one regime to another depends on whether the non-cooperative equilibrium produces a lower or higher stock of R&D capital than is optimal from society's point of view. The implementation mechanism also contains two separate time-dependent lump-sum subsidies (taxes). One is correcting the shadow price of the accumulated hazard, and the other is netting out the revenues from the subsidy or the cost of the tax.

The seemingly complicated implementation mechanism is, loosely speaking, created by the fact that each firm underestimates society's ability to make the innovation, since they only care about their own chances of winning the patent race. Technically this means the difference between the post- and pre-discovery value of the firm is scaled by the number of firms. At the same time, the pre-discovery value is scaled by the number of firms (there are more firms pre than post). This value is directly related to the negative of the shadow price of the accumulated hazard. The latter is negative, because the accumulated hazard enters the problem as an extra discount factor.

The analysis conducted above is, to a large extent, simplified by our treatment of entry behavior. One of the most important generalizations would be to introduce the free entry of firms.

NOTES

1. Loury (1979) has a similar approach, although he only treats the steady state, which is approached instantaneously.
2. See also Aronsson and Löfgren (1996).
3. We assume that it is cost free for the firm to move its R&D capital to other uses once the patent race is terminated.
4. Kamien and Schwartz (1991, p. 281) assume that $\alpha = h = 0$ and that $c(t) = h_i^2/2$. The optimal control is then a function of time, but independent of the stocks of R&D capital of the firm and its competitors, so that the open and feedback strategies coincide. Scherer (1967) is an early attempt to treat the problem of R&D expenditure as a Cournot–Nash game.
5. Equation (2.13) means, ignoring the post-discovery value, that a discovery at s implies a loss equal to the present value of the value function. See also Clark and Reed (1994).
6. For a theorem developed by Atle Seierstad, see Aronsson et al. (1997, appendix to chapter 4).
7. Note that the number of firms is being treated as exogenously given. The reason is that we are not modeling the decision to enter.
8. See also Aronsson and Löfgren (1996).

REFERENCES

Aronsson, T., P.O. Johansson and K.G. Löfgren (1997), *Welfare Measurement, Sustainability and Green National Accounting*, Cheltenham, UK and Northampton, MA, USA: Edward Elgar.

Aronsson, T. and K.G. Löfgren (1996), 'Social accounting and welfare measurement in a growth model with human capital', *Scandinavian Journal of Economics*, **98**, 185–201.

Başar, T. and G.J. Olsder (1982), *Dynamic Noncooperative Game Theory*, London: Academic Press.

Bhattacharya, S. and D. Mookherjee (1986), 'Portfolio choice in research and development', *Rand Journal of Economics*, **17**, 594–605.

Caputo, M.R. (1990), 'How to do comparative dynamics on the back of an envelope in optimal control theory', *Journal of Economic Dynamics and Control*, **14**, 655–83.

Clark, H.R. and W.J. Reed (1994), 'Consumption and pollution tradeoffs in an environment vulnerable to pollution-related catastrophic collapse', *Journal of Economic Dynamic and Control*, **18**, 991–1010.

Dasgupta, P. and J.E. Stiglitz (1980), 'Industrial structure and the nature of innovative activity', *Economic Journal*, **90**, 266–93.

Gilbert, R. and C. Shapiro (1990), 'Optimal patent length and breadth', *Rand Journal of Economics*, **21**, 106–12.

Grossman, G.M. and E. Helpman (1991), 'Quality ladders in the theory of economic growth', *Review of Economic Studies*, **58,** 43–61.

Grossman, G.M. and C. Shapiro (1986), 'Optimal dynamic R&D programs', *Rand Journal of Economics*, **17**, 581–93.

Gruver, G.W. (1991), 'Optimal R&D policy for a patent race with uncertain duration', *Mathematical Social Sciences*, **22**, 69–85.

Jensen, H. and B. Lockwood (1998), 'A note on discontinuous value functions and strategies in affine quadratic differential games', *Economic Letters*, **61**, 301–6.

Johansson, P.-O. and K.G. Löfgren (1994), 'Comparative dynamics in health economics: some useful results', Mimeo, Stockholm School of Economics.

Jovanovic, B. and G.M. MacDonald (1994), 'Competitive diffusion', *Journal of Political Economy*, **102**, 24–52.

Kamien, M.I. and N.L. Schwartz (1991), *Dynamic Optimization*, Amsterdam: North-Holland.

Klemperer, P. (1990), 'How broad should the scope of patent protection be?', *Rand Journal of Economics*, **21**, 113–30.

Klette, T. and D. de Meza (1986), 'Is the market biased against risky R&D?', *Rand Journal of Economics*, **17**, 133–9.

LaFrance, J.T. and D.L. Barney (1991), 'The envelope theorem in dynamic optimization', *Journal of Economic Dynamics and Control*, **15**, 355–85.

Loury, G.C. (1979), 'Market structure and innovation', *Quarterly Journal of Economics*, **93**, 395–410.

Malliaris, A.G. and W. Brock (1991), *Stochastic Methods in Economics and Finance*, Amsterdam: North-Holland.

Romer, P.M. (1990), 'Endogenous technological change', *Journal of Political Economy*, **98**, S71–S102.

Scherer, F.M. (1967), 'Research and development resource allocation under rivalry', *Quarterly Journal of Economics*, **81**, 359–94.

Segerstrom, P.S. (1999), 'Endogenous growth without scale effects', *American Economic Review*, **88**, 1290–1310.

Seierstad, A. (1981), 'Derivatives and subderivatives of the optimal value function in control theory', Memorandum, Institute of Economics, University of Oslo, 26 February.

Seierstad, A. and K. Sydsaeter (1987), *Optimal Control Theory with Economic Applications*, New York: North-Holland.

Tirole, J. (1988), *The Theory of Industrial Organization*, Cambridge, MA: MIT Press.

3. The strategy of treaty negotiation: 'broad but shallow' versus 'narrow but deep'

Scott Barrett

1 INTRODUCTION

This chapter builds on the foundation laid by Karl Göran Mäler's (1989, 1991) pioneering research on the acid rain game. My concern here is with two features of international environmental agreements: that they must be self-enforcing and that they must be fair.

It is obvious why agreements must be self-enforcing. There is no world government that can enforce an agreement between countries. But why should agreements be fair? You could argue that fairness is required on philosophical grounds, but I wish to stress a different motivation. This is that *an agreement is more likely to be self-enforcing if it is fair*. A fair agreement is more likely to be perceived as being legitimate; and, as Bodansky (1999: 603), a professor of international law, argues, 'whether international environmental regimes are perceived as legitimate will play an important role in their long-term success'.

I shall take it that the underlying problem is to supply either a regional or global public good. It is not in any country's interests to supply the public good unilaterally, but all countries would be better off if every country supplied the good. There is thus a gap between the non-cooperative and full cooperative outcomes. The purpose of an international agreement is to close this gap – or at least to narrow it. This is essentially the same game that Mäler (1989, 1991) analysed, the only difference being that the acid rain game is asymmetric and I shall assume that countries are symmetric. As Mäler emphasized, when countries are asymmetric, it may not be in every country's interests to sustain full cooperation in the absence of side-payments. However, side-payments are only a necessary condition for sustaining full cooperation when countries are strongly asymmetric. A self-enforcing agreement also requires that free riding be deterred, and this is as much a problem for symmetric as for asymmetric games. Side-payments may help in sustaining more cooperation when countries are strongly asymmetric, but they cannot be relied upon to sustain full cooperation (Barrett, 2001).

I shall now give some definitions. An agreement to limit pollution emissions is *self-enforcing* if is satisfies the following properties:

1. no party can do better by withdrawing, or by failing to comply, given the terms of the agreement, the participation by others, and the behavior of non-parties;
2. no non-party can gain by acceding, given the terms of the agreement, the participation and compliance by others, and the behavior of the other non-parties;
3. all the parties collectively cannot gain by renegotiating the terms of the agreement, given their participation and compliance and the behavior of the non-parties; and
4. no non-party can gain by changing its own emission level, given the behavior of both the parties to the agreement and the other non-parties.

In general, fairness is a more elusive concept. When countries are symmetric, however, it is pretty obvious what a fair agreement should require. An agreement is *fair* if no country would prefer to switch places with any other country. That is, an agreement is fair if it is *envy free*.

Here, then, is the rub. The literature on self-enforcing agreements typically finds that environmental agreements are incomplete as regards participation. Some countries participate, and some free ride. These agreements are fair only in the sense that no signatory could do better by switching places with another signatory. They are unfair in the sense that every signatory would prefer to switch places with a non-signatory. Remember, by assumption, all countries are symmetric. They all benefit the same from the provision of the public good. However, only signatories pay for this provision. The only fair agreement, by this reckoning, is one that attracts full participation. And yet full participation may not be self-enforcing.

To reconcile these twin requirements, we need to determine whether the conditions that make a treaty self-enforcing can be modified such that the level of participation can be varied. In particular, we need to determine whether a self-enforcing agreement can sustain full participation – a consensus treaty – under a wide range of circumstances. I shall show that this requirement can be satisfied provided the standard assumption about rationality is weakened slightly. The constraint of self-enforcement can then bite on the provision level rather than on the level of participation. Essentially, full participation can only be bought at the cost of lowering each party's provision of the public good. Such an agreement might be called 'broad but shallow'.

The difficulty here is that once the rationality assumption is weakened, a great variety of other agreements will also be self-enforcing. However, only one of the alternatives is compelling (in the sense of being focal). This is a partial agreement in which the signatories maximize their collective payoff, taking the participation level as given, but in which participation is incomplete. This is the standard kind of agreement considered by the literature (see Barrett, 1999); it might be called a 'narrow but deep' agreement. In having to choose between these two agreements, the 'broad but shallow' agreement might seem especially focal because it is fair. However, in this chapter I shall show that this consensus agreement has yet another advantage. I shall show that, under certain conditions, every negotiating party will *prefer* to negotiate a 'broad but shallow' agreement as compared to the 'narrow but deep' alternative. When we see countries negotiate by consensus, the reason may not be only that they are seeking to negotiate a fair agreement. The reason may rather be that the consensus agreement better serves their national interests. In this sense, the twin objectives of fairness and efficiency may not conflict. They may rather be self-reinforcing.

2   WEAKENING COLLECTIVE RATIONALITY

As in Barrett (1999), I shall employ a repeated game framework in this chapter and rely on the concept of a renegotiation-proof equilibrium developed by Farrell and Maskin (1989). They consider only two-player games, and I need to extend this concept for N-player games. In doing so, I ignore potential objections from coalitions of arbitrary size. I also assume that countries select from the set of all renegotiation-proof agreements the one that sustains the maximum payoff for its signatories.[1] To emphasize these features, I refer to agreements that satisfy these properties as being *collectively rational*.

Like Farrell and Maskin's concept of a renegotiation-proof equilibrium, collective rationality is compatible with two different kinds of punishment. The self-enforcing treaties studied in Barrett (1999) might best be called *strongly collectively rational* (SCR). For these treaties, the countries called upon to punish a defector or cheater would collectively prefer to impose the prescribed punishments than to revert to cooperation or to play any alternative, feasible punishment. A *weakly collectively rational* (WCR) treaty narrows this choice. For these treaties, the countries called upon to punish a unilateral deviation would collectively prefer to behave as the treaty instructs them to behave rather than to ignore the deviation and revert to cooperation. In other words, a WCR treaty cannot be rewritten after a deviation has occurred. It can only be obeyed or ignored.

An example best illustrates the difference between the concepts. Suppose that a country that benefits from the provision of a public good withdraws from an agreement seeking to supply it, or fails to accede to this agreement in the first place, as it is entitled to do under international law. Suppose, too, that the countries that *are* parties to the agreement are required by the treaty to punish this free rider. Since self-enforcing agreements must be individually rational, we know that each such party will impose the punishment prescribed by the treaty, given that all other parties do so.[2] But punishing a deviator is costly to the countries imposing the punishment, and there is nothing to stop these countries from proposing a change in the treaty at the next scheduled conference of the parties, or even from convening an extraordinary meeting to discuss the defection. This is why the punishments prescribed by a self-enforcing treaty must be renegotiation-proof. If, at such a meeting, the aggrieved countries can only choose between imposing the prescribed punishment or not, and they cannot do better, either individually or collectively, except by imposing the punishment, then the treaty is WCR. If, however, these countries can choose to impose different punishments than required by the treaty, but cannot gain by doing so, then the treaty is SCR. As suggested by this example, all SCR treaties are WCR, but the reverse is not true. SCR treaties are more credible.

However, this additional credibility comes at a cost. The countries called upon to punish a defection invariably harm themselves when they do so, and so SCR treaties will tend to prescribe only small punishments. As a consequence, they will not be very effective in deterring free riding.

I should emphasize that an agreement that seeks merely to sustain the equilibrium in unilateral policies will not normally be SCR. So the concept of an SCR treaty is incompatible with the view that treaties are showpieces, serving only to codify non-cooperation. Essentially, the SCR concept compels countries to cooperate but prevents them from cooperating very much.

3 ALTERNATIVE APPROACHES

Weakening the rationality assumption is one way to get a consensus agreement, but it is not the only way.

One alternative is to make different assumptions about the beliefs of the players. Chander and Tulkens (1997) show in a static game that a consensus agreement can sustain full cooperation if the parties believe that, in the event that one of them should deviate, the agreement will be nullified and all the other parties will thereafter behave non-cooperatively. However, this only begs the question of why countries might hold such beliefs – especially as they are unlikely to be confirmed by how states actually behave.

Another approach is to alter the payoffs of the players. In a static game, Hoel and Schneider (1997) add to each country's payoff a cost to not cooperating that increases in the number of countries that do cooperate. This can be interpreted as a penalty for not conforming, or for deviating from the legal norm that says that countries ought to cooperate. It has the consequence that, if enough other countries participate, then each will be inclined to participate. If the cost of not conforming is big enough, the underlying game will not be a prisoners' dilemma. It will rather be a coordination game, and the full cooperative outcome is easy to sustain for these kinds of games. It is important to note as well that, within the Hoel–Schneider framework, the penalty imposed on non-conformers does not cost the cooperators a penny. Nor is imposition of the penalty willful. The mechanism that triggers the punishment is hard-wired into the treaty. The assumption about payoffs is thus equivalent to an assumption about preferences: countries are assumed to prefer to conform.

The approach I take here has an advantage over these alternatives. I shall show that it may be in the interests of countries to *choose* to conform. All countries may do better if they negotiate a 'broad but shallow' treaty (in which all countries behave symmetrically) as opposed to a 'narrow but deep' agreement (in which some countries cooperate and some do not). Crucially, the punishments needed to sustain such an agreement are determined endogenously. Deviations are not punished automatically in this construction; they are punished only when the countries asked by the treaty to impose a punishment gain collectively by doing so.

4   CONCEPTS

Let me now provide a more formal description of the alternative concepts of collective rationality.

There are N countries in total. Suppose that there are k signatories ($k \leq N$) to a self-enforcing agreement and that each signatory gets a payoff of Π_s every period in a cooperative phase. Suppose further that any non-signatories behave non-cooperatively. Indeed, suppose that they have a dominant strategy: to play q^u. The latter assumption is a simplification; it allows us to ignore strategic interactions between signatories and non-signatories. To simplify matters even more, assume $q^u = 0$.

A self-enforcing agreement must be able to deter unilateral deviations. So suppose party j cheats. Then a punishment phase will be triggered. The treaty tells J that it must play q_j^j every period in the punishment phase. The treaty also instructs the other $k - 1$ signatories to provide Q_{-j}^j of the public good in this phase (to punish j for cheating). For discount factors very close to one, country j cannot lose by obeying this strategy provided:

$$\max_{q_j} \Pi_j (q_j; Q_{-j}^j) \leq \Pi_s. \tag{3.1}$$

In words, given that the other $k - 1$ signatories provide Q_{-j}^j of the public good in the punishment phase, the best payoff that j can secure for itself in the punishment phase is no greater than the payoff it gets by complying with the treaty and thus re-establishing a cooperative phase. If (3.1) holds, then j can thus do no better than to play q^j_j.

We must also be sure that, when push comes to shove, the k – 1 other parties to the agreement will carry out their side of the bargain and actually provide Q^j_{-j} of the public good in the punishment phase. That is, we require:

$$\Pi_m (Q^j_{-j}; q^j_j) \geq \Pi_s \qquad (3.2)$$

for every signatory m, $m \neq j$. If condition (3.2) is satisfied, then the signatories other than j cannot do better by ignoring the deviation and reverting immediately to a cooperative phase (note that if this condition is satisfied for every signatory then it will also be satisfied for the summation of all the k – 1 aggrieved signatories as a group). They cannot lose – and they may gain – by carrying out the punishment that the treaty asks them to carry out. Condition (3.2) thus makes the threat to impose the punishment credible.

Conditions (3.1) and (3.2) are rather easily satisfied. For example, if the agreement requires that signatories play q^u always (that is, in every cooperative and punishment phase), then condition (3.1) will be satisfied, since by assumption play q^u is a dominant strategy of the one-shot game. Condition (3.2) will also be satisfied. And, of course, a player could only lose by departing from q^u in the first place. So a treaty that satisfies these two conditions may merely codify the non-cooperative outcome.

However, this begs the question of why countries would bother to negotiate a treaty that did not increase welfare. It thus makes more sense to tighten up on this definition, and insist that signatories exploit every opportunity for collective gain – that is, that they choose the abatement level that, for k given, maximizes the value of Π_s in (3.1) and (3.2). I shall assume that this is the payoff that every signatory to a WCR treaty consisting of k signatories will get every period.

An SCR treaty must also satisfy (3.1). But condition (3.2) must be strengthened for an SCR treaty. For this kind of treaty it must not be possible for the countries other than j collectively to do better by choosing any feasible abatement level other than q^j_m in a punishment phase. That is, for an SCR treaty, Q^j_{-j} must be the solution to:

$$\max_{Q_{-j}} \sum_{m, m \neq j} \Pi_m(Q_{-j}; q^j_j) \geq (k-1)\Pi_s. \qquad (3.3)$$

Condition (3.3) tells us that the aggrieved countries would not only prefer to impose the promised punishment rather than ignore the deviation, as required by (3.2). They would also prefer to impose the promised punishment rather than play any alternative, feasible level of abatement in the punishment phase. It is easy to see that if condition (3.3) is satisfied then (3.2) will be satisfied but that the reverse is not true. In general, SCR treaties are more credible than WCR treaties.

5   THE UNDERLYING GAME

To illustrate the approach, I shall take the simplest possible game structure. In particular, I shall assume that the payoffs and feasible actions are given by:

$$\Pi_i = bQ - cq_i, \text{ where } Q = \sum_{j \neq i} q_j, \; q_i \in [0,1], \text{ and } bN > c > b > 0.$$

Π_i is country i's payoff, the difference between its gross benefit of public good provision and its own cost of supply; Q is the quantity of the public good provided; q_i is country i's supply of the public good, which can vary between 0 and 1; N is the total number of countries that can both supply and benefit from the public good; and b and c, respectively, are the constant marginal benefits and costs of public good supply to i.

The restrictions on the parameter values coupled with the payoff specification means that the problem being studied here is a linear, N-player prisoners' dilemma. The Nash equilibrium of the one-shot game is $q^u = 0$ with $\Pi_i^u = 0$; the full cooperative outcome is $q_i^c = 1$, with $\Pi_i^c = bN - c$ for all i. If we instead assumed $b > c$, then all countries would supply the public good unilaterally. If we assumed $c > bN$, then countries would not supply the public good even if they cooperated fully. In neither of these cases would an agreement be needed. Assuming $bN > c > b$ introduces a conflict between what countries will choose to do unilaterally and what they would prefer that all countries do collectively. It is the tension that this literature has rightly focused on.

6   SUSTAINING FULL COOPERATION

Under what conditions can full cooperation be sustained? Condition (3.1) requires:

$$b(N - 1)q_m^j \leq bN - c.$$

Taking $q_j^j = 1$, condition (3.2) requires:

$$q_m^j[b(N - 1) - c] \geq b(N - 1) - c.$$

Plainly, if $b(N - 1) > c$, then the countries called upon to punish a deviation must play $q_m^j = 1$; otherwise (3.2) will not be satisfied. However, in this case condition (3.1) implies $b \geq c$, which is untrue by assumption. If $b(N-1) \leq c$, however, then (3.2) will hold for *any* feasible q_m^j. Condition (3.1), then, requires $q_m^j \leq (bN-c)/(bN-b)$. Since $c > b > 0$ and $bN - c > 0$ by assumption, the denominator on the RHS of this weak inequality exceeds the numerator; q_m^j must therefore be strictly less than one though it may exceed zero. Hence, full cooperation can be sustained by a WCR treaty provided $b(N-1) \leq c$ or $N \leq (c+b)/b$. The same condition holds for an SCR treaty (see Barrett 1999).[3] The only difference is that, when $b(N-1) < c$, an SCR treaty insists that j be punished by having the other $N-1$ countries play zero abatement. A WCR treaty can sustain full cooperation using smaller punishments.

For this particular game, being able to impose weaker punishments does not buy us anything. The maximum N that can sustain full cooperation is the same for both WCR and SCR treaties. This turns out not to be a general result, but it is true that allowing treaties to be WCR rather than SCR makes no qualitative difference within this framework. The distinction only makes a material difference when we consider the possibility that the countries may seek to negotiate by consensus. I examine this problem below.

7 CONSENSUS TREATIES

If N is small enough, we need not compromise between choosing a high level of abatement and sustaining wide participation. However, if N is sufficiently large, something will have to give.

A consensus treaty must satisfy (3.1). If the treaty is WCR, condition (3.2) must also be accommodated. In the previous section I set the payoff in these inequalities equal to the full cooperative payoff and solved for the maximum value of N capable of sustaining this payoff. Here, I turn things around. I shall fix N and solve for the maximum payoff that can be sustained by a self-enforcing agreement. Denote this payoff by $\overline{\Pi}_s$.

Condition (3.1) now requires:

$$b(N-1)q_m^j \leq \overline{\Pi}_s. \tag{3.4}$$

If (3.4) holds, then for discount factors close to one, the deviant cannot lose and may gain by re-establishing cooperation. The LHS of (3.4) is the best payoff j can get by continuing to 'cheat'. The RHS of (3.4) is the average payoff j will get if it plays the strategy allowing a new cooperative phase to become established.

Similarly, condition (3.2) requires:

$$b[q_j^j + (N-1)q_m^j] - cq_m^j \geq \overline{\Pi}_s. \tag{3.5}$$

If (3.5) holds, each of the $N - 1$ countries called upon to punish j cannot do better to carry out their threat. Given that j plays q_j^j, the others are no worse off, and may be better off, playing q_m^j as opposed to ignoring the deviation and reverting to the cooperative phase without punishing j.

Setting $q_j^j = 1$ and rearranging, conditions (3.4) and (3.5) together require:

$$\frac{\bar{\Pi}_s - b}{b(N - 1) - c} \leq q_m^j \leq \frac{\bar{\Pi}_s}{b(N - 1)}$$

or

$$\bar{\Pi}_s \leq \frac{b^2(N - 1)}{c}. \tag{3.6}$$

The RHS of (3.6) is the maximum payoff that can be sustained by a self-enforcing, consensus agreement.

It might seem strange that this maximum value should be increasing in N. Remember, however, that the payoff to full cooperation is increasing in N, too. The ratio of the former payoff to the latter can be shown to be decreasing. Thus (3.6) tells us that, if the payoff each country realizes in the cooperative phase is lowered by enough relative to the full cooperative payoff, then a consensus agreement can be made WCR for *any* N. Lowering the payoff to cooperation reduces the incentive to renegotiate and thus makes more credible the threat to punish unilateral deviations.

It can now be seen why an SCR treaty cannot in general sustain a consensus. If N is large enough, the SCR concept requires that the countries other than j play $q_m^j = 1$ in a punishment phase. This is no punishment. Hence, for N large enough, an SCR consensus treaty does not exist.

8   CREDIBILITY VERSUS FAIRNESS

This raises an important question: must treaties be WCR or SCR? The answer is not obvious. SCR treaties are more credible. But that does not mean that they are more likely to be negotiated. The extra credibility of an SCR treaty can only be obtained at the cost of reduced flexibility. An agreement backed up by credible threats is compelling, but so is an agreement that is perceived to be 'fair'. Suppose that the players held strong beliefs that all countries should play their part – that the equilibrium for symmetric players should itself be symmetric. Strict adherence to the SCR concept would require that this concern for fairness take a back seat to credibility. But why should credibility outweigh concerns for fairness?[4]

The experimental game theory literature suggests that concerns for fairness often dominate. Consider, for example, the ultimatum game. In this game, two people have a fixed sum of money to divide – say, $100. One person, the Proposer, is able to make a proposal for how to divide the money. The other person, the Responder, can either accept or reject the proposal. If the proposal is rejected, both players get nothing. If the proposal is accepted, both players get the amounts specified by the proposal. If the Proposer were to look forward and reason backward, s/he would offer $99 (assuming that the proposal must be in whole dollar increments). S/he would make this offer because s/he would know that the Responder would prefer to get $1 than nothing, and so would accept the proposal. However, in experiments with real people, most proposals are in the range of 40–50 percent ($40–50). Proposals offering less than 30 percent of the total money available are almost always rejected. Almost never does a Proposer offer less than 20 percent or more than 50 percent. I stress that these are common findings. It has been observed in countries as diverse as Indonesia, Russia, Japan, Israel, the United States and several European countries (see Fehr and Gächter 2000). The reason: low offers seem unfair.

One reason low offers may seem unfair is that these games do not explain *why* one party should be the Proposer and the other the Responder; it just happens that one party is the Proposer and the other the Responder. But why should one party have an advantage? Here is another way in which a sum of money can be divided. The Proposer chooses a division, and the Responder chooses which piece of the division s/he wants. Obviously, in this situation, the Proposer will propose a 50–50 allocation, and it will not matter which piece of the sum the Responder chooses. This allocation mechanism results in a fair allocation. In particular, it results in an allocation that is *envy-free*, meaning that neither player prefers the other person's allocation to his/her own. It also results in an allocation that is *role-neutral*, meaning that the equilibrium payoffs do not depend on how the roles are assigned to the two players.[5]

My guess is that the players in the ultimatum game recognize that the 50–50 split is the fair allocation, and that, moreover, each recognizes that the other player recognizes the 50–50 split as being the fair allocation. The Responder will punish deviations from this fair allocation, and the Proposer can anticipate this response (this explains why the Proposer offers more than $1). Why then is the 60–40 division more common? I think the reason has to do with the asymmetry of the ultimatum game. The Proposer not only moves first; s/he can also choose any division from 0–100 to 100–0 in whole dollar increments. The Responder, by contrast, has only a very blunt punishment to hand: s/he can only accept or reject. If the Responder could impose a separate penalty in whole dollar increments, s/he might choose a value that was broadly proportional to the deviation from the 50–50 division. Being able only to wield his/her blunt weapon, however, s/he will only punish deviations that deviate *enough* from the fair division.

In the ultimatum game, concerns for fairness upset the subgame perfect equilibrium. The theory tells us that the threat to punish offers below, say, 40 percent, should not be credible; and yet, based on how real people play this game, the threat is credible. A similar logic may support a WCR consensus treaty. The threat to impose the WCR sanctions against a deviant may not be credible in the SCR sense. However, if the WCR sanctions are perceived as being necessary to enforce an inherently fair allocation, then they may be credible in a different sense; when push comes to shove, the players in this treaty game may carry out their threat rather than renegotiate, to sustain the outcome they perceive to be fair.

Having made this argument, it might be tempting to weaken the collective rationality assumption even further. After all, the full cooperative outcome is a symmetric outcome with symmetric players, and this 'fair' outcome can be sustained as a subgame perfect equilibrium, a concept only a bit less credible than WCR punishments. However, as I have argued elsewhere (Barrett, 1999), subgame perfection is too weak a requirement for international agreements. It suppresses the collective nature of the negotiation enterprise. The WCR concept strikes a kind of compromise.

Even if we believe that the SCR concept has special merit, there is virtue in considering the WCR alternative. Doing so allows us to test robustness. It also allows us to examine the implications of negotiation by consensus. If the SCR concept is believed to be more appropriate, then in general, countries will be unable to sustain consensus agreements. This is important to know. If, however, the WCR concept seems compelling, partly because it is better suited to sustaining a consensus, then we have learned an important lesson: agreements sustaining full participation may not sustain full cooperation. This, too, is important to know.

9 'BROAD BUT SHALLOW' VERSUS 'NARROW BUT DEEP'

If we accept the relevance of the WCR concept, cooperation can be manifest in a number of ways. Parties to an agreement may maximize their collective payoff, taking their participation as given; or they may instead decide that participation must be full, and maximize their collective payoff subject to meeting the constraint of self-enforcement (obviously, intermediate outcomes are also sustainable). What are the implications of these alternatives?

Let $\bar{N}$ denote the maximum number of countries able to sustain full cooperation. For the model we have been using, $\bar{N}$ is the largest integer not greater than $(b + c)/b$. Now, if $N \leq \bar{N}$, then it seems pretty obvious that the full cooperation will be sustained. Suppose, however, that $N > \bar{N}$. Then a partial agreement may be formed, with $k = \bar{N}$ signatories (this is more clearly seen in a stage-game framework; see Barrett, 1999). Of course, if there are $\bar{N}$ signatories, and if $N > \bar{N}$, then there must be $N - \bar{N}$ non-signatories. Assume that these non-signatories behave non-cooperatively, setting $q_n = 0$. Signatories will of course play $q_s = 1$. Denote the payoff to a non-signatory by $\Pi_n(\bar{N}; N)$ and the payoff to a signatory by $\Pi_s(\bar{N}; N)$. On substituting we get $\Pi_n = b\bar{N}$, $\Pi_s = b\bar{N} - c$.

From (3.6) we know that a consensus treaty can support a payoff of $\overline{\Pi} = b^2(N - 1)/c$. So, which kind of agreement will countries prefer to negotiate, a 'narrow but deep' partial agreement or a 'broad but shallow' consensus treaty?

Put yourself in the shoes of a signatory to a partial agreement. Broadening participation gets non-participants to supply more of the public good, which helps you. Moreover, since the abatement by each party is lower for a consensus treaty than a partial treaty, your costs fall. This is all for the good. However, your country would lose to the extent that other signatories to the partial agreement reduce *their* abatement under the consensus alternative. Taken together, it is not obvious which kind of agreement signatories to a partial agreement will prefer. However, for the model we are using it is easy to confirm that signatories to a partial agreement will always prefer the consensus alternative. To be precise, it can be shown that $\overline{\Pi}(N) > \Pi_s(\bar{N}; N)$ for $N > \bar{N}$.[6] In other words, the signatories to a partial agreement consisting of $\bar{N}$ countries will *always* prefer a consensus treaty.

What about the non-signatories to the partial agreement? Since these countries free ride, it might seem that they would prefer the status quo. If a consensus agreement were negotiated, these countries would now have to incur a cost for abatement. Moreover, the signatories to the partial agreement would lower their provision of the public good as participation increased, and this would harm the non-signatories to a partial agreement. On the other hand, however, the *other* non-signatories to the partial agreement would have to supply some of the public good if a consensus agreement were formed instead, and this would benefit each such non-participant. On reflection, non-signatories to a partial agreement may be better off with a consensus agreement provided N were sufficiently greater than $\bar{N}$. Indeed, it can be shown that $\overline{\Pi}(N) \geq \Pi_n(\bar{N}; N)$ for $N \geq (c\bar{N} + b)/b$.[7] Since $b < c$ by assumption, N must be at least two countries greater than $\bar{N}$ for non-signatories to prefer a consensus agreement.

Now imagine that all countries around the negotiation table can look forward and calculate the implications of negotiating a partial versus a consensus agreement. As the negotiations get under way, no country will know whether it will be a signatory or a non-signatory to a partial agreement (this will be true so long as countries must choose to be a signatory or a non-signatory independently – that is, without knowing how the others have chosen). If a partial agreement is negotiated, each party can expect to get a payoff of $\hat{\Pi}=[\bar{N}\Pi_s + (N - \bar{N})\Pi_n] \div N$. This payoff is obviously less than Π_n and so a consensus agreement is more likely to be preferred by all countries from this *ex ante* perspective. Indeed, it can be shown that, from this *ex ante* perspective, all countries will prefer the consensus alterative provided $N \geq (c/b)^2$.[8]

Note that there is no time-inconsistency problem here. *Ex ante*, all countries would rather that there be a consensus agreement provided that $N \geq (c/b)^2$. *Ex post*, no country could gain by deviating since the consensus treaty is self-enforcing.

I have also analysed this problem for a model with increasing marginal costs and find that a consensus treaty is especially favored (see Barrett, 2000). From an *ex ante* perspective, all countries will prefer to negotiate by consensus *for any N*. The reason is that, with marginal costs increasing, broader participation lowers the total cost of achieving any given level of participation.

To sum up, if agreements need only be WCR, countries may gain by negotiating by consensus. A consensus treaty will appear especially attractive when non-participation in a partial agreement would be substantial or when marginal costs increase in the level of provision. Consensus agreements are not only fair; from the perspective of the negotiating table, they hold the prospect of making every country better off as compared with the (focal) partial agreement alternative.

10   CONCLUSION

The notion that agreements will typically be incomplete sits rather awkwardly next to the facts. Most agreements attract something close to full participation. And where participation is less than full, the reason is usually not that the non-participants are free riding. Iceland, an active whaling nation, withdrew from the Whaling Convention in 1992 only after other parties objected to a resumption of whaling on animal welfare rather than conservation grounds, the basis on which the treaty was originally negotiated. Though Rwanda and Somalia have yet to sign the Montreal Protocol, the reason is not that they aspire to free ride; the reason is that they lack an effective municipal government. The United Kingdom and the United States failed to participate in the first sulfur protocol, the focus of Mäler's (1989, 1991) acid rain game. However, the UK argued that the agreement could not be relied upon to reduce the acid rain problem, and the US claimed that the base year was chosen arbitrarily and did not reflect emission reductions undertaken previously by the US. Neither country gloated at being so fortunate as to free ride on the abatement efforts of others.

There are probably many reasons why participation tends to be full or nearly full. It may be that states have a preference to conform, or that there is a price to be paid for failing to conform, or that moral reasoning compels states to cooperate if enough others do so. Or it may be that, from the *ex ante* perspective, states realize that they could do better by negotiating by consensus. In this chapter I have emphasized this last explanation. That such an agreement is also fair only adds to its appeal.

NOTES

1. Since I assume that symmetric countries impose symmetric punishments, whenever all aggrieved countries cannot gain collectively from renegotiation, none can gain individually from renegotiation.
2. Throughout this chapter, I take discount factors to be close to one. By the folk theorem, we can thus be sure that any feasible outcome can be sustained as a subgame perfect equilibrium.
3. Note, however, that this is not a general result. For alternative spcifications of payoffs, the maximum value of N for which the full cooperative outcome can be sustained by a self-enforcing agreement increases when treaties need only be WCR. See Barrett (2000).
4. Binmore (1998) makes a different criticism. He argues that a negotiated equilibrium should resist demands for renegotiation *on* the equilibrium path, but that it is unreasonable to demand that negotiated agreements be renegotiation-proof *off* the equilibrium path, too. By this reasoning also WCR treaties are more appealing.
5. See Young (1994) for a discussion of fair allocation processes.
6. Suppose that this claim is false. Then, upon substituting, we must have $b^2(N-1)/c \leq b\bar{N} - c$. The RHS of this inequality is increasing in $\bar{N}$ and $\bar{N}$ cannot exceed $(b+c)/b$. Hence, if the inequality holds for $\bar{N} = (b+c)/b$ then it will hold for any $\bar{N}$. Substitution and a little algebra shows that this implies $N \leq (b+c)/b$. Since $\bar{N}$ is the largest integer not greater than $(b+c)/b$, this implies $N < \bar{N}$. By assumption $N > \bar{N}$. Hence, the claim must be true.
7. On substituting, $\overline{\Pi}(N) \geq \Pi_n(\bar{N}; N)$ implies $b^2(N-1)/c \geq b\bar{N}$, which on rearranging proves the claim.
8. A consensus agreement will be preferred to a partial agreement if $\overline{\Pi} \geq \hat{\Pi}$. On substituting we get $b^3 \underline{N}^2 - b[b^2 + c(b+c)]N + c^2(b+c) \geq 0$. The LHS of this inequality in quadratic. Let $\underline{N}$ and $\overline{N}$ denote the two values of $\underline{N}$ for which the quadratic term equals zero. By inspection, the inequality holds for $\underline{N} \geq N \geq \overline{N}$. Solving the quadratic yields $\underline{N} = (b+c)/b$ and $\overline{N} = (c/b)^2$. Since $\bar{N}$ is the largest integer less than or equal to $(b+c)/b$, and since $\underline{N}$ and $\overline{N}$ need not be integers, it follows that $\underline{N} \geq \bar{N}$. But the proposition holds for $N > \hat{N}$. Hence, $\overline{\Pi} \geq \hat{\Pi}$ only holds for $N > \bar{N}$ if $N \geq \bar{N}$ or $\bar{N} \geq (c/b)^2$.

REFERENCES

Barrett, S. (1999), 'A theory of full international cooperation', *Journal of Theoretical Politics*, **11** (4): 519–41.

Barrett, S. (2000), 'Consensus treaties', mimeo, Paul H. Nitze School of Advanced International Studies, Johns Hopkins University, Baltimore, MD.

Barrett, S. (2001), 'International cooperation for sale', *European Economic Review*, **45**: 1835–50.

Binmore, K. (1998), *Game Theory and the Social Contract, Volume 2: Just Playing*, Cambridge, MA: MIT Press.

Bodansky, D. (1999), 'The legitimacy of international governance: a coming challenge for international environmental law?' *American Journal of International Law*, **93**: pp. 596–624.

Chander, P. and H. Tulkens (1997), 'The core of an economy with multilateral environmental externalities', *International Journal of Game Theory*, **26**: 379–401.

Farrell, J. and E. Maskin (1989), 'Renegotiation in repeated games', *Games and Economic Behavior*, **1**: 327–60.

Fehr, E. and S. Gächter (2000), 'Fairness and retaliation: the economics of reciprocity', *Journal of Economic Perspectives*, **14** (3): 159–81.

Hoel, M. and K. Schneider (1997), 'Incentives to participate in an international environmental agreement', *Environmental and Resource Economics*, **9**: 153–70.

Mäler, K.-G. (1989), 'The acid rain game', in H. Folmer and E. van Ierland (eds), *Valuation Methods and Policy Making in Environmental Economics*, Amsterdam: Elsevier, pp. 231–52.

Mäler, K.-G. (1991), 'The acid rain game II', mimeo, Stockholm School of Economics.

Young, H.P. (1994), *Equity*, Princeton, NJ: Princeton University Press.

4. A CGE analysis of sulfur deposition and Sweden's 'green' net national product

Lars Bergman*

1 INTRODUCTION

Conventional measures of macroeconomic performance such as national income (NI) and net national product (NNP) do not take into account the impact on welfare of environmental pollution and the depletion of natural resources. For this reason it is often argued that these measures tend to over-estimate significantly both the level of real income and the rate of economic growth. Thus, with proper adjustments for the deterioration of environmental quality and the depletion of natural resources, the rate of economic growth, it is claimed, would be considerably lower than actually indicated by the national accounts. Empirical support for this view is given by, for instance, Repetto et al. (1989) who, in a study of Indonesia found that the depletion of natural resources would call for a rather significant downward adjustment of the conventional measure of the national product. Further evidence on significant deviations between conventional and 'green' national accounts is given in the survey by Dasgupta et al. (1995).

Generally speaking 'greening' of the conventional measure of NNP amounts to adding the consumption value of environmental quality and deducting the value of natural resource depletion. As the scaling of any measure of environmental quality tends to be somewhat arbitrary, the positive consumption value of environmental quality alternatively can take the form of a deduction of the value of environmental damage in relation to some exogenous environmental quality standard. Needless to say there are a host of empirical and methodological problems related to the practical implementation of these ideas. However, there are also issues about principles: how should the green NNP be defined and what can such a measure be used for?

In an article in *Environmental and Resource Economics*[1] in 1991, Karl-Göran Mäler sketched answers to both of these issues. Thus, on the one hand he indicated how the conventional NNP could be adjusted in order to take resource depletion and environmental damage into account. On the other hand he extended the discussion in Weitzman (1976) on NNP as a measure of welfare. Similar ideas were presented in Hartwick (1990), and further developments are presented in Dasgupta et al. (1995). However, the approach to environmental and economic accounting proposed by Mäler differed quite significantly from the one proposed within the national accounting community.

The UN Statistical Office, for instance, aimed at establishing a satellite system to the System of National Accounting for environmental and resource accounting, called the *System for Integrated Environmental and Economic Accounting* (SEEA). The views on conceptual issues underlying this work are presented in Bartelmus et al. (1991). One of the key conceptual issues is related to the principles for determination of the consumption value of environmental quality. Another is related to the treatment of so-called defensive expenditures, that is, expenditures aimed at eliminating or counteracting environmental deterioration or natural resource degradation.

The purpose of this chapter is to compare some potentially competing definitions of green NNP in a model simulation framework and in the case of sulfur.[2] Thus a computable general equilibrium (CGE) model of the Swedish economy, in which both the emissions of sulfur and the damage caused by sulfur depositions are endogenously determined, is developed. The model, which is a revised and elaborated version of the model presented in Bergman (1995), is used for comparative static analyses as well as for projections of the economy's development over time. Three competing measures of green NNP are used for the evaluation of the resulting resource allocation patterns.

In Section 2 the core model is presented, while the modeling of economy–environment interactions is described in Section 3. In Section 4 the environmental policy measures of the model economy are discussed. Then, in Section 5, different measures of green NNP are defined and discussed, and in Section 6 some model simulation results are presented. This includes a comparison of the different green NNP measures. Section 7 concludes the chapter.

2   THE CGE MODEL

2.1   General Features

The model depicts the Swedish economy as a small open economy that is price-taker both on international product markets and on the international capital market. Production and consumption generate emissions of sulfur emissions that are partly deposited within Sweden. Sulfur depositions accumulate over

Table 4.1   Production sectors

T-sectors	NT-sectors
Forestry, paper and pulp industry	Trade, construction, services and communication
Mining, steel and chemicals industries	Water and district heating
Export-oriented manufacturing industries	Public services
Import-competing manufacturing industries	

time, and the accumulated stock of sulfur negatively affects both the level of environmental quality and the overall productivity of the economy's resources. As 'environmental quality' is a public good that affects the utility of the households, the accumulation of sulfur negatively affects welfare both directly via the utility functions and indirectly via productivity losses.

Although time and the accumulation of sulfur in the environment are essential aspects of the analysis to be presented later on in this chapter, the model is not dynamic in the sense that it explicitly incorporates forward-looking behavior. Instead it is solved for one period at a time, and the closing stocks in one period are taken as the opening stocks in the following period. Thus, the accumulation of real capital is exogenous to the model, and within each period the equilibrium prices reflect only the current preferences, technological constraints and resource availability.

In the model the Swedish economy is aggregated to one single consuming sector and seven producing sectors of which one is the public sector. As can be seen in Table 4.1, four of the production sectors produce tradables, while three sectors produce non-tradables. In the formal description of the model the number of production sectors is set equal to n, and each production sector either belongs to the set of tradables-producing sectors, T, or the set of non-tradables-producing sectors, NT.

The tradables-producing sectors are assumed to produce an aggregate of goods for the international market and goods for the domestic market and the elasticity of transformation between the two varieties of output is assumed to be constant in all sectors.[3] The prices of internationally traded goods are exogenously determined, while prices of goods for the domestic market are determined by domestic supply and demand conditions.

2.2   Factors, Technology and Prices

There is an inelastic supply of internationally immobile and intersectorally perfectly mobile labor. In addition to labor there are two domestic resources, which are both sector specific. The first is fixed capital in the form of existing hydro and nuclear power capacity. As essentially all power production in

Sweden is based on hydro or nuclear power, one could alternatively say that
the supply of electricity is exogenously given. The second sector-specific
domestic resource is forest resources, used as input in the forest industry. It is
assumed that the supply of forest resources is completely price inelastic, but
depends on the accumulated deposition of sulfur.

The production technology of all sectors exhibits constant returns to scale
in labor, capital, energy and intermediate goods. The production functions are
nested Leontief and constant elasticity of substitution (CES) functions. The
total factor productivity changes over time due both to exogenous technological change at a sector-specific rate and the change in a measure of environmental quality, *ENQ*.[4] 'Environmental quality' is a public good, but the impact
of changes in environmental quality on total factor productivity differs across
sectors. Thus, for each production sector the technological constraints are
described by a production function of the form:

$$X_j = \min \left(\frac{Y_j}{A_j e^{-\lambda_j t}}, \frac{M_{ij}}{a_{ij}}, \frac{M_j}{m_j} \right) g_j(ENQ_t) \, j \in T \cup NT, \qquad (4.1)$$

where X_j is gross output in sector j, Y_j is the input in of an aggregated input
consisting of labor, capital, electricity, fuels and, in the forest industry, forest
resources. M_j is the input of (aggregated) imports in sector j. The coefficients
A_j, a_{ij} and m_{ij} indicate the input per unit of gross output of the three types of
inputs, while the parameter λ_j indicates the rate of sector-specific technical
change. The function $g_j(.)$ defines the sector-specific relation between environmental quality and total factor productivity. The parameter t, finally, is an
index for time, equal to zero at the base year.

The production of goods and services generates sulfur emissions.[5] The
possibility of emitting sulfur into the environment can be seen as a kind of
input in the sectoral production processes, and substitution between this particular input and capital, labor, energy and intermediate inputs could be envisaged. However, the empirical basis for estimation of the relevant elasticities of
substitution is insufficient with a wide margin. Thus the emissions of sulfur are
assumed to be proportional to the use of fossil fuels,[6] and sulfur is not explicitly included in the description of the sectoral production functions.

On the basis of the production function (4.1) the unit, and marginal, cost of
production in sector j becomes:

$$C_j = (P_{Yj} A_j e^{-\lambda_j t} + \sum_i P_i^D a_{ij} + P^M m_j + b_j) \frac{1}{g_j(ENQ_t)}; \, j \in T \cup NT, \qquad (4.2)$$

where P_{Yj} is the sector-specific price of the labor–capital–energy aggregate
input, P_i^D is the price of 'domestic' good i, and P^M is the price of imported
inputs.

The price of the aggregated labor–capital–energy input is defined as the unit cost of a nested CES aggregate of these inputs, and for all sectors except except the forest sector it can be written:

$$P_{Yj} = P_{Yj}\{P_L, P_{Uj}[P_k, P_{Qj}(P_E, P_{Fj})]\}; \, j \in T \cup NT. \tag{4.3a}$$

In equation (4.3a) P_{Fj} is the sector-specific price[7] of imported fuels, while P_E is the price of electricity. Consequently P_{Qj} is the price of the CES aggregate of electricity and fuels. Together with capital with the price P_K this aggregate forms another CES aggregate of capital and energy, U_j, with the price P_{Uj}. Finally the capital–energy aggregate is combined with labor, with the price P_L, to become a CES aggregate of labor, capital, electricity and fuels.

In the case of the forest industry ($j = FOREST$) the capital–energy aggregate forms a CES aggregate, H, with forest resources, N. Thus, in the case of the forest industry the price of the aggregate input can be written:

$$P_{Y,FOREST} = P_{Y,FOREST}(P_L, P_H\{P_N, P_{U,FOREST}[P_K, P_{Q,FOREST} \atop (P_E, P_{F,FOREST})]\}). \tag{4.3b}$$

The input 'fuel' is an aggregate of imported fossil fuels. The world market price of fuels is assumed to be exogenously determined, but the domestic user price includes a tax (positive or zero) on sulfur emissions. As the composition of the aggregated fuel commodity differs across sectors, including the household sector, the content of sulfur per unit of fuel also differs across sectors. This means that a uniform tax on sulfur emissions will affect the sectoral user prices of fuel in a non-uniform way. This is the reason for the sectoral index on the fuel price variable in equations (4.3a) and (4.3b), which is defined in the following way:

$$P_{Fj} = P_F + PEM f_j; \, j \in T \cup NT, \tag{4.4}$$

where P_F is the world market price of fuels, PEM is the endogenously determined tax (to be defined later) on sulfur emissions, and f_j is the emission of sulfur per unit of fuels in sector j. The user price of fuels for the household sector is defined in a parallel way (with the coefficient f_D being the emission of sulfur per unit of fuels used in the household sector).

As was indicated above, the output of sector j is a constant elasticity of transformation (CET) aggregate of goods for international markets, denoted, X_j^Z, and goods for the domestic market, X_j^D. Thus the price of sector j output can be written as a price-possibility frontier defined by:

$$P_j = P_j(P_j^D, P_j^Z); \, j \in T \cup NT, \tag{4.5}$$

with obvious notation.

2.3   Producer Behavior, Supply and Factor Demands

Producer behavior is modelled on the basis of the standard assumption about
profit maximization. The level of output is determined by the usual condition
on price and marginal cost, that is:

$$P_j = C_j; \, j \in T \cup NT. \tag{4.6}$$

In the T-sectors the profit-maximizing mix of total output in terms of domestic and international goods is determined in accordance with the following
conditions:

$$X_j^D = \frac{\partial P_j(P_j^D, P_j^Z)}{\partial P_j^D} X_j; \, j \in T; \tag{4.7}$$

$$X_j^Z = \frac{\partial P_j(P_j^D, P_j^Z)}{\partial P_j^Z} X_j; \, j \in T. \tag{4.8}$$

As was mentioned above, the domestic producers of tradables face given
prices in foreign currency units on world markets. The price of tradables in
domestic currency units is defined by:

$$P_j^Z = \Omega P_j^W; \, j \in T, \tag{4.9}$$

where Ω is the exchange rate. In the same way the domestic price of imports
is defined by:

$$P_M = \Omega P_M^W. \tag{4.10}$$

In the following the exchange rate is taken to be the numeraire of the price
system and set equal to unity.

The production sector demand for intermediate inputs, domestically
produced as well as imported, is directly given by the fixed input coefficients
defined in connection with equation (4.1) and the level of output. The demand
for the 'substitutable' inputs, that, labor, capital, fuels and electricity, is given
by Shephard's lemma in conjunction with the cost function defined in equation (4.2). Thus, with obvious notation and suppressing the structure of the
nesting of the cost function, the demand for these four factors can be written:

$$L_j = \frac{\partial C_j(P_L, P_K, P_{Fj}, P_E)}{\partial P_L} X_j; \, j \in T \cup NT; \tag{4.11}$$

$$K_j = \frac{\partial C_j(P_L, P_K, P_{Fj}, P_E)}{\partial P_K} X_j; \, j \in T \cup NT; \tag{4.12}$$

$$F_j = \frac{\partial C_j(P_L, P_K, P_{Fj}, P_E)}{\partial P_{Fj}} X_j; \, j \in T \cup NT; \tag{4.13}$$

$$E_j = \frac{\partial C_j(P_L, P_K, P_{Fj}, P_E)}{\partial P_E} X_j; \, j \in T \cup NT. \tag{4.14}$$

In addition to these factors, the forest industry also uses forest resources as an input, and the demand for forest resources is given by:

$$N_{FOREST} = \frac{\partial C_{FOREST}(P_L, P_K, P_N, P_{F,FOREST}, P_E)}{\partial P_N} X_{FOREST}. \tag{4.15}$$

2.4   Utility and Final Demand

It is assumed that individual welfare is affected by environmental quality defined by the index *ENQ*. Thus the preferences of the aggregated household sector is represented by a utility function of the form:

$$U = u(D)v(ENQ), \tag{4.16}$$

where the function $u(D)$ has the Cobb–Douglas form. D is an $n + 3$ vector of private goods (n domestically produced goods, fuels, electricity and imports) and $v(ENQ)$ is an exponential function. The vector of private goods includes the output of the public sector. By the structure of the utility function the supply of the public good 'environmental quality' affects the level of utility generated by a given vector of private goods, but it does not affect the marginal rates of substitution between different private goods. Thus the household sector demand for domestically produced goods can be written:

$$D_j = D_i(P_1^D, \ldots, P_n^D, P_F, P_E, P_M, I); \, j = 1, 2, \ldots, n + 3. \tag{4.17}$$

where good $n + 1$ is fuels, good $n + 2$ electricity and good $n + 3$ imports.

The variable I is the total expenditures of the household sector. It should be noted that there is no explicit tax and transfer system in the model. The revenues from sulfur emission taxes, as well as the few other taxes that are incorporated, are assumed to be paid back to the household sector as lump-sum transfers.

2.5 Equilibrium Conditions

In addition to the intermediate and final demand for goods discussed so far, there is also an exogenously determined demand for good i, G_i, for investment purposes. The equilibrium conditions for the $n + 3$ goods demanded both by the producing sectors and the household sector, that is, for tradables (T), non-tradables (NT) and imports, fuel and non-fuel, can now be written:

$$X_i^D = \sum_i a_{ij}X_j + D_i + G_i; \, j \in T \cup NT; \quad (4.18)$$

$$F = \sum_i F_j + D_F; \quad (4.19)$$

$$E = \sum_j E_j + D_E; \quad (4.20)$$

$$M = \sum_j m_j X_j + D_M. \quad (4.21)$$

The equilibrium conditions for the labor, capital and forest resources markets can be written:

$$L = \sum_j L_j + L_{def}; \quad (4.22)$$

$$K = \sum_j K_j + K_{def}; \quad (4.23)$$

$$N(ENQ) = N_{FOREST}, \quad (4.24)$$

where L, K and N represent the supply of the resources in question.

The supply of labor is exogenously determined and entirely inelastic, while the supply of capital is perfectly elastic at the internationally determined rate of interest. As was mentioned before, the supply of forest resources depends on the environmental quality index ENQ. More precisely the rate of forest growth, and thus the annual supply of forest resources, is a decreasing function of the accumulated stock of sulfur in the environment. The labor and capital demands denoted L_{def} and K_{def} represent the quantities of labor and capital used for so-called 'defensive' activities, that is, activities aimed at protecting the environment from the negative impact of sulfur deposition. The determination of these quantities will be discussed in Section 3.

2.6 Current Account and Macroeconomic Closure

The current account surplus is exogenously determined and equal to B. Thus the budget constraint of the economy, is exogenously determined. Formally it holds that:

$$\sum_j P_j^Z X_j^Z - P_M M - P_F F + P_K(AS - K) = B, \tag{4.25}$$

where AS is the exogenously determined domestic accumulated savings and K, which is defined in equation (4.23) above, is the aggregate domestic use of capital. Thus the last term on the left-hand side represents the (positive or negative) return on international net lending at the internationally determined rate of interest. Walras's law in conjunction with equation (4.25) determines aggregate household spending, that is, the variable I. As the aggregate investment expenditures (the G variables in equation (4.18)) are exogenously determined, the equality between current period savings and investments is brought about by a suitable adjustment of aggregate consumption expenditures.

This completes the description of the 'core' of the CGE model. It remains to describe the relation between economic activity and environmental quality.

3 EMISSIONS, DEPOSITIONS AND ENVIRONMENTAL QUALITY

The first step in the chain from economic activity to environmental quality is the emissions of pollutants, in this particular case sulfur. As was indicated above the emissions of sulfur, in the form of SO_2, are proportional to the use of fuels in the production sectors and the household sector. Thus the total emissions of sulfur dioxide, TEM, are defined by the following linear function:

$$TEM = \sum_j f_j F_j + F_D D_F. \tag{4.26}$$

All the emissions sooner or later become depositions in various receptors within or outside Sweden. In the same way part of the emissions outside Sweden are deposited in Swedish receptors. In the model the entire area of Sweden is divided into four types of land: agricultural land, forest land, lakes and rivers, and urban areas, and each type of land is defined as a 'receptor'. Thus, the set of receptors, R, has four elements defined in Table 4.2.

Table 4.2   Elements of the set of receptors (R)

Element	Definition
AGR	Agricultural land
FOR	Forest land
WAT	Lakes and rivers
URB	Urban areas

The deposition of sulfur in receptor R is denoted DEP_R and defined in accordance with:

$$DEP_R = \theta_R(\alpha TEM + IMP), \tag{4.27}$$

where α is the share of domestic emissions deposited within Sweden, IMP is the deposition resulting from foreign emissions, and the coefficients θ_R both convert sulfur dioxide to sulfur and allocate the total depositions across receptors.

The sulfur that is being deposited in the environment is gradually neutralized over time. The rate of neutralization depends partly on the buffering capacity of the soil and partly on the extent to which active environmental protection measures (such as liming) are implemented. In the following these active environmental protection measures somewhat incorrectly will be called 'removal activities' and denoted REM_R, while the natural rate of neutralization in receptor R is denoted δ_R.

The output of the 'removal activities' can be regarded as the services produced by firms specialized in environmental protection and cleanup activities. In the national accounts the output of environmental protection and cleanup services bought by the production sectors would be regarded as 'intermediate goods', while the services bought by households, government or foreign buyers would be regarded as 'final goods', that is, included in NNP. In the numerical experiments carried out with the model and reported below, the environmental protection and cleanup services are *not* included in the utility function of the aggregated household sector. In other words the household sector is assumed to benefit from environmental protection and cleanup activities only to the extent that these activities improve the environmental quality, that is, *ENQ*.

Using the notation introduced so far, the accumulated stock of sulfur in receptor R in year t, that is, the variable S_R^t, is given by the stock accumulation equation:

$$S_R^t = (1 - \delta_R)S_R^{(t-1)} + DEP_R^t - REM_R^t; \ R = AGR, FOR, WAT, URB. \tag{4.28}$$

The environmental quality index *ENQ* introduced in Section 2 is a function of S_R^t for one or several receptors. Normally this means that the numerical value of *ENQ* depends on how much of a given pollutant has accumulated in the environment. However, for some aspects of environmental quality, such as urban air quality, the annual deposition rather than the accumulated stock of pollutants is the critical factor. In terms of equation (4.28), such a case would correspond to $\delta_R = 1$ and $REM_R^t = 0$ so that $S_R^t = DEP_R^t$ for the receptor *URB*.

Turning next to the removal activities it is assumed that the technology in this sector of the economy exhibits constant returns to scale in capital and labor.[8] It is also assumed that the input coefficients for these factors of production are constant and equal to k_R and l_R, respectively. In the following the cost of removing depositions in receptor R is called 'defensive expenditures' and denoted DE_R. Thus the defensive expenditures related to receptor R are defined by:

$$DE_R^t = (P_K k_R + P_L l_R)\, REM_R^t;\ R = AGR, FOR, WAT, URB. \qquad (4.29)$$

For the receptor *FOR* we shall later on refer to the 'hypothetical defensive expenditures', that is, the hypothetical cost of removing the current deposition on forest land. This variable will be denoted DE^*, and defined in accordance with equation (4.29).

Suppressing the time index, the total amounts of capital and labor used for removal activities are consequently determined by:

$$L_{def} = \sum_R l_R REM_R; \qquad (4.30)$$

$$K_{def} = \sum_R k_R REM_R. \qquad (4.31)$$

To sum up, the formulation of the model implies that sulfur emissions can lead to welfare losses in two different ways. First, real resources might be allocated to removal activities. Second, sulfur depositions, directly or indirectly through the accumulation of sulfur in the environment, cause welfare losses by reducing total factor productivity and by reducing the quality of the environmental services 'consumed' by the household sector. What actually happens depends partly on a number of parameters in production and utility functions, and partly on the degree to which removal activities are carried out. It remains to introduce a mechanism, or a set of assumptions, such that the extent of removal activity is determined.

For the simulation experiments carried out in this particular study, several simplifying assumptions are made in order to determine the values of the *REM* variables. Thus, for two of the receptors, *AGR* and *WAT*, we assume that all depositions are neutralized by liming, that is, a removal activity. This corresponds roughly to the current reality. In urban areas, that is, receptor *URB*, the deposition of sulfur in the form of acid rains tends to damage buildings, bridges and monuments, while accumulation is not a problem. In order to counteract the damage caused by sulfur deposition, real resources have to be allocated to repair and maintenance, that is, a removal activity has to be carried out. In our simulations we assume that all depositions in the receptor *URB* are counteracted by removal activities.

Thus, for the receptors *AGR*, *WAT* and *URB* it is assumed that $REM_R^t = DEP_R^t$ for all t. Consequently there is no accumulation of sulfur in these receptors, and the welfare cost of sulfur deposition is given by the opportunity cost of the resources used for removal activities.

In the case of sulfur deposition on forestland, that is, in the receptor *FOR*, we make the simplifying, and reasonably realistic, assumption that there are no significant removal activities. In other words we assume that $REM_{FOR} = 0$. Moreover, the natural rate of neutralization, that is, the parameter δ_{FOR}, is considerably smaller than unity. This means that sulfur tends to accumulate in the receptor *FOR* unless the annual deposition is very small. Concerning the effects of sulfur deposition we utilize the empirical evidence suggesting that the accumulation of sulfur in *FOR* negatively affects both the growth of forests and the amenity value of forests.

The environmental quality index *ENQ* is the crucial link between, on the one hand, the stock of sulfur in *FOR* and, on the other hand, forest growth and the amenity value of forests. It is defined by:

$$ENQ_t = \left(\frac{S^{max} - S_t}{S^{max} - S_0} \right), \qquad (4.32)$$

where S^{max} is the stock of sulfur that would reduce the rate of forest growth to zero in all parts of the country. It follows from this definition that the value of the environmental quality index at the base year, that is, ENQ_0, is equal to unity.

Extensive empirical studies by Skånberg (1994) and Sverdrup et al. (1994) of the impact of sulfur accumulation on forest growth suggest that there is a threshold level at which additional sulfur accumulation would have a negative impact on forest growth. Moreover, the actual base year value of the stock of sulfur was very close to that threshold level. Thus, to the extent that the stock of sulfur would continue to grow over the model simulation period, forest growth would be reduced. More precisely, additional net deposition of sulfur would gradually increase the area of forest land where there is essentially no growth. In the model we have made the simplifying assumption that, in the aggregate, the negative impact of sulfur deposition on forest growth is linear between the threshold level and the level S^{max}. Thus the annual supply of forest raw material is given by the following function:

$$N(ENQ_t) = \bar{N}\,ENQ_t \equiv \bar{N}\left(\frac{S^{max} - S_t}{S^{max} - S_0}\right), \qquad (4.33)$$

where $\bar{N}$ is the annual supply of forest raw material provided the accumulated stock of sulfur does not exceed the threshold level.

Concerning the amenity values of healthy forests the empirical basis is more uncertain. To begin with, the environmental quality index is normalized in such a way that the factor $v(ENQ_0)$ in the utility function (4.16) is equal to unity. (This particular normalization will be discussed in the following section.) In other words it holds that:

$$U(D,ENQ_0) = u(D)v(ENQ_0) = u(D). \qquad (4.34)$$

It follows from the definition of *ENQ* and the utility function that an increase in the accumulated stock of sulfur will decrease the utility associated with a given consumption vector. It should also be noted that the utility function implies a well-defined measure of the marginal willingness to pay for environmental quality, in the following denoted $MWTP^{ENQ}$. A socially efficient tax on sulfur deposition should be equal to the aggregate marginal willingness to pay for the relevant environmental quality.

Lacking better data, however, we have turned the procedure around and simply assumed that the base year tax on sulfur emissions (SEK 30 per kg sulfur), after conversion to a tax on sulfur deposition within Sweden, was a socially efficient tax. On the basis of this assumption the relevant parameter of the utility function of the household sector was calibrated so that the base year marginal willingness to pay for a reduction of sulfur deposition became equal to the actual base year tax on sulfur deposition.

Finally a word on the impact of sulfur deposition and/or accumulation on total factor productivity in the production sectors, that is, the functions $g_j(ENQ_t)$ in equations (4.1) and (4.2). Given the assumption that all depositions in the receptors *AGR*, *WAT* and *URB* are entirely counteracted by removal activities, it would be double counting to include productivity effects as well. However, as that assumption, after all, is not very realistic for the receptor *URB*, it would have been desirable to represent the cost of increased corrosion of buildings and bridges as a productivity loss in the relevant production sectors. For the moment, however, the empirical basis for such a treatment of sulfur deposition in urban areas is too shaky.

4 ENVIRONMENTAL POLICY

In the model the total emissions of sulfur can be constrained. The exogenously imposed constraint is implemented through a system of tradable emission permits. Trade among the emitters leads to a unique price, *PEM*, of emission permits. As the market for emission permits is assumed to be competitive, this price is equal to the marginal cost of emission reduction in all sectors. Formally the system is defined by the following set of equations and inequalities where $\overline{TEM}$ is the exogenous supply of emission permits, that is, the predetermined level of total emissions:

$$(TEM - \overline{TEM}) \le 0;\ PEM\ (TEM - \overline{TEM}) = 0;\ PEM \ge 0. \qquad (4.35)$$

5 DEFINITIONS OF 'GREEN' NNP

In the following the model presented in the preceding sections will be used for comparative static experiments and for projections of the development of the Swedish economy over time. The resulting resource allocations in the model economy will be evaluated using different macroeconomic indicators, that is, conventional NNP as well as various measures of green NNP. Three specific measures of green NNP will be used. In the following these measures are defined for the particular case we are investigating, that is, a case where sulfur is the only pollutant and where the depletion or deterioration of other natural resources than forest resources is ignored.

The first measure, which seems to be in line with the measure proposed by Mäler, can be written:

$$ENP_t = NNP_t + MWTP_t^{ENQ}(ENQ_t - ENQ_0) + P_t^N(N_t^S - N_{t-1}^s), \quad (4.36)$$

where conventional NNP is adjusted with respect to the consumption value of environmental quality (the second term on the right-hand side) and the deterioration of forest resources (the third term on the right-hand side). In other words, using this measure the impact of increased deposition of sulfur will have two components. First, there will be an immediate loss of welfare due to reduced environmental quality. Second, there will be a long-term loss due to reduced forest yield in the future.

A couple of points should be noted to relation to expression (4.36). First, environmental quality is evaluated with $MWTP^{ENQ}$, that is, the marginal willingness to pay for *ENQ*. This measure is derived from the utility function of the aggregated household sector. In fact, the first two terms in the expression are just the result of a first-order linearization of the utility function around a given consumption vector and ENQ_0. This also implies that *ENP* can be used to evaluate changes in *ENQ* which are sufficiently small to keep all prices and the *MWTP* approximately constant.

Second, the variable *ENQ* is normalized by its base year value ENQ_0. The reason for this is that there is no obvious choice of scaling in the case of environmental quality; while zero consumption of potatoes, French wines and other private goods can easily be envisaged, zero consumption of environmental quality is not a well-defined quantity. However, the choice of scaling affects only the level of green NNP and thus does not affect its rate of change in response to environmental deterioration. Our particular choice of scaling implies that the consumption value of environmental quality is positive whenever *ENQ* is greater than its base year value, and negative in the opposite case.

The second measure of environmental quality, for convenience denoted *ENQ2* in the following, is something in between the above-defined *ENP* and the definition adopted in the SEEA. Thus, as in our *ENP* measure, there is no deduction for actual 'defensive' expenditures during the period. But as in the SEEA, the damage caused by non-abated sulfur deposition is evaluated in monetary terms with the hypothetical defensive expenditures that would have been necessary in order to keep the environmental quality at the same level as at the beginning of the year. As the cost for defensive activities is a lot easier to estimate than the marginal willingness to pay for environmental quality, *ENP2* is an attractive alternative to *ENP* (provided that it gives approximately the same result). *ENP2* can be written in the following way:

$$ENP2_t = NNP_t - DE_t^* + P_t^N(N_t^S - N_{t-1}^s), \qquad (4.37)$$

where DE^* is the hypothetical defensive expenditure that would have neutralized sulfur deposited on forestland and thus kept *ENQ* constant during the year.

One important differences between *ENP* and *ENP2* should immediately be pointed out. That is, whereas *ENP* depends on the stock of sulfur that accumulates over time, *ENP2* only takes into account sulfur depositions within the current period. In other words *ENP* reflects the entire history of sulfur deposition, while *ENP2* takes the level of environmental quality at the beginning of each individual year as the point of departure. Not surprisingly this difference between the two measures will turn out to be quite important.

Another important issue is whether the value of *ENP* will differ from the value of *ENP2* at a given initial stock of sulfur. To elucidate this issue, it should be noted that by an appropriate rescaling the value of environmental quality can be defined in terms of the accumulated stock of sulfur. Thus it holds that:

$$MWTP_t^{ENQ}(ENQ_t - ENQ_0) \equiv MWTP_t^S(S_t - S_0). \qquad (4.38)$$

Moreover, if we let $C(S)$ be the marginal cost of counteracting accumulating sulfur depositions, it holds that:

$$DE_t^* = C(S_t)(S_t - S_0). \qquad (4.39)$$

It follows that for a given S_0 the value of *ENP* is equal to the value of *ENP2* if and only if $C(S)$ is equal to $MWTP^S$ around S_0. In other words, if the actual stock of sulfur is efficient in the sense that the marginal cost of reducing the stock is equal to the value of the marginal damage of additional sulfur deposition, the two measures of green NNP attain the same numerical value. But in the more likely case of an inefficient stock of sulfur the two measures differ.

Our third measure of green NNP is simply the one proposed in the SEEA. It can be written in the following way:

$$SEEA_t = NNPt - DE_t^* - \sum_{R \neq FOR} DE_t^R + P_t^N (N_{t-1}^S), \qquad (4.40)$$

where the index R denotes the receptor where the sulfur is deposited, and DE_R is the cost of the measures actually undertaken to counteract or neutralize the sulfur depositions in receptor R. At a given level of accumulated sulfur, *SEEA* is lower than *ENP* whenever there are defensive expenditures. However, as *SEEA*, unlike *ENP*, fails to take stock accumulation into account, the ranking between the two measures might be reversed along a trajectory where sulfur is accumulated.

6   COMPARISONS OF DIFFERENT MEASURES OF GREEN NNP

The main conceptual differences between the competing measures of green NNP have already been indicated. It remains to investigate whether these differences are of any practical importance, that is, if, for a given development of the economy, there is any significant quantitative difference between *ENP*, *ENP2* and *SEEA*. In order to shed some light on that issue, a number of simulations with the model presented in Sections 2 and 3 have been carried out. In this section the main findings are summarized.

The first model simulation was a comparative static experiment aimed at elucidating the impact on various macroeconomic indicators of increased sulfur deposition. More precisely it was assumed that, *ceteris paribus*, the sulfur emissions outside Sweden increased to the extent that the depositions in Sweden would increase by 100 percent in relation to the base year depositions.

Given the construction of the model this exogenous change would produce both direct and indirect negative welfare effects. The direct welfare effects reflect the loss of environmental quality due to additional accumulation of sulfur. The indirect welfare effects reflect both productivity losses in forestry due to additional sulfur deposition and the use of real resources for counteracting the damage otherwise caused by sulfur deposition on agricultural land, in lakes and rivers and on buildings and bridges in urban areas.

The quantitative results are summarized in Table 4.3. It should be noted that both environmental quality and forest yield, the variables *ENQ* and *N* in the model, are scaled in such a way that conventional *NNP* and all three measures of green NNP attain the same base year value. Moreover, the base year marginal cost of counteracting sulfur deposition, the variable $C(S)$ discussed above,[9] is equal to the base year value of $MTWP^S$. This is not a coincidence; the tax-rate was chosen on the basis of an estimate of the cost of reducing sulfur emissions. The consequence of the base year equality between $C(S)$ and $MWTP^S$ is that, for small changes in the accumulated stock of sulfur, there should be no difference between *ENP* and *ENP2*.

Several observations can be made on the basis of the results presented in Table 4.3. First, the impact on ENQ of significantly increased depositions during one year is quite small. The reason for this is that the impact of the depositions during one single year on the accumulated stock of sulfur is very small. As a result of the small change in the stock of sulfur there is no measurable difference between $C(S)$ and $MWTP^S$ and thus between *ENP* and *ENP2*. Second, in spite of the small change in *ENQ* there is an impact on NNP as well as a difference between conventional NNP and *ENP*. This reflects the reduction of forest yield due to the accumulation of sulfur on forestland. Third, *SEEA* is considerably lower than *ENP* and *ENP2*. In other words the deduction of defensive expenditures seems to make a rather significant difference.

Table 4.3   *Comparative static impact of doubled deposition on macroeconomic (in SEK10^9) and environmental quality indicators*

	Base year values	Doubled deposition case
NNP	918.8	918.6
ENP	918.8	918.4
ENP2	918.8	918.4
SEEA	918.8	916.5
ENQ	1.000	0.990

Table 4.4   Calculated development over time of various macroeconomic and environmental quality indicators

	$t = 0$	$t = 5$	$t = 10$	$t = 15$
NNP	918.8	1005.1	1098.2	1198.2
ENP	918.8	1005.0	1097.7	1197.0
ENP2	918.8	1005.1	1098.2	1198.1
SEEA	918.8	1004.8	1097.5	1197.2
ENQ	1.000	0.996	0.985	0.967

Next we turn to the development over time. On the assumption that the domestic growth of capital and labour resources and productivity would allow an annual growth of GDP by 2 percent, and that sulfur emissions outside Sweden grow by 2 percent per annum, the model was solved for 15 consecutive years. The developments over time for the macroeconomic and environmental quality indicators are summarized in Table 4.4.

Again several observations can be made. First, the annually small accumulation of sulfur over a 15-year period does have a non-negligible impact on the index of environmental quality. And as a result there is a clear, although small, difference between conventional NNP and *ENP* at the end of the period.

Second, as the stock of sulfur grows and the index of environmental quality declines there is a growing difference between *ENP* and *ENP2*. This reflects a growing difference between $C(S)$ and $MWTP^S$ as the quality of the environment deteriorates the latter increases while the former remains approximately constant. However, there is also another reason for the difference between *ENP* and *ENP2*. Whereas *ENP* reflects the environmental damage caused by the growing stock of sulfur, *ENP2* by definition only reflects the deposition during each particular year. As a result the adjustment of conventional NNP with DE^* remains very small in spite of the gradual deterioration of the environment.

Third, as in the comparative static experiment summarized in Table 4.3, *SEEA* initially implies a greater adjustment of conventional NNP than *ENP*. Again this primarily reflects the deduction of defensive expenditures. However, by the end of the simulation period the ranking of the two measures is reversed. The reason is that the underestimation (in relation to *ENP*) of the environmental and natural resource deterioration effects on economic growth, due to the neglect of sulfur stock accumulation, in the long run dominates over the overestimation due to the deduction of defensive expenditures.

The results presented so far indicate the obvious, namely that in an economy with environmental pollution there is a difference between conventional

Table 4.5   Calculated development of ENP *and NNP with and without productivity effects of sulfur deposition*

	$t = 0$	$t = 5$	$t = 10$	$t = 15$
ENP	918.8	1005.0	1097.7	1197.0
NNP 'with'	918.8	1005.1	1098.2	1198.2
NNP 'without'	918.8	1005.2	1099.0	1200.4

NNP and the environmental quality-adjusted NNP, that is, *ENP*. However, environmental deterioration and natural resource degradation and depletion affect the productivity of capital and labor, and these productivity reductions are reflected in the conventional measure of NNP. In order to elucidate the impact on capital and labor productivity of sulfur deposition and accumulation, another set of model simulations were carried out. In these simulations it was, somewhat unrealistically, assumed that all sulfur deposition could be counteracted at no cost. The results, which are summarized in Table 4.5, indicate that a significant share of the total economic impact of sulfur deposition in fact reflected in the conventional NNP measure.

A slightly different issue concerns the scope for, as well as the costs and benefits of, policy measures aimed at reducing the domestic emissions of sulfur. Currently only about 10 percent of the sulfur deposited in Sweden originates from Swedish sources. Thus, reducing domestic emissions may have a rather limited impact on the long-run accumulation of sulfur as long as the domestic measures, in one way or another, induce similar measures in other countries.

In order to elucidate this issue the model was used to simulate the development of the economy over a 15-year period, during which the domestic emissions were kept at the base-year level. This policy objective was implemented by means of a system of tradable emission permits. As no transaction costs or monopolization of the permit market were assumed, the equilibrium prices of emission permits, the variable *PEM* in the model, is equal to the marginal cost of reducing sulfur emissions. (It should be noted that in Sweden, since 1991, there has been a tax of SEK 30 per kg of emitted sulfur.) The results of the model simulations are summarized in Table 4.6.

The results suggest that a constraint on domestic emissions in the long run have a non-negligible impact on the accumulation of sulfur. However, the results also suggest that zero growth of domestic emissions does not prevent positive growth of the stock of sulfur. Moreover, according to the model results the benefits of a better environment are lower than the costs of attaining the zero emission growth.

Table 4.6   Calculated impact on macroeconomic and environmental quality indicators of a 'zero-growth' constraint on domestic sulfur emissions

	$t = 0$	$t = 5$	$t = 10$	$t = 15$
Without policy				
ENP	918.8	1005.0	1097.7	1197.0
ENQ	1.000	0.996	0.985	0.967
PEM (SEK/kg)	0.00	0.00	0.00	0.00
With policy				
ENP	918.8	1004.0	1093.8	1192.2
ENQ	1.000	0.997	0.989	0.976
PEM (SEK/kg)	0.00	10.00	26.00	49.60

7   CONCLUDING REMARKS

Needless to say the model and the results presented above are just a first step towards a CGE model of economy–environment interactions. More pollutants need to be included in order to give better estimates of the environmental costs of pollution. In order to be able to say something about 'double-dividend' issues, an elaborated representation of the tax and transfer system should be incorporated. As environmental damage is often related to the accumulation of stocks rather than to the instantaneous flow of pollutants, the model should be fully dynamic rather than quasi-dynamic.

In spite of all this, however, the results reported in the preceding section do suggest that conceptual issues are important when environmental and economic accounting systems are designed. Compromises between what is theoretically desirable and what is practically feasible obviously have to be made. But the first step towards a good compromise is solid understanding of the underlying theoretical issues. The contributions by Mäler and others have elucidated the fundamental issues that national accountants are faced with when they extend the conventional national accounts to include environmental resources.

NOTES

*   The author is grateful for contributions by Sofia Ahlroth and Kristian Skånberg to an earlier version of this chapter. Financial support from the National Swedish Energy Administration is gratefully acknowledged.
1.   Mäler (1991). Similar ideas were independently put forward in Hartwick (1990).

2. Needless to say sulfur is not the only pollutant of importance in relation to a measure of green NNP. However, most of the key issues related to green national accounting can be elucidated within a case study of sulfur.
3. For a discussion on this and alternative approaches to the treatment of tradables-producing sectors in CGE models, see Bergman (1985).
4. The environmental quality index *ENQ* is further discussed in Section 3, below.
5. In this particular study, sulfur is the only pollutant considered, but the model is designed to incorporate several different pollutants.
6. It should be noted, however, that other inputs can be substituted for fossil fuels and thus the emission of sulfur per unit of output is *not* a fixed coefficient in the model.
7. The reason for the sectoral differentiation of fuel prices will be explained below.
8. The use of intermediate inputs in removal activities is disregarded.
9. It should be pointed out that in the model, measures to counteract accumulation of sulfur is assumed to be a constant returns to scale activity. Thus, at given factor prices the marginal cost of those measures, $C(S)$, is constant.

REFERENCES

Bartelmus, P., C. Stahmer and J. van Tongeren (1991), 'Integrated environmental and economic accounting: framework for a SNA satellite system', *Review of Income and Wealth*, Series 37, No. 2.

Bergman, L. (1985), 'Extensions and applications of the MSG-model: a brief survey', in F.R. Førsund, M. Hoel and S. Longva, *Production, Multi-Sectoral Growth and Planning*, Amsterdam: North-Holland, pp. 127–61.

Bergman, L. (1995), 'Environment–economy interactions in a computable general equilibrium model: a case study of Sweden', in P.O. Johansson, B. Kriström and K.-G. Mäler, *Current Issues in Environmental Economics*, Manchester and New York: Manchester University Press, pp. 153–70.

Dasgupta, P., K.-G. Mäler and B. Kriström (1995), 'Current issues in resource accounting', in P.O. Johansson, B. Kriström and K.-G. Mäler, *Current Issues in Environmental Economics*, Manchester and New York: Manchester University Press, pp. 117–52.

Hartwick, J. (1990), 'Natural resources, national accounting and economic depreciation', *Journal of Public Economics*, **43**: 291–304.

Mäler, K.-G. (1991), 'National Accounts and Environmental Resources', *Environmental and Resource Economics*, **1**, 1–15.

Repetto, R.W. Magrath, M. Wells, C. Beer and F. Rossini (1989), *Wasting Assets: Natural Resources in the National Income Accounts*, Washington DC: World Resources Institute.

Skånberg, K. (1994), 'En beräkning av skogsförsurningens skadekostnader' (An estimate of the damage cost of forest acidification), mimeo, Statistics Sweden and National Institute of Economic Research.

Sverdrup, H., P. Warfinge and B. Nihlsgård (1994), 'Assessment of soil acidification effects on forest growth in Sweden', *Water, Air and Soil Pollution*, **78**, 1–36.

Weitzman, M. (1976), 'On the welfare significance of national product in a dynamic economy', *Quarterly Journal of Economics*, **90**, 156–62.

5. Biodiversity management under uncertainty: species selection and harvesting rules

William Brock and Anastasios Xepapadeas

1 INTRODUCTION

The significance of biodiversity and the value of resource conservation to society is an issue that has drawn considerable attention both from the economists' and ecologists' point of view.[1] One of the major questions associated with this issue is the value of biodiversity loss due to anthropogenic influences.

There is a high degree of uncertainty associated with species diversity, the rate at which diversity is lost and the implications of such loss, which makes the analysis of the problem extremely complicated. Given, however, the significance of the issue, there is an ever-increasing need to develop systematic models capable of dealing with some aspects of biodiversity. The purpose of this chapter is to develop a model for analysing biodiversity management.

In particular we consider the problem of an ecosystem manager or planner that seeks to allocate a given amount of land to different species. Uncertainty is reflected in the stochastic growth rates of the species biomasses. We associate a total economic value with each species in the landscape. This value includes components such as ecological, genetic, social, economic, scientific, educational, cultural, recreational and aesthetic (Pearce and Perrings 1995). More compactly, biodiversity values can be classified in four broad categories (Ehrlich and Ehrlich 1992, Daily and Ehrlich 1995): (i) existence values, (ii) aesthetic values, (iii) direct economic values or direct use values, and (iv) non-substitutable ecosystem services.

Direct economic values are mainly associated with harvesting of species that requires removal of a certain amount of the biomass of the harvested species from the ecosystem. On the other hand the other types of values are mainly associated with the biomass of the species remaining in the ecosystem. Thus harvesting and conservation reflect a fundamental trade-off in the ecosystem management. If we define values associated with direct economic (use) values as economic or market values, and those associated with existence values, aesthetic values, and non-substitutable ecosystem services as indirect (non-use) values, then the relative use/non-use values should determine the desired trade-off.

In this chapter we model the desired trade-off as a problem of maximizing expected utility from both the use and non-use values of the ecosystem. A two-stage approach is used. In the first stage the optimal allocation of land to each species is defined. This implies the development of a static biological portfolio selection model, along the lines of the financial capital asset pricing model (CAPM), with species portfolios characterized by the land allocation.[2] In the second stage the optimal harvesting of species conditional on the land allocation is determined.

To determine the value of the ecosystem we need both use and non-use values. However, while the use values can in principle be observed from market prices, non-use values are in general non-observable. Thus in order to obtain an approximation of the ecosystem's value we assume that some part of the non-use values, such as existence or aesthetic values, can be associated with a set of prices obtained from contingent valuation studies. These prices might not capture values associated with non-substitutable service values arising from species interactions, since little is known about these issues, but can be regarded as a first-order approximation of non-use values that allow the development of a biological CAPM (B-CAPM).

The B-CAPM is used to determine efficient species portfolios. It is shown that a range of expected ecosystem values exists which correspond to efficient species portfolios that fully preserve biodiversity. In the second stage we also characterize the optimal harvesting rule contingent on the selection of an efficient biodiversity-preserving species portfolio. Furthermore, we show that it is possible to construct diversified species portfolios in the presence of two weather regimes (dry and wet) that dominate both the dry and the wet species portfolios.

We extend the B-CAPM to a continuous time dynamic framework and we characterize optimal harvesting and species portfolio rules by stochastic dynamic programming methods. In particular we characterize optimal species portfolios for the social and the private optimum under: (i) the assumption that species biomasses were fluctuating continuously and that these stochastic influences were adequately represented by the geometric Weiner processes and (ii) that catastrophic events like fires or floods could affect the biomass of species in a discrete way to that we introduce the possibility of discrete jumps in species biomasses, which are modeled by Poisson processes.

Finally we show how our portfolio management approach can be linked with intercropping theory, and agroecological theory.

2   A MEAN-VARIANCE MODEL OF SPECIES SELECTION

We consider a landscape of a given size which is normalized to unity. In the landscape, $i = 1, \ldots, n$ species could potentially coexist. Let B_{0i} be the biomass of species i at the beginning of the period and let $\tilde{g}_i$ denote the one-period random growth rate of the species. If the whole landscape were devoted exclusively to the growth of species i, then its end-of-period biomass would be $\tilde{B}_i = \tilde{g}_i B_{0i}$. If only a proportion $w_i \in [0, 1]$ is devoted to the growth of species i, then its end-of-period biomass would be $w_i \tilde{B}_i$.

We assume that the end-of-period biomass can be either left in the landscape or harvested. If harvested, then a unit of the harvested biomass has a value determined by a known exogenous market price $p_i^m \geq 0$.[3] If left in the landscape, a unit biomass has a positive value $p_i > 0$, which reflects the species existence value.[4] This existence value can be determined by contingent valuation studies of conservation programs associated with the given species.

Assume a harvesting rule according to which the landscape manager or planner harvests a proportion $h_i \in [0, 1]$ of the end-of-period biomass. Thus the value of the biomass of a species, for which a proportion w_i of the landscape is devoted, at the end of the period is defined as:

$$p_i^m h_i w_i \tilde{B}_i + p_i (1 - h_i)\, w_i \tilde{B}_i \text{ or } w_i x_i \tilde{B}_i$$
$$x_i = p_i + (p_i^m - p_i)\, h_i$$

where x_i reflects the unit biomass value for species i associated with the given harvesting rule h_i. For exogenous market and existence values, x_i is completely determined by the harvesting rule. Assuming that species with zero market price are never fully harvested, or $h_i < 1$ if $p_i^m = 0$, then $x_i > 0$.

Let $\bar{\mathbf{B}} = (\bar{B}_1, \ldots, \bar{B}_n)$ be the vector of expected end-of-period biomasses if the whole landscape is devoted to each of the species, and let $\mathbf{w} = (w_1, \ldots, w_n)$ be an arbitrary allocation rule of the landscape to each species and $\mathbf{x} = (x_1, \ldots, x_n)$ be an arbitrary harvesting rule. Then the expected value of the landscape, defined in terms of both harvesting and existence values for the given allocation and harvesting rule, can be defined as:

$$e = \sum_{i=1}^{n} w_i x_i \bar{B}_i = \mathbf{w} \bar{\mathbf{B}}_{\mathbf{x}}$$

where $\bar{\mathbf{B}}_{\mathbf{x}} = (x_1 \bar{B}_1, \ldots, x_n \bar{B}_n)$ is the harvest-adjusted vector of expected returns. It should be noted that in this static framework we assume no interactions among species. This can be interpreted in Vandermeer's (1989, Figure 2.1) setting as a collection of n monocultures, each monoculture setting on w_i units of land. In Section 6 we generalize our model to allow polycultures on some parts of the land as well as monocultures to parallel Vandermeer's (1989,

p. 158) discussion of using a mixture of monocultures and polycultures on one's land as an additional device to increase average yield while controlling risk. So, for this section, the growth of one species does not depend on the relative abundance of another. The corresponding variance of the landscape value is defined as:

$$\sigma^2 = \sum_{i=1}^{n} w_i^2 (x_i^2 \sigma_{B_i}^2) + \sum_{i=1}^{n} \sum_{j \neq i}^{n} w_i w_j (x_i x_j \sigma_{B_i B_j})$$

where $\sigma_{B_i}^2$ is the variance of the species i biomass and $\sigma_{B_i B_j}$ is the covariance between the biomasses of species i and j. Denoting by $\Omega^x = [x_i x_j \sigma_{B_i B_j}]$, $i, j = 1, \ldots, n$, the variance covariance matrix of the species biomasses for the harvesting rule x, then σ^2 is defined as:

$$\sigma^2 = \mathbf{w}' \Omega_x \mathbf{w}$$

where $\mathbf{w}$ is the column vector of land allocation. We assume that the harvest-adjusted variance–covariance matrix is positive definite.

Denote by $\tilde{e} = \sum_{i=1}^{n} w_i x_i \tilde{B}_i$ the end-of-period landscape value and assume that the planner's preferences are characterized by preference for expected values and aversion for variance as in the standard mean-variance model of financial analysis. Let $u(\tilde{e})$ denote the planner's second-period utility function. Expanding as a Taylor series around the end-of-period expected landscape value e we obtain:

$$u(\tilde{e}) = u(e) + u'(e)(\tilde{e} - e) + \frac{1}{2} u''(e)(\tilde{e} - e)^2 + R$$

where the remainder R includes all higher-order derivatives. Then under standard assumptions the landscape manager's expected utility can be written as:

$$E[u(\tilde{e})] = u(e) + \frac{1}{2} u''(e) \sigma^2 + E(R)$$

where $E(R)$ contains all central moments of order higher than two.

Assuming strictly increasing and concave utility function and multivariate normal distribution for the species growth and that $u''(e)$ is constant in e, the planner's preferences are completely specified in terms of the expected landscape value and its variance, or:

$$E[u(\tilde{e})] = U(e, \sigma^2), \text{ with } \frac{\partial U}{\partial e} > 0, \frac{\partial U}{\partial \sigma^2} < 0, \frac{\partial^2 U}{\partial \sigma^2} > 0. \qquad (5.1)$$

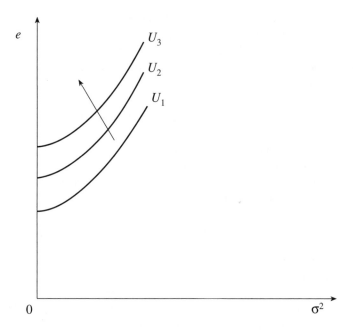

Figure 5.1   Indifference curves for landscape expected value and variance

The indifference curves in the (e, σ^2) are increasing and convex as in the standard financial CAPM (see Figure 5.1).

2.1   Efficient Species Portfolios

For any given harvesting rule $\mathbf{x}$, a land allocation vector $\mathbf{w}$ defines a portfolio of species. A frontier species portfolio, or a minimum variance portfolio, p, is the portfolio that has the minimum variance from all portfolios that correspond to the given harvesting rule. The frontier species portfolio is the solution to the following optimization problem:

$$\min_{\mathbf{w} \geq 0} \frac{1}{2} \mathbf{w}' \Omega_x \mathbf{w} \qquad (5.2)$$
$$\text{s.t. } \mathbf{w}' \bar{\mathbf{B}}_x = e_p$$
$$\mathbf{w}' \mathbf{1} = 1$$

where e_p is the expected landscape value for the species portfolio p, and $\mathbf{1}$ is an n-vector of ones. The Lagrangian for problem (5.2) is defined as:

$$\mathcal{L} = \frac{1}{2}\,\mathbf{w}'\Omega_x\mathbf{w} + \delta_1(e_p - \mathbf{w}'\bar{\mathbf{B}}_x) + \delta_2\,(1 - \mathbf{w}'\mathbf{1}).$$

The necessary and sufficient conditions for a global minimum are:

$$\frac{\partial \mathcal{L}}{\partial \mathbf{w}} = \Omega_x\mathbf{w} - \delta_1\bar{\mathbf{B}}_x - \delta_2 \geq \mathbf{0}\ (= \mathbf{0}\ \text{if } \mathbf{w} > \mathbf{0}) \qquad (5.3)$$

$$\frac{\partial \mathcal{L}}{\partial \delta_1} = e_p - \mathbf{w}'\bar{\mathbf{B}}_x = 0 \qquad (5.4)$$

$$\frac{\partial \mathcal{L}}{\partial \delta_2} = 1 - \mathbf{w}'\mathbf{1} = 0 \qquad (5.5)$$

where $\mathbf{0}$ is an n-vector of zeroes.

It should be noted that the above optimality conditions are similar to the standard financial CAPM, with one exception. The non-negativity constraint on the portfolio weights $\mathbf{w} \geq \mathbf{0}$ is equivalent to a no-short sales assumption in the financial CAPM, and distinguishes the biological CAPM from the financial CAPM.

Assume that for a given harvesting rule $\mathbf{x}$, a set of expected landscape values $E = \{e_p : \underline{e}_p \leq e_p \leq \bar{e}_p\}$ exists, such that problem (5.2) has a solution. In general some allocation weights could be zero at the solution indicating that these species will be extinct at the period's end.

We are interested in characterizing solutions that can fully conserve biodiversity, in the sense that if all n species are present at the beginning of the period, the same number of species exist at the period's end after harvesting takes place. Thus we are looking for conditions that characterize solutions $\mathbf{w}^* > \mathbf{0}$, for all $h_i < A$.

Assume that a solution $\mathbf{w}^* > \mathbf{0}$ exists for some $E^* \subseteq E$ and given $\mathbf{x}$. Then (5.3) should be satisfied as equality. Solving the linear system (5.3)–(5.5) we obtain:[5]

$$\mathbf{w}_p^* = \delta_1(\Omega_x^{-1}\bar{\mathbf{B}}_x) + \delta_2(\Omega_x^{-1}\mathbf{1}) \qquad (5.6)$$

where:

$$\delta_1 = \frac{Ce_p - A}{D}, \ \delta_2 = \frac{B - Ae_p}{D} \qquad (5.7)$$

$$A = \mathbf{1}'\Omega_x^{-1}\bar{\mathbf{B}}_x$$
$$B = \bar{\mathbf{B}}_x'\Omega_x^{-1}\bar{\mathbf{B}}_x$$
$$C = \mathbf{1}'\Omega_x^{-1}\mathbf{1}$$
$$D = BC - A^2 > 0. \tag{5.8}$$

Since Ω_x^{-1} is positive definite by the assumption on Ω_x, $B > 0$ and $C > 0$. Furthermore as shown by Huang and Litzenberger (1988, p. 64), $D > 0$. The frontier portfolio that conserves all species can then be written as:

$$\mathbf{w}_p^* = \mathbf{g} + \mathbf{h}e_p \tag{5.9}$$

$$\mathbf{g} = \frac{1}{D}[B(\Omega_x^{-1}\mathbf{1}) - A(\Omega_x^{-1}\bar{\mathbf{B}}_x)]$$

$$\mathbf{h} = \frac{1}{D}[C(\Omega_x^{-1}\bar{\mathbf{B}}_x) - A(\Omega_x^{-1}\mathbf{1})].$$

Standard results obtained for frontier portfolios in the financial CAPM extend naturally to the B-CAPM. Thus any frontier portfolio that conserves biodiversity can be represented by (5.9). Conversely any portfolio that is presented by (5.9) is a frontier portfolio, although not necessarily biodiversity preserving. The set of all frontier portfolios is the portfolio frontier of the B-CAPM.

Consider a species frontier portfolio characterized by (5.9). The portfolio will be a biodiversity-preserving frontier portfolio if $\mathbf{w}_p^* = \mathbf{g} + \mathbf{h}e_p > 0$. But then (5.6) implies for the biodiversity-preserving frontier portfolio that:

$$\delta_1(\Omega_x^{-1}\bar{\mathbf{B}}_x) + \delta_2(\Omega_x^{-1}\mathbf{1}) > 0. \tag{5.10}$$

Assume that all covariances are non-negative so that Ω_x being a variance–covariance matrix will have all non-negative elements, then premultiplying by Ω_x we obtain, $\delta_1\bar{\mathbf{B}}_x + \delta_2\mathbf{1} > \mathbf{0}$. Since $\bar{\mathbf{B}}_x > \mathbf{0}$, a sufficient condition for a biodiversity-preserving frontier portfolio is $(\delta_1, \delta_2) > 0$ or:

$$Ce_p - A > 0, B - Ae_p > 0.$$

Both inequalities are satisfied if:

$$\frac{A}{C} < e_p < \frac{B}{A}.$$

For the set $E^* = \{e_p : A/C < e_p < B/A\}$ to be non-empty, it is required that $A/C < B/A$, or $(A^2 - CB)/AC < 0$. But $A^2 - CB = -D < 0$ by (5.8). So $E^* \neq \emptyset$ if $A > 0$. Therefore if Ω_x has non-negative elements, and:

$$A = \mathbf{1}'\Omega_x^{-1}\bar{\mathbf{B}}_x \tag{5.11}$$

then an interval of expected landscape values $e_p \in (A/C, B/A)$ exists such that the frontier portfolio conserves all species by the period's end.

The next step in this analysis is to locate the biodiversity-preserving frontier portfolio on the portfolio frontier locus. Assume that $\underline{e}_p < A/C$ and $\bar{e}_p > B/A$. Then the frontier portfolio defined for $e_p \in (\underline{e}_p, \bar{e}_p)$ could include zero weights for some species. The frontier portfolios will be determined as vectors:

$$\mathbf{w}_p = [\mathbf{g} + \mathbf{h}e_p \mid \mathbf{0}]$$

where the zero vector corresponds to the species with zero weight. The portfolio frontier for $e_p \in (\underline{e}_p, \bar{e}_p)$ is defined in the variance-expected landscape value space by the parabola:

$$\sigma^2 = \frac{1}{D}(De_p^2 - 2Ae_p + B)$$

which is shown in Figure 5.2. The minimum variance species portfolio (*mvsp*) corresponds to the point $(1/C, A/C)$.[6] Thus the biodiversity-preserving portfolio

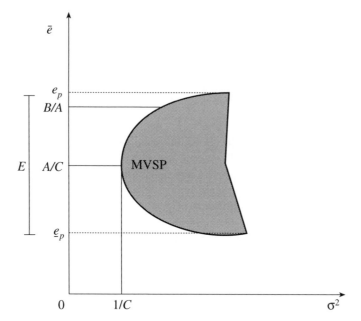

Figure 5.2   Biodiversity-preserving portfolio frontier

frontier (BPPF) is located between the *mvsp* and the expected landscape value
B/A.

Since portfolios on the BPPF have expected landscape value higher than
the expected value of the *mvsp* they are *efficient species portfolios*. This result
essentially implies that biodiversity conservation can be combined with efficiency in the selection of species portfolios. The difference $(A/C - B/A)$ can be
regarded as the window of expected landscape values for which biodiversity
can be preserved with efficient species portfolios.

Efficient species portfolios can be also defined in the case where existence
values are not taken into account. Assume that the landscape is managed by a
utility-maximizing agent which does not attach any existence values to species
biomasses at the period's end. This implies that $p_i = 0$ for all i, and since no
interactions between the existing biomasses and the species growth rates are
taken into account in this essentially static approach, it is natural to set the
harvesting rates at $h_i = 1$ if a positive landscape proportion is allocated to the
species. Then the unit biomass value is determined by the market price of the
harvested biomass or $\hat{x}_i = p_i^m$. The change in the unit biomass value when existence values are set to zero is:

$$\hat{x}_i - x_i = \Delta x_i = (p_i^m - p_i)(1 - h_i).$$

If we define $\hat{\bar{\mathbf{B}}}_x = (p_1^m \bar{B}_1, \ldots, p_n^m \bar{B}_n)$, $\hat{\Omega}_x = (p_i^m p_j^m \sigma_{B_i B_j})$ then we can define
the frontier portfolio as above. The interval of expected landscape values that
could allocate positive weight to all species can be defined as:

$$\hat{e}_p \in \left(\frac{\hat{A}}{\hat{C}}, \frac{\hat{B}}{\hat{A}} \right).$$

It should be made clear that the above interval does not define a biodiversity-
preserving window, since all species are harvested to exhaustion at the
period's end, but a condition where landscape is allocated to all species, so that
all species coexist before final harvesting.

To obtain an idea of the different magnitudes characterizing the efficient
species portfolios, we consider a simple numerical example with only two
species, so that $n = 2$. The rest of the parameters are defined as follows:

P_1	P_2	p_1^m	p_2^m	$\sigma_{B_1}^2$	$\sigma_{B_2}^2$	$\sigma_{B_1 B_2}$	h_1	h_2	$\bar{B}_1$	$\bar{B}_2$	e_p
5	3	6	2	50	15	0.1	0.6	0.7	130	140	650

The optimal landscape allocation weights for the above parameter configuration are $(w_1^*, w_2^*) = (0.81, 0.19)$. The portfolio frontier is defined as:

$$\sigma^2 = 1.25802(1119.1 - 5.78514e_p + 0.00818)e_p^2.$$

The variance corresponding to $e_p = 650$, is $\sigma^2 = 1082.67$. The optimal allocation weights as functions of the existence values are shown in Figure 5.3.

It is clear that specialization may occur. For example for low existence

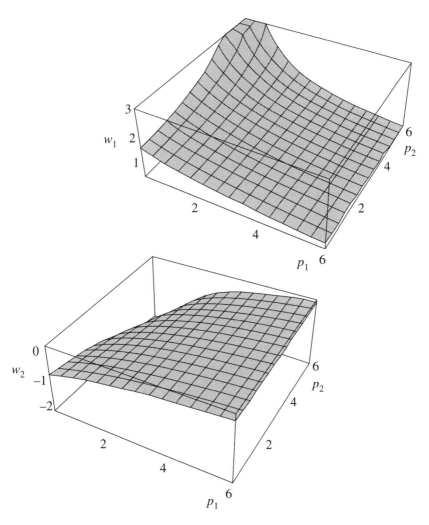

Figure 5.3   Optimal allocation weights

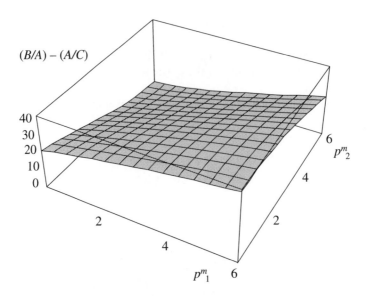

Figure 5.4   Window of biodiversity preservation

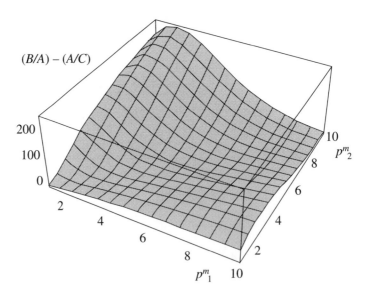

Figure 5.5   Window of positive landscape allocation with zero existence values

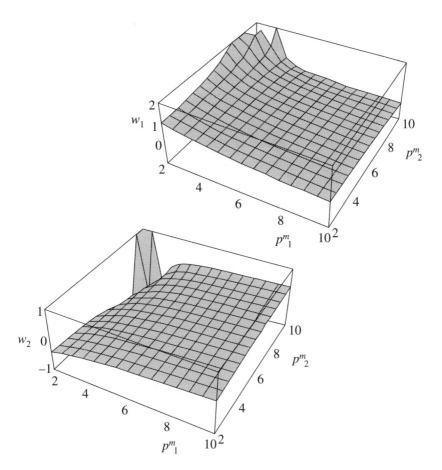

Figure 5.6   Optimal allocation weights with zero existence values

values, we have $(w_1^*, w_2^*) = (1, 0)$, thus only species one survives at the period's end.

The window of biodiversity preservation or $(B/A - A/C)$ is shown in Figure 5.4.

We also derive numerical results for the case where existence values are set to zero and $h_1 = h_2 = 1$. The window of positive landscape allocation to both species with zero existence values is shown in Figure 5.5, while the optimal landscape allocation weights are shown in Figure 5.6.

By comparing the shapes of the surfaces in Figures 5.4 and 5.5, there are indications that specialization is more likely to occur when existence values are set to zero.

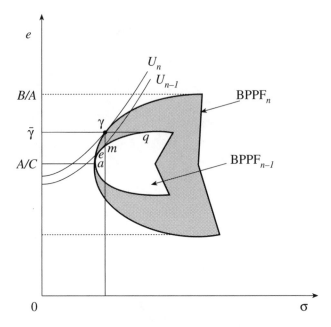

Figure 5.7   Valuation of species loss

2.2   Choice of Efficient Species Portfolios and Valuation of Species Loss

The specific species portfolio chosen by the planner will be determined by the planner's indifference map and the portfolio frontier. The planner's equilibrium is shown in Figure 5.7.

The planner will always choose efficient portfolios. The specific choice in Figure 5.7 is such that the utility-maximizing portfolio is also a biodiversity-preserving frontier portfolio. However, if the shape of the indifference curves is different, such that the tangency point is above B/A, some species will become extinct in equilibrium.

Assume now that equilibrium takes place at point γ on the $BPPF_n$ with an efficient biodiversity-preserving frontier portfolio w_γ. Consider a portfolio w_q with the same return as γ and the same weights, except for one weight which is set equal to zero. Clearly $w_\gamma \neq w_q$, and since w_γ is a frontier portfolio, the variance of w_q should be greater than the variance of w_γ. Thus w_q should be, say at q, on the line γq to the right of γ. Then it can be shown (Huang and Litzenberger 1988) that there exists a portfolio frontier passing from q and the *mvsp* portfolio a that lies inside the $BPPF_n$. The portfolio frontier through q and a, BPPF_{n-1}, touches the BPPF_n portfolio at the *mvsp* portfolio a.

However, the BPPF_n contains all n species while the BPPF_{n-1} portfolio contains $n-1$ species so the loss of one species can be valued on the portfolio frontiers in the following ways.

- If we want to value in terms of the loss in expected returns while keeping the risk of the portfolio constant, then the value of the extinct species is γm in terms of Figure 5.7.
- If we want to value in terms of the increase in the variance of the portfolio while keeping expected returns constant, then the value of the extinct species is γq in terms of Figure 5.7.
- If we consider the utility-maximization problem with utility defined by the mean-variance model, then equilibrium on the BPPF_n is at point γ, while equilibrium on the BPPF_{n-1} is on point e. Therefore the value of the extinct species in utility terms is $U_n - U_{n-1}$.

  In the same way, when more than one species have zero weights, portfolio frontiers can be generated and the loss of species can be valued relative to equilibrium on the BPPF.

We apply the above approach to the numerical example of the previous section, where the equilibrium values were, $w_1^* = 0.807882$, $w_2^* = 0.195118$, $\sigma^2 = 1028.67$, and $e_p = 650$. By 'losing' species 2, that is setting its weight equal to zero and keeping the variance constant, the loss in expected return is 9.3 percent. On the other hand by 'losing' species 2 and keeping the expected return constant the increase in variance is 21.5 percent.

3 EFFICIENT SPECIES PORTFOLIOS AND OPTIMAL HARVESTING RULES

The analysis in the previous section suggests that the minimum variance defined as the solution of problem (5.2) for expected landscape values in the interval $(A/C, B/A)$, depends on the harvesting rule. Then the value function of the problem, the minimum variance function, will be defined as:

$$V(\mathbf{x}, e_p) = \min_{\mathbf{w} \geq 0} \left\{ \frac{1}{2} \mathbf{w}' \Omega_x \mathbf{w} : \mathbf{w}' \overline{\mathbf{B}}_x = e_p, \mathbf{w}' \mathbf{1} = 1 \right\}. \tag{5.12}$$

A set of harvesting rules $\mathbf{x} \in X$, where $X = \{ \mathbf{x} : x_i = p_i + (p_i^m - p_i)h_i) \}$ is a closed and bounded set,[7] under which problem (5.2) has a unique solution for strictly positive $\mathbf{w}$, will define a family of BPPF, one for each harvesting rule.

Since $(1/2)\mathbf{w}'\Omega_x\mathbf{w}$ is continuous and is defined in the compact set $[0, 1]^n \times X$ the value function (5.12) is continuous. Therefore since X is compact $V(\mathbf{x}, e_p)$ achieves a minimum (and a maximum) in a compact subset of X. Let

$$\mathbf{x}^* = \arg \min_{\mathbf{x} \in X} V(\mathbf{x}, e_p)$$

then $\mathbf{x}^*$ is the harvesting rule that minimizes the variance over all harvesting rules that correspond to a positive solution of problem (5.2). For the solution to be an admissible one it should hold that:

$$x_i : h_i = \frac{x_i - p_i}{p_i^m - p_i} \in [0, 1].$$

We examine the variance minimizing harvesting rule for our numerical example. For admissible solutions the values for $\mathbf{x}$ should be $x_1 \in [5, 6]$, $x_2 \in [2, 3]$. Variance is minimized at the boundary of the feasible set for:

$$(x_1^*, h_1^*) = (6, 1), (x_2^*, h_2^*) = (3, 0)$$
$$\text{minimum} V = 764.853, (w_1, w_2) = (0.639, 0.361).$$

The variance minimizing harvesting rule is to fully harvest species 1 and not harvest at all species 2. Thus the variance minimizing harvesting rule for this case is not biodiversity preserving.

If we make the assumption that $V(\mathbf{x}, e_p)$ has a global interior minimum in $\mathbf{x}$, then the variance minimizing harvesting rule will be determined by:

$$\frac{\partial V(\mathbf{x}, e_p)}{\partial \mathbf{x}} = 0.$$

This derivative can be evaluated using the envelope theorem as

$$\frac{\partial V(\mathbf{x}, e_p)}{\partial \mathbf{x}} = \frac{\partial L(\mathbf{w}^*, \delta_1^*, \delta_2^*)}{\partial \mathbf{x}}$$

where

$$L(\mathbf{w}^*, \delta_1^*, \delta_2^*) = \frac{1}{2} \left(\sum_{i=1}^{n} w_i^{*2} x_i^2 \sigma_i^2 + \sum_{\substack{i,j \\ i \neq j}} w_i^* w_j^* x_i x_j \sigma_{ij} \right)$$

$$+ \delta_1^* \left(e_p - \sum_{i=1}^{n} w_i^* x_i \bar{B}_i \right) + \delta_2^* \left(1 - \sum_{i=1}^{n} w_i^* \right).$$

Using this Lagrangian function we obtain:

$$\frac{\partial L(\mathbf{w}^*, \delta_1^*, \delta_2^*)}{\partial \mathbf{x}} = (w_i^{*2}\sigma_i^2)x_i + \sum_{\substack{i,j=1 \\ i \neq j}}^{n} w_i^* w_j^* x_j \sigma_{ij} - \delta_1^* w_i^* \bar{B}_i = 0, \, i = 1, \ldots, n.$$

Define the matrix $\Omega_{\mathbf{w}^*} = [w_i^* w_j^* \sigma_{ij}]$ $i, j = 1, \ldots, n$ and the column vector $\mathbf{w}_B^*$ = $[\delta_1^* w_i^* \bar{B}_i]$ $i = 1, \ldots, n$. Then the variance minimizing harvesting rule is obtained as

$$\mathbf{x}^* = \Omega_{\mathbf{w}^*}^{-1} \mathbf{w}_B^*. \tag{5.13}$$

Since $\Omega_{\mathbf{w}^*}^{-1}$ and $\mathbf{w}_B^*$ are themselves functions of x through (5.6), the variance minimizing harvesting rule will be a fixed point of (5.13).

Assume now that for set $E_p \subseteq (A/C, B/A)$ a variance minimizing harvesting rule exists. Then this rule will determine a minimum variance BPPF as an outer envelope of the BPPF's corresponding to non-variance minimizing harvesting rules (Figure 5.8). As also indicated in Figure 5.8, the equilibrium

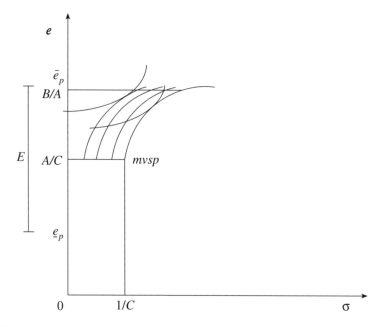

Figure 5.8   Optimal harvesting and biodiversity-preserving portfolio frontier

species portfolio on the minimum variance BPPF will maximize utility over all admissible harvesting rules.

The procedure described above specifies therefore a two-stage approach by which both the optimal species portfolio and the optimal harvesting rule can be determined.

4   OPTIMAL SPECIES DIVERSIFICATION UNDER ALTERNATIVE EXTERNAL REGIMES

In the previous section the optimal species portfolio and the optimal harvesting rules were obtained following a two-stage approach. Conditions under which the equilibrium species portfolio and harvesting rules lead to biodiversity preservation were also determined.

Management of ecosystems in the sense of harvesting, but also having as an objective the preservation of biodiversity, often takes place in a framework which is heavily affected by external factors, which may significantly affect the growth rates of species as well as the covariance of growth rates among species. If, for example, we consider two weather regimes – a dry regime and a wet regime – it is most likely that there will be species better suited to one regime than the other, thus the respective growth rates will be different when the wet or the dry regime prevails.

Consider an ecosystem manager that manages the landscape by determining the optimal portfolio of species and the optimal harvesting rule by the two-stage approach defined above. The expected growth rates of species are different in the two regimes; thus the equilibrium portfolios will be different for the two regimes.[8]

The question is whether the ecosystem manager can diversity between the two regimes in the sense of constructing a new species portfolio from a combination of dry and wet portfolios that will dominate both the dry and wet portfolios. Dominance here is defined in the sense of second-order stochastic dominance, which means that the new portfolio will dominate both the dry and wet portfolios if it has at least the same expected landscape value and smaller variance than both.

Let e_d, σ_d^2 and e_w, σ_w^2 be the expected landscape value and the variance of species portfolios in the dry and wet regimes, respectively, and let e_D, σ_D^2 be the expected landscape value and the variance of species portfolio after diversification. Portfolio D will dominate the wet and dry regimes portfolios if:

$$e_D = \max\{e_d, e_w\} \tag{5.14}$$

$$\sigma_D^2 < \min\{\sigma_d^2, \sigma_w^2\} \tag{5.15}$$

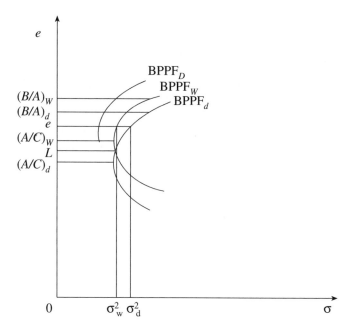

Figure 5.9   Diversification under alternative external regimes

when (5.14) and (5.15) are satisfied, portfolio D dominates d and w in the sense of the second-degree stochastic dominance and for all concave utility functions,

$$\mathrm{E}[U(e_D)] > \mathrm{E}[U(e_j)], j = w, d.$$

Consider the two BPPF on Figure 5.9 with BPPF_d, BPPF_w corresponding to the dry and wet regimes, respectively. For expected landscape values above L, the wet regime dominates in the sense of the second-degree stochastic dominance. Let there be two portfolios a and b on the wet and dry frontiers such that $e_{aw} = e_{bd} = e$ and $\sigma^2_{aw} < \sigma^2_{bd}$ so that the wet regime portfolio dominates. The manager's problem is whether it is possible to construct a diversified portfolio D that includes both a and b such that

$$e_D = e_{aw} = e_{bd} = e \tag{5.16}$$

$$\sigma^2_D < \min\{\sigma^2_{aw}, \sigma^2_{bd}\} < \sigma^2_{aw}. \tag{5.17}$$

The diversified portfolio will have expected landscape value:[9]

$$e_D = \lambda e_{aw} + (1 - \lambda)e_{bd}, \ \lambda \in (0, 1) \tag{5.18}$$

$$\sigma_D^2 = \lambda^2 \sigma_{aw}^2 + 2\lambda(1 - \lambda)\sigma_{ab} + (1 - \lambda)^2 \ \sigma_{bd}^2 < \sigma_{aw}^2 \tag{5.19}$$

where σ_{ab} is the covariance between the wet and the dry portfolios. It is clear that since $e_{aw} = e_{bd} = e$ from (5.16), condition (5.18) is satisfied if $\lambda = 1/2$. Thus in order to know whether a stochastically dominating diversified portfolio can be constructed, we need to determine conditions under which (5.19) is satisfied for $\lambda = 1/2$. From (5.19) the following quadratic function can be defined:

$$\phi(\lambda) = (\lambda^2 - 1)\sigma_{aw}^2 + 2\lambda(1 - \lambda)\sigma_{ab} + (1 - \lambda)^2 \ \sigma_{bd}^2 \tag{5.20}$$

with

$$\phi'(\lambda) = 2(\sigma_{aw}^2 + \sigma_{bd}^2 - 2\sigma_{ab}) \ \lambda + 2 \ (\sigma_{ab} - \sigma_{bd}^2) \tag{5.21}$$

$$\phi''(\lambda) = 2(\sigma_{aw}^2 + \sigma_{bd}^2 - 2\sigma_{ab}). \tag{5.22}$$

The roots of (5.20) are:

$$\lambda_1 = 1, \ \lambda_2 = \frac{\sigma_{bd}^2 - \sigma_{aw}^2}{\sigma_{aw}^2 + \sigma_{bd}^2 - 2\sigma_{ab}}.$$

Assume that σ_{ab} is sufficiently small so that $\phi''(\lambda) > 0$, then for $\lambda \in (\lambda_2, \lambda_1)$ the quadratic (5.20) is negative or, equivalently, inequality (5.19) is satisfied. Then the dominating diversified portfolio can be constructed if:

$$\frac{1}{2} \in (\lambda_2, \lambda_1), \text{ or } \lambda_2 < \frac{1}{2} \Rightarrow 3\sigma_{bd}^2 - 3\sigma_{aw}^2 + 2\sigma_{ab} < 0. \tag{5.23}$$

On the other hand if $\phi''(\lambda) < 0$, then the dominating portfolio can be constructed if:

$$\frac{1}{2} \in (0, \lambda_2), \text{ or } \lambda_2 > \frac{1}{2}. \tag{5.24}$$

Assume that λ_2 satisfies either (5.23) or (5.24) and consider the set

$$\left\{ \begin{array}{l} (e_D, \sigma_D^2) : e_D = e_{aw} = e_{bd} = e, \ \sigma_D^2 < \min \ \{\sigma_{aw}^2, \sigma_{bd}^2\} \\ \sigma_D^2 = \dfrac{1}{4} \sigma_{aw}^2 + \dfrac{1}{2} \sigma_{ab} + \dfrac{1}{4} \sigma_{bd}^2 \end{array} \right\}$$

This set is a convex combination of two convex sets and therefore it is convex itself. The diversified frontier BPPF$_D$ will dominate both the wet and the dry frontiers as shown in Figure 5.9.

5 OPTIMAL SPECIES PORTFOLIOS IN CONTINUOUS TIME

In this section we consider the same normalized landscape, but we assume, as is more realistic, that species evolve and interact among themselves over time in a continuous time dynamic set-up.

We examine two problems. In the first the ecosystem manager or social planner seeks to maximize utility derived both from harvesting and biomass existence. In the second problem we assume that the landscape is managed by a profit-maximizing agent who maximizes solely utility from harvesting. We call the solution to the first problem the socially optimal species portfolio (SOSP) and the solution to the second the privately optimal species portfolio (POSP).

We characterize the solutions of these two problems by the first-order necessary conditions associated with the dynamic programming equations. Approximating solutions of the nonlinear partial differential equations resulting from these conditions is beyond the scope of this chapter. However, formulating the problem in these terms and exploring the implications of the first-order conditions can be regarded as providing a useful conceptual framework for analysing biodiversity management problems under uncertainty.

5.1 The Socially Optimal Species Portfolio

In analysing the species portfolio selection problem in the continuous time dynamic framework, land can be regarded as a limiting resource in fixed supply. The allocation of this limiting resource among species determines the evolution of their biomasses within the planning horizon. This formulation is consistent with the mechanistic resource-based models of species competition (Tilman 1982, 1988), where the growth rates of species biomasses depend on the limiting resource consumed by the species. Since in our case the amount of the resource, the land, is fixed, our model is a special case of the more general Tilman models where the resource evolves in time according to the amount supplied per unit time and the consumption by the competing species.

Let $\mathbf{w}(t) = [w_1(t), \ldots, w_n(t)]$ be an arbitrary land allocation at time t, where w_i is the proportion of landscape allocated to species i with $\sum_i w_i = 1$, $w_i \geq 0$. By normalizing the size of land to unity the growth of species biomass can be modeled by a system of stochastic differential equations which are indepen-dent of the size of the land:

$$\frac{dB_i}{B_i} = [f_i(\mathbf{w}) - h_i]dt - \sigma_i(\mathbf{w})dz_i, \; B_i(0) = B_i^0 > 0, \; i = 1, \ldots, n \quad (5.25)$$

where $\mathbf{B} = (B_1, \ldots, B_n)$ is the vector of biomasses, h_i is the harvest rate for species i, and $z_i(t)$ is a Brownian motion. Thus, $f_i(\mathbf{w}) - h_i$ is the instantaneous net of harvesting percentage change in the biomass of species i and $\sigma_i^2(\mathbf{w})$ is the conditional variance per unit time. Total harvesting at time t is defined as $H_i(t) = h_i(t)B_i(t)$. If no land is allocated to a species at any point in time then we assume that its biomass is driven to zero without cost and that no replant-ing is possible at any later date or,[10]

$$\text{if } w_i(\tau) = 0, \text{ then } B_i(t) = H_i(t) = 0, \; \forall t \geq \tau.$$

The introduction of the land allocation weights $\mathbf{w}$ in the growth equations takes into account interactions among species. For example, if two species i and j are strictly complementary then $f_i(\mathbf{w}) = 0$ if $w_j = 0$.

Assume that the existing biomasses at any point in time have non-negative existence values. So the existence value of landscape is $\Sigma_i p_i(t)B_i(t)$. The ecosystem manager's or social planner's objective is to allocate land to each species and to determine a harvesting rule that will maximize an objective functional within a finite time horizon $t \in [0, T]$. To simplify the exposition we assume that both the price of harvested species and their existence values are fixed within the planning horizon.

The instantaneous utility functions from harvesting or biomass existence are assumed to be represented by strictly concave utility functions:

$$U^H\left(\sum_{i=1}^n p_i^m H_i\right), \; U^B\left(\sum_{i=1}^n p_i B_i\right).$$

The ecosystem manager's objective is to solve the maximization problem:

$$\max_{(\mathbf{w},\mathbf{H})\geq 0} J(\mathbf{B}; \mathbf{w}, \mathbf{H}) = \mathrm{E}_0\int_0^T \left[U^H\left(\sum_{i=1}^n p_i^m H_i\right) + U^B\left(\sum_{i=1}^n p_i B_i\right) \right] dt$$

$$+ \; b[B(T)] \text{ subject to } (5.25) \quad (5.26)$$

where $b[B(T)]$ is a bequest function assumed to reflect the manager's attitudes regarding the existence values left to future generations. For example, if

$b[B(T)] = \sum_{i=1}^{n} p_i B_i^0$, for some initial landscape allocation $\mathbf{w}^0$, then the planner's attitude is to leave resources to the future generation sufficient to give the landscape the same total existence value the manager had when the planning started.[11]

Problem (5.26) is a stochastic control problem. Then, the differential generator for the stochastic processes B_i, is defined as

$$\mathcal{L}_{B_i}^{\mathbf{w},\mathbf{H}} = \frac{\partial}{\partial t} + [f_i(\mathbf{w})B_i - H_i]\frac{\partial}{\partial B_i} + \frac{1}{2}\sum_{i=1}^{n}\sum_{j=1}^{n}\sigma_{ij}B_iB_j\frac{\partial^2}{\partial B_i \partial B_j} \quad (5.27)$$

where $\sigma_{ij} = \sigma_i(\mathbf{w})\sigma_j(\mathbf{w})\rho_{ij}$, with ρ_{ij} being the instantaneous correlation coefficient between the Weiner processes dz_i and dz_j.

Let $(\mathbf{w},\mathbf{H})\in \mathcal{U}$ where $\mathcal{U} \subset \mathcal{R}_+^{2n}$ is a compact control space. The value function of the ecosystem's manager is defined as:

$$V(\mathbf{B},t) = \max_{(\mathbf{w},\mathbf{H})\in \mathcal{U}} J(\mathbf{B}, t; \mathbf{w}, \mathbf{H}). \quad (5.28)$$

Then the dynamic programming equation is obtained as:

$$0 = \max_{(\mathbf{w},\mathbf{H})\in \mathcal{U}} \left\{ U^H + U^B + \sum_{i=1}^{n} \mathcal{L}_{B_i}^{\mathbf{w},\mathbf{H}}[V(\mathbf{B}, t)] \right\}, \ t\in [0, T] \quad (5.29)$$

For any control process $(\mathbf{w},\mathbf{H})\in \mathcal{U}$, (5.29) is a partial differential equation with boundary condition $V(\mathbf{B}, T) = b[B(T)]$.

A verification theorem (Fleming and Soner 1993, p. 163) states that if v is a twice differentiable solution of (5.29) with boundary condition $b[B(T)]]$, then:

1. $v(\mathbf{B}, t) \le J(\mathbf{B}, t; \mathbf{w}, \mathbf{H})$ for an initial condition and control process $(\mathbf{w}, \mathbf{H})$.
2. If for any initial data there exists a control process $(\mathbf{w}^*, \mathbf{H}^*)$ such that

$$(\mathbf{w}^*, \mathbf{H}^*) \in \arg\max \left\{ \begin{array}{l} U^H(\sum_{i=1}^{n}p_i^m H_i^*) + U^B(\sum_{i=1}^{n}p_i B_i^*) \\ +\sum_{i=1}^{n}\mathcal{L}_{B_i^*}^{\mathbf{w}^*,\mathbf{H}^*}[V(\mathbf{B}^*, t)] \end{array} \right\}$$

then $v(\mathbf{B}, t) = J(\mathbf{B}, t; \mathbf{w}^*, \mathbf{H}^*)$, where $\mathbf{B}^*$ is a solution of (5.25) with control process $(\mathbf{w}^*, \mathbf{H}^*)$.

To obtain therefore the optimal feedback harvesting and land allocation rule we solve the maximization problem associated with the right-hand side of the dynamic programming equation. The Lagrangian for this problem is:

$$L = U^H + U^B + \sum_{i=1}^{n} \mathcal{L}_{B_i}^{\mathbf{w},\mathbf{H}}[V(\mathbf{B}, t)] + \delta\left(1 - \sum_{i=1}^{n} w_i\right).$$

The first-order conditions imply for $i = 1, \ldots, n$:[12]

$$\frac{\partial L}{\partial H_i} = U'^H p_i^m - V_{B_i} \leq 0 \ (= 0 \text{ if } H_i^* > 0) \tag{5.30}$$

$$\frac{\partial L}{\partial w_i} = V_{B_i} B_i \frac{\partial f_i}{\partial w_i} + \sum_{j \neq i}^{n} V_{B_j} B_j \frac{\partial f_j}{\partial w_i} +$$

$$\sum_{i=1}^{n} \sum_{j=1}^{n} V_{B_i B_j} B_i B_j \frac{\partial \sigma_{ij}}{\partial w_i} - \delta \leq 0 \ (= 0 \text{ if } w_i^* > 0) \tag{5.31}$$

$$\frac{\partial L}{\partial \delta} = 1 - \sum_i w_i = 0 \tag{5.32}$$

where U'^H is the first derivative of the U^H function with respect to the total harvest, and V_{B_i}, $V_{B_i B_i}$ are the partial derivatives of the value function. The static $2n + 1$ equations (5.30)–(5.32) can be used to solve for the $2n + 1$ unknowns, the harvesting rule H_i^*, the land allocation rule w_i^* ($i = 1, \ldots, n$), and the multiplier δ as functions of the derivatives of the value function.

The static first-order conditions can be interpreted by noting that V_{B_i} is the marginal value of the biomass of species i, with the value including both values arising from harvesting and values arising from existence. Then (5.30) indicates that optimal harvesting at each point in time is undertaken up to the point where the marginal utility from harvesting equals the species biomass marginal value. So a sufficiently high V_{B_i} because, for example, of very high existence values, could imply $H_i^* = 0$. Condition (5.31) defines optimal weights. The term $V_{B_i} B_i \, \partial f_i / \partial w_i$ reflects the change in the value of the species i biomass resulting from changing the land allocation w_i to this species. The cross-product term $\sum_{j \neq i}^{n} V_{B_j} B_j \, \partial f_j / \partial w_i$ reflects the change in the value of all other species biomasses resulting from changing the land allocation w_i to species i. Thus these terms reflect changes due to species interactions. The other terms reflect similar effects on the variance of species evolutions. These terms can be regarded as generalized risk premia. A solution to the system (5.30)–(5.32) will determine solutions of the form:

$$H_i^* = H_i^*(\mathbf{B}, V_{\mathbf{B}}, V_{\mathbf{BB}}; \mathbf{p}, \mathbf{p}^m) \tag{5.33}$$

$$w_i^* = w_i^*(\mathbf{B}, V_{\mathbf{B}}, V_{\mathbf{BB}}; \mathbf{p}, \mathbf{p}^m).$$ (5.34)

Substituting these solutions into (5.29) we obtain the fundamental partial differential equation for the value function:

$$
0 = \frac{\partial V(\mathbf{B}, t)}{\partial t} + U^H \left(\sum_{i=1}^n p_i^m H_i^*(\cdot) \right) + U^B \left(\sum_{i=1}^n p_i B_i \right)
$$

$$
+ \sum_{i=1}^n \{ f_i[\mathbf{w}^*(\cdot)]B_i - H_i^* \} \frac{\partial V}{\partial B_i}
$$

$$
+ \frac{1}{2} \sum_{i=1}^n \sum_{j=1}^n \sigma_{ij}[\mathbf{w}^*(\cdot)]B_i B_j \frac{\partial^2 V}{\partial B_i \partial B_j}
$$ (5.35)

If the partial differential equation were solved[13] with boundary condition $V(\mathbf{B}, T) = b[\mathbf{B}(T)]$, the solution when substituted back into (5.33) and (5.34) would obtain the optimal feedback harvesting and land allocation rules.

There is a similarity between the above solution and Merton's (1971, 1973) continuous time consumption–portfolio rules, with harvesting corresponding to the consumption rule and land allocation corresponding to the portfolio rule. It should be noted, however, that our continuous IB-CAPM model seems to be more complicated than Merton's I-CAPM model since the objective function depends on the valuation of biomasses due to the positive existence values, and species interactions prevent the transition equation from being linear in the allocation weights $\mathbf{w}$, thus equation (5.31) is not linear in the portfolio weights $\mathbf{w}$.

It should also be noted that the introduction of non-negativity constraints may cause some additional problems in defining in appropriate solution, if some class of utility functions require negative harvesting or allocation weights, so that the policy seems to be to set them equal to zero. As noted by Cox and Huang (1989) for the I-CAPM, setting consumption equal to zero in case the utility function requires negative consumption, and following the decision rules for the weights as long as wealth is not negative, may not be the optimal policy for some members of the hyperbolic absolute risk aversion (HARA) family. This result indicates that the policy rules derived here should be regarded with caution when zero solutions regarding w_i and H_i are examined.

Biodiversity preservation at the social optimum
The optimal land allocation rule $\mathbf{w}^*$ determines the socially optimal portfolio of species. All species will enter this portfolio if $\mathbf{w}^* > 0$. The extent that this

result is possible depends on the magnitude of the marginal values V_{B_i}. Intuitively if $w_i \to 0$ then $B_i \to 0$. If in this case $V_{B_i} \to M$, where M is a large positive number, possible infinity, then $w_i^* = 0$ cannot be a solution of (5.31), $w_i^* > 0$ is an optimal solution, and biodiversity is preserved.

5.2 The Privately Optimal Species Portfolio

We consider the case of a private agent that takes harvesting prices as fixed and seeks to maximize utility from harvesting subject to the dynamics of the species growth.[14] In this case the dynamic programming equation becomes:

$$0 = \max_{(\mathbf{w},\mathbf{H}) \in \mathcal{U}} \left\{ U^H + \sum_{i=1}^{n} \mathcal{L}_{B_i}^{\mathbf{w},\mathbf{H}}[V^p(\mathbf{B}, t)] \right\}, \ t \in [0, T].$$

It is clear that the structure of this problem is the same as the structure of the social optimization problem, so that the optimality conditions and the solution concepts are the same. However the value function is different, and this has implications for the possibility of having species go extinct during the planning horizon or equivalently $w_i^* = 0$. Thus there is a deviation between the socially optimal and the privately optimal species portfolio. Since the existence values of species biomasses do not affect the private species portfolio, some species may go extinct at the optimal portfolio of the private agent.

Another potential source of deviation between the private and the socially optimal solution is the possibility that the private agent will not take into account species interactions. In this case the f_i and the σ_i functions are functions of w_i alone and the optimality conditions that determine the optimal allocation $\mathbf{w}$ will not contain the interaction terms of (5.31). There are many striking examples in resource management where ignoring species interactions could lead to species specialization with possibly disastrous effects for the whole ecosystem (Scott, 1998, Brock and Xepapadeas, 1999).

Some insight into the nature and the characteristics of a solution can be obtained by considering a special case. Let the utility functions from harvesting and biomass existence be defined as:

$$U^H = \sum_i \left(p_i^m H_i - \frac{1}{2} \kappa_i H_i^2 \right), \ U^B = \left(\sum_i (p_i B_i)^\beta \right)^{\frac{1}{\beta}}$$

where $\beta \leq 1$ determines the elasticity of substitution between species existence values, and let $f_i(\mathbf{w}) = \alpha_i w_i$, $\sigma_i(\mathbf{w}) = \sigma_i w_i$, so that no species interactions are allowed. Then the optimality conditions are:

$$p_i^m - \kappa_i H_i^* - V_{B_i} \leq 0, H_i^* \geq 0 \tag{5.36}$$

$$a_i B_i V_{B_i} + w_i^* \sigma_i^2 B_i^2 V_{B_i B_i} + \sum_{j \neq i} w_j^* \sigma_{ij} B_i B_j V_{B_i B_j} - \delta \leq 0, w_i^* \geq 0 \tag{5.37}$$

$$\sum_i w_i^* = 1. \tag{5.38}$$

System (5.36)–(5.38) is linear in **w** and δ so the weights can be obtained and then substituted back into (5.36) to obtain the harvesting rule. For example, if $i = 1, 2$ then

$$w_1^* = \frac{a_1 B_1 V_{B_1} - a_2 B_2 V_{B_2} - \sigma_2^2 B_2 V_{B_2 B_2} + \sigma_{12} B_1 B_2 V_{B_1 B_2}}{\sigma_1^2 B_1^2 V_{B_1 B_1} - 2\sigma_{12} B_1 B_2 V_{B_1 B_2} + \sigma_2^2 B_2^2 V_{B_2 B_2}}$$

$$w_2^* = 1 - w_1^*.$$

If V_{B_1} is sufficiently small when B_1 is small then w_1^* could be zero and the private solution specializes to species 2. The fundamental partial differential equation for the value function is determined in the same way as above.

5.3 Species Selection when Catastrophic Events are Possible

The analysis in the previous sections was based on the assumption that species biomasses were fluctuating continuously and that these stochastic influences were adequately represented by the geometric Weiner processes. This is not, however, always the case in ecosystems where catastrophic events like fires or floods could affect the biomass of species in a discrete way. To model these effects we introduce the possibility of discrete jumps in species biomasses, which are modeled by Poisson processes. Thus we assume that species biomasses evolves according to:

$$\frac{dB_i}{B_i} = [f_i(\mathbf{w}) - h_i]dt - \sigma_i(\mathbf{w})dz_i + g_i(\mathbf{w})dq_i$$

where $q_i(t)$ is a Poisson process. In this way the biomass evolution is modeled by a mixed Brownian motion–Poisson process.

The discrete jumps implied by the Poisson processes can be interpreted in the following way.[15] Let λ_i be the mean arrival time of a possible catastrophic event causing a downward jump in the biomass of species i of a random amplitude $\hat{u}$ with density function $p(u)$. That is $p(u)d(u)$ is the probability of a jump amplitude contained in $(u, u + du)$. Then the probability of an event causing a jump in the species biomass of random size u_i is $\lambda_i dt$. Therefore,

$$dq_i = \begin{cases} 0 \text{ with probability } 1 - \lambda_i dt \\ -u_i \text{ with probability } \lambda_i dt. \end{cases}$$

Let $\mathcal{D}_{B_i}^{\mathbf{w},\mathbf{H}}$ be the differential generator for the mixed processes characterizing the growth of biomasses. Then,

$$\mathcal{D}_{B_i}^{\mathbf{w},\mathbf{H}}[V(\mathbf{B}, t)] = \frac{\partial V(\mathbf{B}, t)}{\partial t} + [f_i(\mathbf{w})B_i - H_i] \frac{\partial V(\mathbf{B}, t)}{\partial B_i}$$

$$+ \frac{1}{2} \sum_{j=1}^{n} \sum_{i=1}^{n} \sigma_{ij} B_i B_j \frac{\partial^2 V(\mathbf{B}, t)}{\partial B_i \partial B_j}$$

$$+ \lambda_i \int_{u_i} \{V[\mathbf{B} + g_i(\mathbf{w})B_i u_i, t] - V(\mathbf{B}, t)\} p(u_i) du_i.$$

The dynamic programming equation for the mixed process can be written as (Malliaris and Brock 1982):

$$0 = \max_{(\mathbf{w},\mathbf{H}) \in \mathcal{U}} \left\{ U^H + U^B + \sum_{i=1}^{n} \mathcal{D}_{B_i}^{\mathbf{w},\mathbf{H}}[V(\mathbf{B}, t)] \right\}, \ t \in [0, T].$$

The Lagrangian for the optimal feedback rules is:

$$L^{\mathcal{D}} = U^H + U^B + \sum_{i=1}^{n} \mathcal{D}_{B_i}^{\mathbf{w},\mathbf{H}}[V(\mathbf{B}, t)] + \delta \left(1 - \sum_{i=1}^{n} w_i \right).$$

The first-order conditions imply for $i = 1, \ldots, n$:[16]

$$\frac{\partial L^{\mathcal{D}}}{\partial H_i} = U'^H p_i^m - V_{B_i} \leq 0 \ (= 0 \text{ if } H_i^* > 0)$$

$$\frac{\partial L^{\mathcal{D}}}{\partial w_i} = \sum_{j=1}^{n} V_{B_j} B_j \frac{\partial f_j}{\partial w_i} + \sum_{i=1}^{n} \sum_{j=1}^{n} V_{B_i B_j} B_i B_j \frac{\partial \sigma_{ij}}{\partial w_i}$$

$$+ \lambda_i \int_{u_i} V_{B_i} \frac{\partial g_i}{\partial w_i} B_i u_i p(u_i) du_i$$

$$+ \sum_{j \neq i}^{n} \lambda_j \int_{u_j} V_{B_j} \frac{\partial g_j}{\partial w_i} B_j u_j p(u_j) du_j$$

$$- \delta \leq 0 \ (= 0 \text{ if } w_i^* > 0)$$

$$\frac{\partial L}{\partial \delta} = 1 - \sum_i w_i = 0.$$

Assume that u_i is non-stochastic, so that $u_i = -\bar{u}_i$ with probability one and that $g_i(\mathbf{w}) = g_i(w_i)$, with $\partial g_i(w_i)/\partial w_i < 0$. The rationale behind the negative derivative is that the mixed process can be controlled with respect to the jump by allocating more land to the species experiencing the catastrophic event, so that the effects of the downward jump in the biomass can be partly offset. In this case the optimality condition characterizing the optimal allocation weights becomes:

$$\frac{\partial L^D}{\partial w_i} = \sum_{j=1}^{n} V_{B_j} B_j \frac{\partial f_j}{\partial w_i} + V_{B_i B_i} B_i^2 \frac{\partial \sigma_{ii}^2}{\partial w_i}$$

$$+ \sum_{j \neq i}^{n} V_{B_i B_j} B_i B_j \frac{\partial \sigma_{ij}}{\partial w_i}$$

$$- \lambda_i V_{B_i} \frac{\partial g_i(w_i)}{\partial w_i} B_i \bar{u}_i$$

$$- \delta \leq 0 \; (= 0 \text{ if } w_i^* > 0).$$

Since $\partial g_i(w_i)/\partial w_i < 0$ the term $-\lambda_i V_{B_i} [\partial g_i(w_i)/\partial w_i] B_i \bar{u}_i$ is positive so that the possibility of a catastrophic event makes less likely the possibility of having $w_i^* = 0$ even when V_{B_i} does not tend to infinity as the species is close to extinction. If we further simplify for the case of two species without interactions the optimal weights are determined as:

$$w_1^* = \frac{\left[a_1 - \lambda_1 \frac{\partial g_1(w_1)}{\partial w_1} \bar{u}_1 \right] B_1 V_{B_1} - \left[a_2 - \lambda_2 \frac{\partial g_2(w_2)}{\partial w_2} \bar{u}_2 \right] B_2 V_{B_2}}{\Delta}$$

$$+ \frac{-\sigma_2^2 B_2 V_{B_2 B_2} + \sigma_{12} B_1 B_2 V_{B_1 B_2}}{\Delta}$$

$$w_2^* = 1 - w_1^*, \; \Delta = \sigma_1^2 B_1^2 V_{B_1 B_1} - 2\sigma_{12} B_1 B_2 V_{B_1 B_2} + \sigma_2^2 B_2^2 V_{B_2 B_2}.$$

The weights can be compared to those obtained in Section 5.2. The extra term $-\lambda_1 [\partial g_1(w_1)/\partial w_1]\bar{u}_1$ is positive and contributes to the preservation of species 1.

The above analysis suggests the existence of deviations between the socially optimal and the privately optimal solutions regarding the selection of species portfolios. There are two main sources of deviations. One is that the private agents ignore existence values, thus setting $\mathbf{p}^m = \mathbf{0}$, and the other is the possibility that the private agent ignores the fact that species interaction is possible and therefore that private agents might opt for monocultures with many spillovers when a polyculture with fewer spillovers might be socially optimal. Of course, this fact raises the issue of whether the socially optimal solution can be obtained through regulation.

The discussion and analysis of regulatory schemes are beyond the scope of the present chapter and might constitute a fruitful area for further research. It should be noted, however, that regulation can be approached from two ways. One is the classical way of economic incentives, which might suggest different tax schemes. Another way of approaching the problem is to examine the possibility of introducing land set-aside or zoning programs.[17] A number of zones are set aside and are not harvested for profit maximization, but are managed according to the social optimum. Securing optimal biodiversity in some zones of the landscape might counterbalance the adverse effects of the monocultures emerging from profit-maximizing agents in the other zones.

6 GENERALIZATIONS AND SUGGESTIONS FOR FUTURE RESEARCH

In Section 2 we developed a theory of B-CAPM under the assumption that monoculture i is on w_i units of land and no polyculture was allowed. It can be argued that this assumption totally violates the very substance of biodiversity theory if we interpret our model as a national park and/or intercropping system and/or dual-purpose facility under management. We show here how easy it is to usefully extend our model once we have identified what we think is a fruitful conceptual framework. Before we begin we wish to describe the essence of the role of biodiversity in an example – the prairie. Consider the following material which we quote at length from a book chapter about Wes Jackson and the Land Institute which works on 'natural systems' agriculture (Benyus 1997, p. 23):

> Though never planted by human hands, the prairie is choked by blossoms, grasses gently pouring over, seeds setting, new shoots growing, runnings crisscrossing the earth in a web of decay, growth, and new life. . . . Every plant – 231 species in this patch alone – has a role and cooperates with linked arms with the plants nearby. . . . Piper talks about the plants as if they are neighbors in a community – the nitrogen fixers, the deep-rooted ones that dig for water, the shallow-rooted ones that make the most of a gentle rain, the ones that grow quickly in the spring to shade out weeds, the ones that resist pests or harbor heroes such as beneficial insects. . . .

Beneath this unruly mob lies 70 percent of the living weight of the prairie – a thick weave of roots, rootlets, and runners – that captures water and pumps nutrients up from the depths . . . There are thousands of species in a single teaspoon [of prairie soil] . . . The secret of the prairie is its ability to maintain both above ground and below ground assemblies in a dynamic steady state . . .

We sketch here how one might usefully extend the theory of B-CAPM to model polycultural interactions of a natural system like the prairie which the above quotation captures. Consider an example of $n = 2$ species. The only possible polyculture is the biculture 12. All we need to do is to relabel the biculture 12 as '3', treat it as a third 'species' and repeat the treatment in Section 2 with three 'species'. There is a complication, however. As in Vandermeer (1989, pp. 144–54) we need to relate the expected yield of 12 and its variability to the monocultural yields and variabilities. The easiest way to do this is to adapt Vandermeer's treatment. If we initially have 12 with (B_{01}, B_{02}) initial biomasses of 1, 2 respectively, we obtain $(\tilde{B}_1, \tilde{B}_2)$ at the end of the period where:

$$
\begin{aligned}
\tilde{B}_1 &= \tilde{g}_1 B_{01} - a_{(1,2)} \tilde{B}_2 \\
\tilde{B}_2 &= \tilde{g}_2 B_{02} - a_{(2,1)} \tilde{B}_1 \\
\tilde{B}_1 &= \tilde{g}_{(1/12)} B_{01} \\
\tilde{B}_2 &= \tilde{g}_{(2/12)} B_{02}
\end{aligned}
\tag{5.39}
$$

where the notation is self-explanatory. For example, the bicultural growth rates $\tilde{g}_{(i/12)}$ are defined by the equations above. Note that $\tilde{g}_i B_{i0}$, $i = 1, 2$ in (5.39) are the monocultural yields and $a_{(i,j)}$ are interaction coefficients as in Vandermeer (1989, p. 149, equation (9.1)). The pair 12 is called 'competitive' if the a's are positive, and 'facilitative' if the a's are negative. There are also cases where one 'a' is positive and the other 'a' is negative. Vandermeer stresses that there is a strong tendency for the intercrop to be more variable than the monoculture, as can be seen if we place restrictions on the a's so that (5.39) translates into a stable discrete time dynamical system. The reason is that the a's end up magnifying the variability of the monocultural yields. This is especially so in the competitive case (see Vandermeer 1989, especially equation (9.2) for the details). This observation is important for us because it argues for monoculture unless there is strong facilitation coupled with substantial intercrop overyield (Vandermeer 1989, p. 24, income equivalent ratio) in revenue to compensate for the extra variance. Of course intercropping may economize on other costs such as pest and weed control.

We shall say more about this below. After the random variables $\tilde{g}_{(i/12)}$, $i = 1, 2$ are calculated from (5.39) we may label 12 as 'species' 3 and copy the analysis in Section 2 with $n = 3$. We have to calculate the covariances of the monoculture biomasses $w_i g_i B_{i0}$, $i = 1, 2$ with the bicultural '12' biomass:

$$w_{12}[\tilde{B}_1 + \tilde{B}_2] = w_3[g_{(1/12)}B_{10} + g_{(2/12)}B_{20}]$$

recalling the relabeling that $w_{12} = w_3$. This framework not only extends the B-CAPM to include biculture, but it also allows us to evaluate the value of the option of including biculture following the treatment of valuation of species loss in Section 2.2.

We extend our two species numerical example by considering the possibility of intercropping. As shown in Figure 5.10, in this two-species intercropping the polyculture is constructed by planting half of the positions in the polyculture with species 1 and half with species 2 (Vandermeer 1989, p. 16).

In treating the intercrop as the third species we assume the following parameter values:[18]

$\bar{B}_3$	$\sigma^2_{B_3}$	$\sigma_{B_1B_3} = \sigma_{B_2B_3}$	h_3	p_3	p_3^m
145	70	0.6	0.65	4	4

Setting again e_p = 650 the optimal land allocation is $(w_1^*, w_2^*, w_3^*) =$ (0.472943, 0, 0.527027), $\sigma^2 = 668.556$. Therefore the optimal allocation keeps part of the land as a monoculture of the first species, and the rest as an intercrop of the two species. By 'losing' species 3, the intercrop, while keeping the variance constant, the loss in expected return is 27 percent. On the other hand by 'losing' the intercrop while keeping the expected return constant the increase in variance is 87 percent.

The extension to n larger than 2 is now clear but messy. We list all the possible polycultures as well as the monocultures and create an 'artificial' species for each possible polyculture. We work out yields for each polyculture using an obvious multivariate generalization of the bivariance system (5.39). Then we set up an analog of problem (5.2) in Section 2 for this expanded allocation problem. We may now use this conceptual apparatus to pose and solve problems of valuation of intercropping options, facilitative biodiversity, and the like. It is beyond the scope of this chapter to do more here.

One component of intercropping advantage and biodiversity advantage is the possible savings of costs associated with pest control such as insects, weeds, and the like. Now that our conceptual framework is in place it is easy to generalize it to include costs. For example, imagine that each species in a cropping system (including polycultures treated as a 'species' as detailed above) produces output on w units of land as a Leontief production process of the w units of land and a vector of inputs including weeding, spraying, tending, cultivating, and the like. If we assume that, for example, for monoculture i, B_{i0} plays the role of 'seed input' and this is in fixed proportion to the rest of the inputs then the cost function will be linear for each 'species' (that is, each monoculture and each possible polyculture)

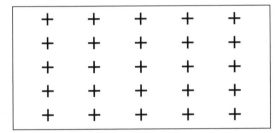

Monoculture: Species 1

Monoculture: Species 2

Polyculture: Constructed by planting half of the positions in the polyculture with one species and half with the other (substitutive design, Vandermeer 1989, p. 16)

Figure 5.10   Monocultures and polyculture

and we can simply subtract that cost from x_i for each species i and adapt the treatment above to include these costs. If costs are low enough for a particular polyculture, the yield could be low and variance high relative to the 'equivalent' set of monocultures using Vandermeer's land equivalent ratio measure (Vandermeer (1989, p. 19). This is why Vandermeer stresses the use of other measures of intercrop advantage or disadvantage such as the income equivalent ratio.

But there is an extra issue in our problem, which is that of the differential between private and social optimization incentives. Intercrops that economize on social spillover effects such as well-water pollution (for example, the intercrop might economize on the herbicides and pesticides needed for an income equivalent set of monocultures) might well be socially more efficient. Some discussion of this issue is given in Section 5.

Finally our general theoretical approach to landscape allocation of mixtures of monocultures and polycultures suggests posing the question: what does Nature optimize if anything? Students of natural systems like prairies suggest: 'The secret of the prairie is its ability to maintain both above ground and below ground assemblies in a dynamic steady state. . . . The first thing that strikes us is . . . that ninety-nine point nine percent of the plants are perennials' (Benyus, 1997, pp. 24, 25). Benyus quotes tropical agroecologist Jack Ewel: 'Imitate the vegetative structure of an ecosystem and you will be granted function' (ibid., p. 24).

Ecologist Jon Piper stresses three key features of a prairie: (i) most of the grasses are perennials; (ii) there is much diversity with much 'redundancy' of function (for example, many warm-season grasses, many nitrogen-fixing legumes, and so on); (iii) there are four classic plant types – warm-season grasses, cool-season grasses, legumes and composites (Benyus 1997, p. 26). Perennials sink deep roots, hold the soil together, and are self-fertilizing and self-weeding. To put it another way, it is as though the prairie was designed to maximize some measure of resilience, that is, survivability, in the face of highly variable weather and other disturbances.

Indeed the emphasis of research at the Land Institute discussed in Benyus (1997) and Soule and Piper (1992) is design of a nature-mimicking agroecosystem based upon herbaceous seed-yielding perennials that runs on sunlight and 'pays its own bills' in the sense of not requiring external inputs such as fertilizer, pesticides, herbicides and other negative externality inputs associated with conventional high-input fossil fuel-based monoculture.

Tilman et al. (1996) report on experiments at Cedar Creek which document benefits of biodiversity (that is, polycultures). In order to make contact with polyculture research and sustainable ecosystems research such as Tilman et al. (1997), we can generalize equation (5.25) by defining each polyculture as a new 'species' as we did in generalizing Section 2 above and locate sufficient conditions for this generalized version of equation (5.25) to be 'sustainable' in the sense that the assembly persists forever through time. A notion of 'sustainable function' could be defined so that we could locate sufficient conditions for maximizing the probability of sustainable function forever through time. If a plausible one-dimensional index of sustainable function, call it I, which is a time-stationary function of the biomasses in (5.25) (including the artificial 'species' which correspond to polycultures) could be defined, then optimal stopping theory as in Malliaris and Brock (1982) could be used to study the assembly of species that maximizes the probability of I not falling below a 'critical' level I_c. This might make a useful 'working model' of Nature for comparison with private and social optimization of humans studied in Section 5.

In conclusion, this chapter has laid out only a conceptual approach to the study of biodiversity management which suggests that it might be useful to unify ideas from portfolio management, intercropping theory and agroecological theory. Exploration of this type of framework must await future research.

NOTES

1. See, for example, Perrings et al. (1995).
2. There are a number of empirical studies relating the number of species in ecosystems to plant productivity (Naeem et al. 1996; Tilman et al. 1996; Hooper and Vitousek 1997 which have found that functional diversity is a principal factor explaining plant productivity. Vandermeer (1989), in a similar type of problem, seeks to allocate a given area to different plants so as to minimize the variance of the sum of crops from all plants.
3. Zero price can be associated with 'weeds'.
4. The price vectors are assumed to belong to some compact subset of $\mathcal{R}^{2n}$.
5. For the solution see, for example, Huang and Litzenberger (1988, Section 3.8) or Campbell et al. (1997, Section 5.2).
6. It should be clear from Figure 5.2 that condition (5.10) requires that the *mvsp* corresponds to a positive expected landscape value.
7. The set is closed and bounded because the harvest rates are between zero and one and the p's are fixed.
8. If some expected growth rates are zero in one regime, then the equilibrium portfolios in each regime will not in general contain the same number of species.
9. This diversification is similar to the international diversification of investment portfolios (for example, Grubel 1968, Levy and Sarnat 1970).
10. This assumption can be relaxed by allowing the possibility of introducing a species later on by allowing replanting at a cost.
11. This type of motive can be related to sustainability notions.
12. Second-order conditions will be satisfied if the value function is concave in **B**.
13. It can be shown (Soner 1997, p. 148) that the value function $V(\mathbf{B}, t)$ is a unique continuous viscosity solution of the dynamic programming equation.
14. The analysis can be extended to many utility-maximizing agents allowing for strategic interactions among them.
15. See, for example, Kushner (1967) and Malliaris and Brock (1982) for details.
16. Second-order conditions will be satisfied if the value function is concave in **B**.
17. For policy schemes where required species are planted in specific strips of land, see Carlson et al. (1991).
18. Due to the substitutive design of the intercrop we assume the market and existence values are the simple arithmetic means of the corresponding values of the two species.

REFERENCES

Benyus, J. (1997), *Biomimikry: Innovation Inspired by Nature*, New York: W. Morrow & Company.

Brock, W. and A. Xepapadeas (1998), 'Optimal management in Tilmania: a competitive species assembly constrained by a limiting factor', *Fondazione ENI Enrico Mattei, Working Paper*, 68/98, Milan, Italy.

Brock, W. and A. Xepapadeas (forthcoming), 'Optimal ecosystem management when species compete for limiting resources', *Journal of Environmental Economics and Management*.

Campbell, J., A. Lo and A. MacKinlay (1997), *The Econometrics of Financial Markets*, Princeton, NJ: Princeton University Press.

Carlson, D.A., A.B. Hauries and A. Leizarowitz (1991), *Infinite Horizon Optimal Control*, 2nd edn, Berlin: Springer-Verlag.

Cox, J. and C.-F. Huang (1989), 'Optimal consumption and portfolio choices when asset prices follow a diffusion process', *Journal of Economic Theory*, **49**, 33–83.

Daily, G. and P. Ehrlich (1995), 'Population extinction and biodiversity crisis', in Perrings et al. (eds), pp. 45–56.

Ehrlich, P. and A. Ehrlich (1992), 'The value of biodiversity', *Ambio*, **21**, 219–26.

Fleming, W. and H.M. Soner (1993), *Controlled Markov Process and Viscosity Solutions*, New York: Springer-Verlag.

Grubel, H. (1968), 'Internationally diversified portfolios: welfare gains and capital flows', *American Economic Review*, **58**, 1299–314.

Hooper, D. and P. Vitousek (1997), 'The effects of plant composition and diversity on ecosystem processes', *Science*, **277**, 1302–5.

Huang, Chi-fu and R. Litzenberger (1988), *Foundations for Financial Economics*, New York: North-Holland.

Kushner, H. (1967), *Stochastic Stability and Control*, New York: Academic Press.

Levy, H. and M. Sarnat (1970), 'International diversification of investment portfolios', *American Economic Review*, **60**, 668–75.

Malliaris, A.G. and W.A. Brock (1982), *Stochastic Methods in Economics and Finance*, Amsterdam: North-Holland.

Merton, R. (1971) 'Optimum consumption and portfolio rules in a continuous time model', *Journal of Economic Theory*, **3**, 373–413.

Merton, R. (1973), 'An intertemporal capital asset pricing model', *Econometrica*, **41**, 867–87.

Naeem, S., K. Hakansson, J. Lawton, M. Crawley and L. Thompson (1996), 'Biodiversity and plant productivity in a model assemblage of plant species', *Oikos*, **76**, 259–64.

Pearce, D. and C. Perrings (1995), 'Biodiversity conservation and economic development: local and global dimensions', in Perrings et al. (eds).

Perrings, C.A., K.-G. Mäler, C. Folke, C.S. Holling and B.O. Jansson (eds) (1995), *Biodiversity Conservation*, Dordrecht: Kluwer Academic.

Scott, J.C. (1998), *Seeing Like a State*, New Haven, CT: Yale University Press.

Soner, M. (1997), 'Controlled Markov processes, viscosity solutions, and applications to mathematical finance', in I. Capuzzo Dolcetta and P.L. Lions (eds), *Viscosity Solutions and Applications*, Berlin: Springer, pp. 134–85.

Soule, J. and J. Piper (1992), *Farming in Nature's image: An Ecological Approach to Agriculture*, Washington, DC: Island Press.

Tilman, D. (1982), *Resource Competition and Community Structure*, Princeton, NJ: Princeton University Press.

Tilman, D. (1988), *Plant Strategies and the Dynamics and Structure of Plant Communities*, Princeton, NJ: Princeton University Press.

Tilman, D., J. Knops, D. Wedin, P. Reich, M. Richie and E. Siemann (1997), 'The influence of functional diversity and composition on ecosystem processes', *Science*, **277**, 1300–302.

Tilman, D., D. Wedin and J. Knops (1996), 'Productivity and sustainability influenced by biodiversity in grassland ecosystem', *Nature*, **379**, 718–20.

Vandermeer, J. (1989), *The Ecology of Intercropping*, Cambridge: Cambridge University Press.

6. The Kyoto Protocol: an economic and game-theoretic interpretation

Parkash Chander, Henry Tulkens, Jean-Pascal van Ypersele and Stephane Willems[*]

1 INTRODUCTION: COOPERATION AT THE WORLD LEVEL, FROM RIO TO KYOTO

Our central theme in this chapter is the one of cooperation at the world level on the issue of climatic change. We start from the facts and then try to enlighten them by means of ideas provided by economics and game theory.

The negotiations on climate change that have been taking place since the late 1980s within the United Nations institutions[1] are obviously a quasi-worldwide process, judging by the length of the list of countries[2] participating. But these negotiations, prior to the Kyoto meeting, had led only to a 'framework convention', signed in 1992 in Rio de Janeiro, that was little more than a declaration of intentions. The real issue was then: are the continuing negotiations eventually going to lead to a sustainable agreement bearing on effective actions that is also worldwide? Or will they lead to a breaking up of the countries into separate blocs, each acting to the best of its own interests?

The Kyoto Protocol, signed in December 1997, is the major development in the post-Rio evolution of these negotiations. Its importance lies mainly in the fact that it bears on effective actions to be taken by countries, actions that are recognized as binding commitments by them.

However, according to the Protocol, not all countries have to take specific actions. As our summary presentation will report more in detail below, commitments to quantified emissions reduction or limitation are mentioned only for the so-called 'Annex I' parties.[3] The role of the other countries in the agreement, while not ignored, is much less precisely specified.

The natural question that then arises is whether the Kyoto Protocol is to be considered as just an 'Annex I' Protocol; or is it to be seen, after further thought and beyond the appearances, as a worldwide Protocol? Below, we defend the second thesis, first on the basis of our own conviction, but also because we think we can support it by means of well-established conceptual tools of economics and game theory.

For the applied economist, the Kyoto Protocol offers an exceptionally rich combination of opportunities to put theory into use, both in a positive and a normative way – that is, for explaining events as well as for advising on decision making. Indeed, several strands of theory are involved as we shall show: externalities of the Samuelsonian public good type, Nash non-cooperative equilibria, worldwide Pareto optimality, cooperative solution concepts, and finally Walrasian market equilibria with their Edgeworthian coalitional stability. All these are involved!

2   MAIN FEATURES OF THE PROTOCOL

We briefly state here what the main features of the Protocol are, from the point of view of our arguments to follow:

1. Dated *emission quotas*, expressed in percentages of 1990 emissions, are established for Annex I countries, to be met around 2010.
2. The principles of (a) *emissions trading* by countries (or by their nationals) and of (b) *joint implementation* are established for Annex I countries.
3. A *clean development mechanism* (CDM) is established as a way to involve non-Annex I countries (especially developing ones) in some particular form of joint implementation and emissions trading.

No explicit provision in the Protocol mentions the introduction of targets for non-Annex I countries. But it is expected that this will take place in the future through the general review clauses of the Protocol and of the Convention.

Trade in emissions will be allowed only among countries that do ratify. It is also expected that it will not be allowed with the countries that would not fulfill their obligations under the Protocol.

Finally, the Protocol comes into force automatically[4] only if (i) at least 55 parties to the Convention have ratified it, and (ii) these 55 parties include a number of Annex I parties accounting for at least 55 percent of the base year CO_2 emissions of all Annex I parties to the Convention.

While parties are committing themselves to proceed to enforcement within their country, no sanctions are specified if a ratifying country does not fulfill its obligations under the Protocol, except for the above provision on being excluded from emissions trading. A compliance regime, including possible sanctions for non-compliance, is yet to be specified in the process of future negotiations.

3 ECONOMICS OF THE ISSUES AT STAKE

Consider the n countries of the world (indexed below $i = 1, \ldots, n$), who each enjoy an aggregate consumption level x_i, equal to the aggregate value of their production activities y_i, minus the damage D_i consisting in lost production that results from global pollution. Each country i's productive activity entails some amount of polluting emissions e_i, which are related to production according to the increasing and strictly concave production function[5] $y_i = g_i(e_i)$. Damages in each country are generated by the total of such emissions, $\Sigma_{i=1}^n e_i$; they affect production possibilities in each country[6] in a way that is usually represented by an increasing damage cost function $D_i = d_i(\Sigma_{j=1}^n e_j)$ which for simplicity we assume to be linear. Each country's consumption possibilities are thus given by the expression:

$$x_i = g_i(e_i) - d_i \sum_{j=1}^n e_j, \tag{6.1}$$

where $d_i > 0$ is thus the damage cost per unit of emission or, equivalently, the benefit per unit of abatement (for decreasing Σe_j).

3.1 World Optimality

Ignoring distributional issues, world consumption optimality can then be represented by the consumption levels that maximize $\Sigma_{i=1}^n x_i$ with respect to the n variables $e_1, \ldots, e_n$. Let $(e_1^*, \ldots, e_n^*)$ be the vector of emission levels in the n countries that achieve such a world optimum. First-order conditions for a maximum are given by the following system of equations expressing equality between the marginal cost of global damages and the marginal abatement cost of each party i:

$$g_i'(e_i^*) - \sum_{j=1}^n d_j = 0, \ i = 1, \ldots, n. \tag{6.2}$$

We shall develop our arguments below under the assumption that climate change negotiations are aiming at achieving such a world optimum. Attaining it requires coordination among the countries, so as to ensure that each one of them does take into account the effect of its emissions on the other countries as reflected by their damage cost functions.

3.2 Non-cooperative Equilibrium

It is indeed often argued[7] that in the absence of coordination, countries choose emission policies that best suit their own interest, taking as given what the other countries do. This leads us to consider that a non-cooperative equilibrium of some sort prevails between countries if no negotiations take place.

How would a country determine its best emissions levels? The answer is not immediate since imposing low emissions on itself implies low net production according to the function g_i, whereas allowing for high emissions entails high damage costs according to the function D_i. Classical economic reasoning suggests that a rational domestic optimum for each country would be one that best balances these two aspects; it is achieved by maximizing its own consumption level x_i with respect to e_i as defined in (6.1), taking as given all variable e_j with $j \neq i$. If all countries adopt such a behavior, a Nash-type equilibrium between countries prevails, which we represent by the vector of emissions[8] $(\bar{e}_1, \ldots, \bar{e}_n)$. For each country i, the first-order condition of its maximizing behavior is given by the equation:

$$g_i'(\bar{e}_i) - d_i = 0 \qquad (6.3a)$$

while its achievable consumption level is:

$$\bar{x}_i = g_i(\bar{e}_i) - d_i \sum_{j=1}^{n} \bar{e}_j . \qquad (6.3b)$$

Two characteristics of the non-cooperative equilibrium so defined are essential for our purposes: (i) the equilibrium emissions $(\bar{e}_1, \ldots, \bar{e}_n)$ are clearly not a world optimum as can be seen from comparing (6.2) and (6.3a and b): that is why negotiations are necessary; and (ii) $\bar{e}_i > e_i^*$ for each i since g_i is concave and $\sum_{j=1}^{n} d_j > d_i$ for all i's; thus, world optimal emissions are lower than those prevailing at the non-cooperative equilibrium.

3.3 Coalitional Stability for the Treaty

The basic reason for the non-optimality of the Nash equilibrium is a well-known externality argument. Each country decides its emission level $\bar{e}_i$ without concern for the effects on other countries: it thus equates its marginal abatement cost, $g_i'(\bar{e}_i)$, to its own marginal damage cost, d_i, whereas a world optimum requires each country to equate its marginal abatement cost to the aggregate world marginal damage cost, $\sum_{i=1}^{n} d_i$.

Furthermore, a world optimum may require from the various countries different levels of abatement $\bar{e}_i - e_i^*$, entailing costs and benefits that are a priori by no means identical across them: some may have high abatement costs while having only small damage costs to avoid, whereas other countries may have low abatement costs while facing high damage costs. To have the world optimum voluntarily agreed upon by all countries requires in addition that *for each country* and *for each group of countries* the benefits exceed the costs of abatement. Because of the asymmetries just mentioned, this can be achieved only by means of appropriately designed resource transfers from the net gainers to the net losers.

To that effect Chander and Tulkens (1997) have proposed that the optimal emission levels $(e_1^*, \ldots, e_n^*)$ specified in the treaty be accompanied by a scheme of transfers $(T_1, \ldots, T_n)$ which are of the form:

$$T_i = [g_i(\bar{e}_i) - g_i(e_i^*)] - \frac{d_i}{\displaystyle\sum_{j=1}^{n} dj} \left[\sum_{j=1}^{n} g_j(\bar{e}_j) - \sum_{j=1}^{n} g_j(e_j^*) \right], \tag{6.4}$$

$$i = 1, \ldots, n,$$

where $T_i > 0$ if the transfer is received by country i, while $T_i < 0$ if the transfer is paid.[9] The first expression within square brackets is equal to the abatement cost borne by country i from moving from its Nash equilibrium level of emissions $\bar{e}_i$ to the level e_i^* prescribed by world optimality. As this amount is positive in (6.4), the role of this part of the transfer appears to be to cover that cost increase for i. The second expression within square brackets is the *world total* over all countries of their emissions abatement cost from the Nash equilibrium levels to the world optimal ones – also a positive magnitude. With the ratio $d_i/\sum_{j=1}^{n} d_j$ and taking account of the negative sign, the second term in (6.4) thus determines a contribution of country i, which is specified as a fraction of the aggregate abatement cost.

Clearly $\sum_{i=1}^{n} T_i = 0$, so that these transfers would ensure a balanced budget if an international agency were established for implementing them. Note also the role played by the reference emission levels $\bar{e}_i$ in the design of the transfers – a feature whose importance will be highlighted below.

The 'coalitional stability' property claimed above for the Chander–Tulkens proposal of optimality with transfers is that, in addition to making each country *individually* better off compared to the Nash equilibrium, it also makes every *group* of countries better off, compared to what they could get by adopting any alternative arrangement among themselves, be it in terms of emissions, or transfers, or both. For further reference in our arguments below, let us be more precise on this property. Let $W = \{i = 1, \ldots, n\}$ denote the set of all countries of the world and $S \subset W$ be any subset, or 'coalition' of countries. Then the best outcome that the members of S could obtain by making arrangements among themselves only – to be called a 'partial agreement Nash equilibrium with respect to S' (PANE w.r.t. S) – is the one resulting from the emissions policy $(\tilde{e}_1, \ldots, \tilde{e}_n)$ defined by, for the members of S,

$$(\tilde{e}_i)_{i \in S} = arg\ max \left[\sum_{i \in S} g_i(e_i) - (\sum_{i \in S} d_i)(\sum_{i \in S} e_i + \sum_{j \in W \setminus S} \tilde{e}_j) \right],$$

and for the countries not in S:

$$\tilde{e}_j = arg\ max\ \left[g_j(e_j) - d_j(e_j + \sum_{i\neq j}^{n}\tilde{e}_i)\right], j\in W\backslash S.$$

A PANE w.r.t. S is thus a Nash equilibrium between the countries in S acting jointly and the remaining countries acting individually. It can be characterized by the first-order conditions:

$$g_i'(\tilde{e}_i) = \sum_{j\in S}d_j,\ i\in S$$

and

$$g_i'(\tilde{e}_i) = d_i,\ i\in W\backslash S.$$

A comparison of these conditions with (6.2) implies $\sum_{i\in S}\tilde{e}_i \leq \sum_{i\in S}\bar{e}_i$ and $\tilde{e}_j = \bar{e}_j, j\in W\backslash S$. Since in a PANE w.r.t. S the countries within the coalition coordinate their emissions so as to take into account their effect on each other, their emissions are lower compared to the Nash equilibrium. The emissions of the countries outside of the coalition are, however, not lower. In fact, they might be higher if the damage function is convex but not linear.[10] Moreover, since total world emissions are lower in a PANE w.r.t. S, the countries outside the coalition are better off, although that is not the intention of the coalition.

3.4 Statistics versus Dynamics

Thus far, and for most of the sequel, the above quantities x_i and e_i are considered to be flows per unit of time. The damages from climate change are, however, induced less by the flow of greenhouse gas emissions than by the increase[11] ΔS in their accumulated stock S in the atmosphere. At each time t, ΔS_t is thus determined by a relation of the form:

$$\Delta S_t = -\delta S_{t-1} + k\sum_{i=1}^{n}e_{it},\ t = 1, 2 \ldots$$

where according to climatic science common wisdom $\delta \cong 0.01$ and k is of the order of 0.5 (and slowly increasing over time).

The issues at stake have thereby an inherently dynamic component that is by no means ignored in the economics literature on climate change; see, for example, Nordhaus and Yang (1996), or, for our part, Germain et al. (1998). One might therefore consider that world optimality is not to be defined in terms of just one-period emission, production and consumption levels as we have done but, instead, of multiperiod emission trajectories $\{(e_{1t}, \ldots, e_{nt})_{t=1,2,\ldots}\}$ and similarly for production and consumption.

While this more elaborate modeling has its merits, it turns out to be unnecessary for our purposes. Indeed, one may have noted that the specific object of the Kyoto Protocol is *not* trajectories of emissions: it is emissions *levels* at some point in time (around 2010[12]). We therefore feel justified in working, in the present chapter, with the usual 'static' or one-period model.[13]

4   NON-COOPERATIVE CHARACTERIZATIONS OF THE PRE-AGREEMENT STAGE

The non-cooperative behavior described in Section 3.2 is not the only one conceivable of this kind. Indeed, the fulfillment of conditions (6.3a) and (6.3b) which characterize it requires domestic policies to be designed and implemented, involving an energy tax or appropriately priced pollution permits, so that the energy price including the tax or the permit unit price is equal to the domestic marginal damage cost d_i. These belong to the class of what is often called 'no-regrets policies'. However, not all countries can be said to have adopted such a nationally rational course of action.

For instance, industrial firms in some countries may have strong lobbying power and use it so as to obtain low energy prices. While still choosing, as profit maximizers, energy use and emissions so that g_i' is equal to the price of energy (denoted henceforth as p_i), this results into emissions $\bar{\bar{e}}_i$ higher than $\bar{e}_i$ and such that $g_i'(\bar{\bar{e}}_i) < d_i$, thus successfully preventing the nationally rational policy to be adopted. If this behaviour is assumed to prevail in all countries, a different equilibrium – equally non-cooperative – results, called by Nordhaus and Yang (1996) the 'market solution' (or 'business as usual', according to others).

Alternatively, energy-importing countries facing balance of payments problems may have introduced high taxes and domestic prices of energy: their emission levels $\bar{\bar{e}}_i$ are then likely to be such that $g_i'(\bar{\bar{e}}_i) > d_i$.

Finally, another reason why a nationally rational policy may not come about is that firms in a country may simply not be profit maximizers, as is particularly the case with large public sector enterprises of non-market economies. In such cases, the domestic equilibria are neither of the 'market' nor of the 'nationally rational' type, and energy prices do not induce any well-defined emissions policy – except for the fact of a generally low concern for economical use of energy.

Our point in this section is that in the situation prevailing at the pre-negotiation stage, all three types of country behaviour are likely to be present, and we wish to illustrate this empirically with the data in Table 6.1.

We first note a similarity between the structure, across some major countries, of the average energy prices for three kinds of fossil fuels (first three

Table 6.1 Retail prices (in US$ per unit) of industrial fossil fuels, marginal abatement cost and damage cost in selected countries or regions

	Heavy fuel oil for industry[*] (per ton)	Steam coal for industry[*] (per ton)	Natural gas for industry[*] (per 10kcalGCV)	Marginal abatement cost/ton of carbon for first 100Mton reduction ($)[**]	Annual damage cost as % of GDP[***]	Type of domestic equilibrium
USA	138.00	35.27	136.62	12	1.3	$g_i'(\overline{e}_i) = p_i < d_i$
EU	187.40	76.00	182.00	40	1.4	$g_i'(\overline{e}_i) = p_i \geq d_i$
Japan	172.86	49.90	423.12	350	1.4	$g_i'(\overline{e}_i) = p_i \geq d_i$
India	191.15	19.36	na	22	na	?
FSU	na	na	na	22	0.7	?
China	na	na	na	3.5	4.7	?

Sources: [*]*Energy Prices and Taxes* (1996); [**]Ellerman and Decaux (1998); [***]Fankhauser (1995).

columns) on the one hand, and of the marginal abatement costs (fourth column) on the other hand. In particular, it is seen that the energy prices in the US are systematically lower and so is the marginal cost of abatement.[14] Moreover, for the three developed regions the USA, the European Union (EU) and Japan which are also market economies, the higher the energy prices, the higher the marginal abatement costs.[15] For the other countries we cannot say much, not only because of lack of data but also because they are either non-market or less developed, or both.

Second, we have an opportunity to characterize some domestic policies by using equations (6.3a) and (6.3b) – according to which in countries that choose their emission levels rationally, that is, in the 'no-regrets' sense, the marginal damage cost from emissions must be equal to the marginal abatement cost and also to the average energy prices. Indeed, the data in the table reveal that marginal abatement costs are lower in the USA compared to the EU and Japan (they are even lower than those of a developing country like India). Now, it can hardly be the case that the marginal damage cost for the USA, the largest economy, is lower than that of the EU or of Japan. Therefore, we have an indication that in the USA, decisions regarding emissions are determined by the business-as-usual policy rather than optimized at the national level.

We indicate in the last column the type of pre-negotiation domestic equilibrium we conjecture from the data to prevail in each region.

What is the relevance of these observations for our purposes in this chapter? While the optimum emissions $(e_1^*, \ldots, e_n^*)$ are, as seen from (6.2), independent of those at the pre-negotiation stage, the transfers T_i defined in (6.4) may have to be modified with the $\bar{e}_i$'s substituted by the actual emission levels of each country i as they are described here. Does such a substitution affect the coalition stability property of the transfers? The answer is no,[16] as long as one can assume that countries do adopt the same behavior at the pre-agreement stage and at a PANE when not in the coalition. For the sake of simplicity, however, we shall continue to consider the $\bar{e}_i$'s as Nash equilibrium emission levels.

5   KYOTO QUOTAS AND WORLDWIDE TRADING: EFFICIENCY AND COALITIONAL STABILITY OF THE SCHEME

5.1   The Kyoto Quotas: Not Optimality, but a Step in the Right Direction

While it is straightforward to define and characterize a world optimum in theory, as we have done in Section 3, implementing it is undoubtedly difficult in practice, for several reasons among which we identify four. First, determining optimal emissions at the world level requires knowledge of, and agreement on, what the aggregate marginal damage costs $\sum_{i=1}^{n} d_i$ are, as well as the countries' marginal abatement costs $g_i'(e_i)$. While 'objective' technical studies can provide some of that information, one can expect that, due to the huge interests at stake in many segments of all concerned economies, pressures are exerted for either concealing or simply not collecting the statistical material required.

Second, because the achievement of a stable world optimum may require, as noted earlier, resource transfers between the countries to compensate those for which net benefits, that is, benefits minus costs, are low or negative, institutions or mechanisms that hardly exist today are needed to implement such transfers.

Third, the reference emission levels $\bar{e}_i$, which play a role in the design of the transfers (6.4) ensuring coalitional stability, may themselves be considered unfair, typically by those countries that are in the early stages of their economic development: they currently have comparatively low emission levels, while developed countries have high ones. In the future, when they will be developed, currently developing countries will have higher emissions and they might argue that these should be used as reference levels instead of those of today.

Finally, if reductions in emissions $\bar{e}_i - e_i^*$, are very large (as proposed by some countries), they are simply not politically feasible, at least in the short run. In fact, the Kyoto Protocol requires only relatively small reductions for the immediate future (the next 15 years), leaving further reductions for later periods.

For all these reasons it is difficult to assess whether the emissions reduction chosen by the Kyoto signatories correspond to world optimal emissions.

Yet, countries in Kyoto have agreed upon *some* scheme of quotas on their emissions. Denote this scheme by the vector $(\hat{e}_1, \ldots, \hat{e}_n)$ where $\hat{e}_i$ is the quota on emissions of country i and write $\hat{e} = \sum_{i=1}^{n} \hat{e}_i$ for the so-induced aggregate reduced emissions.[17] Because $\hat{e}$ is lower than $\bar{e} = \sum_{i=1}^{n} \bar{e}_i$, that is, the total sum of emissions in 1990, these aggregate reduced emissions are certainly a step in the right direction since irrespective of whether 1990 emissions are business-as-usual or no-regrets policies, both imply too large emissions with respect to the world optimum.

5.2   Emissions Trading: Efficiency of Equilibrium

If the Kyoto aggregate emissions reduction to $\hat{e}$ is achieved by letting each country abide by its emissions quota and simply emit up to $e_i = \hat{e}_i$, the ensuing aggregate gross world production, $\hat{y} =_{\text{def}} \sum_{i=1}^{n} \hat{y}_i = \sum_{i=1}^{n} g_i(\hat{e}_i)$, may not be the highest achievable level. If so, the national policies $e_i = \hat{e}_i$ for each i would be inefficient. Alternative specifications of the countries' emissions e_i all achieving $\hat{e}$, are conceivable. In fact, recalling (6.1), the highest possible world consumption levels compatible with $\hat{e}$ would be those given by the vector $\hat{e}^* = (\hat{e}^*_1, \ldots, \hat{e}^*_n)$, which solves the problem:

$$\max \sum_{i=1}^{n} x_i = \sum_{i=1}^{n} [g_i(e_i) - d_i \sum_{j=1}^{n} \hat{e}_j] \tag{6.5}$$

$$\text{subject to } \sum_{i=1}^{n} e_i = \sum_{i=1}^{n} \hat{e}_i. \tag{6.6}$$

How are these efficient emission levels to be determined? With appropriate information on the production (or abatement cost) functions g_i, this could be done by computation. However, having argued above that such information is hard to come by, it is likely that strong opposition would arise against the computed emission levels, and in particular against those that would be larger than $\hat{e}_i$, which is indeed a possibility!

We want to show presently that the desired efficient emission levels are precisely those that a competitive market equilibrium in tradable emission quotas would determine; in other words, that tradability of quotas automatically solves the problem (6.5)–(6.6).

To this effect, note first that the vector $\hat{e}^* = (\hat{e}^*_1, \ldots, \hat{e}^*_n)$ we are interested in identically solves the problem of maximizing aggregate gross production:

$$\max \sum_{i=1}^{n} [g_i(e_i)] \text{ subject to } \sum_{i=1}^{n} e_i = \sum_{i=1}^{n} \hat{e}_i, \tag{6.7}$$

because the dropped term $d_i \sum_{j=1}^{n} \hat{e}_j$ is a constant in (6.5).

Next, define a *competitive emissions trading equilibrium* with respect to $(\hat{e}_1, \ldots, \hat{e}_n)$ as a vector of national emissions $(\hat{e}'_1, \ldots, \hat{e}'_n)$ and a price $\hat{\gamma} > 0$ for CO_2 (expressed in units of consumption goods per unit of CO_2 emission) such that for each country $i = 1, \ldots, n$,

$$\hat{e}'_i = \arg \max [g_i(e_i) + \hat{\gamma}(\hat{e}_i - e_i)], \tag{6.8}$$

and

$$\sum_{i=1}^{n} \hat{e}'_i = \sum_{i=1}^{n} \hat{e}_i. \tag{6.9}$$

In such a competitive emissions trading equilibrium, the countries (typically their firms, but conceivably also other economic agents) freely trade in their pollution rights, equal to their emissions quotas $(\hat{e}_1, \ldots, \hat{e}_n)$, at the given price $\hat{\gamma}$, and at that price, demand and supply of pollution rights are equal.[18] The magnitudes $\hat{\gamma}(\hat{e}_i -$

$\hat{e}'_i$) represent the value, in private goods, of payments for the purchase, at world price $\hat{\gamma}$, of quotas if $(\hat{e}_i - \hat{e}'_i)$, the amount purchased, is negative, or of receipts from the sale of quotas if $(\hat{e}_i, \ldots, \hat{e}'_i)$, the amount sold, is positive.

Clearly the vector $(\hat{e}'_i - \hat{e}'_n)$ defined by (6.8)–(6.9) is also the one that solves (6.7), hence (6.5)–(6.6) and thereby maximizes world consumption, since:

$$\sum_{i=1}^{n} g_i(\hat{e}'_i) + \hat{\gamma} \sum_{i=1}^{n} (\hat{e}_i - \hat{e}'_i) = \max \sum_{i=1}^{n} g_i(e_i) \text{ subject to } \sum_{i=1}^{n} e_i = \sum_{i=1}^{n} \hat{e}_i.$$

As a confirmation, it can be seen from the first-order condition for (6.8) that at the price $\hat{\gamma}$ the equality $g_i(\hat{e}'_i) = \hat{\gamma}$ is satisfied for all i's, implying that $g_i(\hat{e}'_i) = g_j(\hat{e}'_j)$ for all $i, j = 1, \ldots, n$, a necessary condition for a solution of (6.5)–(6.6).

Trading thus allows countries to achieve the aggregate emissions reduction $\hat{e}$ with the highest level of world consumption compatible with this reduction or, in other words, at the lowest opportunity cost for the world. This holds even if for some countries $(\hat{e}_i - \hat{e}'_i)$ is negative: the point is indeed that world consumption be maximized and not that all countries necessarily emit $\hat{e}'_i$ lower than $\hat{e}_i$.

5.3 Emissions Trading: Coalitional Stability of Equilibrium

If trade in emissions is allowed another question arises: will there be blocs of countries forming in emissions trading? We answer the question in this section by means of a simple argument based on the theory of market games.

Let $S \subset W$ be a bloc of countries whose members would decide, given the vector $(\hat{e}_i)_{i \in S}$ of their individual Kyoto quotas, to adopt some joint policy of their own for meeting their aggregate quota, $\sum_{i \in S} \hat{e}_i$, such as, for example, trading only among themselves, or engaging in other bilateral or multilateral agreements that fulfill the same condition. To characterize the economic effect of the formation of such a bloc, define:

$$\upsilon(S) = \max \sum_{i \in S} g_i(e_i) \text{ subject to } \sum_{i \in S} e_i = \sum_{i \in S} \hat{e}_i, \tag{6.10}$$

that is, is the maximum total gross[19] output that the countries in bloc S can hope to achieve jointly, given their aggregate emissions constraint.

Consider now again $(\hat{e}'_1, \ldots, \hat{e}'_n)$, the world competitive emissions trading equilibrium with respect to $(\hat{e}_1, \ldots, \hat{e}_n)$. If we can show that the members of S are better off at that worldwide competitive equilibrium than at their best actions as a separate bloc (as identified in (6.10)), we shall have established that bloc S has no interest in forming, thus answering in the negative the question raised in this section.

This is in fact straightforward. Indeed, with our notation it is equivalent to showing that:

$$\Sigma_{i \in S}[g_i(\hat{e}'_i) + \hat{\gamma} + (\hat{e}_i - \hat{e}'_i] \geq \upsilon(S), \qquad (6.11)$$

that is:

$$\sum_{i \in S}[g_i(\hat{e}'_i) + \hat{\gamma}(\hat{e}_i - \hat{e}'_i)] \geq \sum_{i \in S} g_i(\tilde{e}_i),$$

where $(\tilde{e}_i)_{i \in S}$ is the solution to (6.10). Clearly, we have $\Sigma_{i \in S}\hat{e}_i = \Sigma_{i \in S}\tilde{e}_i$. Hence we must show that:

$$\sum_{i \in S} g_i(\hat{e}'_i) + \hat{\gamma}(\sum_{i \in S}\tilde{e}_i - \sum_{i \in S}\hat{e}'_i) \geq \sum_{i \in S} g_i(\tilde{e}_i).$$

But this inequality is true since from concavity of g_i we have for each i in S:

$$g_i(\hat{e}'_i) + \hat{\gamma}(\tilde{e}_i - \hat{e}'_i) \geq g_i(\tilde{e}_i), \qquad (6.12)$$

using the fact that $\hat{\gamma} = g'_i(\hat{e}'_i)$ at the world competitive emissions trading equilibrium.[20]

Repeating this argument for any conceivable bloc of countries leads to the conclusion that no bloc has an interest in forming,[21] once a competitive emissions trading equilibrium prevails at the world level.

We have thus shown that the outcome of competitive trade in emissions among the countries cannot be improved upon by the formation of coalitions of countries, such as, for example, trading blocs. We are thereby rediscovering – in fact, just applying – a general property of market equilibria known as their 'core' property, which says that such equilibria belong to the core of some appropriately formulated cooperative game.[22]

5.4 Desirability of Worldwide and Competitive Trading

While the Kyoto Protocol can be seen as allowing for trading in emissions among the Annex I or more parties, it leaves open the questions of the extent and nature of such trading.[23] Economic and game-theoretic considerations can be further called upon to resolve these questions.

As to the extent of trading, that is, the number of participants in the trade, market equilibrium theory makes a case in favor of emissions trading *with the largest number of traders* possible. Thus, *worldwide* emissions trading is desirable. This is implied by the previous argument on subgroups, be they trading blocs or any other form of 'coalitions'. Indeed, if it is not to the benefit of any such subgroup of countries to form and act independently of the other countries, the outcome is also not more beneficial for these other countries, if a subgroup were to form. This is because their only best actions would be to act also as a subgroup, and for this subgroup the inequality (6.11) also applies.

We claim on that basis that it is in the world's overall economic interest that non-Annex I countries, whose emissions are not subject to quotas, nevertheless be allowed to participate in the trading process. The CDM contains provisions to that effect. A policy implication of our claim is that this mechanism be designed so as to make it as open as possible to the largest number of countries. The fact that no quota was assigned to many countries is irrelevant to the beneficial property, both for the world in general and for those countries in particular, of a worldwide emissions trading equilibrium.

As to the nature of trading, the same body of theory advocates that the institutions governing the trades be designed so as to ensure that they are as *competitive* as possible – competitiveness meaning here that all participants behave as price takers. It is indeed only for markets with that property that efficiency, coalitional stability and worldwide maximal benefits are established.

Regulatory provisions that would result in restricting competitiveness in the emissions trading process are thus to be avoided, and absence of regulations designed to prevent restrictions to competition should be avoided as well. For example, provisions allowing for market power to be exerted by some traders so as to influence price formation to their advantage, as well as regulatory controls that would impede sufficient price flexibility; or, as proposed by some, the capping of the quantities that participants are allowed to trade on.

As is well known, the larger the number of participants, the more competitive the market is likely to be: our argument favoring a large extension of the market is thus also one that favors competition.[24] Large numbers are admittedly neither the only way nor a sufficient condition to ensure the competitive character of a market, but they are a powerful factor.

5.5 A Numerical Illustration

Using the carbon emissions reduction commitments made by the Annex I parties to the Kyoto Protocol, as well as the marginal cost abatement curves generated by MIT's EPPA model (which is a multiregional, multisectoral computable general equilibrium model of economic activity, energy use and carbon emissions), Ellerman and Decaux (1998) develop a method for estimating quantitatively the outcome in 2010 of various trading regimes, including the world competitive emissions trading equilibrium. They highlight the substantial differences in the outcome of the various trading regimes – confirming our theoretical claim of maximal efficiency of worldwide trading, but they leave open the question of which one might be agreed upon by the parties to the Protocol.

Table 6.2 *The Ellerman and Decaux characterization of the world competitive emissions trading equilibrium with respect to the Kyoto quotas*

	Annex I countries						Non-Annex I countries						World
	USA	JPN	EEC	OOE	EET	FSU	EEX	CHN	IND	DAE	BRA	ROW	
Reference non-cooperative emissions in 2010 (Mton) $\bar{e}_i$	1838.25	424.24	1063.27	472.04	394.76	873.32*	927.39	1791.96	485.76	308.32	97.27	531.61	9208.63
Kyoto quotas of permitted emissions (Mton) $\hat{e}_i$	1266.67	280.05	756.51	300.66	247.45	873.32	927.39	1791.96	485.76	308.32	97.27	531.61	7866.95
Post-trading emissions reductions (Mton) $\bar{e}_i - \hat{e}'_i$	186.22	12.33	74.96	60.07	52.98	213.36	52.54	447.93	104.87	42.78	2.50	91.07	1341.61
Emission permits (Mton) imported (+)/exported (−) $\hat{e}'_i - \hat{e}_i$	385.36	131.86	232.25	111.31	94.33	−213.36	−52.54	−447.93	−104.87	−42.78	−2.50	−91.07	0.07
Marginal cost of abatement ($/ton) $\hat{\gamma} = g'_i(\hat{e}'_i)$	24.75	24.75	24.75	24.75	24.75	24.75	24.75	24.75	24.75	24.75	24.75	24.75	24.75
Total cost of own abatement ($ bn) $g_i(\bar{e}_i) - g_i(\hat{e}'_i)$	1.77	0.15	0.76	0.44	0.46	0.86	0.57	4.49	1.01	0.47	0.03	0.86	11.86
Cost (+)/receipt (−) of emission permits exports/imports ($ bn) $\hat{\gamma} = (\hat{e}'_i - \hat{e}_i)$	9.54	3.26	5.75	2.75	2.33	−5.28	−1.30	−11.09	−2.60	−1.06	−0.06	−2.25	0.00

Notes:

Annex I countries: USA; Japan (JPN); European Union, 12 countries (EEC); other OECD countries (OOE); Eastern Economies in Transition (EET); Former Soviet Union (FSU).

Non-Annex-I countries: Energy Exporting Countries (EEX); China (CHN); India (IND); Dynamic Asian Economis (DAE); Brazil (BRA); Rest of the World (ROW).

For non-Annex-I countries: Kyoto quotas of permitted emissions $\hat{e}_i$ have been taken to be equal to their estimated non-cooperative emissions in 2010, that is, $\bar{e}_i$, since it was agreed that their emissions need not be capped in this round of negotiations.

*For FSU, we have taken the reference emissions, $\bar{e}_i$, to be equal to the Kyoto commitment (873.32), although the actual emissions have been estimated to be only (762.79). This is equivalent to giving credit for emission reductions that would happen in any case.

Source: Ellerman and Decaux (1998, Table G; August version).

Our analysis above brings an answer to this question, again in favor of world competitive emissions trading, based on showing that strategic behavior of coalitions of countries cannot be more beneficial to them than worldwide emissions trading. For illustrative purposes we reproduce here (see Table 6.2) Elleman and Decaux's estimate of the world competitive emissions trading equilibrium in 2010 and of its price $\hat{\gamma}$ at that time 24.75 US$/ton.

6   BEYOND THE KYOTO QUOTAS: THE POSSIBILITY OF A SCHEME ACHIEVING A WORLD COALITIONALLY STABLE OPTIMUM

The outcome of the competitive emissions trading equilibrium with respect to the Kyoto quotas $(\hat{e}_1, \ldots, \hat{e}_n)$ is described in the last row of Table 6.2. It is seen that it results in monetary transfers among the countries and equalizes their marginal costs of abatement. This equilibrium thus very much looks like the worldwide treaty described above (Chander and Tulkens 1997) which also requires transfers among the countries and equalizes their marginal costs of abatement (see (6.2) and (6.4)), except for the fact that that treaty leads to the worldwide optimal emissions $(e_1^*, \ldots, e_n^*)$ while the Kyoto quotas do not.

This prompts our final question: could an appropriate emission quotas and trading scheme of the Kyoto type nevertheless be used to reach a world optimum with the same coalitional stability property as ensured by the Chander–Tulkens transfers? The answer is yes, because that optimum can be shown to be equivalent to an emission quotas and trading scheme.

To that effect define quotas $(\hat{e}_1^*, \ldots, \hat{e}_n^*)$ from the optimal emissions $(e_1^*, \ldots, e_n^*)$ and the reference emissions $(\bar{e}_1, \ldots, \bar{e}_n)$ such that for each country i,

$$(\hat{e}_i^* - e_i^*) \sum_{j \in W} d_j = g_i(\bar{e}_i) - g_i(e_i^*) - \frac{d_i}{\sum_{j \in W} d_j} [\Sigma_{j \in W} g_j(\bar{e}_j)$$
$$- \Sigma_{j \in W} g_j(e_j^*)]. \tag{6.13}$$

The left-hand side of this expression is what country i pays (or receives) if it buys (sells) emission rights amounting to $(\hat{e}_i^* - e_i^*)$ at a price $\hat{\gamma} = \Sigma_{j \in W} d_j$. This suggests that $(e_1^*, \ldots, e_n^*)$ and $\hat{\gamma} = \Sigma_{j \in W} d_j$ are nothing more than a competitive emissions trading equilibrium with respect to the quotas $(\hat{e}_1^*, \ldots, \hat{e}_n^*)$, in the sense of (6.8)–(6.9). And the right-hand side is precisely the Chander and Tulkens transfer T_i advocated in Section 3 (see (6.4)) above to achieve optimality in a coalitionally stable way.

Note that while the world optimum emissions $(e_1^*, \ldots, e_n^*)$ as defined in (6.2) are independent of the reference emission levels $(\bar{e}_1, \ldots, \bar{e}_n)$ as defined in (6.3a) and (6.3b), the emission quotas $(\hat{e}_1^*, \ldots, \hat{e}_n^*)$ as defined in (6.13) are not. In fact, since the optimal emissions are independent of reference emissions, there is a one-to-one correspondence between $(\hat{e}_1^*, \ldots, \hat{e}_n^*)$ and $(\bar{e}_1, \ldots, \bar{e}_n)$. This means that if the reference emission levels $(\bar{e}_1, \ldots, \bar{e}_n)$ are not in dispute, then the emission quotas $(\hat{e}_1^*, \ldots, \hat{e}_n^*)$ along with competitive emissions trading would also be acceptable to all countries since by definition these would not only lead to the optimum emissions $(e_1^*, \ldots, e_n^*)$ but also to transfers that would make each country or group of countries better off compared to $(\bar{e}_1, \ldots, \bar{e}_n)$.

The significance of this shift in perspective lies in the fact that, as noted earlier, the currently considered reference emission levels $(\bar{e}_1, \ldots, \bar{e}_n)$ are felt to be unfair, typically by the countries that are in the early stages of economic development with comparatively low emission levels. Therefore, the emissions of such countries may not be subjected to quotas, as agreed upon at Kyoto, at least until the time when their emission levels become comparable to those of Annex I countries. With time their emissions will rise as a result of economic development and those of the Annex I countries will fall as a result of abatement. While the Kyoto Protocol is a step in the right direction in terms of the actual emissions, we are suggesting here that the effective ultimate aim should in fact be to reach an agreement on appropriate reference emission levels (or pollution rights) $(\bar{e}_1, \ldots, \bar{e}_n)$ at some future round of negotiations.

The discussion in the preceding paragraph clarifies that once an agreement is reached regarding reference emissions $(\bar{e}_1, \ldots, \bar{e}_n)$ then an agreement would also be reached regarding the target emission quotas $(\hat{e}_1^*, \ldots, \hat{e}_n^*)$ and competitive emissions trading which by definition lead to optimum emissions $(e_1^*, \ldots, e_n^*)$ and transfers that ensure coalitional stability.

Such an agreement requires the countries first to agree on equity principles to be adopted, as for instance per capita or per unit of GDP emissions. The currently considered baselines of business-as-usual Nash equilibrium or historically grandfathered emissions are known to be problematic. Something else seems to be required, making explicit room, for instance, for principles such as 'common but differentiated responsibilities'. If such new reference levels can be agreed upon, our analysis suggests that a quotas and trading scheme of the kind pioneered in Kyoto is an appropriate tool to reach stable world optimality in the future.

NOTES

*   The authors are especially indebted to their Massachusetts Institute of Technology (MIT) colleague Denny Ellerman who kindly informed them of the state of his work and provided key numerical information. They also thank their colleague Jean Gabszewicz for a careful reading of an earlier version. Seminar presentations and discussions of this study have been made in 1999 at the third Fondazione Enrico Matteeni Center for Operations Research and

Econometrics (FEEM/CORE) Workshop on coalition formation held at Greqam, Aix en Provence (January 1999), at the United Nations Capacity Building Workshop, New Delhi (March 1999), at the Coventry conference on Environmental Economics (May 1999), as well as at the third Toulouse conference on Environmental and resource economics (June 1999). This paper was circulated earlier as CLIMNEG working paper No. 12, April 1999.

The research on which it is reported here is part of the program 'Changements climatiques, Négociations internationales et Stratégies de la Belgique' (CLIMNEG), supported by the Belgian State's Services du Premier Ministre, Services fédéraux des Affaires scientifiques, techniques et culturelles (SSTC), Brussels. See www.core.ucl.ac.be/climneg.

1. For a thorough account of the scientific evidence on the state of the problem, the reader is referred to the work of the Intergovernmental Panel on Climate Change (IPCC), and in particular to the contribution of its Working Group III (IPCC 1995).

2. There were 178 in Rio, 159 in Kyoto and 161 in Buenos Aires.

3. 'Annex I' (to the Rio Convention text) countries are the Organization for Economic Cooperation and Development (OECD) countries, those of the former Soviet Union and those of the Eastern European economies in transition.

4. In Kyoto, the text of the Protocol was adopted unanimously by the delegates of the 159 countries that participated in the negotiations. Signature of the text by governments and ratification by parliaments are the following stages of the process.

5. We may think of e_i either as the energy input in the production, or as the pollution emission, assuming that a unit of energy generates a unit of pollutant as a byproduct. Accordingly, $g_i'(e_i)$ $(= dg_i(e_i)/de_i)$ may be interpreted either as the marginal product of energy or (for decreasing e_i) the marginal cost of abatement, depending upon the context.

6. Numerical estimates of damages in some regions of the world are given in Table 6.1 below.

7. See, for example, Chander and Tulkens (1992).

8. Uniqueness of this vector is ensured under our assumptions of concavity of the functions g_i and of linearity of the functions D_i.

9. The transfers are expressed here in units of physical goods. The issue whether it is preferable that such transfers be financial rather than in real terms is an important one, but we cannot deal with it here.

10. This might also happen when the countries outside the coalition are not acting rationally but following the business-as-usual policy, since the abatement by the coalition S might result in lower energy prices in the rest of the world. Ellerman and Decaux (1998) observe this phenomenon in their computable general equilibrium model, and call it 'leakages'.

11. Usually taken with respect to pre-industrial times.

12. Actually an average over the years 2008–12.

13. Nash equilibrium and optimal trajectories are determined and discussed in Germain et al. (1998).

14. In the case of Japan, the marginal cost of abatement may look exceptionally high, but this is because of its large dependence on nuclear energy and natural gas.

15. Coal in Japan is a noticeable exception; but its use there is considerably lower.

16. In technical terms, this is because levels of the $\bar{e}_i$'s higher than those of a Nash equilibrium induce a larger core for the game whereby Chander and Tulkens (1997) establish the coalitional stability property of the transfers (6.4).

17. Note that for all non-Annex I countries, we have $\hat{e}_i = \bar{e}_i$.

18. Existence and uniqueness of a competitive emissions trading equilibrium follow from concavity of the functions g_i and continuity arguments.

19. We need not subtract damages as they are already fixed in the aggregate by the aggregate emissions constraint.

20. This is irrespective of whether $(\bar{e}_i - \hat{e}_i')$ is positive or negative.

21. Not only no bloc S taken *in the aggregate*, as formulated in (6.11), but also *each member* of the bloc, as (6.12) shows.

22. In technical game-theoretical terms, the expression $\upsilon(S)$ defined above is the payoff that S can achieve for its members and any vector $(e_i)_{i \in S}$ that meets the condition $\sum_{i \in S} e_i = \sum_{i \in S} \hat{e}_i$ is an emissions strategy for S. Then the pair $[W, \upsilon]$ satisfies the definition of an n-person game in characteristic function form where υ is the function $\upsilon : 2^W \to \mathfrak{R}$ defined by (6.10).

A strategy for the grand coalition W, $(e_i)_{i \in W}$, is said to be in the core of this game if for each $S \subset W$, $\Sigma_{i \in S} g_i(e_i) \geq \upsilon(S)$. That there exists such a strategy, that is, that the core of our game is non-empty can be asserted in general terms by showing that the game is balanced (in the sense of Shapley 1967). But we provide above the same positive answer in an economically more interesting way by exhibiting an actual strategy for W – namely the equilibrium outcome of worldwide competitive emissions trading – that we show to belong to the core. Note that the cooperative game defined here (and hence its core) is *not* the same as the one proposed in Chander and Tulkens (1995, 1997). The present game is a pure market game in the sense of Shapley and Shubik (1969), where externalities play no role since, once the quotas are fixed, the public good aspect of the problem disappears. One is left with only the private goods-type problem of allocating the emissions between the countries. It is worth pointing out, finally, that the game is one for an economy with production, and not of the usual pure exchange type.

23. These were addressed at the subsequent Conferences of Parties.
24. With large numbers, our previous argument on the role of markets to achieve coalitional stability is also reinforced by a central result in economic theory (due to Debreu and Scarf 1963, elaborating on Edgeworth 1881) according to which the *only* coalitionally stable outcome (in our case, the only emissions allocation with that property) is the competitive one.

REFERENCES

Chander, P. and H. Tulkens (1992), 'Theoretical foundations of negotiations and cost sharing in transfrontier pollution', *European Economic Review*, **36** (2/3), 288–99 (April).

Chander, P. and H. Tulkens (1995), 'A core-theoretic solution for the design of coop- erative agreements on transfrontier pollution', *International Tax and Public Finance*, **2** (2), 279–94.

Chander, P. and H. Tulkens (1997), 'The core of an economy with multilateral envi- ronmental externalities', *International Journal of Game Theory*, **26**, 379–401.

Debreu, G. and H. Scarf (1963), 'A limit theorem on the core of an economy', *International Economic Review*, **4**, 235–46.

Edgeworth, F.Y. (1881), *Mathematical Psychics*, London: Paul Kegan.

Ellerman, A.D. and A. Decaux (1998), 'Analysis of post-Kyoto CO_2 emissions trading using marginal abatement curves', MIT Joint Program on the Science and Policy of Global Change, report No. 40, Massachusetts Institute of Technology (October).

Energy Prices and Taxes (1998), Paris: International Energy Agency.

Fankhauser, S. (1995), *Valuing Climate Change: The Economics of the Greenhouse*, London: Earthscan.

Germain, M., Ph. Toint, H. Tulkens, and A. de Zeeuw (1998), 'Transfers to sustain cooperation in international stock pollutant control', CLIMNEG Working Paper No. 6, Center for Operations Research and Econometrics, Université Catholique de Louvain, Louvain-la-Neuve (also available as CORE Discussion Paper No. 9832, and Report 98/08, Publications du Départment de Mathématiques, Facultés univer- sitaires de Namur).

Intergovernmental Panel on Climate Change (IPCC) (1995), *Climate Change 1995: The Economic and Social Dimensions of Climate Change*, Contribution of Working Group III to the Second Assessment Report of the Intergovernmental Panel on Climate Change, Cambridge: Cambridge University Press.

Nordhaus, W.D. and Z. Yang (1996), 'A regional dynamic general equilibrium model of alternative climate-change strategies', *American Economic Review*, **86** (4), 741–65.

Shapley, L. (1967), 'On balanced sets and cores', *Naval Research Logistics Quarterly*, **14**, 453–60.

Shapley, L. and M. Shubik (1969), 'On market games', *Journal of Economic Theory*, **1**, 9–25.

7. A model of fertility transition

Partha Dasgupta

1 INTRODUCTION

In order to understand fertility behaviour, economic demographers have presumed that parents regard children as both ends and means. Children are ends in all cultures: we are genetically endowed to want and to value them. Viewing them as ends ranges from the desire to have offspring because they are playful and enjoyable, to a desire to obey the dictates of tradition and religion. One such injunction emanates from the cult of the ancestor, which, taking religion to be the act of reproducing the lineage, requires women to have many children. And there are many more such injunctions in various cultures.

But children can also be a means to economic betterment. In the extreme, they can be a means to survival. Children offer two such means. First, in the absence of capital markets and social security, children can be a source of private security in old age. There is evidence that in poor countries children do offer such security.[1] It leads to a preference for male offspring if males inherit the bulk of their parents' property and are expected to look after them in their old age. Second, in agriculture-based economies children are valuable in household production. Evidence of this also is extensive.[2]

Caldwell (1981, 1982) put forward the interesting hypothesis that the intergenerational transfer of resources is from children to their parents in societies experiencing high fertility and high mortality rates, but that it is from parents to their children when fertility and mortality rates are low. Assuming it to be true, the relationship should be interpreted to be an association only. The direction of intergenerational resource transfers would be endogenous in any general theory of demographic behaviour; it would not be a causal factor in fertility transitions.

The historical change in the North in parents' attitudes towards their children (from regarding children as a 'means' to economic ends, to regarding them simply as an 'end') can seem to pose a deep puzzle, as can differences between the attitudes of parents in the North and South today. Some demographers claim that some fundamental shift in adults' 'world view' must have been involved in such changes in attitudes, a shift that some have called an 'ideational change'.[3]

They may be right. On the other hand, not only is the explanation something of a *deus ex machina*, it is also very difficult to test. A different sort of explanation, one which is testable, is that children cease being *regarded* as productive assets when they cease *being* productive assets. When schooling is enforced, children are not available for household and farm chores. If the growth of urban centres makes rural children less reliable as old-age security (children are now able to leave home and not send remittances), children cease being sound investment for old age. And so on. In the limit, if children were to become relatively unproductive in each of their possible roles as an economic asset, their only remaining value would be as an end. No change in world view would necessarily be involved in this transformation.

The above argument does not rely on economic growth. What it involves is a comparison of the productivity of different forms of capital assets. Children could cease being a sound economic investment even if the economy remained poor.

Elsewhere (Dasgupta, 2000) I have tried to bring these considerations together for the purposes of explaining fertility behaviour in today's poor regions, namely, the Indian sub-continent and sub-Saharan Africa. That fertility rates there are high is a commonplace observation. What is less appreciated is that there are signs of fertility decline in parts of the poor world (see Table 7.1). How has that come about?

Women's education is widely regarded as the key explanation. In this chapter I want to explore a second, complementary, explanation: imitative behaviour, arising from a spread of information about other lifestyles through newspapers, radio and television.

It has proved hard to obtain direct evidence of imitative behaviour as there

Table 7.1   Total fertility rates and GNP per head in a sample of countries

	Total fertility rates	
	1980	1996
China	2.5	1.9
Bangladesh	6.1	3.4
India	5.0	3.1
Pakistan	7.0	5.1
Sub-Saharan Africa	6.6	5.6
(Nigeria)	6.9	5.4
USA	1.8	2.1

Source: World Bank (2000, Table 1.1).

is not much of it. The famous experiments of Sherif and Asch, where subjects were set visual discrimination tasks (the task of comparing lengths without the aid of a measuring rod), showed not only that people are more influenced by others' opinions when the facts in question are more uncertain, but also that people may conform simply to avoid censure, ridicule and social disapproval.[4] Psychologists have classified the findings in a way that implies that conformity is lower in the 'individualistic' cultures thought to embody North American and North-West European societies than in the 'communitarian' cultures widely taken to represent societies in Africa, Asia, Oceania and South America.[5] This may appear intuitively plausible to many. To me, however, it hints at how difficult it is to separate various types of conformism, and how problematic it is to talk of conformism unless the domain of behaviour over which conformism is thought to prevail has been specified. The point is that a society could be individualistic in some respects even while it is deeply conformist in others.

People conform in their purchase of such goods as the telephone, the fax machine and the personal computer, because there are interpersonal 'complementarities' in their use-value. (My use for a telephone increases as the number of others who rely on telephones increases, and so on.) But other patterns of conformism could be due to shared disposition.

What follows is a sketch of a process, triggered by conformism, that may well be significant in bringing about fertility transitions. The model is not as neat and tidy as Karl-Göran Mäler, rightly, likes them to be. But I believe it is suggestive enough to hold his attention. For me, that alone would be enough to justify this chapter.

2   CONFORMITY AND 'CONTAGION'

That children are an end in themselves provides a mechanism by which reasoned fertility decisions at the level of every household can lead to an unsatisfactory outcome from the perspective of all households. The mechanism arises from the possibility that traditional practice is perpetuated by conformity. Procreation in closely-knit communities is not only a private matter, it is also a society activity, influenced by both family experiences and the cultural milieu. Formally speaking, behaviour is conformist if, other things being the same, every household's most desired family size is the greater, the larger is the average family size in the community.[6] This is a 'reduced form' of the concept, and the source of a desire to conform could lie in reasons other than an intrinsic desire to be like others. For example, it could be that similar choices made by households generate mutual positive externalities, say, because people care about their status, and a household's choice of actions signals its predispositions (for example, its willingness to belong) and so affects its status.[7] In a world where people conform, the desire for children is endogenous.

Whatever the basis of conformism, there would be practices encouraging high fertility rates which no household would unilaterally desire to break. Such practice could well have had a rationale in the past, when mortality rates were high, rural population densities were low, the threat of extermination from outside attack was large, and mobility was restricted. But practices can survive even when their original purposes have disappeared. So, it can be that as long as all others follow the practice and aim at large family size, no household on its own wishes to deviate from the practice; however, if all other households were to restrict their fertility rates, each would desire to restrict its fertility rate as well. In short, conformism can be a reason for the existence of *multiple* reproductive equilibria.[8] It can even be that they are Pareto rankable, in which case a community could get stuck at an equilibrium mode of behaviour even though there is another equilibrium mode of behaviour which is better for all.

3 A MODEL

Figure 7.1 depicts fertility choices in a stylized community where households are identical and are conformists. We imagine that the government has no population policy in place. The horizontal axis denotes $\bar{n}$, which is the average number of children per household. It represents the total fertility rate (TFR) in the community.[9] The vertical axis denotes n^*, which is the desired number of children of the representative household.[10] Since households are identical, every household is representative. As n^* is a function of $\bar{n}$, we write it as $n^*(\bar{n})$. It is drawn as an increasing function, the distinctive feature of conformism. In Figure 7.1 it is so drawn that it cuts the 45° line at three points, $\bar{n}_1$, $\bar{n}_2$, and $\bar{n}_3$. Each is an equilibrium. To confirm this, imagine for example that each household *expects* all other households to have $\bar{n}_3$ children. Then $\bar{n}_3$ will be each household's choice, thus confirming the expectations. And so on for $\bar{n}_1$ and $\bar{n}_2$. Note as well that $\bar{n}_1$, $\bar{n}_2$ and $\bar{n}_3$ are the only equilibria. Let us assume now that out of equilibrium households expect the TFR in each period to be the previous period's TFR (this is a special form of what are known as 'adaptive expectations'). It is then easy to check that $\bar{n}_1$ and $\bar{n}_3$ are (locally) stable, while $\bar{n}_2$ is unstable. So interest lies in $\bar{n}_1$ and $\bar{n}_3$.

I have not offered a micro-foundation for $n^*(\bar{n})$. The model is of a reduced form. But it can be that all households are better off at $\bar{n}_1$ than at $\bar{n}_3$. However, in view of the externality, neither equilibrium is a socially optimal state of affairs.[11] It may be that the optimal TFR lies somewhere between $\bar{n}_1$ and $\bar{n}_3$

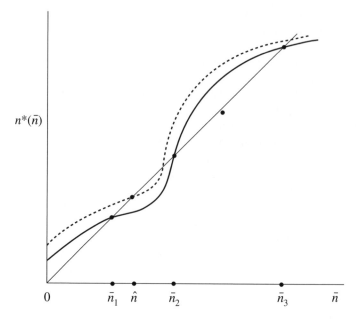

$n^*(\bar{n})$

0          $\bar{n}_1$ $\hat{n}$ $\bar{n}_2$ $\bar{n}_3$ $\bar{n}$

Figure 7.1   Desired number of children in a representative household,
n[*](n̄), *as a function of average number of children born per*
household, n̄

(say, at $\hat{n}$). If this were so, then from the social point of view, TFR would be
too low at $\bar{n}_1$ and too high at $\bar{n}_3$. In either situation there would be a need for
government policy (for example, tax-subsidy policy), of a kind that would
sustain equilibrium TFR at $\hat{n}$. In Figure 7.1 the broken curve is the representative household's most desired number of children as a function of the community's TFR when the optimum policy is in place. It cuts the 45° line at $\hat{n}$.

These are theoretical possibilities. Testing for multiple equilibria is a most
difficult matter. For the moment it is analytical reasoning which tells us that a
society could in principle get stuck at a self-sustaining mode of behaviour
characterized by high fertility (and low educational attainment), even when
there is another, potentially self-sustaining, mode of behaviour characterized
by low fertility (and high educational attainment).

This does not mean that society would be stuck with high fertility rates for
ever. External events could lead households to 'coordinate' at $\bar{n}_1$ even though
they had earlier 'coordinated' at $\bar{n}_3$.[12] The external events could, for example,
be a programme of public exhortations aimed at altering household expectations about one another's behaviour (for example, family-planning campaigns
run by women). This is a case where the community 'tips' from one mode of

behaviour to another, even though there has been no underlying change in household attitudes ($n^*(\bar{n})$ has not changed) to trigger the change in behaviour.

In a well-known paper, Cleland and Wilson (1987: 9) argued that the only plausible way to explain the recent onset of fertility transitions among countries at widely different levels of economic development was an *ideational change*, 'a psychological shift from, *inter alia*, fatalism to a sense of control of destiny, from passivity to the pursuit of achievement, from a religious, tradition-bound, and parochial view of the world to a more secular, rational, and cosmopolitan one'. The authors may be right that societies have undergone ideational changes. But they are not right to think that ideational change needs to be invoked to explain recent fertility transitions. The tipping phenomenon I have just discussed does not appeal to ideational changes. This said, I know of no evidence that is able to discriminate between the two types of explanation.

4 APPLICATION TO DEMOGRAPHIC TRANSITIONS

The tipping phenomenon can also occur because of changes in the peer group on whose behaviour households base their own behaviour. This amounts to the function $n^*(\bar{n})$ shifting slowly. Such shifts may also fall short of an ideational change. However, as we see below, the process can precipitate a demographic transition.

One pathway by which $n^*(\bar{n})$ can shift arises from the fact that people differ in their absorption of traditional practice. There are inevitably those who for one reason or another experiment, take risks, and refrain from joining the crowd. They subsequently influence others. They are the tradition-breakers, often leading the way. It has been observed that educated women are among the first to make the move towards smaller families.[13] The middle classes can also be the trigger, becoming role models for others.

A possibly even stronger pathway is the influence that newspapers, radio, television and now the Internet play in transmitting information about other lifestyles.[14] The analytical point here is that the media may be a vehicle through which conformism increasingly becomes based on the behaviour of a wider population than the local community: the peer group widens.

Such pathways can give rise to demographic transitions, in that fertility rates display little-to-no trend over extended periods, only to cascade downward over a relatively short interval of time, giving rise to the classic logistic curve of diffusion processes. To illustrate this, consider Figure 7.2, which is based on Figure 7.1. Begin with an isolated community. The curve ABCDE is the representative household's demand for children as a function of the community's total fertility rate ($n^*(\bar{n})$). As with Figure 7.3, there are three equilibria, $\bar{n}_1$, $\bar{n}_2$, and $\bar{n}_3$, of which $\bar{n}_1$ and $\bar{n}_3$ are (locally) stable, and $\bar{n}_2$ is

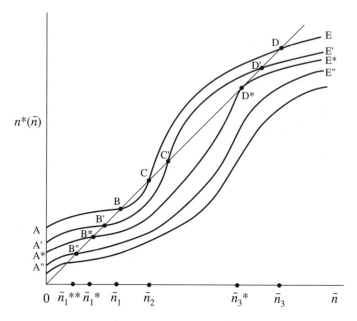

Figure 7.2   A model of demographic transition

unstable. We are to imagine that households have equilibrated at D, where the total fertility rate is $\bar{n}_3$. Imagine now that the community begins to have expo-sure to the outside world. To make the point I wish to make in the simplest possible way, assume that the rate at which the community is exposed to outside influence (as measured, say, by the rate of increase in the number of radio sets in the community) is small and steady. It is natural to assume next that, as outside influence increases, $n^*(\bar{n})$ shifts downward slowly. This means that equilibrium TFR declines slowly. In Figure 7.2 the curve A'B'C'D'E' represents one such transitional demand schedule. The corresponding equilib-rium TFR is associated with D'. Since D' is locally stable, the assumption that the community equilibrates to D' is correct. The underlying hypothesis is that outside influence is a slow-moving variable and that the community equili-brates quickly to changes in the extent of outside influence.

What would statistical demographers make of the process thus far? They would record that the community's TFR had declined in response to increas-ing exposure to the outside world. But they would record that the decline was slow. Now let time pass. The schedule in Figure 7.2 continues to shift down-ward slowly and the TFR declines slowly, until eventually, the schedule attains the position where there are only two equilibria: $\bar{n}_1^*$ and $\bar{n}_3^*$. (The intermedi-ate equilibrium point has vanished at this critical juncture.) This is represented by the curve $A^*B^*D^*E^*$. Since the community will have equilibrated at D^*, statistical demographers would observe that there had so far been no dramatic decline in fertility.

But what happens when the curve shifts down a tiny bit more, say to become the curve $A''B''E''$ in Figure 7.2? Well, now the schedule cuts the 45° line only once, at the stable equilibrium B'' (at TFR, $\bar{n}_1^{**}$). But as TFR had only recently been substantially above $\bar{n}_1^{**}$, households will display disequilibrium behaviour for a while, as they 'seek' $\bar{n}_1^{**}$. Demographers would record a substantial decline in TFR to $\bar{n}_1^{**}$. Subsequent declines in TFR (one such decline is depicted in the lowest curve in Figure 7.2) would be observed again to be slow. Statisticians would record the period in which TFR declined sharply as a 'demographic transition'. In our model the transition would be an extended period of disequilibrium behaviour.

It is worth noting that, in showing how fertility cascades can occur, we have not assumed the flow of outside exposure to be 'non-linear'. Rather, we have assumed household responses to changes in outside exposure to be non-linear: the shape of $n^*(\bar{n})$ has the non-linearity built into it.[15]

In a pioneering article, Adelman and Morris (1965) found 'openness' of a society to outside ideas to be a powerful stimulus to economic growth. It is possible that the fertility reductions that have been experienced in India and Bangladesh in recent years (see Table 7.1) were due to the wider influence that people there have been subjected to via the media or to attitudinal differences arising from improvements in family planning programmes. To be sure, fertility reductions have differed widely across the Indian sub-continent (there has not been much reduction in Pakistan so far), but we should not seek a single explanation for so complex a phenomenon as fertility transition.[16]

5 EVIDENCE

Demographers have made few attempts to discover evidence of behaviour that is guided in part by an attention to others. The two exceptions with which I am familiar are Easterlin et al. (1980) and Watkins (1990). The former studied intergenerational influence in a sample of families in the United States. They reported a positive link between the number of children with whom someone had been raised and the number of children they themselves had.

In her study of demographic change in Western Europe over the 1870–1960 period, Watkins (1990) showed that differences in fertility and nuptiality within each country declined. She found that in 1870, before the large-scale declines in marital fertility had begun in most areas of Western Europe, demographic behaviour differed greatly within countries. Provinces (for example, counties and cantons) within a country differed considerably, even while differences *within* provinces were low. There were thus spatial clumps within each country, suggesting the importance of the influence of local communities on behaviour. In 1960, differences within each country were less than they were in 1870. Watkins explained this in terms of increases in the geographical reach national governments enjoyed over the 90 years in question. The growth of national languages could have been the medium through which reproductive behaviour was able to spread.

There is one recent finding which could also point to contagious behaviour. Starting in 1977 (when the TFR in Bangladesh was in excess of 6), 70 'treatment' villages were serviced by a massive programme of birth control in Matlab Thana, Bangladesh, while 79 'control' villages were offered no such special service. The contraceptive prevalence in the treatment villages increased from 7 to 33 percent within 18 months, and then more gradually to a level of 45 percent by 1985. The prevalence also increased in the control villages, but only to 16 percent in 1985. Fertility rates in both sets of villages declined, but at different speeds, with the difference in fertility rates reaching 1.5, even though there had been no difference to begin with (Hill, 1992). If we were to assume that, although influence travels, geographical proximity matters, we could explain why the control villages followed those 'under treatment', but did not follow them all the way. Contagion did not spread completely.[17]

6   CAUTION

In this chapter I have sketched a model of fertility transition that is based on conformist behaviour. The trigger for the transition is a widening of the peer group that influences behaviour. That said, it is as well to emphasize that fertility transitions in all probability are not brought about by a single cause. Nor are the various causes of equal force in every place and in every period. Earlier demographic transitions in France and England may have had little to do with the mechanism I have presented here. Nor are all contemporary transitions likely to have been caused by a widening basis of conformism. Nevertheless, the process identified here is suggestive. It calls for further work.

NOTES

1. See Dasgupta (2000) for references.
2. See Dasgupta (2000) for references.
3. Cleland and Wilson (1987). See below.
4. Hogg and Vaughan (1995, Ch. 6).
5. See Smith and Bond (1993) for a review of a number of such studies. For simplicity, I am using 'imitation' and 'conformity' interchangeably.

6. See Dasgupta (1993, Ch. 12).
7. Bernheim (1994) and Bongaarts and Watkins (1996).
8. Dasgupta (1993, Ch. 12).
9. TFR is the number of live births a woman would expect to have if she were to live through her childbearing years and to bear children at each age in accordance with the prevailing age-specific fertility rates. If the TFR were 2.1 or thereabouts, population in the long run would stabilize.
10. n^* is taken to be a continuous variable as a way of acknowledging that realized household size is not a deterministic function of the size the household sets for itself as a target.
11. As households are identical in this stylized model, by a collective optimum I mean a Pareto optimum.
12. In game theory, Figure 7.1 is called a coordination game.
13. See Farooq et al. (1987) for a commentary on West Africa.
14. Freedman (1995); Bongaarts and Watkins (1996); and Iyer (2000).
15. Formally, the above is a model of demographic transitions viewed as 'relaxation phenomena'. The mathematical structure I have invoked is similar to one that has recently been used by oceanographers and ecologists in their exploration of tipping phenomena in ocean circulation and lake turbidity, respectively. See Rahmstorf (1995) and Scheffer (1997).
16. In this connection, the Indian state of Andhra Pradesh offers an interesting example. Female illiteracy there is high (55 percent) and some 75 percent of the population have access to radio or television. The fertility rate there is now 2.3.
17. I am grateful to Lincoln Chen for a helpful 1996 correspondence on this point.

REFERENCES

Adelman, I. And C.T. Morris (1965), 'A factor analysis of the interrelationship between social and political variables and per capita gross national product', *Quarterly Journal of Economics*, **79** (2), 555–78.
Bernheim, B.D. (1994), 'A theory of conformity', *Journal of Political Economy*, **102** (4), 841–77.
Bongaarts, J. and S.C. Watkins (1996), 'Social interactions and contemporary fertility transitions', *Population and Development Review*, **22** (4), 639–82.
Caldwell, J.C. (1981), 'The mechanism of demographic change in historical perspective', *Population Studies*, **35** (1), 5–27.
Caldwell, J.C. (1982), *The Theory of Fertility Decline*, New York: Academic Press.
Cleland, J. and C. Wilson (1987), 'Demand theories of the fertility transition: an iconoclastic view', *Population Studies*, **41** (1), 5–30.
Dasgupta, P. (1993), *An Inquiry into Well-being and Destitution*, Oxford: Clarendon Press.
Dasgupta, P. (2000), 'Population and resources: an exploration of reproductive and environmental externalities', *Population and Development Review*, **26**, 643–89.
Easterlin, R., R. Pollak and M. Wachter (1980), 'Toward a more general model of fertility determination: endogenous preferences and natural fertility', in R. Easterlin (ed.), *Population and Economic Change in Developing Countries*, Chicago: University of Chicago Press, pp. xx.
Farooq, G., I. Ekanem and S. Ojelade (1987), 'Family size preferences and fertility in South-Western Nigeria', in C. Oppong (ed.), *Sex Roles, Population and Development in West Africa*, London: James Currey, pp. xx.
Freedman, R. (1995), 'Asia's recent fertility decline and prospects for future demographic change', Asia–Pacific Population Research Report No. 1, East–West Center, Honolulu.

Hill, K. (1992), 'Fertility and mortality trends in the developing world', *Ambio*, **21** (1), 79–83.

Hogg, M.A. and G.M. Vaughan (1995), *Social Psychology: An Introduction*, London: Prentice-Hall/Harvester Wheatsheaf.

Iyer, S. (2000), 'Religion and the economics of fertility in South India', PhD Dissertation, Faculty of Economics, University of Cambridge.

Rahmstorf, S. (1995), 'Bifurcations of the Atlantic thermohaline circulation in response to changes in the hydrological cycle', *Nature*, **378**, 145–9.

Scheffer, M. (1997), *The Ecology of Shallow Lakes*, New York: Chapman & Hall.

Smith, P.B. and M.H. Bond (1993), *Social Psychology Across Cultures: Analysis and Perspectives*, London: Harvester Wheatsheaf.

Watkins, S.C. (1990), 'From local to national communities: the transformation of demographic regions in Western Europe 1870–1960', *Population and Development Review*, **16** (2), 241–72.

World Bank (2000), *World Development Indicators*, Washington, DC: World Bank.

8. Notes on irreversibility, sustainability and the limits to growth

Anthony C. Fisher and Jinhua Zhao

1 INTRODUCTION

The concept of 'sustainability', of sustainable development, has become well known, and indeed generally accepted as a criterion for resource allocation, among researchers, at least some policy makers, and the general public, in recent years. A watershed document here, though certainly not the first articulation of the theme, was the 1987 report of the World Commission on Environment and Development, *Our Common Future*, also known as the Brundtland Report after the Commission's chair, former Prime Minister of Norway, Gro Harlem Grundtland. As the Commission put it: 'Sustainable development is development that meets the needs of the present without compromising the ability of future generations to meet their own needs' (page 8). Although this does not explicitly address the natural environment, most of the subsequent discussion of sustainability has focused on limits, or constraints on development, imposed by the environment.

A notable exception to the general acceptance of the sustainability criterion has been the reaction of economists, the people who are professionally concerned with resource allocation. Economists, though not opposed to sustainability, have subjected the concept to rigorous scrutiny in attempting to determine its relationship to other accepted criteria for resource allocation, principally economic efficiency. Environmental and resource economists, in particular Karl-Göran Mäler (1991) in his seminal article in the first issue of the journal *Environmental and Resource Economics*, have also explicitly considered the implications of constraints imposed by nature, such as limited stocks of extractive natural resources and limited assimilative capacity of environmental reservoirs for the residuals of production and consumption activities. The object of our chapter is to explore the relationship to sustainability of a concept from the earlier environmental economics literature, namely *irreversibility*, the idea that decisions about resource use, or their consequences, may not be technically reversible, regardless of the amounts of conventional inputs, such as labor and reproducible capital devoted to the purpose. The seminal work here, at least for economists, is probably Krutilla's (1967) 'Conservation reconsidered'. Interestingly, Krutilla focused on what might be called extractive resources *in situ*, that is, the 'grand geomorphological features', the standing virgin forests, and other examples of natural environments that could be tapped to provide conventional extractive resources, such as electric power, irrigation water and timber. Krutilla's point was that it was the resources *in situ*, rather than as inputs to production, that were especially vulnerable to irreversible depletion – and also increasingly valuable, though that is another story.

In the next section, we lay out a model in which production and utility depend on inputs of both reproducible capital and what we might call natural capital, which embodies both extractive and *in situ* resources, both flows and stocks, and use it to study the precise meanings of sustainability and irreversibility, their relationship to each other, and to efficiency in resource use. Anticipating the results of the discussion, our main point will be that an economy is not sustainable if there are resources that are both (a) non-renewable, in the sense that their depletion is irreversible, and (b) non-substitutable in the production of utility. This may seem obvious, but there are some interesting distinctions to be made, and we believe that there is also value in elucidating the relationships precisely in the context of a recognizable model. We also consider the role of irreversibility in the widely influential analysis of resources as limits to growth, developed by Meadows et al. (1972) and Meadows et al. (1992). It appears that here too the key issue is the degree of substitutability between (a component of) natural capital and other inputs.

2   MODEL

Consider an economy, which may be competitive, but may also have a government that tries to internalize externalities, with one production sector and one consumption sector, over an infinite time period indexed by t.

2.1   Production

The factor of production is capital, including reproducible capital K^m, natural capital extracted from renewable resources K^r, and natural capital extracted from non-renewable resources K^n. We ignore the labor input, which is assumed to be constant.[1] The production function is given by:

$$y_t = f(K^m_t, K^n_t, K^r_t, A_t), \tag{8.1}$$

where A_t is the technology level at time t.

Equations of motion for stocks of natural resources S^n and S^r are:

$$\dot{S}^n_t = -K^n_t \qquad (8.2)$$

$$\dot{S}^r_t = g(y^r_t, S^r_t, B_t) - K^r_t, \qquad (8.3)$$

where g is the growth function of the renewable resource, y^r is the amount of output that is used to 'restore' (help enhance the growth of) the stock of renewable resources, and B_t is the level of 'restoration technology' at time t.[2]

The equation of motion of reproducible capital is:

$$\dot{K}^m_t = y_t - c_t - y^r_t - \delta K^m_t, \qquad (8.4)$$

where c_t is the level of consumption and δ is the rate of depreciation. The first three terms on the right-hand side constitute saving (and investment) in period t.

We assume f is increasing and concave in each of its arguments, as is g in y^r and B. We also assume that the two functions are smooth, permitting substitutability among the three types of capital in production. Substitutability in intermediate production seems reasonable given the availability of backstop resources (or technologies) but, as we shall see, is a crucial assumption. Note that, even if some resources are essential in the production of some goods (that is, there are no substitutes in production), these goods may have substitutes in final consumption. Production of the substitute goods may not require the 'essential' natural capital. Since we use a scalar y to represent produced goods, the assumption of substitutability of produced goods in final consumption directly translates into substitutability in production. Note that use of the First Law of Thermodynamics to show limited substitutability of reproducible capital for natural capital needs to be considered in the context of substitutability in final consumption. The distinction between substitutability in intermediate production and in final consumption is discussed further later on.[3]

2.2 Consumption

Let the utility function for the representative individual be:

$$u(c_t, S^r_t - S^{rc}, S^n_t), \qquad (8.5)$$

where S^{rc} is the critical stock level of the renewable resource below which the individual cannot survive. We make the usual assumptions of monotonicity and concavity and assume that the utility function is smooth so that there is substitutability among the three factors. Again, the assumption of substitutability is crucial. We further assume that the marginal utility of each argument goes to infinity as the argument goes to zero.

Renewable resources can be thought of in a general way as the natural environment (clean air, clean water and so on), a minimum amount of which is essential for life. Above this minimum amount, there are substitutes: living in Los Angeles (with low air quality) can be compensated by more consumption of other goods (such as higher income, good weather, beaches and so on); having the money to buy water filters can compensate for polluted water. A critical level, or minimum viable population, for, say, a particular fish species of $S^{rc} = 0$, would be a special case of our more general representation.

The non-renewable resource stock enters the utility functions of at least some individuals and therefore that of the representative individual. Damming and filling Yosemite Valley would surely hurt some who value this environment. However, these resource stocks may also have substitutes. While we cannot enjoy the Hetch Hetchy Valley in Yosemite Natural Park as people did 100 years ago, we have instead faster transportation to the Yosemite area and other amenities offered by a modern economy. Many people would choose to live today rather than 100 years ago even though Hetch Hetchy Valley was around at that time. The reason for substitutability is that, generally, though there may, of course, be exceptions, our lives do not depend on the non-renewable resources. Without these resources, we can survive even though we may suffer a utility loss that can be (at least partially) compensated in some way. Note, however, that the compensation may be 'expensive' in the sense that many other resources may be needed due to the high marginal utility of S^n when it is low.

3 CONCEPTS

There are several related concepts used in the literature, including irreplaceability, substitutability, irreversibility and sustainability. Now we study what they mean in our model.

Clearly, the renewable resource is non-substitutable in consumption if its stock is below the critical level. However, above some level, which may be critical level S^{rc}, the process of decreasing its stock is not irreversible: the stock can grow, and grow faster if we invest in restoration, that is, in accelerating regeneration. But note the converse: below some level, which could lie above the critical level, the renewable resource may irreversibly decline, in effect becoming non-renewable.

Krutilla et al. (1972) argue that irreplaceability is 'a function of the closeness of substitutes in final consumption' (page 70). In this sense, irreplaceability is equivalent to non-renewability and non-substitutability in final consumption. A stronger version of irreplaceability would define an asset as irreplaceable if its attributes cannot be reproduced. For example, what Krutilla et al. called 'gifts of individual genius' would fall into this category: the works of Leonardo da Vinci cannot be replicated by any device, however ingenious, as the result would not have the desired characteristic of authenticity. Also, by this definition, any species would be irreplaceable unless its entire genetic pattern could be identified and reproduced. However, this definition of irreplaceability may be too strong for the study of sustainability.

Depletion of the non-renewable resource is of course by definition irreversible: its stock cannot be increased in any way. In a sense, irreversibility corresponds to a *one-way substitutability*: in the utility function, given the current c_t and S_t^n levels, the only direction of substitution is to substitute consumption or the renewable resource stock (assuming this has not fallen below the level from which it cannot recover) for the non-renewable resource stock. The other direction does not work because the stock cannot be increased. Similarly, in the production process, there is no way to use more K^m or K^r so that the stock of S^n is raised, although, at least for a time, it is possible to substitute K^n for K^m or K^r in production (thereby decreasing S^n).

There are many versions of the definition of sustainability, including non-decreasing consumption, non-decreasing utility, and non-decreasing resource or capital stock). A distinction is also made between strong sustainability and weak sustainability. Pearce and Atkinson (1993) and Victor (1991) define weak sustainability as preserving aggregate capital (when natural capital and other kinds of capital are substitutable) and strong sustainability as preserving the natural capital stock (on the presumption that natural capital is not substitutable). As we assume substitutability, we shall be implicitly discussing weak sustainability.[4] Our model indicates that non-decreasing consumption is not adequate, at least for the case when the renewable resource becomes not substitutable. That is, consumption alone is not enough for sustainability if there is non-substitutability in the utility function.

The most intuitive definition is non-decreasing utility through generations. We see that sustainability is potentially possible, as long as there is a sufficiently rapid rate of technological progress. Increased production leads to more K^m and more restoration of the renewable resource. Then both consumption and the renewable resource can be augmented and used to substitute for the non-renewable resource in the utility function. Note that non-substitutability does not necessarily mean no sustainability as long as the non-substitutable resource is not irreversible (so that its stock can be increased). Similarly, irreversibility does not lead to no sustainability either, as long as the irreversibly depleted resource has substitutes. However, the economy is not sustainable if there are resources that are both irreversible and non-substitutable in final consumption. Thus, failure of sustainability is a function of both non-substitutability in consumption (or irreplaceability) and irreversibility.

As noted earlier, in evaluating sustainability we need to distinguish between non-substitutability in production of intermediate goods and in final consumption. Non-substitutability in intermediate production does not pose as much of a threat to sustainability when the final goods have substitutes. However, non-substitutability in final consumption does threaten sustainability when coupled with irreversibility. The literature seems to be unclear about this when it addresses substitutability (see, for example, the review in Toman et al. 1995). Critics of substitutability invoke the First Law of Thermodynamics to argue that there should not be much substitutability between natural and reproducible capital. However, if there is substantial substitution in consumption between the goods produced using mainly reproducible capital and those produced using mainly natural capital, substitutability in production between the two forms of capital will be greater once the economy's production mix is adjusted according to price signals as the natural resource stock changes. The literature seems to have ignored the adjustment of production mix and its effect on substitutability.[5] That said, we acknowledge that there may be goods or services produced with natural capital that do not in fact have adequate substitutes, such as medicines developed from the stock of genetic information embodied in existing plant and animal species, or the amelioration of climate produced by the atmospheric system.

4   THE LINK TO *LIMITS TO GROWTH*

Recall that in the original *Limits to Growth* model (Meadows et al., 1972), two key equations (rewritten using our notation, where relevant, and in slightly simpler form) are:

$$S_t^n = S_{t-1}^n - \theta(c_t)\, P_t, \quad \theta'(c_t) > 0, \tag{8.6}$$

where c_t now refers specifically to per capita consumption, and P_t is population, and:

$$c_t = \frac{\alpha\, S_t^n\, K_t^m}{P_t}. \tag{8.7}$$

Equation (8.6) means that the non-renewable resource stock must be declining – and at an increasing rate, with increases in population or per capita consumption. This is not in itself unreasonable; what is less reasonable is that the effects of depletion cannot be mitigated by substitution or technical change. As equation (8.7) is written, non-renewable resources and capital are in fact complements, not substitutes. As resources are depleted and population increases, the economy needs ever more producible capital to maintain a given level of per capita consumption or, in other words, an increase in the flow of extraction must be accompanied by an increase in the capital stock.

Nordhaus (1973), in a critical analysis of the *Limits* model, proposes instead to model substitution and technical change in accord with economic theory and empirical findings, specifying a nested Cobb-Douglas production function of the form:

$$y_t = ke^{ht}[P^{\beta 1}(K^m)^{\beta 2}(-\dot{S}^n)^{\beta 3}L^{\beta 4}]^{1-b} \prod^b \qquad \sum_{i=1}^{4}\beta_i = 1, \qquad (8.8)$$

where $h = 0.025$ = the rate of technical change, L is land, $\prod$ is pollution, and other symbols are as before. As he shows, with this specification of production relations, the simulated economy does not collapse as in *Limits*; instead there is indefinite growth in per capita consumption. But this result depends on substitution not just among conventional inputs to production, P, K^m, $-\dot{S}^n$, and L, as is certainly well supported by a half century of empirical evidence, but also between the conventional inputs and pollution. The latter is not well supported but seems plausible. One can certainly imagine producing a given output 'using' a certain amount of air pollution, say, or alternatively producing that output using less pollution but more labor and producible capital, to control the pollution.

But this is not the only plausible scenario. Suppose we broaden the definition of non-renewable resouce capital and disaggregate it into a conventional extractive resource K_1^n and 'true' natural capital K_2^n, where K_2^n represents something like the assimilative capacity of the atmosphere or, perhaps, an ecosystem that provides services such as amelioration of climate or control of crop pests, or a stock of genetic information. Now equation (8.8) can be rewritten, substituting K_2^n, natural capital, for pollution and K_1^n for $-\dot{S}^n$

$$y_t = ke^{ht}[P^{\beta 1}(K^m)^{\beta 2}(K_1^n)^{\beta 3}L^{\beta 4}]^{1-b}(K_2^n)^b. \qquad (8.9)$$

The question is whether, or to what degree, it is possible to substitute conventional resource inputs, especially producible capital, for natural capital. If the latter is irreversibly depleted, and cannot be substituted, as implied by equation (8.9), there may indeed be a limit to growth – or even to indefinitely sustainable production of the composite good. Thus, non-renewability or irreversibility (depletion of natural capital K_2^n, combined in this case with non-substitutability in production, will preclude sustainability – again, unless the depletion of natural capital can be compensated by a shift in the mix of composite output away from goods intensive in natural capital to goods that do not depend on this input.

5 CONCLUSIONS

We have set out a model in which production depends on inputs of natural capital from both renewable and non-renewable resources, as well as reproducible capital, and utility depends on consumption (of the produced good) along with the stocks of renewable and non-renewable resources. The renewable resource is non-substitutable in the utility function if the stock falls below a critical level; a minimum level of, say, air quality, is essential for life. Depletion of the non-renewable resource is by definition irreversible, but an economy is sustainable if the produced good and the renewable resource stock are substitutable for the non-renewable resource stock in the utility function. Technical change, which makes possible both increases in output and additional restoration of renewable resources, obviously improves the prospects for sustainability. Given that there is no resource that is both irreversible and non-substitutable, there is in principle a minimum speed of technological progress and a necessary amount of saving (or level of consumption) that can achieve sustainability. Note that the Hartwick rule does not work here: we need increasing consumption or renewable resource stock to substitute for the decreasing stock of non-renewable resources. Further, the level of consumption cannot be too high since the stock of renewable resources cannot fall below the critical level.

NOTES

1. This assumption can be relaxed if we also consider population changes.
2. For simplicity, we may ignore the impact of B_t. More realistically, sustainability should depend on both types of technologies: in production and in restoring the environment.
3. Alternatively, we can model two produced goods, one of which requires a type of natural capital that has no substitutes. However, in final consumption, there is substitutability of these two goods in the utility function.
4. A somewhat different distinction is drawn by Barbier et al. (1990), who define strong sustainability as non-positive net damages to environmental capital along the whole time path of resource exploitation and weak sustainability as non-positive present value of damages (see Toman et al., 1995).
5. The First Law of Thermodynamics states that mass and energy cannot be reduced, and the Second Law states that the entropy cannot be reduced. The First Law implies that the economy cannot run on zero or a vanishingly small quantity of energy. This limits the substitutability of reproducible capital for natural capital in the production process. The Second Law then limits the restoration efforts and pollution abatement. However, these physical laws do not limit substitutability in final consumption, for example, the case where a good using a small quantity of natural capital substitutes for one using a large quantity of natural capital.

For the literature on physical limits, see Kneese et al. (1971); Perrings (1986); Anderson (1987); and Gross and Veendorp (1990).

REFERENCES

Anderson, C.L. (1987), 'The production process: inputs and wastes', *Journal of Environmental Economics and Management*, **14** (1), 1–12.

Barbier, E.B., A. Markandya and D.W. Pearce (1990), 'Environmental sustainability and cost–benefit analysis', *Environment and Planning A*, **22** (9), 1259–66.

Gross, L.S. and E.C.H. Veendorp (1990), 'Growth with exhaustible resources and a materials-balance production function', *Natural Resource Modeling*, **4** (1), 77–94.

Kneese, A.V., R. Ayres and R. d'Arge (1971), *Economics and the Environment*, Baltimore, MD: Johns Hopkins University Press, Resources for the Future.

Krutilla, J.V. (1967), 'Conservation reconsidered', *American Economic Review*, **54** (4), 777–86.

Krutilla, J.V., C.J. Cicchetti, A.M. Freeman and C.S. Russell (1972), 'Observations on the economics of irreplaceable assets', in A.V. Kneese and B.T. Bower (eds), *Environmental Quality Analysis*, Ch. 3, Baltimore, MD: Johns Hopkins University Press, Resources for the Future.

Mäler, K.G. (1991), 'National accounts and environmental resources', *Environmental and Resource Economics*, **1** (1), 1–15.

Meadows, D.H., D.L. Meadows, J. Randers and W. Behrens (1972), *The Limits to Growth*, New York: Universe Books.

Meadows, D.H., D.L. Meadows and J. Randers (1992), *Beyond the Limits*, Post Mills, VT: Chelsea Green Publishing Company.

Nordaus, W.D. (1973), 'World dynamics: measurement without data', *Economic Journal*, **83**, 1156–83.

Pearce, D.W. and G.D. Atkinson (1993), 'Capital theory and the measurement of sustainable development: some empirical evidence', *Ecological Economics*, **8** (2), 103–8.

Perrings, C. (1986), 'Conservation of mass and instability in a dynamic economy–environmental system', *Journal of Environmental Economics and Management*, **13** (3), 199–211.

Toman, M.A., J. Pezzey and J. Krautkraemer (1995), 'Neoclassical economic growth theory and "sustainability"', in D. Bromley (ed.), *The Handbook of Environmental Economics*, Ch. 7, Oxford, UK; Cambridge, MA: Blackwell.

Victor, P.A. (1991), 'Indicators of sustainable development: some lessons from capital theory', *Ecological Economics*, **4** (3), 191–214.

World Commission on Environment and Development (1987), *Our Common Future*, The Brundtland Report, Oxford, UK: Oxford University Press.

9. The acid rain game: a formal and mathematically rigorous analysis

Henk Folmer and Pierre von Mouche[*]

1 INTRODUCTION

Until the late 1980s environmental economics was almost exclusively restricted to environmental problems that take place within national borders. The year 1989 marked a major change in that international environmental problems became more visible due to the publication of Mäler's (1989) 'Acid rain game'. The death of forests and lakes in Scandinavia and Central Europe inspired Mäler to present a first analysis of the problem of acidification and to put it on the economic research agenda. In this paper he takes into account that acidification is a transboundary pollution process, that is, the environment in one country is affected by emissions generated in one or more other countries. The paper focuses on the efficiency of and obstacles to international cooperation with respect to acid rain abatement, taking into account the geographical pattern of the sources of emissions of sulphur and nitrogen oxides, their transportation and their depositions.

Mäler's rationale for analysing acid rain and its impacts was not only guided by ecological and economic motives, but was also triggered by the 'multitude of intellectual challenges' inherent to the acid rain problem. One challenge relates to the fact that the information on causes and effects is highly uncertain. Not only does this have consequences for policy making and its analysis, but it also gives rise to empirical problems, such as estimating damage cost functions. A second challenge relates to the fact that acid rain concerns the use of a common property resource in a very asymmetric way and that the parties involved are sovereign countries. The latter implies that there is no international institution that can implement and enforce acid rain abatement policy. Hence, international cooperation must be based on voluntary agreements.

In the above-mentioned paper, Mäler develops a skeleton of an analytical model in the form of a game in strategic form relating to the net benefits of abatement and applies it to the acid rain problem among European countries. On the basis of a data set relating to European countries in the mid-1980s, he numerically determines (using the General Algebraic Modelling System (GAMS)) the[1] non-cooperative (Nash) equilibrium and social optimum (full cooperative emission vector) and then, on the basis of these results, considers how the net benefits associated with the non-cooperative equilibrium and the social optimum relate to each other. In this way he illustrates that from a welfare point of view the social optimum is preferable to the non-cooperative equilibrium in the sense that it leads to higher total net benefits. Furthermore, the numerical results show that some countries may incur negative net benefits under the social optimum, which forms a major obstacle to implement it.[2] Finally, he discusses some instruments to overcome this obstacle, particularly side-payments.

Mäler's paper has not only put acid rain but also international environmental problems in general in the limelight. Although it is difficult to establish a causal link, research on acid rain was soon followed by a rapidly growing flow of publications on such problems as the pollution of international rivers and seas, photochemical smog, ozone layer depletion, and, particularly, global warming. The acid rain model framework developed by Mäler can be applied to all these transboundary pollution problems. We explicitly mention Finus (2001), Welsch (1993), and Mäler and de Zeeuw (1998) (who deal with a differential game approach), and refer to Folmer and von Mouche (2000) for further references.

Mäler's acid rain game has undoubtedly also stimulated application of game theory to environmental economics. This applies not only to international environmental problems but also to the implementation and enforcement of domestic environmental policy, the exploitation of natural resources, and the implementation of environmental policy at the firm level. In particular the special case of global pollution has been explored.

Not only is the acid rain game an important tool to analyse environmental problems, it also offers a variety of interesting problems for game-theoretical research. The acid rain game is also a powerful pedagogical tool. It offers students the opportunity to familiarize themselves with the characteristics of transboundary pollution and with (an application of) game theory. To sum up, when Mäler developed his acid rain game in 1989, he made a far greater contribution to the (environmental) economics literature than he was probably aware of at that time.

In spite of its important contributions to the environmental economics literature, Mäler's paper (and several subsequent contributions) lacks precision and rigor.[3] The purpose of the present chapter is to present the acid rain game in a self-contained,[4] formal and mathematically rigorous way and to address some unexplored characteristics. In order to do so we introduce in Section 2 the notion of a formal transboundary pollution game. We also present some specific vocabulary that is instrumental to the analysis which is presented in

Section 3. Proofs that are not too technical or too long will be given in passing; otherwise they will be given in the appendix. The latter type is indicated with a frownie: ⊗. In Section 4 we present the main conclusions and some suggestions for further research.

2 DEFINITIONS

Definition 1   A (supersmooth, regular) formal transboundary pollution game, abbreviated as FTPG, is a game in strategic form

$$(X^1, \ldots, X^N; f^1, \ldots, f^N)$$

where for each player j:[5]

1. $X^j := [0, M^j]$ with $M^j > 0$;
2. $f^j(x^1, \ldots, x^N) := \theta^j(x^j) - \mathcal{D}^j(\sum_{l=1}^{N} T_{jl} x^l)$ with all $T_{jl} \geq 0$, $\theta^j : [0, M^j] \to \mathbb{R}$, $\mathcal{D}^j : [0, r^j] \to \mathbb{R}$ where $r^j := \sum_{l=1}^{N} T_{jl} M^l$;
3. $T_{jj} > 0$;
4. $\mathcal{D}^j$ and θ^j are continuous;
5. $\mathcal{D}^j$ is strictly increasing and convex;
6. θ^j is strictly increasing and strictly concave;
7. $\mathcal{D}^j$ is twice continuously differentiable and $\theta^j : [0, M^j] \to \mathbb{R}$ is twice continuously differentiable with a negative second derivative;
8. For each fixed multi-action $\mathbf{x}^{\hat{\jmath}} \in \mathbf{X}^{\hat{\jmath}}$ of the other players, there exists a right (left) neighbourhood of 0 (of M^j) where the function f^j as a function of $x^j \in X^j$ is strictly increasing (strictly decreasing) and there exists a right (left) neighbourhood of 0 (of M^j) where the function $\sum_{l=1}^{N} f^l$ as a function of $x^j \in X^j$ is strictly increasing (strictly decreasing).

Moreover:

9. The $N \times N$-matrix $T := (T_{kl})$ is not diagonal. ◇

We introduce the following correspondence between standard game-theoretical terminology and FTPG terminology: Player ↔ *country*; action ↔ *emission level*; multi-action ↔ *emission vector*; action space ↔ *emission space*; payoff (function) ↔ *net benefits (function)*. Moreover, for each country j we call θ^j its *production function* and $\mathcal{D}^j$ its *damage cost function*. Finally we call T the *transport matrix*.

A possible real-world interpretation of an FTPG is the following. N countries, denoted by $1, \ldots, N$, produce emissions that cause damage in the home country and abroad. X^j is the set of country j's possible emission levels. The transboundary pollution process is assumed to be linear and is represented by means of the transport matrix T. The 'portion' $T_{ij}x^j$ of country j's emission level x^j is deposited in country i. Country j incurs (monetary) benefits $\theta^j(x^j)$ and faces (monetary) damage costs $\mathcal{D}^j(\sum_{l=1}^{N}T_{jl}x^l)$. This leads to the above net benefits function f^j.[6]

We complete our vocabulary with the following definitions. Let $\mathcal{N} := \{1, \ldots, N\}$.

Definition 2

1. We speak of *uniformly distributed transboundary pollution*, or, more precisely of *α-uniformly distributed transboundary pollution*, if there exists an $\alpha \in \mathbb{R}_{++}^N$ such that $T_{jl} = \alpha_j T_{1l}(j, l \in \mathcal{N})$.[7]
2. Country j is said to be *sensitive to emissions* from country l if $T_{jl} \neq 0$.[8] If country j is not sensitive to emissions from any other country, we say that country j is *insensitive to foreign emissions*. ◇

The following observations related to the (mathematical and real-world) structure of an FTPG apply. (i) 'Regular' refers to Assumption 8 in Definition 1. This technical assumption guarantees among other things (see Section 3) that there is no country whose emission level in a Nash equilibrium or in a full cooperative emission vector[9] is at the border of its emission space. 'Supersmooth' refers to Assumption 7 in Definition 1, that is, to the differentiability properties of the production and damage cost functions.[10] (ii) Assumption 9 in Definition 1 implies that there is at least one country that is sensitive to emissions from another country and thus that $N \geq 2$. (iii) We do not assume that each column sum of the transport matrix is equal to 1. Therefore, our model framework includes non-closed systems (where the column sums are less than or equal to 1) as well as global pollution processes (where all transport matrix coefficients are identical). (iv) We do not assume $\mathcal{D}^j(0) = 0$ or $\theta^j(0) = 0$. Moreover, payoffs can be negative. (v) Our setting differs from Mäler's acid rain game in the sense that we do not allow arbitrarily high emission levels (which is unrealistic) by assuming that the emission spaces are bounded. Other differences are that we set up the game in terms of emission levels instead of abatement levels[11] and the payoffs as net benefits (production – damage costs) instead of total costs (abatement costs + damage costs).

If not stated otherwise, in the rest of this chapter we always consider an FTPG:

$$Z := (X^1, \ldots, X^N; f^1, \ldots f^N)$$

and use notations as in Definition 1.

Observe that in an FTPG differentiability of a production function θ^j at 0 is not assumed.[12] However, since θ^j is concave, the number $\theta^{j\prime}(0) := \lim_{x^j \downarrow 0}(\theta^j(x^j) - \theta^j(0))/(x^j - 0) \in \mathbb{R} \cup \{+\infty\}$ is well defined. Elementary results from the theory of convex functions show that for each FTPG:

a. $\theta^{j\prime}(x^j) > 0$ $(x^j \in (0, M^j))$ and $\mathcal{D}^{j\prime}(Q^j) > 0$ $(Q^j \in (0, r^j))$,
b. $\theta^{j\prime\prime}(x^j) < 0$ $(x^j \in (0, M^j))$ and $\mathcal{D}^{j\prime\prime} \geq 0$.

Moreover, a game in strategic form $(X^1, \ldots, X^N; f^1, \ldots, f^N)$ is an FTPG if for each player j the Assumptions 1–4, 7, 8 in Definition 1 hold, Assumption 9 in Definition 1 applies, and for each player j the above properties a, b hold.

We introduce the following notations:

$$\mathbf{X} := X^1 \times \ldots \times X^N.$$

Moreover, we define $\mathbf{X}^{\hat{i}} := \prod_{j=1,\, j \neq i}^{N} X^j$, identify $\mathbf{X}$ with $X^i \times \mathbf{X}^{\hat{i}}$ and accordingly write $\mathbf{x} \in \mathbf{X}$ as $\mathbf{x} = (x^i; \mathbf{x}^{\hat{i}})$. For $\mathbf{z} \in \mathbf{X}^{\hat{j}}$ we define the function $g_{\mathbf{z}}^j : X^j \to \mathbb{R}$, by

$$g_{\mathbf{z}}^j(x^j) := f^j(x^j; \mathbf{z})$$

and refer to it as the *conditional net benefits function* of country j. Note that each $g_{\mathbf{z}}^j$ is strictly concave. Given a weight[13] λ, we define the function $F_\lambda : \mathbf{X} \to \mathbb{R}$ by

$$F_\lambda := \sum_{j=1}^{N} \lambda^j f^j.$$

Finally, we define the function $Q^j : \mathbb{R}^N \to \mathbb{R}$ by

$$Q^j(\mathbf{a}) := \sum_{l=1}^{N} T_{jl} a^l$$

and call for an emission vector $\mathbf{x}$ the number $Q^j(\mathbf{x})$ the *deposition* (*level*) in country j caused by $\mathbf{x}$. Note that in the case of $\boldsymbol{\alpha}$-uniformly distributed transboundary pollution we have $Q^j = \alpha^j Q^1$ for each country j.

3   ANALYSIS

3.1   Best Reply Functions

Since a conditional net benefits function $g_{\mathbf{z}}^j$ is strictly concave and continuous, it assumes a maximum at a unique point. Thus, for each country j its best reply correspondence B^j is singleton-valued and therefore can be interpreted as a function $B^j : \mathbf{X}^{\hat{j}} \to X^j$. Due to its strict concavity, the function $g_{\mathbf{z}}^j$ is strictly increasing on $[0, B^j(\mathbf{z})]$, strictly decreasing on $[B^j(\mathbf{z}), M^j]$ and is maximal in $B^j(\mathbf{z})$. Assumption 8 in Definition 1 implies that $0 < B^j < M^j$.

For further analysis it will be useful to define for an FTPG the function $Q_*^j : \mathbf{X}^{\hat{j}} \to [0, \infty)$ by:

$$Q_*^j(\mathbf{x}^{\hat{j}}) := \frac{1}{T_{jj}} \sum_{l=1, l \neq j}^{N} T_{jl} x^l.$$

Furthermore, for each country j we define for each $c \in [0, L^j]$, with

$$L^j := Q_*^j(\mathbf{M}^{\hat{j}}),$$

the function $h_c^j : X^j \to \mathbb{R}$ by

$$h_c^j(x) := \theta^j(x) - \mathcal{D}^j(T_{jj}(x + c)).$$

Finally, since h_c^j is strictly concave and continuous, one can define $\mathcal{B}^j : [0, L^j] \to [0, M^j]$ by:

$\mathcal{B}^j(c)$ is the unique point where h_c^j assumes its maximum.

The introduction of h_c^j and $\mathcal{B}^j$ is indeed useful: because of the identities

$$g_{\mathbf{z}}^j = h^j_{Q_*^j(\mathbf{z})} \text{ and } B^j(\mathbf{z}) = \mathcal{B}^j(Q_*^j(\mathbf{z})),$$

the best reply function of country j can be analysed as a function of one variable $(\mathcal{B}^j(\cdot))$ and the conditional net benefits of country as a function of two variables $(h_c^j(\cdot))$.

Theorem 1

1. $\otimes$ $\mathcal{B}^j$ is continuously differentiable.
2. $\mathcal{B}^j$, and (hence) the best reply function B^j, are decreasing. $\diamond$

Proof Because $0 < \mathcal{B}^j < M^j$, we have $h^{j\prime}(\mathcal{B}^j(c)) = 0$ $(0 \leq c \leq L^j)$, that is, $\theta^{j\prime}(\mathcal{B}^j(c)) = T_{jj} \mathcal{D}^j(T_{jj}(\mathcal{B}^j(c) + c))$ $(0 \leq c \leq L^j)$. Partially differentiating this identity with respect to c leads to the formula

$$\mathcal{B}^{j\prime}(c) = -\frac{T_{jj}^2 \mathcal{D}^{j\prime\prime}(T_{jj}(\mathcal{B}^j(c) + c))}{T_{jj}^2 \mathcal{D}^{j\prime\prime}(T_{jj}(\mathcal{B}^j(c) + c)) - \theta^{j\prime\prime}(\mathcal{B}^j(c))}. \tag{9.1}$$

We observe that $\mathcal{B}^{j\prime} \geq 0$ and thus that $\mathcal{B}^j$ is decreasing.

By

$$\bar{K}^j, \underline{K}^j$$

we denote the best reply of country j to the emission vectors $\mathbf{0}$ and $\mathbf{M}^j$ of the other countries, respectively. Because B^j is decreasing it follows that $\underline{K}^j \leq B^j \leq \bar{K}^j$.

3.2 Dominant Emission Levels

Since for an FTPG a best reply correspondence is singleton-valued, it follows that dominant emission levels are strictly dominant. It is easy to see that a best reply function is in general not constant. Thus, a country does in general not have a dominant emission level. Of course, if a country has a strictly dominant emission level this emission level has to be $\bar{K}^j$ and in this case $n^j = \bar{K}^j$ for each Nash equilibrium $\mathbf{n}$.

Theorem 2   Each of the following two conditions is sufficient for a country j to have a strictly dominant emission level:

1.   Country j has an affine damage cost function.
2.   Country j is insensitive to foreign emissions. ◇

Proof   The conditional net benefits function $g_{\mathbf{z}}^j$ is equal to $g_{\mathbf{0}}^j$ plus a constant that only depends on $\mathbf{z}$. Thus the point where this function is maximal is independent of $\mathbf{z}$.

Finally we observe that there exists an FTPG for which country j is sensitive to foreign emissions with a piece-wise affine (instead of an affine) damage cost function such that country j has a strictly dominant emission level.

3.3 Nash Equilibria

Next we consider the existence and uniqueness of Nash equilibria. Recall from Definition 1 that each emission space is a compact and convex subset of $\mathbb{R}$ and that each conditional net benefits function is quasi-concave. These conditions are sufficient to ensure:

Theorem 3   Each FTPG has a Nash equilibrium. ◇

Moreover, for each emission vector $\mathbf{n}$:

$$\mathbf{n} \text{ is a Nash equilibrium} \Rightarrow (D_j f^j)(\mathbf{n}) = 0 \ (j \in \mathcal{N}), \tag{9.2}$$

where $D_j f^j$ denotes the partial derivative of f^j with respect to its j-th variable. Observe that $(D_j f^j)(\mathbf{n}) = \theta^{j\prime}(n^j) - T_{jj} \mathcal{D}^{j\prime}(Q^j(\mathbf{n}))$. Because $\underline{K}^j \leq B^j \leq \bar{K}^j$, we have for each Nash equilibrium $\mathbf{n}$ that $\underline{K}^j \leq n^j \leq \bar{K}^j$ ($j \in \mathcal{N}$).

We now consider the uniqueness of Nash equilibria of an FTPG. For that purpose we make use of a simple principle and two theorems relating to games in strategic form in general. We start with the following simple principle: an N-player game in strategic form with singleton-valued best reply correspondences for which there is a permutation π of the players such that for each i the best reply function of player $\pi(i)$ does not depend on the actions of players $\pi(i + 1)$, $\pi(i + 2)$, ..., $\pi(N)$ has at most one Nash equilibrium. This leads to Theorem 4 for which we introduce the following notation: for a permutation π of $\mathcal{N}$ and a $N \times N$-matrix A, $\pi(A)$ denotes the $N \times N$-matrix with coefficients $(\pi(A))_{ij} := A_{\pi(i),\pi(j)}$:

Theorem 4 Each FTPG for which there exists a permutation π of the countries such that $\pi(T)$ is lower triangular, has a unique Nash equilibrium.[14] ◇

Second, according to the fixed point theorem of Banach–Picard, an FTPG has a unique Nash equilibrium if the mapping

$$\mathbf{B} : \mathbf{X} \to \mathbf{X},$$

defined by $\mathbf{B}(\mathbf{x}) := (B^1(\mathbf{x}^{\hat{1}}), \ldots, B^N(\mathbf{x}^{\hat{N}}))$ is a contraction.

Finally, from a 'Rosen-like theorem' (see, for instance, Forgó et al. 1999), it follows that an FTPG has a unique Nash equilibrium if for each $\mathbf{x}$ in the interior of $\mathbf{X}$ the symmetric $N \times N$ matrix $J(\mathbf{x})$ defined by

$$J_{ij}(\mathbf{x}) := \frac{\partial^2 f^i}{\partial x^i \partial x^j} + \frac{\partial^2 f^j}{\partial x^j \partial x^i}$$

is negative definite. These conditions can be further analysed. We will not do this here, but will consider more specific uniqueness results instead. The most interesting specific case is presented in Theorem 5(2).

Theorem 5

1. ⊗ For $W := \cap_{j=1}^N \{\mathbf{x} \in \mathbb{R}^N \mid Q^j(\mathbf{x}) \geq 0\}$ and E the set of Nash equilibria we have $(E - E) \cap W = \{\mathbf{0}\}$.
2. For an FTPG with uniformly distributed transboundary pollution, there is a unique Nash equilibrium. ◇

Proof   From 1 we have $W = \{\mathbf{x} \in \mathbb{R}^N \mid Q^1(\mathbf{x}) \geq 0\}$. If $\mathbf{n}$, $\mathbf{z}$ are two Nash equilibria, then $\mathbf{n} - \mathbf{z} \in W$ or $\mathbf{z} - \mathbf{n} \in W$. It now follows $\mathbf{n} - \mathbf{z} \in \{\mathbf{0}\}$ or $\mathbf{z} - \mathbf{n} \in \{\mathbf{0}\}$, thus $\mathbf{z} = \mathbf{n}$.

Symmetric Nash equilibria may facilitate the analysis. In order to have a look at their existence and uniqueness we consider an FTPG $\mathcal{Z}$ with identical emission spaces, say, X. For all $a \in X$ one has: $B^j(a, \ldots, a) = a (j \in \mathcal{N}) \Leftrightarrow (a, \ldots, a)$ is a symmetric Nash equilibrium. Define $B : X \to X$ by

$$B(x) := B^1(x, \ldots, x).$$

Because B is continuous and decreasing, B has a unique fixed point. And for the existence of a symmetric Nash equilibrium it is sufficient that

$$B^j(x, \ldots, x) = B(x) \ (j \in \mathcal{N}, x \in X). \tag{9.3}$$

Summarizing we have:

Theorem 6   An FTPG $\mathcal{Z}$ with identical emission spaces has at most one symmetric Nash equilibrium; it has exactly one if $\mathcal{Z}$ satisfies (9.3) (which is in particular the case if $\mathcal{Z}$ is symmetric[15]). ◇

In Theorem 7 we prove for a class of not necessarily symmetric FTPGs with identical emission spaces that they have a symmetric Nash equilibrium which, moreover, is the unique Nash equilibrium.

Theorem 7   ⊗ The unique Nash equilibrium of an FTPG with **1**-uniformly distributed transboundary pollution,[16] proportional production functions and proportional damage cost functions,[17] say $\theta^i = \beta_{ir}\theta^r$ and $\mathcal{D}^i = \gamma_{ir}\mathcal{D}^r$, such that $\beta_{j1}/\gamma_{j1} = T_{jj}/T_{11}$ ($j \in \mathcal{N}$), is symmetric. ◇

Let us call an FTPG *strongly symmetric* if all diagonal transport matrix coefficients are the same (say t); all off-diagonal transport matrix coefficients are the same (say s);[18] the emission spaces are identical; for each pair of countries i, j the function $\theta^i - \theta^j$ is constant and the function $\mathcal{D}^i - \mathcal{D}^j$ also equals this constant.[19]

Theorem 8   ⊗ A strongly symmetric FTPG with $t \geq s$ has a unique Nash equilibrium. This Nash equilibrium thus is the unique symmetric one. ◇

3.4 Weighted Full Cooperative Emission Vectors

Now we consider the existence and uniqueness of λ-weighted full cooperative emission vectors.[20]

Because production functions are strictly concave and damage cost functions are convex, each net benefits function f^j is concave, but not necessarily strictly concave as the following result implies.

Theorem 9 ⊗ For an FTPG with at least three countries, no net benefits function is strictly quasi-concave. In the case of two countries a net benefits function of a country is strictly concave if that country is sensitive to emissions from the other country and its damage cost function is strictly convex. ◇

If λ is a strict weight, then $F_\lambda := \sum_{j=1}^N \lambda^j f^j$ is strictly concave, since production functions are strictly concave. Because $\sum_{j=1}^N \lambda^j f^j$ is continuous and **X** is compact, there exists an λ-weighted full cooperative emission vector. For a strict weight λ, we obtain that Z, because of the strict concavity of F_λ, has a unique λ-weighted full cooperative emission vector. In the sequel we shall pay special attention to the full cooperative emission vector. We denote this emission vector by **y**. Due to Assumption 7 in Definition 1, **y** is interior, that is, $0 < y^j < M^j$ $(j \in \mathcal{N})$.

Let **z** be a λ-weighted full cooperative emission vector. Then:

$$z^j \text{ is in the interior of } X^j \Rightarrow \sum_{r=1}^N \lambda^r (D_j f^r)(\mathbf{z}) = 0. \tag{9.4}$$

Note that in (9.4) $(D_j f^r)(\mathbf{z}) = \theta^{j\prime}(z^j)\delta_{jr} - T_{rj}\mathcal{D}^{r\prime}(Q^r(\mathbf{z}))$, where δ_{jr} is the Kronecker symbol.

Because the full cooperative emission vector **y** is unique, it is symmetric if the FTPG is symmetric. Less evident is:

Theorem 10 Consider an FTPG with **1**-uniformly distributed transboundary pollution and proportional production functions. Suppose that $\beta_{j1} = T_{jj}/T_{11}$ $(j \in \mathcal{N})$. Then **y** is symmetric. ◇

Proof From (9.4) one obtains that

$$\theta^{1\prime}(y^j) = \frac{T_{jj}}{B_{ji}T_{11}}\sum_{r=1}^N T_{r1}\mathcal{D}^{r\prime}(Q^r(\mathbf{y})) = \sum_{r=1}^N T_{r1}\mathcal{D}^{r\prime}(Q^r(\mathbf{y})) = \theta^{1\prime}(y^1) \ (j \in \mathcal{N}).$$

The injectivity of $\theta^{1\prime}$ implies that **y** is symmetric.

For several further results Theorem 11 is crucial.[21]

Theorem 11 ⊗ For each λ-weighted full cooperative emission vector **z** the following inequalities hold for a country j for which there is a country k in supp(λ) that is sensitive to emissions from country j:

1. $z^j \leq B^j(\mathbf{z}^{\hat{j}})$;
2. $z^j < B^j(\mathbf{z}^{\hat{j}})$ if there is such a country k with $k \neq j$. $\diamond$

3.5   Social welfare loss

Let $\mathbf{z}$ be a λ-weighted full cooperative emission vector. Theorems 11(1) and B^j $\leq \bar{K}^j$ imply that $z^j \leq \bar{K}^j$ ($j \in$ supp(λ)); in particular $\mathbf{y} \leq \bar{\mathbf{K}}$. Together with the fact that the conditional net benefits function $g^j_{\mathbf{z}}$ is strictly increasing on [0, $B^j(\mathbf{z})$], Theorem 11(2) implies that each country j for which there is another country from supp(λ) that is sensitive to emissions from j, can increase its net benefits by increasing its emission level by a sufficiently small amount (while the other countries do not change their emission levels). Because for an FTPG there is always a country that is sensitive to emissions from another country this implies:

Theorem 12   A λ-weighted full cooperative emission vector cannot be a Nash equilibrium if each country is sensitive to emissions from at least one other country or if λ is strict. $\diamond$

Theorem 12 implies that for an FTPG the full cooperative emission vector is not a Nash equilibrium. This result together with the fact (obtained from general results for games in strategic form) that the set of Nash equilibria of an FTPG is compact, implies Theorem 13.

Theorem 13   Each FTPG has a positive social welfare loss.[22] $\diamond$

Note that the proof of Theorem 13 is not based on the argument that a Nash equilibrium is Pareto inefficient; as we shall see in Theorem 15, this argument is false.

3.6   Pareto Efficiency of Nash Equilibria

We now address Pareto efficiency of Nash equilibria. Before going into detail, we observe that if there is a country that is insensitive to foreign emissions, each Nash equilibrium is weakly Pareto efficient. (Observe that this already proves the 'necessary' in Theorem 14.) And that (see Theorem 15) a weakly Pareto-efficient emission vector is not necessarily (strongly) Pareto efficient.[23]

It is worthwhile pointing out that if each net benefits function were strictly concave, the set of Pareto-efficient and the set of weakly Pareto-efficient emission vectors would be the same. However, in this regard we already have the (negative) result of Theorem 9.[24]

Theorem 14   Sufficient and necessary for each Nash equilibrium of an FTPG to be weakly Pareto inefficient is that each country is sensitive to emissions from at least one other country. ◇

Proof   We prove the 'sufficient' in this theorem by contradiction: assume **n** were a Nash equilibrium that is weakly Pareto efficient. Then there exists a weight λ such that **n** is λ-weighted full cooperative. But this is in contradiction with Theorem 12.

Theorem 15   ⊗ The unique Nash equilibrium of an FTPG for which there exists a permutation π of $\mathcal{N}$ such that $\pi(T)$ is lower triangular is Pareto efficient. Moreover, such an FTPG has a weakly Pareto-efficient emission vector that is not strongly Pareto efficient. ◇

Each prisoners' dilemma game[25] has a positive social welfare loss, but an FTPG with a positive social welfare loss is of course not necessarily a prisoners' dilemma. However, with Theorems 2 and 14 we may conclude that:

Theorem 16   Sufficient conditions for an FTPG to be a prisoners' dilemma game is that each country has an affine damage cost function and that each country is sensitive to emissions from at least one other country. ◇

3.7   Comparing Emission Levels

Next we consider a Nash equilibrium **n** and the following questions: is the total emission level in **y** (that is $\sum_{j=1}^{N} y^j$) always less than or equal to that in **n**? And: is the total deposition level caused by **y** (that is $\sum_{j=1}^{N} Q^j(\mathbf{y})$) always less than or equal to that in **n**? Although there exists a widespread belief in environmental economics that the answer to both questions is affirmative, Theorem 17 shows that this is a misunderstanding. Before going into detail, we remark that there is a simple relationship between total emission levels and total deposition levels in the case when each column sum of the transport matrix is the same. If this sum is c, then for each emission vector **x** we have

$$\sum_{j=1}^{N} Q^j(\mathbf{x}) = c\sum_{j=1}^{N} x^j.$$

Theorem 17   ⊗ There exists an FTPG with a (unique) Nash equilibrium **n** and a (not individually rational) full cooperative emission vector **y** for which the inequality $\sum_{j=1}^{N} y^j > \sum_{j=1}^{N} n^j$ holds. ◇

The explanation for the misunderstanding related to the first question above is that in the environmental economics literature one usually deals with affine (and even linear) damage cost functions. In this regard, Theorem 2(1), $y^j \leq \bar{K}^j = B^j(\mathbf{0})$ and Theorem 11(2) imply:

Theorem 18 If country j has an affine damage cost function, then $y^j < n^j$ for each Nash equilibrium $\mathbf{n}$. Moreover, if there is another country that is sensitive to emissions from country j, then even $y^j < n^j$. ◇

We do not know the answer to the second question. However, the following theorem applies.

Theorem 19 Let $\mathbf{n}$ be the Nash equilibrium of an FTPG with uniformly distributed pollution. Then the deposition level in each country caused by $\mathbf{y}$ is less than its deposition level caused by $\mathbf{n}$. ◇

Proof If there were a country i with $Q^i(\mathbf{n}) \leq Q^i(\mathbf{y})$, then (because of uniformly distributed pollution), one would have $Q^j(\mathbf{n}) \leq Q^j(\mathbf{y})$ ($j \in \mathcal{N}$). With (9.2) and (9.4) we would have $\theta^{j\prime}(n^j) = T_{jj}\mathcal{D}^{j\prime}(Q^j(\mathbf{n})) \leq T_{jj}\mathcal{D}^{j\prime}(Q^j(\mathbf{y})) < \sum_{r=1}^N T_{rj}\mathcal{D}^{r\prime}(Q^r(\mathbf{y})) = \theta^{j\prime}(y^j)$. Thus $\theta^{j\prime}(n^j) < \theta^{j\prime}(y^j)$. Because θ^j is strictly concave, it would follow that $y^j < n^j$. Thus $\mathbf{y} \ll \mathbf{n}$ would follow. But this contradicts $Q^i(\mathbf{n}) \leq Q^i(\mathbf{y})$.

Theorems 20 and 21 further characterize the relationships between the λ-weighted full cooperative emission vector $\mathbf{y}_\lambda$ with strict weight λ and a Nash equilibrium $\mathbf{n}$.

Theorem 20 The inequality $\mathbf{y}_\lambda \geq \mathbf{n}$ never holds. ◇

Proof by contradiction According to Theorem 12 $\mathbf{y}_\lambda \neq \mathbf{n}$. Suppose we had $\mathbf{y}_\lambda > \mathbf{n}$. Because of Theorem 11(1) we have for each country j that $y_\lambda^j \leq B^j(\mathbf{y}_\lambda^{\hat{\jmath}})$. Because $\mathbf{y}_\lambda^{\hat{\jmath}} \geq \mathbf{n}^{\hat{\jmath}}$ and B^j is decreasing, it would follow that $B^j(\mathbf{y}_\lambda^{\hat{\jmath}}) \leq B^j(\mathbf{n}^{\hat{\jmath}})$. But $B^j(\mathbf{n}^{\hat{\jmath}}) = n^j$ and hence $y_\lambda^j \leq n^j$. Thus $\mathbf{y}_\lambda \leq \mathbf{n}$, which is a contradiction.

In the case of an FTPG with symmetric $\mathbf{y}$ and a symmetric Nash equilibrium $\mathbf{n}$ with $\mathbf{n} \neq \mathbf{y}$, the inequality $\mathbf{y} \ll \mathbf{n}$ holds as a consequence of Theorem 20. Here is a less evident result:

Theorem 21 Consider an FTPG with **1**-uniformly distributed transboundary pollution and identical damage cost functions. Then the inequality $\mathbf{y} \ll \mathbf{n}$ holds. ◇

Proof (9.2) and (9.4) imply here that $\theta^{j\prime}(n^j)/\theta^{j\prime}(y^j) = \theta^{i\prime}(n^i)/\theta^{i\prime}(y^i)(i, j\in \mathcal{N})$. Because $\theta^{k\prime}(k\in \mathcal{N})$ is strictly decreasing, $y^i \geq n^i$ would imply that $y^j \geq n^j(j\in \mathcal{N})$ and thus $\mathbf{y} \geq \mathbf{n}$, which is impossible. Thus we have $\mathbf{y} << \mathbf{n}$.

3.8 Pareto Improvements of Nash Equilibria

Reconsidering Theorem 14, the question arises where Pareto improvements of a (weakly) Pareto inefficient Nash equilibrium are located. To answer this question we first mention the following results: (i) The concavity of the net benefits functions implies that for each emission vector $\mathbf{b}$ that is a (unanimous) Pareto improvement of an emission vector $\mathbf{a}$, each emission vector in $(\mathbf{a}, \mathbf{b})$ also is. (ii) If $\mathbf{n}$ is a Nash equilibrium, no emission vector $\mathbf{z}$ for which $Q_*^j(z^{\hat{j}})$ $\geq Q_*^j(\mathbf{n}^{\hat{j}})(j\in \mathcal{N})$ holds[26] is a Pareto improvement of $\mathbf{n}$. (For such an emission vector $f^j(\mathbf{n}) \geq f^j(z^j; \mathbf{n}^{\hat{j}}) \geq f^j(z^j; \mathbf{z}^{\hat{j}})(j\in \mathcal{N})$, thus $\mathbf{f}(\mathbf{n}) \geq \mathbf{f}(\mathbf{z})$.) Next we have the following theorem that deals with 'uniform emissions reductions':

Theorem 22 ⊗ Consider an FTPG where each country is sensitive to emissions from at least one other country and let $\mathbf{n}$ be a Nash equilibrium. Then for small enough $r\in (0, 1)$ the emission vector $(1 - r)\mathbf{n}$ is a unanimous Pareto improvement of $\mathbf{n}$. ◇

Among others for repeated FTPGs it is important to know (because of Folk theorems) whether the net benefits vector corresponding to the full cooperative emission vector $\mathbf{y}$ is individually rational. Theorem 17 shows that $\mathbf{y}$ does not have this property in general. Moreover, the proof of this theorem shows that this property does not even hold in general when all damage cost functions are affine. A related problem is whether $\mathbf{y}$ is a Pareto improvement of a Nash equilibrium. Unfortunately we can only give here the following general result:

Theorem 23 Consider an FTPG $\mathcal{Z}$ with a Nash equilibrium $\mathbf{n}$. If each country has the same net benefits in $\mathbf{n}$ and in $\mathbf{y}$ (which happens for instance if $\mathcal{Z}$ and $\mathbf{n}$ are symmetric), then $\mathbf{y}$ is a unanimous Pareto improvement of $\mathbf{n}$. ◇

Proof This is very simple: by Theorem 12, $\mathbf{n} \neq \mathbf{y}$, which now implies the desired result.

If $\mathbf{n}$ is a Nash equilibrium, it follows from the definition of the full cooperative emission vector $\mathbf{y}$ and the property $\mathbf{y} \neq \mathbf{n}$ that there exists at least one country k such that $f^k(\mathbf{y}) > f^k(\mathbf{n})$. Here is a more interesting result:

Theorem 24 ⊗ Consider the Nash equilibrium $\mathbf{n}$ of an FTPG with $\mathbf{1}$-uniformly distributed transboundary pollution, proportional production functions, identical damage cost functions and, $\beta_{l1} = T_{l1}/T_{11}$ $(l \in \mathcal{N})$.[27] If k is a country with $T_{kk} \leq 1/N \sum_{r=1}^{N} T_{rr}$, then $f^k(\mathbf{n}) < f^k(\mathbf{y})$. If, moreover, $\theta^k(\mathbf{n}) \geq 0$, then for each country j with $T_{jj} \leq T_{kk}$ one has $f^j(\mathbf{n}) < f^k(\mathbf{y})$. $\diamond$

3.9 Regularity

Finally, we turn to the technical Assumption 8 in Definition 1. For a given concrete game in strategic form for which Assumptions 1–7 and 9 in Definition 1 apply one may wish to quickly check that Assumption 8 also holds (that is, that we are dealing with an FTPG). The following result may be instrumental for this purpose:

Theorem 25 $\otimes$ Consider a game in strategic form for which Assumptions 1–7 and 9 in Definition 1 apply for player j. If $\theta^{j\prime}(0) = +\infty$ and if there exists a left neighbourhood of M^j where the function (g_0^j) is negative, then Assumption 8 for player j also holds. $\diamond$

4 SUGGESTIONS FOR FURTHER RESEARCH

The analysis in the previous section motivates the following research problems whose solutions would contribute to a better understanding of formal transboundary pollution games:

1. Does there exist an FTPG with more than one Nash equilibrium? (Compare Theorems 4, 5(2) and 8.)
2. Given a Nash equilibrium $\mathbf{n}$, is the total deposition level caused by the full cooperative emission vector less than or equal to that in $\mathbf{n}$?
3. Analyse the contraction properties of $\mathbf{B}$ and the negative definiteness of $J(\mathbf{x})$ (see § 3.3) in order to obtain uniqueness results for Nash equilibria.
4. Identify other cases of symmetric Nash equilibria and full cooperative emission vectors than the one specified in Theorems 7 and 10 (where the FTPG is not necessarily symmetric).
5. Identify FTPGs other than those in Theorem 23 where the full cooperative emission vector is a (unanimous) Pareto improvement of each Nash equilibrium.
6. Is each weakly Pareto-efficient emission vector strongly Pareto efficient in the case when each country is sensitive to emissions from each other country? (Compare Theorem 15.)
7. How robust are our results against small perturbations?[28]
8. Analyse FTPGs without the regularity and supersmoothness conditions (Assumption 8, respectively 7, in Definition 1).

Finally, we observe that Cornes and Hartley (2000) study games in strategic form with action spaces $[0, \infty)$ and with payoffs functions of the type

$$f^i(x^1, \ldots, x^N) = \psi^i(x^i, \phi^i(x^1, \ldots, x^N)),$$

where $\phi^i(\mathbf{x}) = \sum_{j=1}^{N} x^j$. Such games are called *simply reducible games* there.[29] The framework of simply reducible games applies to, for example, oligopolistic models, open access resource exploitation models and to models of transboundary pollution (with uniformly distributed transboundary pollution). We did not deal with simple reducible games in this chapter, because the present theory of simply reducible games focuses solely on Nash equilibria and not on the other topics in our chapter.[30] More research on simply reducible games would be welcome, however.

APPENDIX   REMAINING PROOFS

Proof of Theorem 1(1)   In order to prove that $\mathcal{B}^j : [0, L^j] \to \mathbb{R}$ is continuously differentiable, we shall prove that for each $c_0 \in [0, L^j]$ there exists an open interval I that contains c_0 such that $\mathcal{B}^j : [0, L^j] \cap I \to \mathbb{R}$ is continuously differentiable.

Well, $h_c^j : [0, M^j] \to \mathbb{R}$ is strictly concave and $h_c^j : [0, M^j] \to \mathbb{R}$ is differentiable. For all $c \in [0, L^j]$, $\mathcal{B}^j(c)$, that is, the unique maximizer of h_c^j, is in the interior of $[0, M^j]$ and therefore the unique zero of the function $(h_c^j)'$ $(0, M^j) \to \mathbb{R}$. With the function $H : [0, L^j] \times (0, M^j) \to \mathbb{R}$ defined by

$$H(c, a) := (h_c^j)'(a) = \theta^{j\prime}(a) - T_{jj}\mathcal{D}^{j\prime}(T_{jj}(a + c)), \qquad (*)$$

$\mathcal{B}^j$ is thus the unique function $\xi : [0, L^j] \to (0, M^j)$ for which $H(c, \xi(c)) = 0$ $(c \in [0, L^j])$. We want to apply the implicit function theorem to H. However, $[0, L^j]$ is not open. In order to handle this we first extend $\mathcal{D}^j$ to a twice continuously differentiable function on $\mathbb{R}$ and extend $[0, L^j]$ to, for example, $(-3, L^j + 5) =: U$. Now define $\tilde{H}: U \times (0, M^j)$ by the formula $(*)$; then $\tilde{H}$ extends H. H is continuously differentiable because it is continuously partially differentiable. Take $c_0 \in [0, L^j]$.

We have

$$\frac{\partial \tilde{H}}{\partial a}(c_0, \mathcal{B}^j(c_0)) = \theta^{j\prime\prime}(\mathcal{B}^j(c_0)) - T_{jj}^2 \mathcal{D}^{j\prime\prime}(T_{jj}(\mathcal{B}^j(c_0) + c_0)) < 0.$$

The implicit function theorem guarantees that there exist an open interval I with $c_0 \in I \subseteq U$ and a continuously differentiable function $\xi : I \to \mathbb{R}$ such that

$\xi(c_0) = \mathcal{B}^j(c_0)$ and $\tilde{H}[c, \xi(c)] = 0 (c \in I)$. Then $H[c, \xi(c)] = 0$ $(c \in I \cap [0, L^j])$. It follows that $\xi(c) = \mathcal{B}^j(c)$ $(c \in I \cap [0, L^j])$ and thus $\mathcal{B}^j : I \cap [0, L^j] \to \mathbb{R}$ is continuously differentiable. $\square$

Proof of Theorem 5(1) '$\supseteq$:' Take $\mathbf{n} \in E$. Then $\mathbf{0} = \mathbf{n} - \mathbf{n} \in (E - E) \cap W$. '$\subseteq$:' Take $\mathbf{n}$, $\mathbf{z} \in E$ with $\mathbf{n} - \mathbf{z} \in W$. Then $Q^j(\mathbf{n}) \geq Q^j(\mathbf{z})(j \in \mathcal{N})$. This implies $n^j \leq z^j$: because of (9.2) we have $\theta^{j\prime}(n^j) = T_{jj} \mathcal{D}^{j\prime}[Q^j(\mathbf{n})] = T_{jj} \mathcal{D}^{j\prime}[Q^j(\mathbf{n})] \geq T_{jj} \mathcal{D}^{j\prime}[Q^j(\mathbf{z})]$ $= \theta^{j\prime}_+(z^j)$, thus $\theta^{j\prime}_-(n^j) \geq \theta^{j\prime}_+ + (z^j)$; because θ^j is strictly concave this implies $n^j \leq z^j$. Thus $\mathbf{n} \leq \mathbf{z}$. This implies $Q^j(\mathbf{n} - \mathbf{z}) \leq 0 (j \in \mathcal{N})$. Thus $Q^j(\mathbf{n} - \mathbf{z}) = 0$ $(j \in \mathcal{N})$ and $\mathbf{n} - \mathbf{z} \leq 0$. From this we derive than $\mathbf{n} - \mathbf{z} = \mathbf{0}$. $\square$

Proof of Theorem 7 Let a be the unique fixed point of B. Thus $B^1(a, \ldots, a) = a \in X^o$. Now we prove that $B^j(a, \ldots, a) = a (j \in \mathcal{N})$ and thus that $(a, \ldots a)$ is a symmetric Nash equilibrium. We have:

$$f^j(\mathbf{x}) = \beta_{j1}\theta^1(x^j) - \gamma_{j1}\mathcal{D}^1(\sum_{l=1}^{N}T_{ll}x^l) = \beta_{j1}[\theta^1(x^j) - \frac{T_{11}}{T_{jj}}\mathcal{D}^1(\sum_{l=1}^{N}T_{ll}x^l)].$$

In particular,

$$g_a^j(x^j) := f^j(x^j; a, \ldots a) = \beta_{j1}\{\theta^1(x^j) - \frac{T_{11}}{T_{jj}}\mathcal{D}^1[T_{jj}x^j + (\sum_{l=1,l\neq j}^{N}T_{ll})a]\}.$$

The function $g_a^j : X \to \mathbb{R}$ is strictly concave and it assumes a maximum in a unique point of X^o. This point is the unique $x \in X^o$ satisfying $(g_a^j)'(x) = 0$, that is, the equality $\theta^{1\prime}(a) = T_{11}\mathcal{D}^{1\prime}[T_{jj}x + (\sum_{l=1,l\neq j}^{N}T_{ll})a]$. Because $B^1(a, \ldots, a) = a$, a is this point and thus $\theta^{1\prime}(x) = T_{11}\mathcal{D}^{1\prime}(\sum_{l=1}^{N}T_{ll}a)$. This identity implies that $x = a$ satisfies the equality for each j. $\square$

Proof of Theorem 8 Suppose $\mathbf{n}$ is a Nash equilibrium. Fix i, $k \in \mathcal{N}$. Let $\theta^i - \theta^k = c$ and $\mathcal{D}^i - \mathcal{D}^k = c$. Denote $\theta = \theta^i$ and $\mathcal{D} = \mathcal{D}^i$. Because of (9.2), $\theta'(n^l) = t\mathcal{D}'(tn^l + \sum_{j=1,j\neq l}^{N}sn^j)(l = i, k)$. From this it follows that:

$$\theta'(n^i) - \theta'(n^k) = t[\mathcal{D}'(tn^i + s\sum_{j=1,j\neq i}^{N}n^j) - \mathcal{D}'(tn^k + s\sum_{j=1,j\neq k}^{N}n^j)].$$

If $t = s$, we have $\theta'(n^i) - \theta'(n^k) = 0$ and thus $n^i = n^k$. Now suppose $t > s$. If $n^i < n^k$ held, then the left-hand side of the above identity would be positive and, because when $tn^i + s\sum_{j=1,j\neq l}^{N}n^j < tn^k + s\sum_{j=1,j\neq k}^{N}n^j$, the right-hand side would be negative which is a contradiction. In the same way $n^i > n^k$ would lead to a contradiction. Thus we may conclude that $n^i = n^k$, and from this that $\mathbf{n}$ is symmetric. Because a symmetric FTPG has a unique symmetric Nash equilibrium, **n** is unique. □

Proof of Theorem 9   First part: fix a country j. The function Q^j is linear and its kernel is a $N - 1$-dimensional linear subspace E of $\mathbb{R}^N$. Let $F := \{\mathbf{z} \in \mathbb{R}^N \mid z^j = 0\}$. Also F is such a subspace. One has dim $(E \cap F) = $ dim $E + $ dim $F - $ dim $(E + F) = 2N - 2 - $ dim $(E + F) \geq N - 2$. Because $N - 2 \geq 1$, there exists $\mathbf{c} \in E \cap F$ with $\mathbf{c} \neq \mathbf{0}$ and even such a $\mathbf{c}$ with $|c^l| < |M^l|$ $(l \in \mathcal{N})$. It is now possible to choose two emission vectors $\mathbf{a}$ and $\mathbf{b}$ such that $\mathbf{c} = \mathbf{a} - \mathbf{b}$. One has $\mathbf{a} \neq \mathbf{b}$, $a^j = b^j$ and $0 = Q^j(\mathbf{c}) = Q^j(\mathbf{a}) - Q^j(\mathbf{b})$. For all $t_1, t_2 \in (0, 1)$ with $t_1 + t_2 = 1$ we have

$$f^j(t_1\mathbf{a} + t_2\mathbf{b}) = \theta^j(t_1 a^j + t_2 b^j) - \mathcal{D}^j(Q^j(t_1\mathbf{a} + t_2\mathbf{b})) = \theta^j(a) - \mathcal{D}^j[Q^j(\mathbf{a})] = f^j(\mathbf{a}).$$

In the same way $f^j(t_1\mathbf{a} + t_2\mathbf{b}) = f^j(\mathbf{b})$. But this implies that f^j cannot be strictly quasi-concave.

Second part: Let j be such a country. Take $t_1, t_2 \in (0, 1)$ with $t_1 + t_2 = 1$ and (x^1, x^2), $(y^1, y^2) \in \mathbf{X}$ with $(x^1, x^2) \neq (y^1, y^2)$. Because T_{j1} and T_{j2} are positive, we have $x^j \neq y^j$ or $\sum_{l=1}^2 T_{jl} x^l \neq \sum_{l=1}^2 T_{jl} y^l$. Using the strict concavity of θ^j and the strict convexity of $\mathcal{D}^j$ we have

$$f^j(t_1\mathbf{x} + t_2\mathbf{y}) = \theta^j(t_1 x^j + t_2 y^j) - \mathcal{D}^j(t_1 \sum_{l=1}^2 T_{jl} x^l + t_2 \sum_{l=1}^2 T_{jl} y^l) > t_1 \theta^j(x^j)$$
$$+ t_2 \theta^j(y^j) - (t_1 \mathcal{D}^j(\sum_{l=1}^2 T_{jl} x^l) + t_2 \mathcal{D}^j(\sum_{l=1}^2 T_{jl} y^l)) = t_1 f^j(\mathbf{x})$$
$$+ t_2 f^j(\mathbf{y}). \ \square$$

Proof of Theorem 11

1. If $z^j = 0$, then this statement holds. Suppose now that $z^j \neq 0$. This is only possible if $\lambda^j \neq 0$ ($\lambda^j = 0$ would imply $z^j = 0$ because $T_{kj} \neq 0$). Since $g_{\mathbf{z}j}^j$ is concave and strictly decreasing on $[B^j(\mathbf{z}^{\hat{}}), M^j]$, $(g_{\mathbf{z}j}^j)' < 0$ on the non-empty $[B^j(\mathbf{z}^{\hat{}}), M^j]$. In order to show $z^j \geq B^j(\mathbf{z}^{\hat{}})$ we can therefore prove that $(g_{\mathbf{z}j}^j)'(\mathbf{z}j) \geq 0$. From (9.4) it follows that

    $$\lambda^j(g_{\mathbf{z}j}^j)'(z^j) = \lambda^j(D_j f^j)(\mathbf{z}) = - \sum_{r=1, r \neq j}^N \lambda^r(D_j f^r)(\mathbf{z})$$
    $$= \sum_{r=1, r \neq j}^N \lambda^r T_{rj} \mathcal{D}^{r\prime}(Q^r(\mathbf{z})) \geq 0.$$

    Thus, because $\lambda^j \neq 0$, we have $(g_{\mathbf{z}j}^j)(z^j) \geq 0$.

2. Take $k \in \text{supp}(\lambda)$ with $T_{kj} \neq 0$ and $k \neq j$. If $z^j = 0$, then, because $0 < B^j(\mathbf{z}^{\hat{}})$, the proof is complete. If $z^j \neq 0$, then (as above) $\lambda^j \neq 0$. As above, $(g_{\mathbf{z}j}^j)' \leq 0$ on the non-empty interval $[B^j(\mathbf{z}^{\hat{}}), M^j]$. So, we can demonstrate that $z^j < B^j(\mathbf{z}^{\hat{}})$ by showing that $(g_{\mathbf{z}j}^j)'(z^j) > 0$. As above, we find:

    $$\lambda^j(g_{\mathbf{z}j}^j)'(z^j) \geq \sum_{r=1, r \neq j}^N \lambda^r T_{rj} \mathcal{D}^{r\prime}(Q^r(\mathbf{z})) \geq \lambda^k T_{kj} \mathcal{D}^{k\prime}(Q^k(\mathbf{z}))$$
    $$\geq \lambda^k T_{kj} \mathcal{D}^{k\prime}(T_{kk} z^k) > 0. \ \square$$

Proof of Theorem 15   Because of Theorem 4 we know that Z has a unique Nash equilibrium $\mathbf{n}$. Define, for $j \neq N$, $S^{\pi(j)} := \{\pi(j+1), \pi(j+2), \ldots, \pi(N)\}$. The lower triangularity of $\pi(T)$ implies for each $j \neq N$ that $f^{\pi(j)}$ is independent of the emission levels of the $(N-j)$ countries in $S^{\pi(j)}$.

We now prove that $\mathbf{n}$ is Pareto efficient by contradiction: suppose that $\mathbf{p}$ would be a Pareto improvement of $\mathbf{n}$. Then

$$f^{\pi(j)}(\mathbf{p}) \geq f^{\pi(j)}(\mathbf{n})(j = 1, 2, \ldots, N-1).$$

Fixing $j = 1$, we had $f^{\pi(1)}(\mathbf{p}) \geq f^{\pi(1)}(\mathbf{n})$. Because $f^{\pi(1)}$ is independent of the emission levels of the other countries and $\mathbf{n}$ is a Nash equilibrium, we have:

$$f^{\pi(1)}(\mathbf{p}) = f^{\pi(1)}(p^{\pi(1)}; \widehat{\mathbf{n}^{\pi(1)}}) \leq f^{\pi(1)}(\mathbf{n}).$$

Therefore $f^{\pi(1)}(\mathbf{p}) = f^{\pi(1)}(\mathbf{n})$ and from $f^{\pi(1)}(p^{\pi(1)}; \widehat{\mathbf{n}^{\pi(1)}}) = f^{\pi(1)}(\mathbf{n})$ it would follow that $p^{\pi(1)} = n^{\pi(1)}$ had to hold. Fixing $j = 2$, we had $f^{\pi(2)}(\mathbf{p}) \geq f^{\pi(2)}(\mathbf{n})$. Because $p^{\pi(1)} = n^{\pi(1)}$, $f^{\pi(2)}$ is independent of the emission levels of the countries $\pi(3), \ldots, \pi(N)$ and $\mathbf{n}$ is a Nash equilibrium we had

$$f^{\pi(2)}(\mathbf{p}) = f^{\pi(2)}(p^{\pi(2)}; \widehat{\mathbf{n}^{\pi(2)}}) \leq f^{\pi(2)}(\mathbf{n}).$$

Therefore $f^{\pi(2)}(\mathbf{p}) = f^{\pi(2)}(\mathbf{n})$ and moreover $p^{\pi(2)} = n^{\pi(2)}$ had to hold. Continuing up to $j = N - 1$ we would obtain $f^{\pi(j)}(\mathbf{p}) = f^{\pi(j)}(\mathbf{n})$ $(1 \leq j \geq N - 1)$ and $p^{\pi(j)} = p^{\pi(j)}$ $(1 \leq j \leq N - 1)$. But then, because $\mathbf{p}$ is a Pareto improvement of $\mathbf{n}$, $f^{\pi(N)}(\mathbf{p}) \geq f^{\pi(N)}(\mathbf{n})$ must hold, that is,

$$f^{\pi(N)}(p^{\pi(N)}; \widehat{\mathbf{n}^{\pi(N)}}) \geq f^{\pi(N)}(n^{\pi(N)}; \widehat{\mathbf{n}^{\pi(N)}}),$$

which is a contradiction because $\mathbf{n}$ is a Nash equilibrium.

Proof of the last statement: with $\mathbf{a} \in X^{\pi(N)}$ defined by $a^j := n^j$, it follows from the above that for all $\mathbf{x} \in X$ and for all $\mathbf{b} \in X$ with $b^k = a^k (k \neq \pi(N))$:

$$f^{\pi(j)}(\mathbf{x}) \geq f^{\pi(j)}(\mathbf{b})(1 \leq j \leq N - 1) \Rightarrow f^{\pi(j)}(\mathbf{x}) = f^{\pi(j)}(\mathbf{b})\ (1 \leq j \leq N - 1).$$

This implies that $\mathbf{b}$ is weakly Pareto efficient. Now take $\mathbf{b}$ such that $b^{\pi(N)} \neq B^{\pi(N)}(\mathbf{a})$. We now show that $\mathbf{c}$ defined by $c^k : b^k (k \neq \pi(N))$ and $c^{\pi(N)} := B^{\pi(N)}(\mathbf{a})$ is a Pareto improvement of $\mathbf{b}$: since $f^{\pi(j)}(\mathbf{c}) = f^{\pi(j)}(\mathbf{b})$ $(1 \leq j \leq N - 1)$ and $B^{\pi(N)}(\mathbf{a}) \neq b^{\pi(N)}$, we have $f^{\pi(N)}(\mathbf{c}) > f^{\pi(N)}(\mathbf{b})$. Thus $\mathbf{b}$ is not strongly Pareto efficient. $\square$

Proof of Theorem 17   We start with the following two preparations.

- *Preparation 1* Given an FTPG. Then $M_i := (m^1, \ldots, m^{i-1}, m^{i+1}, \ldots, m^N)$ with $m^j = M^j$ if $T_{ij} \neq 0$ and $m^j \in [0, M^j]$ arbitrary if $T_{ij} = 0$, is an optimal punishment for country i. This can be seen as follows. Denote the minimax payoff of country i by $\bar{v}^i$. We have to show that $\bar{v}^i = \sup_{x \in X^i} f^i(x; M_i)$. Because '$\leq$' is evident, it remains to show '$\geq$'. For all $z \in X^i$ and for all $x \in X^i$ we have $f^i(x; z) = \theta^i(x) - \mathcal{D}^i(T_{ii}x + \sum_{l=1, l \neq i}^N T_{il}z^l) \geq \theta^i(x) - \mathcal{D}^i(T_{ii}x + \sum_{l=1, l \neq i}^N T_{il}M^l) = f^i(x; M_i)$. From this it follows that $\sup_{x \in X^i} f^i(x; z) \geq \sup_{x \in X^i} f^i(x; M_i)$. This in turn implies $\inf_{z \in X^i} \sup_{x \in X^i} f^i(x; z) \geq \sup_{x \in X^i} f^i(x; M_i)$, thus $\bar{v}^i \geq \sup_{x \in X^i} f^i(x; M_i)$.
- *Preparation 2* Given an FTPG. Because of $(D_i B^j)(\mathbf{z}) = T_{ji}/T_{jj} \cdot \mathcal{B}^{j\prime}[Q_*^j(\mathbf{z})]$, we obtain from (9.1) for $i \neq j$ and $\mathbf{z} \in X^{\hat{j}}$ that:

$$(D_i B^j)(\mathbf{z}) = - \frac{T_{ji}T_{jj}\mathcal{D}^{j\prime\prime}(T_{jj}B^j(\mathbf{z}) + \sum_{l=1, l \neq j}^N T_{jl}z^l)}{T_{jj}^2 \mathcal{D}^{j\prime\prime}(T_{jj}B^j(\mathbf{z}) + \sum_{l=1, l \neq j}^N T_{jl}z^l) - \theta^{j\prime\prime}(B^j(\mathbf{z}))}.$$

Let

$$\bar{a}^j := \min_{x \in [\underline{K}^j, \bar{K}^j]} \theta^{j\prime\prime}(x),$$

$$\underline{b}^j := \min \mathcal{D}^{j\prime\prime}.$$

Note that $\bar{a}^j < 0$. We have

$$\frac{T_{ji}}{T_{jj}} \frac{T_{jj}^2 \underline{b}^j}{T_{jj}^2 \underline{b}^j - \bar{a}^j} \leq \frac{T_{ji}}{T_{jj}} \frac{1}{1 - \theta^{j11}/(T_{jj}^2 \mathcal{D}^{j11})} \leq 1 \, D_i \, B^j 1. \quad (9.5)$$

Now we shall give the proof of the theorem. Consider an FTPG where country i is insensitive to foreign emissions and where there is another country that is sensitive to emissions from country i. From the above it follows that $M_i := \mathbf{0}$ is an optimal punishment for country i. Because of Theorem 11, $y^i < B^i(\mathbf{y}^i)$. Because B^i is decreasing, we obtain $y^i < B^i(M_i)$ and from this it follows that $f^i(\mathbf{y}) = \theta^i(y^i) - \mathcal{D}^i(T_{ii}y^i) = f^i(y^i; \mathbf{0}) < f^i(B^i(M_i); \mathbf{0}) = f^i(B^i(M_i); M_i) = \bar{v}^i$. Thus $\mathbf{y}$ is not individually rational. (Note that all damage cost functions can be affine.)

Now take $N = 2$, $i = 1$ and an affine $\mathcal{D}^1 := c_1 Q^1 + c_2$. We have $T_{12} = 0$. Since $\bar{K}^1$ is a strictly dominant emission level of country 1 and $n^2 = B^2(n^1) = B^2(\bar{K}^1)$, we have that $\mathbf{n} = (\bar{K}^1, B^2(\bar{K}^1))$ is a unique Nash equilibrium. (9.6) and the first mean value theorem imply:

$$\frac{T_{22}T_{21}\underline{b}^2}{T_{22}^2 \underline{b}^2 - \bar{a}^2} \leq \frac{|B^2(c) - B^2(d)|}{|c - d|} \quad (c, d \in (0, M) \text{ with } c \neq d). \quad (\diamond)$$

The emission vector (y^1, y^2) maximizes the function $f^1 + f^2$; hence y^2 maximizes the function $X^2 \to \mathbb{R}$ defined by $a \mapsto (\theta^1(y^1) - (c_1(T_{11}y^1) + c_2)) + f^2(a; y^1)$ and therefore also the function $a \mapsto f^2(a; y^1)$. Thus $y^2 = B^2(y^1)$. We now prove:

$$\frac{T_{22}T_{21}b_-^2}{T_{22}^2 b_-^2 - \bar{a}_-^2} > 1 \Rightarrow y^1 + y^2 > n^1 + n^2.$$

From the above and $y^1 < \bar{K}^1$ (due to Theorem 11(2)) and $B^2(\bar{K}^1) \leq B^2(y^1)$ (due to Theorem 1) we obtain:

$$y^1 + y^2 > n^1 + n^2 \Leftrightarrow y^1 + B^2(y^1) > \bar{K}^1 + B^2(\bar{K}^1) \Leftrightarrow \bar{K}^1 - y^1$$

$$< B^2(y^1 - B(\bar{K}^1) \Leftrightarrow \frac{|B^2(y^1) - B^2(\bar{K}^1)|}{|y^1 - \bar{K}^1|} > 1.$$

($\diamond$) now implies the desired inequality. $\square$

Proof of Theorem 22 Define the function $S^j : [0, 1] \to \mathbb{R}$ by $S^j(r) := f^j((1 - r)\mathbf{n}) = \theta^j((1 - r)n^j) - \mathcal{D}^j((1 - r)Q^j(\mathbf{n}))$. We have $S^{j\prime}(0) = -n^j\theta^{j\prime}(n^j) + Q^j(\mathbf{n})\mathcal{D}^{j\prime}(Q^j(\mathbf{n}))$. With (9.2) this becomes $S^{j\prime}(0) = (\sum_{l=1, l\neq j}^N T_{jl}n^l)\mathcal{D}^{j\prime}(Q^j(\mathbf{n}))$. Using $\mathbf{n} >> \mathbf{0}$ and $T_{jl} \neq 0$ for some $l \neq j$ we see that $S^{j\prime}(0) > 0$. Because $S^{j\prime} : (0, 1) \to \mathbb{R}$ is continuous, $S^{j\prime}$ is positive on some right neighbourhood of 0 and this S^j is strictly increasing there. Therefore for $r \in (0, 1)$ small enough, $S^j(r) > S^j(0)$, that is, $f^j((1 - r)\mathbf{n}) > f^j(\mathbf{n})$, which implies the desired result. $\square$

Proof of Theorem 24 Because of Theorems 7 and 10, $\mathbf{n}$ and $\mathbf{y}$ are symmetric: $\mathbf{y} = (y, \ldots, y)$ and $\mathbf{n} = (n, \ldots, n)$. Because $\beta_{rk} = \beta_{r1}/\beta_{k1} = T_{rr}/T_{kk}$ it follows for each country r that $f^r(\mathbf{n}) = f^k(\mathbf{n}) + (T_{rr}/T_{kk} - 1)\theta^k(n)$ and $f^r(\mathbf{y}) = f^k(\mathbf{y}) + (T_{rr}/T_{kk} - 1)\theta^k(y)$. Because $\mathbf{y} \neq \mathbf{n}$, we have $\sum_{r=1}^N f^r(\mathbf{n}) < \sum_{r=1}^N f^r(\mathbf{y})$. It follows that $Nf^k(\mathbf{n}) + (\sum_{r=1}^N T_{rr}/T_{kk} - N)\theta^k(n) < Nf^k(\mathbf{y}) + (\sum_{r=1}^N T_{rr}/T_{kk} - N)\theta^k(y)$. Thus $f^k(\mathbf{n}) < f^k(\mathbf{y}) + (\sum_{r=1}^N T_{rr}/NT_{kk} - 1)(\theta^k(y) - \theta^k(n))$. Because $\mathbf{y} \neq \mathbf{n}$, Theorem 20 implies $y < n$ and therefore $\theta^k(y) - \theta^k(n) < 0$. Hence $f^k(\mathbf{n}) < f^k(\mathbf{y})$. If also $T_{jj} \leq T_{kk}$, then, using $\theta^k(n) \geq 0$, $f^j(\mathbf{n}) = f^k(\mathbf{n}) + \theta^k(n)(T_{jj}/T_{kk} - 1) \leq f^k(\mathbf{n}) < f^k(\mathbf{y})$. $\square$

Proof of Theorem 25 We shall prove that under the conditions specified in Theorem 25 not only Assumption 8 holds but even that for all $\mathbf{x} \in X^j$ and for each weight λ with $\lambda^j \neq 0$ there exists a right (left) neighbourhood of 0 (of M^j) where the function $F_\lambda = \sum_{l=1}^N \lambda^l f^l$ as a function of $x^j \in X^j$ is strictly increasing (strictly decreasing).

'The existence of a right neighbourhood': $\theta^{j\prime}(0) = +\infty$ implies that $p'(0) = +\infty$, where p denotes the function F_λ as a function of $x^j \in X^j$. Since the function

p is continuous (at 0) and concave (because F_λ is concave) it follows that $\lim_{x^j\downarrow 0} p'(x^j) = +\infty$. Thus there exists a right neighbourhood of 0 where $p' \in [5, \infty]$. This implies that p is strictly increasing on this neighbourhood.

'The existence of a left neighbourhood': now define for $j \in \mathcal{N}$ and $\mathbf{a}$, $\mathbf{b} \in \mathbf{X}^{\hat{j}}$ the function $G^j_{\mathbf{a};\mathbf{b}} : X^j \to \mathbb{R}$ by $G^j_{\mathbf{a};\mathbf{b}}(x^j) := (g^j_{\mathbf{b}} - g^j_{\mathbf{a}})(x^j)$. We first show that for $\mathbf{a} \geq \mathbf{b}$, the function $G^j_{\mathbf{a};\mathbf{b}}$ is increasing. Define

$$R(\xi, \eta) := \frac{\mathcal{D}^j(T_{jj}\xi + \sum_{l=1,l\neq j}^N T_{jl}a^l) - \mathcal{D}^j(T_{jj}\eta + \sum_{l=1,l\neq j}^N T_{jl}b^l)}{(T_{jj}\xi + \sum_{l=1,l\neq j}^N T_{jl}a^l) - (T_{jj}\eta + \sum_{l=1,l\neq j}^N T_{jl}b^l)}$$

and

$$A := \sum_{l=1,l\neq j}^N T_{jl}(a^l - b^l).$$

If $A = 0$, then $G^j_{\mathbf{a},\mathbf{b}} = 0$ and the result holds. $A < 0$ is impossible. Now suppose that $A > 0$. Then $G^j_{\mathbf{a};\mathbf{b}}(x^j) = R(x^j; x^j)A$. $\mathcal{D}^j$ is convex. Therefore, by the three chords lemma, for x^j, $r^j \in X^j$ with $x^j < r^j$ we have $G^j_{\mathbf{a};\mathbf{b}}(r^j) = R(r^j; r^j)A \geq R(x^j; x^j)A = G^j_{\mathbf{a};\mathbf{b}}(x^j)$.

Now take $R \in (0, M^j)$ such that $(g^j_0)'(x^j) < 0$ ($R \leq x^j \leq M^j$). Now g^j_0 is strictly decreasing on $[R, M^j]$. We have

$$p(x^j) := F_\lambda(x^j; \mathbf{x}^j) = \lambda^j g^j_0(x^j) - \lambda^j G^j_{\mathbf{x}^j;0}(x^j) - \sum_{r=1,r\neq j}^N \lambda^r \mathcal{D}^r(T_{rj}x^j$$
$$+ \sum_{l=1,l\neq j}^N T_{rl}x^l) + \sum_{r=1,r\neq j}^N \lambda^r \theta^r(x^r).$$

From the above it now follows that, on $[R, M^j]$, p is equal to the sum of a strictly decreasing, a decreasing, a decreasing and a constant function and thus that p is strictly decreasing on $[R, M^j]$. $\square$

NOTES

* For the most recent comments on this chapter, readers are invited to consult von Mouche's home page (http://www.math.uu.nl/people/mouche/pub.html).

The authors would like to thank M. Finus for substantive comments on a previous version of the chapter and D. Furth for literature references to simply reducible games.

1. There is a unique Nash equilibrium in Mäler's case, because he assumes linear damage cost functions.

2. It should be observed that Mäler also considers other solution concepts.

3. For (almost) mathematical rigorous analyses in the case of global pollution (that is, the case of a transport matrix with identical coefficients) we refer to Chander and Tulkens (1997) and Welsch (1993). The functional form of the payoff functions in Welsch is the same as ours for this case, except that it deals with unbounded emission spaces. Chander and Tulkens use another setting and mainly provide a cooperative analysis.

4. We suppose that the reader has a basic knowledge of the theory of games in strategic form and of the theory of convex functions.

5. Thus X^j is the action space of player j and f^j its payoff function.
6. Of course, the results obtained below are meant to apply to real-world situations where the standard real-world structure assumptions of games in strategic form, such as rationality and complete information, hold.
7. That is, all rows of the transport matrix are positive multiples of each other.
8. Of course, because of the assumption $T_{jj} > 0$ ($j \in \mathcal{N}$), each country j is sensitive to emissions from country j.
9. See note 20 for this notion.
10. The regularity and smoothness properties are not always necessary for the results presented below to hold, but facilitate the presentation.
11. The abatement level associated with emission level x^j is defined as $R^j - x^j$, where R^j represents the status quo for which one usually takes the Nash equilibrium (assuming that there exists only one Nash equilibrium).
12. This implies that (popular) production functions like $\theta^j(x^j) = \sqrt{x^j}$ are not excluded. Moreover, see Theorem 25.
13. For $\mathbf{a}, \mathbf{b} \in \mathbb{R}^N$ we write $\mathbf{a} \geq \mathbf{b}$ if $a_k \geq b_k (1 \leq k \leq N)$, $\mathbf{a} > \mathbf{b}$ if $\mathbf{a} \geq \mathbf{b}$ but $\mathbf{a} \neq \mathbf{b}$ and $\mathbf{a} \gg \mathbf{b}$ if $a_k > b_k (1 \leq k \leq N)$.
    Given N, a weight is an element λ of $\mathbb{R}^N$ with $\lambda > \mathbf{0}$. A weight λ is called *strict* if $\lambda \gg \mathbf{0}$.
14. Observe that $\pi(T)$ being lower triangular implies that $f^{\pi(i)}$ is independent of the emission levels of the $N - i$ countries $\pi(i + 1), \pi(i + 2), \ldots, \pi(N)$.
15. That is, $f^{\pi(j)}(x^1, \ldots, x^N) = f^j(x^{\pi(1)}, \ldots, x^{\pi(N)})$ for all permutations π of $\mathcal{N}$, $\mathbf{x} \in \mathbf{X}$ and $j \in \mathcal{N}$.
16. That is, α-uniformly distributed transboundary pollution where $\alpha_j = 1$ for each j.
17. That is, the production and damage cost functions differ by a positive multiplicative constant. Note that proportional production functions imply that $X^1 = \ldots = X^N$.
18. Note that, because T is not a diagonal matrix, $s \neq 0$.
19. It is straightforward to check that a strongly symmetric FTPG is symmetric.
20. Given a weight λ, we call an emission vector $\mathbf{x} \in \mathbf{X}$ that maximizes $\sum_{j=1}^{N} \lambda^j f^j$ λ-*weighted full cooperative* and an emission vector that maximizes $\sum_{j=1}^{N} f^j$ *full cooperative*.
21. Given a weight λ we denote its *support*, that is the set $\{ j \in \mathcal{N} \mid \lambda^j \neq 0 \}$, by supp($\lambda$).
22. We define the *social welfare loss* of a game in strategic form as the difference between the maximal total payoff and the maximal total Nash equilibrium payoff where 'total' refers to the sum over all players. (The precise definition involves the 'supremum' of course.)
23. To avoid any misunderstanding: an emission vector $\mathbf{x}$ is called *weakly (strongly) Pareto efficient* if there is no emission vector $\mathbf{z}$ such that $\mathbf{f}(\mathbf{z}) \gg \mathbf{f}(\mathbf{x})$ ($\mathbf{f}(\mathbf{z}) > \mathbf{f}(\mathbf{x})$).
24. In order to get around the distinction between strongly and weakly Pareto efficiency, one might deal with the notion of proper Pareto efficiency introduced by Geoffrion (1968). However, we shall not do this because this notion is not so well known.
25. We call a game in strategic form a 'prisoners' dilemma' if each player possesses a strictly dominant action and if the unique dominant equilibrium is weakly Pareto inefficient.
26. This, for instance, is the case if $\mathbf{z} \geq \mathbf{n}$.
27. See Theorem 7 for the notation.
28. For example, in Theorem 4 the coefficients above the diagonal of $\pi(T)$ are exactly equal to 0. (Such coefficients will never occur in the real world.) Does this theorem also hold if these coefficients are slightly different from 0?
29. Also see Corchón (1996).
30. Moreover our FTPG deals with compact action spaces and the more complicated situation that $\phi^i(\mathbf{x}) = \sum_{j=1}^{N} T_{ij} x^j$ depends on i. However, the theory of simply reducible games can be extended to deal with these issues. But more demanding is an extension to more general ϕ^i.

REFERENCES

Chandler, P. and H. Tulkens (1997), 'The core of an economy with multilateral environmental externalities', *International Journal of Game Theory*, **26**: 379–401.

Corchón, L. (1996), 'Theories of Imperfectly Competitive Markets', vol. 442 of *Lecture Notes in Economics and Mathematical Systems*, Springer.

Cornes, R. and R. Hartley (2000), 'Joint production games and share functions', Prepublication, Department of Economics, Keele University, UK.

Finus, M. (2001), *Game Theory and International Environmental Cooperation*, Cheltenham, UK, and Northampton, MA, USA: Edward Elgar.

Folmer, H. and P. von Mouche (2000), 'Transboundary pollution and international cooperation', in T. Tietenberg and H. Folmer (eds), *The International Yearbook of Environmental and Resource Economics 2000/2001*, Cheltenham, UK, and Northampton, MA, USA: Edward Elgar, pp. 231–66.

Forgó, F., J. Szép and F. Szidarovsky (1999), *Introduction to the Theory of Games*, Vol. 32 of *Nonconvex Optimization and its Applications*, Dordrecht: Kluwer Academic Publishers.

Geoffrion, A. (1968), 'Proper efficiency and the theory of vector maximization', *Journal of Mathematical Analysis and Applications*, **22**: 618–30.

Mäler, K. (1989), 'The acid rain game', in H. Folmer and E. van Ireland (eds), *Valuation Methods and Policy Making in Environmental Economics*, Amsterdam: Elsevier, pp. 231–52.

Mäler, K. and A. de Zeeuw (1998), 'The acid rain differential game', *Environmental and Resource Economics*, **12** (2): 167–84.

Welsch, H. (1993), 'An equilibrium framework for global pollution problems', *Journal of Environmental Economics and Management*, **25**: S64–S79.

10. Bridging ecology and economics: reflections on the role of cost–benefit analysis and the design of interdisciplinary research

Ing-Marie Gren, Clifford S. Russell and Tore Söderqvist

1   INTRODUCTION

Cost–benefit analysis (CBA) can be viewed as a quite particular response to decision makers' need for guidance in their selection among different decision alternatives, including the status quo. Suppose that a successful identification of decision alternatives in a certain matter has been accomplished. Following Mäler (1985), suppose also that it is possible to accept an ethical point of departure which says that it is the end states of actions that should determine what actions should be taken in society, rather than the actions in themselves. It is in this case natural to proceed towards a decision by predicting the consequences of each identified decision alternative and finally to base the choice of alternative on a comparison of these consequences. CBA offers a methodology with an elaborated theoretical basis for accomplishing such a comparison, even when both actions and outcomes are complex and multidimensional.

A CBA considers positive and negative aggregate consequences for human well-being. The implication of the aggregation across people and dimensions is that increases (decreases) in one determinant of well-being can be traded off against decreases (increases) in other determinants. The degree of trade-off necessary to remain at a given well-being is then a way of characterizing the consequences in economic terms either as benefits or costs. Such trade-offs can be measured in terms of any determinant of an individual's well-being,[1] but comparing various benefits and costs is greatly facilitated by applying a common measuring unit. A monetary unit is typically used in a CBA. A weighting procedure reflecting distributional concerns is often suggested but only infrequently carried out.

This brief recapitulation of CBA's bases serves as a reminder that it is a quite special tool for guiding decision making. Its points of departure are sometimes controversial, and it is therefore hardly surprising that CBA is as well. For example, it can be argued that not only the end states of actions matter, but also how the end states are achieved. As another example, CBA's focus on *human* well-being seems to many a non-trivial restriction as soon as a full list of consequences involves significant effects on the environment (see, for example, Elliot 1995 and Des Jardins 1997). Moreover, there might be refusals to make trade-offs between some particularly sensitive determinants of well-being (freedom and anything else, for example). And finally, the utilitarian tradition of aggregating measures of changes in well-being over individuals is far from undisputed, to say the least.

These examples show that CBA cannot serve as a universal tool for guiding decision making, and as we might expect, once we get away from fairly straightforward market or market-like settings, we find CBA honored, if at all, in mainly symbolic ways. This is almost certainly because politicians are not anxious to tie their own hands with an aggregate efficiency criterion for decision making. Developed-country politicians are, however, happy enough to tie the hands of decision makers in developing countries with a CBA requirement, a tendency that adds a whiff of hypocrisy to the enterprise.

Political reasons may thus introduce great obstacles to implementing CBA as a decision-making tool. In order to illustrate this, Section 2 briefly describes experience from governments' use of CBA in Europe and the United States. While such politically rooted obstacles may exist, and while it is true that the foundations of CBA restrict its universality, we still believe CBA can be a powerful tool. One reason is the fact that its basis is so clear, making it possible to have a serious discussion of its strong and weak points and contributing to a transparent type of analysis. In this chapter, however, we shall focus on what we perceive as another major advantage of CBA: its reliance on a listing of decision alternatives and predictions of the consequences of the alternatives contributes to the structuring of a comprehensive basis for decisions that is likely to be useful to decision makers *whether they consider the monetized consequences or not.*

Our illustration of this usefulness will be CBA in the case of complex ecosystems. This is a case characterized by great obstacles to carrying out a full CBA, but where the very effort to accomplish a CBA can be instrumental in gaining an improved basis for decisions. Section 3 uses the case of the Baltic Sea to illustrate what data input is needed for a CBA in the case of a complex ecosystem. To be sure, such a CBA cannot be realized without cooperation between researchers from different disciplines. In Section 4, we give examples of such cooperation efforts. Finally, some implications are discussed in Section 5.

2   GOVERNMENTS' USE OF CBA: A BRIEF DESCRIPTION OF US AND EUROPEAN EXPERIENCE

The requirement that CBA be done as a key part of the justification of anything at all arrived on the US scene surprisingly long ago; 1936, in fact, in that year's Flood Control Act, in connection with flood control projects. The act required that the benefits, 'to whomsoever they might accrue', exceed the costs for each project, such as dikes, dams, or stream straightening. Through a decades-long process of extension and refinement, the use of CBA came to be required for all water projects, not just flood control, so that the benefits being estimated came to include those arriving via agriculture product (because of irrigation), power supply (from hydro-power installations), navigation (from systems of locks and dams), and even water-based recreation in addition to flood damages avoided. Because recreation on publicly created reservoirs (and, for that matter, on the streams dammed to make them) is not priced, taking these benefits into account required the exercise of considerable ingenuity and led to the invention and refinement of the 'travel cost method', now a staple of the so-called 'indirect' benefit estimation methods. More generally, a number of outstanding economists, including Otto Eckstein, Harold Hotelling and John Krutilla, contributed to the establishment of a firm conceptual base for the application of CBA. (An interesting early collection of relevant papers may be found in Kneese and Smith (1966).)

This base notwithstanding, when the wave of environmental concern and resulting action washed over the US in the late 1960s and through the 1970s, there was hardly any visible enthusiasm for the application of these techniques to the development of specific regulations to govern the disposal of air, water or solid (land) 'residuals'. Thus, as is painfully well known to economists, the Clean Air Act primary ambient air quality standards are supposed to reflect what is necessary to protect the health of the most vulnerable populations, with not even cost, let alone monetized benefits, considered. The Clean Water Act discharge standards, on the other hand, are in the first instance based on definitions of technological capability, with some consideration of costs implied by phrases in those definitions such as 'economically achievable'. The resulting standard may be adjusted if the technology-based discharge standards are not tough enough to result in the meeting of ambient quality standards. Those in turn were chosen by states, with federal guidance, for the purpose of protecting certain specific uses such as water supply and recreation but with neither costs nor monetized benefits having been considered. More broadly, only a few of the set of environmental acts on the books permit 'balancing' of costs and benefits.

Why this should be so – why well-established methods from a closely related policy field should have been not just ignored, but in some cases actually ruled out explicitly – must to some extent be a matter for speculation and would, in any case, take this chapter too far afield. But as a set of facts, this evidence of antipathy to environmental CBA sets the stage for the Reagan Executive Order (EO) 12–291 of 1981, which established a requirement that CBA be done for all 'major' (defined in money terms) federal actions (regulations, projects and so on) whether or not the result could be used in the ultimate decision. This EO has been reissued in only modestly changed form by each President since, including Bill Clinton, and it is likely to continue under the Bush Administration. It is just as likely that Congress is going to leave the statutes alone, so that there will continue to be a potential mismatch between analysis and actions. This mismatch reflects the deep ambivalence with which politicians regard aggregate efficiency criteria.

In Europe, at least in the mid-1990s according to Navrud and Pruckner (1997, pp. 16–17): 'To our knowledge, there is no legal requirement for doing CBA of projects in any European country'. At the regulatory level these authors asserts that 'Norway seems to be the only European country where CBAs of environmental regulations are now conducted on a regular basis'. Further, these Norwegian estimates have 'either not been used at all when the final decision was made (as in the case with car emission regulations; see Navrud 1991), or they have been used mainly to confirm the environmental goal already set by the environmental authorities (as in the case with the North Sea [pollution reduction] plan ... see Magnussen 1995)'. In fact, the UK seems to be the only European country in which CBA has gained acceptance in practice as a major decision-major tool (Bonnieux and Rainelli 1999).

This experience is despite a long and distinguished set of contributions by European economists to CBA generally and environmental valuation specifically (not least the person honored by this Festschrift). It is also despite quite a few examples of related evaluations for real decisions, such as the fourth London airport study in the UK, and environmental damage estimates made in Germany and the Netherlands as part of a process of justifying policy actions (Navrud and Pruckner 1997).[2] And finally, it is despite language in the European Commission document, *Towards Sustainability* (European Community 1993), with promises that the Commission will analyse 'potential costs and benefits of action and non-action in developing specific formal proposals' at that pan-European level (p. 142).

It thus appears that despite some superficial dissimilarities, Europe and the US are, in fact, behaving in quite similar ways. To put it bluntly, they are not letting CBA stand in the way of, or force, political decisions. Indeed, there seems to be only one set of countries that are actually required to do environmental cost–benefit analysis – the poorer ones, when they apply for environmentally related loans from the multinational lending agencies such as the World Bank (IDB). (For example, guidelines for such analyses for water quality improvement projects are in press at the IDB (Russell et al. 2001a)). These requirements, imposed by the donor countries, would seem to be classic cases of do as we say, not as we do.

3   CBA IN THE CASE OF COMPLEX ECOSYSTEMS: THE CASE OF THE BALTIC SEA

The Baltic Sea and its drainage basin constitute a complex ecological–economic system with interconnections among land-based and sea-based ecosystems and the human economic system. The drainage basin covers about 1.7 million km^2, which is more than four times the surface area of the sea (Sweitzer et al. 1996). Fourteen different countries are fully or partially situated within the drainage basin, and the population in the basin amounts to about 85 million people (ibid). Not surprisingly, the marine environment of the Baltic Sea has been heavily influenced by polluting substances from land-based human activities. Nutrients cause eutrophication – which will be the focus in this chapter – and toxic substances and heavy metals cause toxification of marine organisms. These phenomena are exacerbated by a slow turnover of the total water mass in the sea (10–30 years) (Folke et al. 1991). The multination setting introduces coordination problems in taking actions against the pollutant loads.

The eutrophication and toxification of the Baltic Sea gained attention early in the period of heightened environmental awareness in the closing decades of the twentieth century. The Convention on the Protection of the Marine Environment of the Baltic Sea Area (the Helsinki Convention) was signed in 1974, and aimed at regulating damaging activities carried out around the sea. The associated administrative body HELCOM was responsible for the monitoring of different pollutants, including nitrogen and phosphorus which are regarded as being the main causes of the damages from eutrophication.

Although many environmental targets on the political agenda are expressed as required changes in pollutant emissions or loads to the recipient, the ultimate aim of the policies – certainly policies for the Baltic – is to achieve biological improvements, such as improved functioning of marine ecosystems. This means that the costs of meeting a target should relate costs of emission reductions to associated biological changes, and in the end to the consequences for human well-being, that is, the benefits caused by the emission reductions. In general, conclusions on optimal management hinge crucially on knowledge of properties of the natural systems, in particular ecosystem dynamics such as multiple equilibria and flips from different steady states (Mäler 2000).

In the case of the Baltic Sea recovery, we focus on the option to carry out a CBA and the understanding that such an analysis would require. To be considered here are at least four different systems and their interactions: (i) economic agents' options and costs to reduce nutrient emissions; (ii) the natural systems involved in soil and water nutrient transport in the catchment area of the sea; (iii) the marine nutrient transport mechanisms and resulting concentrations of nutrients; and (iv) the marine ecosystems that respond to the concentrations in ways that have consequences for human well-being. The following subsections expound on the characteristics of these systems.

3.1 Nutrient Abatement Costs, Transport and Transformation of Nutrients in the Catchment

The understanding of the first system, agents' behavior with regard to nutrient abatement, requires knowledge of their adjustment possibilities to achieve different levels of nutrient abatement. In the Baltic Sea we have at least two different types of agents: firms and households. The firms are either private, such as farms, or owned by the public, such as sewage treatment plants. These firms operate under different market conditions, and we would therefore expect them to behave somewhat differently when faced with nutrient abatement requirements. A private firm has to consider reactions in its markets by customers and other firms; and the publicly-owned firm, which covers its costs by households' and firms' water charges, will need to take into account the existence of, for example, the political will to raise water charges. Common to both types of producers is that abatement costs are determined by production technology and prices of other inputs. We thus need to understand firm behavior, production technology, and prices of relevant outputs and inputs.

Once information is obtained on the nutrient abatement costs of different firm types, we need to relate associated reductions in nutrient emissions from the firms to the impacts on the coast of the Baltic Sea. In principle, the transport of nutrients within a land area, or an ecosystem, to the coast may take place along any one or combination of the following pathways: (a) ground-water flow discharging into the catchment stream network that discharges into the coastal water; (b) direct ground-water flow into the coastal water; (c) overland water flow to streams that discharge into the coastal water; and (d) air transport directly to the water mass of the sea and indirectly through deposition in the drainage basin.

Currently, there is annual information on airborne deposition of nitrogen oxides and ammonium on the Baltic Sea and on the drainage basin (Sandnes 1993). The other transport pathways are more difficult or even impossible to quantify deterministically. One important reason for this difficulty is the large natural variability, both in temporal weather patterns driving the flow, and in spatial flow patterns through the different subsurface (soil, aquifers) and surface (overland flow, streams) water systems. To quantify the nitrogen transport from land to coast, both the temporal weather fluctuations and the spatial flow patterns have to be predicted, and this quantification process is subject to uncertainty (see, for example, Destouni 1992, 1993). Obviously then, for all emission sources not discharging directly into the sea, this implies the need to understand the functioning of different types of land and ecosystems with respect to their functioning in the transformation and transport of nutrients. Considering the size of the extensive drainage basin, and number of countries included in it, this is quite a challenging task in practice.

3.2   Effects in Marine Ecosystems

Once the pollutant transport processes to the sea have been successfully modeled, it is necessary to understand the relation between surviving pollutant inputs and ecological functioning in the system being the target for management. One approach would be to combine the loads of nutrients in a differential equation system for predicting such biological impacts as algal growth and fish biomass. We are today, however, far from a complete empirical understanding of the relations between nutrient loads and ecological functioning in the different basins of most water ecosystems. The complexity of the eutrophication phenomenon implies that these relations to a large extent are known only in qualitative terms, if that. A listing of the main eutrophication effects would be the following (Bernes 1988):

1.   more turbid water;
2.   more filamentous algae;
3.   less bladder-wrack and eel-grass;
4.   more fish and other animals above the halocline due to increased plankton production;
5.   fewer fish and other animals below the halocline due to oxygen deficiency situations;
6.   fewer regions available for successful cod reproduction; and
7.   increased frequency of algal/cyanobacteria blooms.

The impact of changes in nutrients is determined by which nutrient, nitrogen or phosphorus, is the limiting one. Sunlight, carbon dioxide and various nutrients, primarily nitrogen (N) and phosphorus (P), are needed for algae and other plants to grow and build up organic matter. The nutrients are needed in certain proportions – for most aquatic organisms 16 nitrogen atoms are used for each atom of phosphorus. This ratio of 16:1 between N and P, the so-called Redfield ratio, is typically found both in organisms and in concentration of inorganic nutrients in most oceans. The ambient ratio is, however, often far from 16:1 in many coastal marine regions.

Adjustments in the sea to reach and maintain the Redfield ratio occur through two biological processes that affect the inorganic nitrogen concentrations in opposite directions: *nitrogen fixation* and *denitrification*. In seas and lakes, nitrogen fixation takes place by the action of cyanobacteria which have the ability to convert inert nitrogen gas (N_2) into useful inorganic nutrients (ammonia, NH_4). Such nitrogen fixation is a highly energy-demanding process being advantageous for these bacteria to deploy only in environments with excess phosphorus and little inorganic nitrogen available. However, nitrogen fixation may not be sufficient to bring the N/P ratio to a balanced 16:1 ratio in a water system. Although there is a relatively large nitrogen input – 40:1 in the case of the Baltic Proper – the N/P ratio may be much lower in the sea.

Why is so much nitrogen lost, reducing the ratio from an input of 40:1 to concentration ratios of 4:1 or even less and creating a nitrogen-limited system with a large excess of phosphorus? This is due to the other important microbial process called denitrification. When organic matter is decomposed, oxygen is utilized by the bacteria and inorganic nutrients, that is, phosphorus and ammonia, are released. Ammonia is further converted (oxidized) to nitrate (NO_3) if oxygen is available. If all oxygen is consumed, the decomposition of organic matter continues, but now the bacteria use nitrate instead of oxygen. By this denitrification process, useful inorganic nitrogen is converted to atmospheric gas. In the case of the Baltic Sea, more than 80 per cent of the annual nitrogen inputs are lost via denitrification. Denitrification occurs primarily in the sediments and the shallow Baltic offers ideal conditions for this process.

It is difficult to estimate the ecological consequences of the low N/P ratio because empirical knowledge of 'the state of the sea' at different concentrations of nutrients is patchy. We would, however, expect to find less primary production of organic matter and thus reduced turbidity and less frequent periods of oxygen deficiency than if the ratio were the ideal 16:1. It is also likely that the relatively high P level encourages cyano-bacterial blooms during late summer, leading to accumulations of sometimes toxic algae on the surface of the Baltic Proper.

3.3   Consequences for Human Well-being

The first three eutrophication effects listed in the previous subsection are easily perceived by people and are likely to affect the quality of seaside recreation and aesthetics. Effects 4–6 concern commercial and recreational fishing. However, the seventh effect has generally attracted more attention than the other ones: summer algal blooms, which possibly have become more intensive in the last decades. To be sure, these 'killer algae that invade the coasts' (as they have been referred to in some media) affect recreational quality and aesthetics. Moreover, some of them are poisonous and thus harmful to marine organisms such as fish, and potentially also to dogs, cows and other animals which happen to drink seawater.

Given this list of main eutrophication effects, a full CBA would require (i) an estimation of the benefits of a reduction of these effects *and* (ii) models of how each of these effects is linked to nutrient concentrations and loads, so that the estimated benefits in fact can be compared to the costs of reducing the nutrient loads to the sea. It is of course possible to study the benefits of reduced eutrophication effects without knowledge of the linkage to nutrient concentration and loads, but there is a great risk that such benefit studies will be carried out in a policy vacuum. Results from benefit studies are simply not useful if it turns out to be impossible to link them to any realistic policy alternative.

There are various approaches available for monetizing the benefits of reduced eutrophication effects. To the extent that a reduced eutrophication affects the production of tradable goods and services, market data can be used for valuing these effects. One example is the consequences for commercial fisheries of a reduced eutrophication. Reduced eutrophication effects might also be an input in household production, and the household production function approach would then be useful for valuation (see, for example, Mäler 1985; Mäler et al. 1994; and Dasgupta and Mäler 1995). For example, recreational trips can be viewed as a commodity produced by households with environmental quality as one of several inputs. The recreational value of quality changes can be studied within the household production function framework by using the travel cost method, relying on the assumption that recreational trips and environmental quality are characterized by weak complementarity (Mäler 1971, 1974). What is needed in order to make this operational is a water quality variable that has a precise relationship both to the recreational quality people experience and to the nutrient concentration. Contingent valuation approaches can also be applied. Valuation scenarios in contingent valuation experiments can to some extent be made precise by the use of water quality variables such as sight depth. On the other hand, there are other eutrophication effects that can only be described in qualitative terms in a valuation scenario. The respondents' answers are likely to reflect a mix of benefits, of which only some are possible to link back to nutrient concentrations and loads in any precise way.

4   INTERDISCIPLINARY RESEARCH EFFORTS

A conclusion that follows from the preceding section is that close cooperation between researchers from different disciplines is needed for realizing CBA efforts in the case of complex ecosystems. Such cooperation is often referred to as 'interdisciplinary', 'transdisciplinary' or 'multidisciplinary' research. The labels vary, and they may reflect different degrees of ambition to communicate, understand and discuss the points of departure of participating disciplines, and to arrive at joint agreements on the focus of the research efforts. For simplicity, we disregard these differences and use the label 'interdisciplinary' below for all research that involves close cooperation between different disciplines. We have been at least tangentially involved in several rather large-scale interdisciplinary environmental research projects, and some of these efforts will now be reviewed. We begin with two projects directly related to the eutrophication of the Baltic Sea, and then move on to two in the US and one, nominally from Europe, which was global in its aspirations.

4.1 The Baltic Drainage Basin Project (BDBP)

In spite of the difficulties noted in Section 3, a few attempts have been made to determine costs and benefits of actions against the eutrophication of the Baltic Sea (Gren et al. 1997a; Turner et al. 1999; Gren et al. 2000a). The BDBP was launched in 1993 as an international and interdisciplinary research project, which adopted a working procedure that to a considerable extent can be illustrated by Figure 10.1. In order to be able to compare benefit and costs,

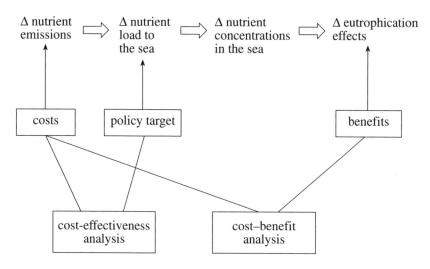

Note: Δ = change in.

Figure 10.1   Linking of costs and benefits in the case of reduced eutrophication effects in the Baltic Sea

the figure suggests the need for detailed knowledge of how measures reducing nutrient emissions in the end influence eutrophication effects. Policy targets about the Baltic Sea have typically concerned the nutrient load to the sea, but also for a cost-effectiveness analysis given such policy targets, there is a need for modeling how measures taken inland result in changed nutrient loads to the sea.

Despite the fact that monitoring of the Baltic Sea was initiated in the 1970s, the data collected was found to be largely irrelevant to the kind of modeling efforts suggested by Figure 10.1. Nutrient concentration ratios measured over so many years had never been related to different nutrient-emitting human activities such as agriculture, or combustion sources such as transportation. Indeed, at the start of the project, there was almost complete ignorance on this issue. The only information available was from experiments on nutrients leaching from arable land at a few scattered locations in Sweden (Elofsson 1997). The role of the landscape for the transport of nutrients from the emission or leaching locations had not been quantified. Although wetlands' capacity as sinks for nitrogen had been investigated in Sweden (Jansson 1994), this important ecosystem service's dependence on the composition of the surrounding landscape was not yet sufficiently well understood. Further, only qualitative scientific knowledge existed on the ecological damages from eutrophication at large-scale levels such as the Baltic Sea. What had been created, and was further developed within the project, was a dynamic model simulating the relation between nutrient loads to the sea and nutrient concentration ratios (Wulff and Niemi 1992).

Given this situation, the project team decided to take a two-step approach with respect to cost-effectiveness. First, minimum costs were calculated for different targets in the reductions of nutrient loads to the coastal waters of the Baltic Sea. In the second step, impacts on steady-state nutrient concentration ratios were simulated for the same targets in nutrient loads as in the cost calculations. It was thus possible to identify an operational relation between minimum costs of nutrient reductions and nutrient concentration ratios.

The project team's estimation of minimum costs of reducing nitrogen and phosphorus discharges to the coastal waters of the Baltic Sea began with relatively accurate data on costs of different nutrient abatement measures (Gren et al. 1997b). On the other hand, they relied on highly simplified data on nutrient leaching in the different drainage basins of the sea. In total, costs and effects of 14 different abatement measures in the nine countries surrounding the Baltic Sea were calculated. Together with data describing airborne transport of nitrogen oxides and ammonium between the countries, minimum costs of different nutrient reductions were estimated. Some interesting results were the following: (i) costs increase rapidly for nitrogen reductions corresponding to more than 40 percent of the load in 1991, and may amount to about SEK

30 billion per year for 50–60 percent reduction levels; (ii) the costs for nitrogen reductions are higher than corresponding phosphorus reductions as measured in percentage decreases; and (iii) the cost estimates are highly sensitive to changes in assumptions on nutrient leaching and retention in the drainage basins.

In order to predict the impact of reducing nutrient discharges to the coastal zones in one sub-basin on nutrient availability in other sub-basins, an existing empirical nutrient budget model of the Baltic Proper was expanded to cover all three sub-basins: Bothnian Bay, the Bothnian Sea and the Baltic Proper. The model consists of the three coupled basins with advective water and nutrient transports between them and with the Kattegat. Empirical relationships among loads, nutrient concentrations and advective transport, based on extensive regional data sets from the last decades, were used to calculate relationships between concentrations and internal nutrient sink terms. The model simulations, although based on very simplistic models and built on empirical relationships and basic physical and biogeochemical properties, show very clearly the basic features and interactions of hydrodynamics and biogeochemistry of nitrogen and phosphorus in the Baltic Sea region. The overall model clearly demonstrates that reduction of inputs to the Baltic Proper is most efficient in reducing concentrations in all the basins. A strategy in which all inputs are reduced to the same degree is not optimal, since the situations in the two northern basins are not critical in terms of eutrophication, with only small amounts exported southwards. From a large-scale perspective, it is also demonstrated that it will take several decades of reduced inputs before the nutrient concentrations return to a level consistent with the situation in the Baltic Sea before eutrophication effects were evident, particularly for phosphorus.

These effects to identify cost-effective combinations of measures against the eutrophication were complemented by estimates of the benefits of reduced eutrophication. Considering the lack of knowledge described above, it should hardly come as a surprise that the rough CBAs that were carried out for the case of actions against the eutrophication of the Baltic Sea rely on a number of assumptions and simplifications (Gren et al. 1997a; Turner et al. 1999). On the benefit side, these CBAs have made use of results of contingent valuation studies that have employed quite vague and qualitative valuation scenarios because of the lack of well-established quantitative links. On the other hand, the studies have reflected the international structure of the project in the sense that large-scale parallel studies were carried out in two Baltic Sea countries (Poland and Sweden). The results of the Polish study were assumed to be representative of the other formerly planned economies around the Baltic Sea; and the results of the Swedish study were assumed to be representative of the established market economies around the sea. The results indicated total benefits that would cover the costs of a 50 percent reduction of the total nutrient load to the sea, given that this reduction is accomplished in a cost-effective way (Gren et al. 1997a).

Moreover, recreational benefits were studied by an application of the travel cost method (Sandström 1996), which was built on a quantification of the link between nutrient concentrations and sight depth. Since it was found that sight depth was a significant determinant for seaside recreation, the recreational benefits from an increased sight depth could be translated to benefits of a reduced nutrient concentration. Recreational benefits are, however, only one of several benefits from reduced eutrophication. A CBA would, of course, have been very informative if the total costs did not exceed such a subset of total benefits, but this did not turn out to be the case.

Given the vagueness, assumptions and simplifications involved, it may be better to view the CBA exercises carried out in the BDBP as 'simulations' (compare Turner et al. 1999). These problems notwithstanding, rough attempts to estimate and compare costs and benefits can also serve as useful points of departure for refinements and policy discussions, as long as the procedure that underlies the 'CBA simulations' is satisfactorily documented and reported.

One experience from the BDBP was the challenging task of balancing policy relevance, that is comparing the costs and benefits of a 50 percent reduction, with the desire to understand more of the single systems, such as marine transports of nutrients. One could regard the BDBP as relatively successful, since it succeeded in finding ways of comparing the different complex systems in order to arrive at a CBA measure. However, this was not a painless achievement, but was associated with hours, days and weeks of discussions among the involved researchers. In principle, these discussions were attributed to the tensions between the policy-oriented researchers, and those whose emphasis was on 'understanding more of each system'. If either of the two forces exercises too much power, the program may get caught in what we shall refer to as the 'interdisciplinary trap'. This means that when the policy-oriented force outweighs the other one, the desire for solving policy problems may lead researchers to compromise too much with scientific relevance – for example, when economists carry out ecological analysis about which they have no training, or vice versa. On the other hand, too much reliance on scientific relevance may result in deep, but policy-irrelevant, understanding of parts of single systems. An example of the latter is the 20 years of monitoring of nutrient concentration ratios in the Baltic Sea, which had little relevance for the policy-relevant CBA discussed above.

The BDBP avoided this trap because of the common interest of all involved researchers to balance the two forces through (i) agreeing on the overall purpose of estimating costs and benefits at the large drainage basin scale, and

(ii) focusing on links between the systems, that is, the nutrient flow paths from emission sources into the Baltic Sea. These two factors helped to avoid too many fruitless discussions on the interpretation of various concepts, such as societal value (see also the discussion in Section 4.3.1 below).

4.2 A Study within the Sustainable Coastal Zone Management Research Program (SUCOZOMA)

As a development of the insights obtained from the BDBP, a research project was begun in 1996 on a relatively well-investigated estuary, the Himmer Bay, South-west of Stockholm, partly as a study within SUCOZOMA. This area had been studied for about 20 years in order to identify the nutrient-limiting biological production in the estuary. Experiments were possible due to the dominance of a single point source, the Himmer Bay sewage treatment plant, where nutrient loads could be changed and associated biological impacts could be monitored. According to the results, the estuary is nitrogen limited (Elmgren and Larsson 1997). The research group, which included economists, hydrologists, mathematicians, oceanographers and marine biologists, then asked the question: how could the estuary and its catchment area be managed in an efficient way?

An important lesson from the BDBP was the impact of changes in drainage basin nitrogen leaching on costs of alternative nitrogen reductions. The project team now decided to focus on the role of uncertainty about the costs and associated policy instruments. Another important task was to identify the impact of coastal zone nitrogen sinks for cost-effective reductions in nitrogen to the marine waters of the Baltic Sea. Results indicate that the uncertainty and its measurement (normal versus lognormal probability distributions of coastal zone deposition from a given nitrogen emission in the drainage basin) have significant impacts on minimum costs of different nitrogen reduction targets and associated charges or permit market designs. It was also shown that the recognition of coastal zones as nitrogen sinks may reduce costs of achieving nitrogen reductions to the marine waters considerably (Gren et al. 2000b, 2000c).

The project also includes more refined efforts at travel cost and contingent valuation approaches than were carried out in the BDBP. The central water quality indicator chosen for both approaches is sight depth. This means that the valuation scenarios used in the contingent valuation studies are now less vague in the sense that water quality improvements caused by measures against nutrient emissions are described in terms of sight depth increases. Moreover, they take into account explicitly the fact that such results cannot be accomplished with certainty, that is, the issue of uncertainty is introduced also in the benefit estimation. In these studies, the Himmer Bay is seen as a part of one of the most important recreational areas along the Swedish Baltic Sea coast, the Stockholm archipelago. The studies make use of more refined relationships between nutrient concentrations and sight depth than those used by Sandström (1996). These relationships make possible the estimation of the benefits of reduced nutrient concentrations in these areas (Söderqvist and Scharin 2000). To subsequently link nutrient concentrations to nutrient loads requires models of water exchange in coastal areas. Such models exist for some smaller coastal areas, such as the Himmer Bay (Engqvist 1997), and efforts are at present being made to develop models for more extensive areas such as the entire Stockholm archipelago (A. Engqvist, Stockholm University, personal communication, 2000).

4.3   Some Other Efforts at Interdisciplinary Work on Complex Ecological/Economics Issues

If the Baltic studies just described illustrate what can be accomplished by interdisciplinary teams, able to collaborate for long periods, with fairly stable funding, experience with analogous efforts in the US suggests some of the modes of failure, as will be evident from the next two subsections.

Relating Environmental Monitoring and Assessment Program (EMAP) indicators to social values

This project originated in a US Environmental Protection Agency (EPA) realization that the language of ecologists is not the language of the public or of public policy. If the public were going to buy into large-scale, long-term programs of 'environmental monitoring and assessment', the potential value had to be made explicit. The call for proposals to help with this challenge came in the summer of 1993, and one of the authors of this chapter (Russell) helped to organize a response involving, originally, three ecologists at Oak Ridge National Laboratories (ORNL). The idea behind the proposal, briefly stated, was to create a translation of technical forest indicator language into visual representations of alternative forests; to see if laypeople could discern and respond to differences in these forests as a way of confirming their usefulness; and thus to present the EPA with a model for 'translation' that could be exported to other ecosystem settings. An extremely ambitious version of the goal motivating the work might be read as the creation of something that could have been put out as an annual 'guide to forest areas', so that potential users could better decide where to go to hike or photograph or even hunt.

In the end, funds were withdrawn from the project by the EPA at, roughly, its mid-point, as part of the massive change in priorities that came with a change in the leadership of the research section of the agency. EMAP itself was shut down for a time at least; and to our knowledge the translation attempt was never resumed.

While the project had nothing explicitly to do with CBA, some of its problems are relevant here – and it led directly into a second project that explored lay respondents' ability to handle vector descriptions of forests.[3] The biggest and most obviously relevant internal problems were, first, a version of the one facing, in our experience, every such ecological/economic collaboration: differences in views of the basis for social prescriptions – science versus individual preferences; and, second, language itself. The latter, especially an endless debate about what 'societal values' meant, was a block to progress from the beginning. In the end, the approach taken was to adapt the scale of values, attributable to Maslow (1970), which organizes wants into a list, ranging from the most fundamental, such as security, shelter and food, to what we might call the most sophisticated, such as aesthetics. The idea was to try to map the esoterica of ecological measurements onto this scale.

The problem of the basis for prescription was never 'solved', but was always a source of tension, with the ecologists mistrustful of the notion that human preferences should be determining. Despite this, they entered energetically into a process of holding focus groups designed to identify what lay respondents 'valued' in their forest experiences. But the notion of a summary measure of 'value' called 'willingness to pay' for differences between described forests, was anathema and never failed to stir up dispute about what relating indicators to values was all about anyway.

Marine Ecosystem Analysis (MESA)

The MESA program was an ambitious effort of the US National Oceanic and Atmospheric Agency (NOAA) initially aimed at understanding several different marine ecosystems, with the original goals including 'policy relevance'. Indeed, MESA might be seen as an early EMAP, with relevance supposed to have been built in from the beginning. The first ecosystem chosen was the New York Bight, the shallow indentation of the Atlantic with its apex at the entrance to New York Harbor, its northern side defined by the south shore of Long Island, and its western edge by the New Jersey shore down to the entrance to Delaware Bay. Its seaward limit was for most purposes taken to be the edge of the continental shelf.

This area has been subject to massive abuse over the last hundred years or more. Pollution from the Hudson and other industrial rivers has been supplemented by the dumping of garbage, sewage sludge and construction debris from barges and the deposition of air pollutants from industrial and powerplant sources to the West, especially in New Jersey and Pennsylvania. At the time the program got underway (in the 1970s), the Bight's water quality was a matter of intense public concern because in the summers the popular Long

Island and New Jersey beaches were being 'polluted' by medical waste such as syringes that presumably had been washed back from dump sites miles at sea. There were also fecal coliform scares and concern that the polluted fresh-water and sewage sludge could be combining to create a 'dead zone' offshore in which normal benthic populations were being wiped out with ill-understood, but presumably undesirable, repercussions further up the water column.

The goals of MESA, while centered on understanding the ecosystem, prominently included developing the ability to explain these phenomena, trace them to specific causes, and suggest practical ways of correcting them. To these multiple ends, the advisory group formed by NOAA included prominent freshwater quality modelers and environmental economists whose task included keeping the NOAA project managers and associated academics focused on the goals.

As the program developed over time, however, the internal scientific dynamics drove it more and more strongly. By this we mean that each new finding created new, and seemingly more esoteric, questions, which required new, more expensive, research techniques. It became less and less important to justify specific sub-enterprises in terms of the original policy problems; instead, a 'full' understanding of the ecosystem became the goal. We might call this the 'scientific capture' of an ostensibly interdisciplinary enterprise. Unlike the Baltic Drainage Basin project, the program was thus caught in the interdisciplinary trap, where the 'understanding more of the system' force was too strong so the program lost sight of the policy relevance.

The International Institute for Applied Systems Analysis
As its name implies, the International Institute for Applied Systems Analysis (IIASA) in Laxenburg, Austria, was organized to approach policy problems defined around mathematical representations of those problems and their possible solutions. This seems to us a potentially very promising way of bridging the disciplinary gaps by forcing problem definition into a common 'language' from the beginning. In the IIASA's case such commonality was always going to be especially important because it was explicitly set up and sited outside Vienna to provide a place in which scholars from East and West could collaborate.

According to Allen Kneese, who was heavily involved as a representative, first of the US National Academy of Sciences, and later of its successor sponsor, the American Academy of Sciences, however, there was from the beginning a mismatch between Western and Eastern views about the balance between the mathematics and the substance. The Soviet scholars were more interested in the mathematics and less in the substance of the problems to be addressed than were their Western counterparts. Add to this that enthusiasm for systems analytic methods of policy problems was waning in the West, certainly in the US, at the time when the IIASA was being set up and you have the setting for different obstacles to collaboration than those stressed elsewhere in this chapter (Kneese 1999). You might call this the mathematical capture of an interdisciplinary effort.

The stresses inherent in such work were exacerbated by the funding problems that were created in the mid-1980s, when the Reagan administration explicitly made the IIASA a pawn in the Cold War chess match, and stopped contributing. The institute was kept alive by the efforts of concerned scholars who solicited funding but, from anecdotal reports, the freedom to pursue ambitious projects was seriously reduced. Realistically, however, it would probably be true in any setting that tensions would surface between the keepers of the mathematics flame and those who stressed realistic substance. Although the IIASA is an institute, this balancing is very similar to that between the two forces of policy relevance and scientific relevance discussed in the context of the Baltic Drainage Basin project. One of the IIASA's endeavors that seems to have achieved this balance is the Regional Air Pollution Information and Simulation Model (RAINS). The development of this integrated assessment tool began in 1983. RAINS has been instrumental in actual international negotiations on restrictions of transboundary air pollution (IIASA 2000), and has also served as a tool in scientific analyses of Baltic Sea nutrient management and other international environmental issues (see, for example, Mäler 1989, 1990).

5   DISCUSSION

This chapter, superficial appearances to the contrary notwithstanding, is not meant as a primer on CBA or on the ecology of the Baltic. Rather we have used what seem to us quite useful Baltic Sea studies to illustrate two complementary observations about the utility of CBA as a basis for collaboration between ecologists and economists. The first observation is that in the right circumstances, the CBA framework can serve as a foundation for such collaboration *despite* the suspicion with which some ecologists approach it and *despite* the deep ambivalence that regulators and politicians have about it as a tool for them. The second observation is that in environmental settings of any but the simplest sort, such collaboration is *essential* to successful CBA – indeed, to successfully informing the policy process.

One might well agree with these observations on principle and still think them quite irrelevant to the practical world of environmental policy and research. Thus, even if a group succeeded in carrying out a full CBA in the case of complex ecosystems, decision makers would not necessarily use this information. As was emphasized in Section 2, the case of the US shows that even legal requirements for CBAs to be carried out do not guarantee that the information obtained will be used. While CBA of projects and policies seems to a large extent independent of the decision process in the short run, however, we believe these CBA exercises can be useful in building a public record that has the potential of allowing broader decisions to be made in the longer run. An example that, in effect, began operating even before environmental concerns became important, was the CBA for dams on the great rivers of the US West. These were repeatedly shown to be inefficient in the CBA sense even without taking account of their pernicious environmental effects, but it was not until the 1980s, 50 years after the great wave of dam building really got started, that the lesson was taken seriously enough that the great pork barrel was shut down.

Further, at the level of the researchers themselves, while to promise inter-disciplinary research is often likely to increase the probability of success in fund-raising efforts, actually doing it can prove costly for the study partici-pants. The dominating career judgment mechanisms in the academic world provide strong incentives to stick to single-discipline research. To establish and pursue cooperation requires communication efforts that take time from the kind of work that will have a more immediate payoff in terms of publication in the single-disciplinary journals that departments 'count' in promotion and tenure decisions. It is thus not very surprising to find that cooperation is some-times used as a strategic façade in the fund-raising stage, with the research groups involved running their own races, once funds are granted.

It may be that this is changing, at least to the extent that a new discipline, 'ecological economics', is becoming more widely recognized. This discipline is characterized by a sensitivity to concerns and techniques of both sides of the eco/eco boundary. Academic positions are now being advertised using this disciplinary label; likewise, there are graduate programs devoted to the production of PhDs. But, as our discussion above has illustrated, the problems of knowledge gaps on the road to environmental CBA involve the ecology as often as the economics. These gaps will probably have to be filled by ecolo-gists – specialists in the modeling of such systems as the eutrophying Baltic (or the Columbia/Snake River salmon runs, or rainforest adjustment to a vari-ety of stressors, or whatever is key to the next policy challenge). Sensitivity, in short, may not be enough; and as long as that is the case, the problem of making successful interdisciplinary work attractive professionally will still be with us.

An important lesson from the BDBP was that successful interdisciplinary research requires careful balancing between policy relevance and scientific relevance. A failure can lead to the project getting caught in the 'interdiscipli-nary trap'. When policy relevance is too strong, there is a risk of losing scien-tific relevance, for example, by scientists from different disciplines doing research in fields where they have no scientific training. Too tight a focus on scientific relevance can, on the other hand, lead to deep understanding of single systems, but not necessarily the links among them, so the policy relevance gets lost.

To increase the status of cooperative efforts in career judgments would encourage cooperation that develops to something more than a façade. One possible way to do this is to establish bodies for cooperative research that employ somewhat different judgments than traditional academic institutions, without compromising scientific quality. One example of such a place is the Beijer Institute, since 1991 an international research institute for ecological economics under the auspices of the Royal Swedish Academy of Sciences. The Beijer Institute has initiated or participated in several research programs in which both natural and social scientists have collaborated. For example, some of the research efforts mentioned above concerning nutrient emissions from land and the eutrophication of the Baltic Sea have been carried out in research programs in which the Beijer Institute was a partner. However, even at such special places, continuous efforts are needed to make theoretical and applied interdisciplinary research into a permanent activity that includes cooperative involvement of both senior ecologists and economists as well as of graduate students from both disciplines.

One important determinant of success (or failure) in this endeavor is the personality of the participating scholars (for example, to what extent each is open-minded). This brings us to the person we are celebrating in this volume. It is very much to Karl-Göran Mäler's credit that he has managed to make and keep the Beijer Institute hospitable to both ecologists and economists and to both junior and senior people in both disciplines. While each of the authors of this chapter is an economist, we have all found the Beijer Institute an exciting place in large part because of the daily informal contacts it affords with ecologists. The sad thing is that the world is still dominated by chauvinists rather than gap closers like KGM, and it strikes us as very important to encourage the latter group of people.

NOTES

1. Our observations suggest that such determinants might be, for example, opera visits, diving, skating, fermented herring meals and bird-watching.
2. In a footnote, Navrud and Pruckner refer to environmental damage estimates for Poland and Spain.
3. This second project also involved ecologists, and was an exploration of the use of multiattribute utility (MAU) questioning techniques in a survey setting, where the object having the attributes was a (hypothetical) forest park that respondents were given information about. The MAU technique allowed construction of value differences between forest descriptions in five dimensions. These were compared to values given in summary form in response to the description vectors (Russell et al. 2001b).

REFERENCES

Bernes, C. (ed.) (1988), *Monitor 1988: Sweden's marine environment – ecosystems under pressure*, Solna: Swedish Environmental Protection Agency.

Bonnieux, F. and P. Rainelli (1999), 'Contingent valuation methodology and the EU institutional framework', in I.J. Bateman and K.G. Willis (eds), *Valuing Environmental Preferences: Theory and Practice of the Contingent Valuation Method in the US, EU, and Developing Countries*, Oxford: Oxford University Press, pp. 585–612.

Dasgupta, P. and K.-G. Mäler (1995), 'Poverty, institutions, and the environmental resource-base', in J. Behrman and T.N. Srinivasan (eds), *Handbook of Development Economics*, Vol. III, Amsterdam: Elsevier Science, pp. 2371–463.

Des Jardins, J.R. (1997), *Environmental Ethics: An Introduction to Environmental Philosophy*, Belmont, CA: Wadsworth.

Destouni, G. (1992), 'Prediction uncertainty in solute flux through heterogeneous soil', *Water Resources Research*, **28**, 793–801.

Destouni, G. (1993), 'Stochastic modelling of solute flux in the unsaturated zone at the field scale'. *Journal of Hydrology*, **143**, 45–61.

Elliot, R. (ed.) (1995), *Environmental Ethics, Oxford Readings in Philosophy*, Oxford: Oxford University Press.

Elmgren, R. and U. Larsson (1997), *Himmerfjärden. Changes in a Nutrient Enriched Coastal Ecosystem* (in Swedish with an English summary), Report No. 4565, Swedish Environmental Protection Agency, Stockholm.

Elofsson. K. (1997), 'Costs of reductions in agricultural nitrogen load to the Baltic Sea', Licentiate thesis, Department of Economics, Swedish University of Agricultural Sciences, Uppsala, Sweden.

Engqvist, A. (1997), 'Water and nutrient exchange in Himmerfjärden', in Elmgren and Larsson (eds), pp. 118–58.

European Community (1993), *Towards Sustainability: A European Community Programme of Policy and Action in Relation to the Environment and Sustainable Development*, Brussels: Office for Official Publications of the European Communities.

Folke, C., M. Hammer and A.-M. Jansson (1991), 'Life-support value of ecosystems: a case study of the Baltic region', *Ecological Economics*, **3**, 123–37.

Gren, I.-M., T Söderqvist and F. Wulff (1997a), 'Nutrient reductions to the Baltic Sea: ecology, costs and benefits', *Journal of Environmental Management*, **51**, 123–43.

Gren, I.-M., P. Jannke and K. Elofsson (1997b), 'Cost effective nutrient reductions to the Baltic Sea', *Environmental and Resource Economics*, **10** (4), 341–62.

Gren, I.-M., K. Turner and F. Wulff (eds) (2000a), *Managing a Sea: The Ecological Economics of the Baltic*, London: Earthscan.

Gren, I.-M., R. Elmgren, A. Engqvist, U. Larsson and H. Scharin (2000b), 'Value of nutrient abatement in sewage treatment and coastal zones', *Vatten*, **56**, 21–7.

Gren, I.-M., G. Destouni and H. Scharin (2000c), 'Cost effective management of stochastic coastal water pollution', *Environmental Modelling and Assessment*, **5**, 193–203.

International Institute for Applied Systems Analysis (IIASA) (2000), 'Cleaner air for a cleaner future: controlling transboundary air pollution', article on IIASA website, http://www.iiasa.ac.at/admin/inf/opt/summer98/feature.htm.

Jansson, M. (ed.) (1994), 'Wetlands and lakes as nitrogen traps', *Ambio*, **23** (6), Special issue.

Kneese, Allen V. (1999), Personal Communication, 9 November.

Kneese, A.V. and S.C. Smith (1966), *Water Research*, Baltimore, MD: Johns Hopkins University Press for Resources for the Future.

Magnussen, K. (1995), 'What is restricting the use of valuation results in public policy?' (in Norwegian), *Sosialøkonomen*, **5**, 2–8.

Mäler, K.-G. (1971), 'A method of estimating social benefits from pollution control', *Swedish Journal of Economics*, **73**, 121–33.

Mäler, K.-G. (1974), *Environmental Economics: A Theoretical Inquiry*, Baltimore, MD: Johns Hopkins University Press.

Mäler, K.-G. (1985), 'Welfare economics and the environment', in A.V. Kneese and J.L. Sweeney (eds), *Handbook of Natural Resource and Energy Economics*, Vol. I, Amsterdam: Elsevier Science, pp. 3–60.

Mäler, K.-G. (1989), 'The acid rain game', in H. Folmer and E. van Ierland (eds), *Valuation Methods and Policy Making in Environmental Economics*, Amsterdam: Elsevier Science, pp. 231–52.

Mäler, K.-G. (1990), 'International environmental problems', *Oxford Review of Economic Policy*, **6**, 80–108.

Mäler, K.-G. (2000), 'Development, ecological resources and their management: a study of complex dynamic systems', *European Economic Review*, **44**, 645–65.

Mäler, K.-G., I.-M. Gren and C. Folke (1994), 'Multiple use of environmental resources: a household production function approach to valuing natural capital', in A. Jansson, M. Hammer, C. Folke and R. Costanza (eds), *Investing in Natural Capital: The Ecological Economics Approach to Sustainability*, Washington, DC: Island Press, pp. 233–49.

Maslow, A.H. (1970), *Motivation and Personality*, Evanston, IL: Harper & Row.

Navrud, S. (1991), 'Norway', in J.-P. Barde and D.W. Pearce (eds), *Valuing the Environment: Six Case Studies*, London: Earthscan, pp. 141–202.

Navrud, S. and G.J. Pruckner (1997), 'Environmental valuation – to use or not to use?', *Environmental and Resource Economics*, **10**, 1–26.

Russell, C.S., W.J. Vaughan, C.D. Clark, D.J. Rodriguez and A.H. Darling (2001a), *Investing in Water Quality: Measuring Benefits, Costs and Risks*, Washington, DC: Inter-American Development Bank.

Russell, C.S., V. Dale, J. Lee, M.H. Jensen, M. Kane and R. Gregory (2001b), 'Experimenting with multi-attribute utility survey methods in a multi-dimensional valuation problem', *Ecological Economics* **36**, 87–108.

Sandnes, H. (1993), 'Calculated budgets for airborne acidifying components in Europe, 1987, 1988, 1989, 1990, 1991, and 1992', Meteorological Synthesizing Centre-West, The Norwegian Meteorological Institute, PO Box 43-Blindern, N-0313 Oslo 3, Norway.

Sandström, M. (1996), 'Recreational benefits from improved water quality: a random utility model of Swedish seaside recreation', Working Paper Series in Economics and Finance No. 121, Department of Economics, Stockholm School of Economics.

Söderqvist, T. and H. Scharin (2000), 'The regional willingness to pay for a reduced eutrophication in the Stockholm archipelago', Beijer Discussion Paper Series No. 128, Beijer International Institute of Ecological Economics, The Royal Swedish Academy of Sciences, Stockholm.

Sweitzer, J., S. Langaas and C. Folke (1996), 'Land cover and population density in the Baltic Sea drainage basin: a GIS database', *Ambio*, **25**, 191–8.

Turner, R.K., S. Georgiou, I.-M. Gren, F. Wulff, S. Barrett, T. Söderqvist, I.J. Bateman, C. Folke, S. Langaas, T. Zylicz, K.-G. Mäler and A. Markowska (1999), 'Managing nutrient fluxes and pollution in the Baltic: an interdisciplinary simulation study', *Ecological Economics*, **30**, 333–52.

Wulff, F. and Å. Niemi (1992), 'Priorities for the restoration of the Baltic Sea: a scientific perspective', *Ambio*, **21** (2), 126–33.

11. Valuing ecosystem services

Geoffrey Heal[*]

The services of natural ecosystems are clearly very important to our societies: we probably could not live without them. (For a review of the importance of ecosystem services, see Daily 1997.) Does this importance translate into economic value? Are these services very valuable in an economic sense? Intuitively it may seem that the answer must be yes. In fact the matter is not so simple as our intuition suggests. Economics is more concerned with *prices* than with *values* or *importance*. To delve into these issues, we need to begin with a discussion of exactly what prices are and what they reflect. For a start, we need to be clear that the price of a good does not reflect its importance in any overall social or philosophical sense. Very unimportant goods can be valued more highly by the market than – have higher prices than – very important goods. The classic illustration of this is the diamonds and water paradox, which perplexed economists through the eighteenth and nineteenth centuries until its resolution by Alfred Marshall. The point here is that water is clearly more important to human society than diamonds, yet diamonds trade in the market at prices far in excess of those fetched by water. Why? Marshall's answer was simple and is by now part of common knowledge: price is set by supply and demand. The market price is the price at which the amount supplied is also the amount demanded. In the case of water, the supply (at least in Marshall's time) was so large as to exceed the amount that could possibly be demanded at any price. Consequently the price was zero: water was free. Now, of course, the demand for water has increased greatly from population growth and raising prosperity, while the supply has remained roughly constant, so that water is no longer free. In the case of diamonds, as they are naturally scarce, the desire for ownership always exceeded that which could be accommodated naturally. The market price was consequently high as a result of competition between rich people for the few diamonds available.

So, in summary, we should not expect that the fact that something is important will ensure that its price is high. If, like water in nineteenth-century England, it is naturally abundant then this will keep down its price. Food in the industrial countries is another good example of this point. Agricultural systems are sufficiently productive that the needs of the populations of the industrial countries can easily be met, and consequently food prices are not high. Indeed, the problem with food in the advanced countries has recently been too much rather than too little production. But food is nevertheless essential to life.

For both water and food, it is likely that if the amounts available were to decrease, then their prices would rise a great deal. If there really were not enough food to go around in the industrial countries, we would all be willing to spend a large fraction of our incomes to try to get enough for our families, in which case there would be a lot of money chasing relatively little food, and prices would be very different. The same is true of water. So the present prices reflect present supply conditions. They tell us nothing about how things would be if a lot less were available. David Ricardo, a famous nineteenth-century British economist, put this nicely. His comment was that:

> The labour of nature is paid, not because she does much, but because she does little. In proportion as she becomes niggardly in her gifts, she exacts a greater price for her work. Where she is munificently beneficent, she always works gratis. (Ricardo 1817, quoted in Siebert, p. 39)

Of course in many developing countries food is not abundant: there are great food shortages. How is this compatible with low food prices? Because the populations of these countries cannot afford to compete for food on world markets. Markets are institutions where, as Paul Samuelson once put it, you vote with your dollars. The populations of developing countries, having few dollars, are disenfranchised in this vote.

This leads naturally to another important aspect of prices: they reflect the distribution of income, the existing social order. To continue with the same example, if the people of Asia and Africa were much richer, they would compete with you and me for the world's food output, and consequently food prices would probably be higher. Going back to diamonds, in a world without very rich people the prices of luxury goods such as diamonds would be a lot lower. The reason of course is that the distribution of income affects the demands for many goods and therefore their prices. In general an increase in the income level of a group will increase the demand for goods that they like and so increase the prices of these goods.

What, then, does the market price of a good reflect? It reflects what the good is worth to what we call the 'marginal buyer'. The marginal buyer is the buyer who is on the verge of not buying the good, the buyer who would drop out if the price were to rise only a small amount. There will typically be many people buying a good for whom that good is worth more than they actually pay: the difference between the price that they pay and what they would be willing to pay is called their 'consumer surplus'. These people do not determine the market price: it is the buyers who might drop out of the market who do this. There is an analogy here with swing voters who determine an election outcome. The market price of a good does not tell us how important that good is to society, or how much some of the people buying it might be willing and able to pay rather than go without. It tells us what it is worth to the 'swing buyer', what economists call the marginal buyer.

In spite of these qualifications, the market price of a good is a very important and informative number. It tells us how much society would gain if a little more of the good were made available. Why? Because a small increase in the supply would not change the price much: the new buyers would therefore be people who valued the good at about the present price. If they valued it at more than the present price they would already be buyers: if they valued it a lot less, then a small drop in price would not bring them in. In other words, if a bit more of a good were available to society, then in a market economy the extra would sell at the current market price and be consumed by people who value it at that price. Accepting the premise that the value of the good to society is the value to those of its members benefiting from the good, this sets its social value at the market price. This of course rests on a utilitarian political philosophy. It sees the good of society as the totality of the well-being of its members. Society has no goals or values not reflected in those of its members. (For the more technically inclined, the price of a good is the partial derivative of social welfare with respect to the availability of that good. In the maximization of social welfare subject to constraints, it is the Lagrange multiplier associated with the constraint posed by the availability of the good.)

To go back to water and Marshall, if more water had been made available to the United Kingdom in the nineteenth century, there would have been no gain to society. Society already had enough. So extra water was of no value. Of course this does not mean that society could have survived the loss of a large part of its water supply. But if the water supply had been a lot less then the price would not have been zero and the market would have indicated a positive value for water.

A key aspect of this interpretation is that price tells us about the value of having a little more (or less) of a good. It does not tell us anything about the importance of having a lot more or a lot less. So the prices of water and food tell us about the values of having a little more or less or each, but emphatically not about the values of having a lot less. Why this focus on small changes, on what economists call marginal changes? The answer is that these are generally the kinds of changes that are under consideration when individuals or policy makers are making decisions. The decision made by a farmer in his crop planning will not have a big effect on the supply of food. His decision is typically whether to increase the output of one crop a little by cutting back on another. He is considering tradeoffs between different crops and their impact on his earnings. For these decisions, which affect the availability to society only a small amount, prices convey the right information. They indicate the social values of small changes in the availability of goods. If farmers and firm managers use these as guides in choosing what to produce then they will be aligning their choices with what is socially desirable.

Now we can return to the issue of valuation. If there are market prices for the services provided by natural ecosystems, then these prices provide an obvious basis for valuing them. So we could value the carbon sequestration services of forests or the water purification services of watersheds by using market prices for these. We could also place some value on their biodiversity support roles by looking at the market prices of ecotourism and of bioprospecting. From these numbers we could try to compute values for the forest as a whole or for the watershed as a whole. Typically we value the asset that provides a flow of services at the present discounted value of the flow of services that it will provide in the future. Corporations, for example, are usually valued for acquisition or investment purposes at the present discounted value of their estimated future earnings. The present discounted value of the future services is a number computed by adding together the values of all of the future services that will ever be provided, after scaling down the values of the future services by numbers called discount factors. Discount factors allow for the fact that investments can earn interest. At 5 percent, $100 set aside today will be worth $105 a year hence. Consequently we can say that $105 a year ahead has a present value of $100 and in present-value calculations scale it down by a discount factor of 100/105. (For a review of the issues raised by discounting see Heal 1998a.) So we could on this principle value a watershed at the present discounted value of the flow of watershed services that it will provide in the future. We could likewise value a forest as the present discounted value of its carbon sequestration and biodiversity support services and its recreational services. Note, of course, that such valuations are likely to be incomplete. There are usually services provided by natural ecosystems for which there are no markets and so no market prices. These will therefore be omitted from the calculations. At best, therefore, we will compute lower bounds for the values of these natural systems. However, even these lower bounds can be strikingly high, high enough to generate action for conservation.

There are methods for attributing prices to services for which there is no market price. By using them some of this omission may be eliminated. In fact there are several quite ingenious ways of doing this. Perhaps the most convincing is the use of hedonic price indices. This is best explained by an example. Suppose we want to value the fertility of soil. Soil fertility is not a good that is bought and sold in a market so we cannot just look up the price. However, farms are bought and sold and we could collect data on farm prices, calculate the prices per hectare of the farmland, and then also collect data on the quality of the soil for these farms. Next we would correlate the land price per hectare with the quality of the soil to see how much the fertility of the soil adds to the price of the land. So indirectly we have estimated a price for soil fertility. We have found what it adds to the market price of land. Securities analysts carry out the same type of analysis daily when they ask how the volatility of a stock's earnings affects its market price. There is no market for volatility directly so they look for comparable stocks with different records of earnings volatility and then attribute the difference to the volatility differences. Indirectly they are placing a market value on volatility. The same techniques are used to place a value on intangibles such as views. What is the value of a beautiful view? To answer this find two comparable houses, one with and one without views, and compare their prices. The difference reflects the value of the view in the marketplace.

In all these examples I have oversimplified to make the point clear. In practice we would rarely find two houses identical except for the view that we want to value. In this case we do the same thing but by a more roundabout route. We relate the prices of many houses to the attributes of those houses, including size, view, quality, neighbourhood and other variables. We use statistical techniques that will tell us how much of the variation in house prices is due to the variation in each of the characteristics. From these we separate out the part of the variation in prices that is due to differences in views. Indirectly, we put a price on the view. The same holds true for analysis of stock prices and farm prices. There is a general principle at work here. The price of a good reflects the valuations people place on all of its characteristics: in the case of a house these will include size, location, quality, views and many more. An important area of economic research is the study of how each of these characteristics contributes to the value that consumers place on the overall package. These techniques sometimes allow us to value properties for which there is no market. However, for this approach to work there has to be a product for which there is a market and in which the characteristic at issue is embedded. So if we want to use this as a way of valuing non-marketed ecosystem services then we can only apply it to cases in which these contribute directly to something that is marketed. (For more details see Rosen 1974.)

Another possibility, perhaps less general, is the use of replacement costs as a way of valuing a natural service. This can work even if there is no marketed service to which the natural service contributes. Again, the best way to start is with an example. Consider the case of New York's decision to preserve the Catskills watershed. In that case the city had an alternative to restoring the watershed: replacing it by a filtration plant. (Details are in Chichilnisky and Heal 1998.) This would have cost about $6–8 billion, plus operating costs and eventually replacement costs. Call the total $9 billion for simplicity. Can we say that because the cost of replacing the watershed would have been $9 billion, this is its value? Certainly this is a tempting strategy.

There are pros and cons to this approach to valuation. Note that as in the cases in which there are markets for some of the services of an ecosystem, at best, we can reach a partial valuation of the watershed via this route. The point is that the filtration plant replaces only a small part of what a watershed does. A filtration plant does not sequester carbon or support biodiversity or provide recreational opportunities. It does not even purify water as well as a natural watershed. So at best we could again reach a partial, a lower-bound estimate of the value of the services of the ecosystem.

In this case there is another argument that goes in the opposite direction. This is that we will not always choose to replace something that is defective: the cost of replacement could be too high. In the New York watershed case, non-replacement was not an option: the city needs drinking water. Suppose instead that the Catskills had just been providing recreational services to the city, and that the replacement of these services was at issue. And suppose that this replacement would cost several billions of dollars. In all probability the city would have decided not to replace the recreational services of the Catskills: it would have decided that at the cost of several billion dollars these were a luxury that they could do without. In this case the replacement cost would not be a proper indicator of the value of the service. Replacement cost can only be a good indicator if it is a cost that will be incurred if a replacement is needed. The same principle operates in many other contexts: we often decide not to replace something that is lost or broken because it is not worth the cost. As I said above, in the case of a watershed supplying a critical life-support service non-replacement is not a possibility. However, even in the new York case we cannot legitimately say that the value of the watershed is $9 billion, as in fact the city never chose to pay this amount: it restored the watershed at a much lower cost of between $1 and $2 billion. We can say that the city saved $9 billion by environmental conservation: that is clear. Perhaps we can even say that environmental conservative enriched the city by $9 billion minus $1.5 billion, the cost of watershed restoration. This is a net enrichment of $7.5 billion. But this is not the same as placing a value on the watershed: it is valuing the consequences of a conservation policy.

In summary, assessing the replacement cost is not a convincing way of valuing natural ecosystems and the services that they provide. Replacements rarely replace all of the services coming from the original system, so that this could capture only a part of the value. But more fundamentally the replacement cost is not a proper estimate of the value unless this cost is incurred. There will be cases in which this does not happen: these are cases in which the replacement will be too expensive to make sense. Replacement costs are certainly interesting, indeed essential, information in the context of evaluating conservation policies, particularly for essential services for which a replacement would surely be needed were the original system to fail. The replacement cost is a benchmark that the decision makers have to keep in mind as they evaluate conservation and restoration options. But, again, this does not make it a good estimate of the economic value of a system or service. To clinch this point let me take one more example, oil. Oil is close to essential to industrial economies. If all oil were to vanish tomorrow, it could (with difficulty) be replaced. We could, for example, extract oil from coal by complex industrial processes, at a cost of about $40 to $50 per barrel (a barrel is 42 US gallons). Or we could extract it from shale or from tar sands, at similar prices. Currently the price of oil is about $18 per barrel. As its replacement cost is at least $40 per barrel, does this mean that its value is $40 per barrel? Clearly not: its value is its market price. Currently the supply is abundant and there is no prospect of having to pay the replacement cost. However, if the supply were to start running out, then the market price would rise towards the replacement cost, which would become more relevant as an indicator of value.

I shall mention briefly another approach to valuing environmental services that are not marketed. This is the travel cost method (see Clawson 1959 for detail). The idea is to estimate how much people value an environmental asset by seeing what costs they will incur to visit it. It has typically been applied in the cases of national parks and ecotourism facilities. The basic idea is simple: if I am willing to incur costs of, say, $500 to visit a forest and spend time there, then being there must provide me with benefits that I value at least this much. It must be worth at least $500 to me. We can think of the access costs as a price that people pay to get to the forest. Across all visitors there will be many different access costs, so that different people are in effect paying different prices for access to the forest. Some may live locally and incur costs of only a few dollars: others may live far away and have to travel for hours at great expense to get there. If there are many different implied prices, then which do we use to value the facility? Which can act like a market place? Recall that the market price tells us the value of having a little more or less of a good. In fact there is no exact equivalent of this for a park: a park is a public good, and there will generally not be a single price that represents its social value. In such cases we have to add up the values attributed to it by all of its users and take this sum as the valuation of the services that it provides. So the sum of the travel costs incurred to visit it would be the natural indicator of the value of providing slightly more of the services of the park.

Market prices, hedonic prices, travel costs and replacement costs as methods of valuing the services of natural systems have an important feature in common: they are based on actual transactions. Hedonic prices are derived from market prices. Travel costs reflect real transactions. And replacement costs, used properly, reflect a cost that will be incurred in the case of a need for replacement. The remaining method of valuation, used when none of these is possible, is called contingent valuation. It is a survey method. In essence it involves asking a carefully-structured sample of people what value they place on a natural asset and then using this data to extrapolate to the population as a whole. The questions posed have to be carefully designed for the answers to have any validity. With this caveat, such methods have been widely used for estimating the value of loss of natural amenities, particularly in high-profile lawsuits such as the *Exxon Valdez* case. I think it fair to say that most economists feel more comfortable with valuations based on actual transactions rather than those given in response to hypothetical questions, however carefully constructed. Intuitively there seems to be a big difference between completing a questionnaire on what you would be willing to pay for something, and actually paying for it. In spite of such reservations, this approach has given quite good predictions of what people might pay on the occasions when it has been possible to compare contingent valuation estimates of what people might pay with what they have subsequently paid for the same service. (For a detailed exposition, see Mitchell and Carson 1989.)

In summary, economists would ideally like to value ecosystem services by attaching market prices to them, or by deriving prices for them from market transactions. There are relatively few cases in which this can be done. But even when this is possible, the market-based valuations resulting need not reflect the social importance of the services or the extent of the losses that we would suffer if these services were removed. The market-based prices tell us the value to society of a small amount more or less of a service, and do not indicate the overall contribution of the service. Operationally, this is usually fine as it is usually small changes in availability that are at issue.

Unfortunately some of the human impacts on important ecosystems are far from small. Overfishing is changing marine food chains radically. Nitrogen fertilizers have already more than doubled natural nitrogen concentrations. We have increased atmospheric concentrations of carbon dioxide and other greenhouse gases significantly. We are driving species to extinction at perhaps one thousand times the natural rate. (For a review of these issues, see Vitousek et al. 1997; Arrow et al. 1995; and Lubchenco 1998.) In such cases market prices, even if they exist, will seriously underestimate the economic value lost by this destruction. Why will market prices give an underestimate? Because typically the price of a good or service rises as it becomes scarcer. This is particularly true of goods and services that are essential to human welfare, such as food, water and clean air. As I noted above, if food or water were scarce in the rich countries, then most of us would spend a significant fraction of our incomes ensuring adequate supplies for our families. In such a world, prices of food, water and access to clean air would rise dramatically, and the prices of other goods would fall as there was less left to spend on them.

Are there any economic measures that would capture better the impact of the loss of a significant amount of a natural life-support system? For example, can we talk sensibly of the value of preserving the climate system intact, or of the value of preserving biodiversity? There are in principle ways of doing this, and recently there have been attempts to apply them and assess the economic value of the biosphere in a comprehensive way. However, we should note immediately some limitations here. It will never make sense to ask about the value that we would lose if an entire and irreplaceable life-support system were to be lost. The point is that if it is indeed a life-support system then its loss would lead to the end of all human life, and to put an economic value on that would seem foolish and inappropriate. (The numbers resulting from a recent attempt to do just this were described by one economist as 'a serious under-estimate of infinity'.)

Could we value instead the loss of a significant part, but not all, of a life-support system? In principle we might be able to do this, but it is very difficult. Take a concrete case, water. Suppose we are concerned to assess the economic costs of a change in the hydrological cycle that would result from a change in the climate system. Assume that this would reduce substantially but not eliminate water supplies to large regions of the earth. Could we value this change by economic techniques? We would have to know how much the price of water would rise as its supply falls, that is, in economic terms we would have to know the demand curve for water. This is not easy: as the price of water rose due to scarcity, many other things would change: food production, food prices, income levels and many other economic variables would all change as the price of water rose in response to a sharp drop in availability. All of these other variables would affect the demand for water, so that estimating how its price would move along a trajectory of declining supply would be immensely difficult. To date, there have been no convincing studies of the economic value of preventing the loss of significant parts of any global life-support systems, although in principle we know how to do this.

The conclusion that emerges from this analysis is that economics probably cannot really value the services of the earth's life-support systems in any way other than by using market prices, which value them in the sense of indicating the value of a small change in their availability. We should not be disappointed with this limited ability to value ecosystem services. If our concern is to conserve these services, then valuation is largely irrelevant. Let me emphasize this: *valuation is neither necessary nor sufficient for conservation; we conserve much that we do not value, and do not conserve much that we value.*

What then is the economic prerequisite for conservation? It lies in incentives: to conserve systems we must give their owners incentives to conserve them. We must make conservation more attractive than any other uses. Conserving forests must be more attractive than clearing them to plant coffee or bananas or cocoa beans. To do this we have to translate some of the social importance of ecosystem services into income and ensure that this income accrues to the owners of the ecosystems as a reward for their conservation.

This is the key theme, the single most important theme, in the conservation of the ecosystems that support human societies. Providing the right incentives is not the same as valuing the services: we can provide the incentives without valuing the services and we can value the services without providing incentives for conserving them. In fact, valuation may sometimes be a byproduct of providing the incentives. If we manage to establish a market in an ecosystem service, then we have a price for it and thus a basis for valuing it. And markets are probably the best ways of providing conservation incentives. So logically incentives come before valuation: *incentives are critical for conservation; valuation is not necessary for establishing the correct incentives.*

To give a concrete example, suppose that when implemented the Kyoto Protocol contains a provision under which owners of tropical forests can be paid for the carbon sequestration services that they provide. Then this will greatly increase the economic returns to forestation and to the preservation of existing forests. I have argued elsewhere (Heal 1998b) that it could lead to payments as high as $100–150 per hectare per year, considerably in excess of the earning potential of land from which tropical rainforests have been cleared. Such a provision would generate strong incentives for the preservation of tropical forests and would change the economics of forestry radically. It would be a major step towards ensuring the preservation of forest ecosystems. The key step would be the provision of incentives, not valuation of services. In this case, valuation would be a byproduct: the market price for carbon sequestration would allow us to calculate a lower bound on the values of forests by computing the present value of their carbon sequestration earnings. In the same vein, suppose that owners of forests were paid for their services as watersheds. These, like carbon sequestration, have great social importance and provide a product, water, for which people are increasingly willing to pay. For the forests that play this role, the economics of conservation versus clear cutting would be changed radically in favor of the former. We should have established a powerful incentive for conservation without valuation, although again the potential to value partially would arise as a result of the provision of incentives. There is one exception to this general statement that valuation is neither necessary nor sufficient for conservation: this occurs in the context of cost–benefit analysis of conservation decisions that are being made via the political process, rather than through economic institutions such as markets. A cost–benefit analysis requires the enumeration and evaluation of the benefits from conserving a natural ecosystem and in this process placing values on the services provided by the system is a necessary step. It is important to remember always that the values that result are likely to be underestimates of the total value provided to society by the system under review.

To conclude: the emphasis on valuing ecosystems and their services is probably misplaced. Economics cannot estimate the importance of natural environments to society: only biology can do that. The role of economics is to help design institutions that will provide incentives for the conservation of important natural systems, and will mediate human impacts on the biosphere so that these are sustainable.

NOTE

*   This chapter was written while I was a visiting scholar at the Center for Environmental Science and Policy at Stanford University. It is based on Chapter Six of my manuscript 'Earthkeeping', which is to be published by Island Press. I am grateful to Gretchen Daily and David Tilman for helping me understand many of the ecological issues involved in the provision of ecosystem services.

REFERENCES

Arrow, K.J., B. Bolin, R. Costanza, P. Dasgupta, C. Folke, C.S. Holling, B.-O. Jansson, S. Levin, K.-G. Mäler, C. Perrings and D. Pimentel (1995), 'Economic growth, carrying capacity and the environment', *Science*, **268**: 520–21.
Chichilnsky, G. and G.M. Heal (1998), 'Economic returns from the biosphere', *Nature*, **391**: 629–30.
Clawson, M. (1959), 'Methods of measuring the demand for and value of outdoor recreation', RFF Reprint 10, Washington, DC: Resources for the Future; Chapter 18 in Wallace Oates (ed.), *The Economics of the Environment*, Aldershot: Edward Elgar, 1992.
Daily, G.C. (1997), *Nature's Services: Societal Dependence on Natural Ecosystems*, Washington, DC: Island Press.
Heal, G.M. (1998a), *Valuing the Future: Economic Theory and Sustainability*, New York: Columbia University Press.
Heal, G.M. (1998b), 'Markets and sustainability', in Richard Stewart (ed.), *Proceedings of the La Pietra Symposium on Environmental Regulation*, Cambridge: Cambridge University Press.
Lubchenco, J. (1998), 'Entering the century of the environment', Presidential address to the American Academy of Arts and Sciences, *Science*, **279**: 491–8.
Mitchell, R.C. and R.T. Carson (1989), *Using Surveys to Value Public Goods: The Contingent Valuation Method*, Washington, DC: Resources for the Future.
Ricardo, David (1817 [1911]), *Principle of Political Economy and Taxation*, London: Everyman's Library; quoted in Horst Siebert, *Economics of the Environment*, Berlin, Heidelberg and New York: Springer-Verlag, 1987.
Rosen, S. (1974), 'Hedonic prices and implicit markets: product differentiation in pure competition', *Journal of Political Economy*, **82**, January/February: pp. 34–35.
Vitousek, P.M., H.A. Mooney, J. Lubchenco and J.M. Melillo (1997), 'Human domination of earth's ecosystems', *Science*, **25**: 494–9.

12. Hotelling (1925) on depreciation

Bengt Kriström[*]

1   ON DEPRECIATION

According to Arrow's (1987) review of Harold Hotelling's contribution to economics, six of Hotelling's ten economics papers became landmarks in the economics literature. Arrow (1987, p. 670) gives Hotelling's (1925) path-breaking paper on depreciation the following acclaim,

> Here, apparently for the first time, he stated the now generally accepted definition of depreciation as the decrease in the discounted value of future returns. This paper was a turning-point both in capital theory proper and in the reorientation of accounting towards more economically meaningful magnitudes.

In this note, which is an exploration into the history of thought, rather than an attempt to provide new results, I show how an application of Hotelling's ideas on depreciation provides several interesting results within a dynamic model. I follow Roos (1928), who gave the calculus of variation version of Hotelling's original idea. The Hotelling result on depreciation is applied to the neoclassical investment model, models of exhaustible and renewable resources, as well as to a current controversy in resource accounting regarding how to value net changes in stocks. This note begins in Section 2 by presenting a model due to Heal (1998). I then provide a study of various special cases as illustrations of the general result in Section 3. The so-called El Serafy model (1999) for depreciation is discussed and its link to Hotelling's theory explored in Section 4. A final section concludes.

2   A MODEL

Let the vector $c_t \in \mathfrak{R}^m$ be a vector of flows of goods consumed and giving utility at time t, and $s_t \in \mathfrak{R}^n$ be a vector of stocks at time t, also possibly but not necessarily sources of utility. Each stock $s_{i,t}$, $i = 1, \ldots, n$, changes over time in a way which depends on the values of all stocks and of all flows:

$$\dot{s}_{i,t} = d_i(c_t, s_t), i = 1, \ldots, n. \tag{12.1}$$

195

The economy's objective is to maximize the discounted integral of utilities (12.2):

$$\max \int_0^\infty u(c_t, s_t)e^{-\delta t}dt \tag{12.2}$$

subject to the rate-of-change equation (12.1) for the stocks. The utility function u is assumed to be strictly concave and the reproduction functions $d_i(c_t, s_t)$ are assumed to be concave. This is flexible formulation, although it should be noted that the objective function is autonomous (except for discounting). For example, if u does not depend on s and if (12.1) takes the form $\dot{s}_{i,t} = -c_{i,t}$, then we have a Hotelling-type model of exhaustible resources. It can also be seen that the Solow model is a special case ($u = u(c)$ and $\dot{s} = f(s) - c$). Thus, while most of the discussion in this chapter revolves around resource economics, other areas of economics could also be addressed. Heal and Kriström (1998) use this set-up to shed light on income measurement in, for example, 'new economy' settings, where the stock of human capital plays an important role.

To solve the maximization problem we construct a current-value Hamiltonian which takes the form:

$$H_t = u(c_t, s_t) + \sum_{i=1}^{n} \lambda_{i,t} d_i(c_t, s_t) \tag{12.3}$$

where $\lambda_{i,t}$ is the shadow price of the stock $i = 1, \ldots, n$. The Hamiltonian in this model is almost by definition ('green') net national product (NNP), because (utility of) consumption and net changes in stocks are added.

Let $V_t = \sup \int_t^\infty u(c_\tau, s_\tau)\exp[-\delta(\tau - t)]d\tau$ be the value function. For the purposes of this chapter, the Hamilton–Jacobi (HJ) equation is useful. For infinite horizon exponentially discounted problems, we can write the HJ equation (for example, Brock 1987, p. 722):

$$\delta V = \max H. \tag{12.4}$$

Since it is natural to interpret V as a wealth indicator, the HJ equation suggests a definition of income as the return on wealth, that is, a definition of income associated with Irving Fisher, E.R. Lindahl and J.R. Hicks.[1]

Furthermore, the HJ equation provides a 'one-line proof' of Weitzman's (1976) fundamental insight on national income, as noted by Lozada (1995, p. 142, Corollary 1). Weitzman showed that the value of the Hamiltonian at t represents a utility level which if maintained for ever from t would give the same present value of utility as the optimal path from t on.[2] This kind of result holds when the Hamiltonian is autonomous. See Asheim (2000) for a recent survey of Weitzman-type results in a variety of settings, including non-autonomous models.

2.1 Defining Depreciation

Hotelling (1925) defines depreciation as the decrease in value of a particular machine, where value is defined as the annual rental value plus a scrap value. Following Hotelling, depreciation is,

$$D_t = -\frac{dV_t}{dt}.$$ (12.5)

Thus, depreciation is the decrease in value over time, where value is defined as the present value of the stream of annual rental value over an infinite horizon (that is, without scrap value). This, of course, is a rather different concept of depreciation compared to the cost-allocation concept used by accountants.

The Hotelling result on depreciation is summarized in the following proposition.

Proposition 1 In an economy described by $\max \int_t^\infty u(c_\tau, s_\tau)e^{-\delta(\tau-t)}d\tau$ s.t. $\dot{s}_{i,t} = d_i(c_t, s_t)$, $i = 1, \ldots, n$, the total depreciation for the stocks of the economy is given by the shadow value of the net change of the economy's stocks. For a particular stock, net change of the stock at time t is multiplied with its shadow price.

$$D_t = -\Sigma \lambda_{i,t}\, \dot{s}_{i,t}$$ (12.6)

$$D_{i,t} = -\lambda_{i,t}\, \dot{s}_{i,t}.$$ (12.7)

Proof $D_t = -dV_t/dt = u(c_t, s_t) - \delta V = u(c_t, s_t) - H = -\Sigma \lambda_{i,t}\, \dot{s}_{i,t}$. ∎

Total depreciation in this economy is the shadow value of the resource needed to keep wealth constant.[3] We can also view the essence of the result as saying that shadow prices are constant for small changes of quantities, which suggests that the result has old roots. I have been unable to pin down a pre-1960 reference, although the economic content of the result seems to have been understood long before the publication of the Pontryagin book on control theory in the beginning of the 1960s.[4] In the resource economics literature, the result can be found in, for example, Lozada (1995, p. 142), who mentions it in passing (in his proof of the Hartwick rule in autonomous settings). Proposition 1 also holds in non-optimizing settings, provided that the shadow prices are reinterpreted. See Dasgupta and Mäler (2000) for a discussion (focusing on net investment, rather than depreciation).

Note, in particular, that the depreciation formula is quite independent of whether or not we allow existence values to be associated with certain stocks. It is also of some interest to note that the national accounts (SNA 93) use a 'Hicks–Hotelling' concept of depreciation, according to Hulten (1995, p. 158, see especially equation (5.15)).[5]

While Hotelling (1925) is to be credited with the basic idea of how depreciation should be defined rigorously at the level of the firm, it was Samuelson (1937) who brought these ideas to bear within economy-wide models. He defines depreciation (his equation (5)), without reference to Hotelling, as the 'loss of value over time'. He argues (p. 471) that 'purely as a matter of formal definition of what is meant by value . . . The rate of depreciation at any instant of time is equal to the difference between net income and the return on value of the Investment Account at that instant of time'.

Samuelson (1937) shows that the fundamental depreciation formula also holds when the discount factor is allowed to vary over time (as can be verified by using the Leibnitz rule).[6] Furthermore, Samuelson (1964) (still without a reference to Hotelling) applied Hotelling's depreciation idea to the measurement of 'true money income' and showed a fundamental tax-invariance result. If a depreciation allowance is admitted when calculating taxable income, then wealth is independent of (a uniform) tax, provided that the allowance is calculated as D_t: 'the only sensible definition of depreciation relevant to measurement of *true money income* is putative decline in economic value' (Samuelson 1964, p. 606).

3   ILLUSTRATIONS

Consider a firm that makes profits according to:

$$\pi_t = pf(K, L) - wL - qI \tag{12.8}$$

where π_t is net profits at time t, p is the output price, $f(K, L)$ is a strictly concave neoclassical production function with positive first partials, K is the capital stock at time t, L is the stock of labor at time t, w is the wage rate and q is the price of a unit of investment I. The net capital stock is given by:

$$\dot{K} = I - dK \tag{12.9}$$

where d is a constant rate of physical depreciation. The value of the firm is:

$$V_t = \int_t^\infty \pi_\tau \exp[-\delta(\tau - t)]d\tau \tag{12.10}$$

so that, from Proposition 1,

$$D_t = -\lambda \dot{K}.$$

Thus, depreciation is simply the (negative of) market value of net investment at time t. This also suggest that the marginal value of the firm is equal to the value of net investments, since $dV_t/dt = -D_t$. This is a natural and intuitively appealing result.

As a second example, take the simplest case with an owner of an exhaustible resource. Suppose that an oil-well of size $Q = \int_t^\infty c(s)ds$ is subject to extraction. The revenues are given by pc and the total costs of extraction are $h(c)$, with $MC \equiv dh/dc > 0$. The profits and the Hamiltonian are, respectively,

$$\pi_t = pc - h(c), \tag{12.11}$$

$$H = pc - h(c) - \lambda c$$

and

$$D_t = \lambda c = (p - MC)c \tag{12.12}$$

where the last equality follows from the first-order conditions. This depreciation concept is often called the net rent method in the literature, and it has been studied in detail by Hartwick (1990). Since $c = -\dot{s}$, depreciation can also be interpreted as the (negative of) the market value of net investment in the non-renewable resource.

Lozada (1995) pointed out that the value of the time is not independent of the market structure. In current-value terms, the value of the remaining stock can be higher in $t + 1$ compared to t in the competitive case; that is, there are capital gains. Capital gains are certainly a gain at the level of the firm, but not for the (closed) economy as a whole. After all, capital gains are of interest in as much as they can contribute to utility at some point in time. Lozada therefore argues that capital gains should not enter the depreciation formulae used for the national accounts. Intuition suggests that capital gains should be included in the national accounts in the open economy, because capital gains can be used to invest in another stock abroad and therefore help in maintaining wealth constant in the economy. (See, for example, Vincent et al. (1997) for further discussion.)

Now let us turn to renewable resources. Depreciation in the case of a firm using a renewable resource follows directly from Proposition 1: net rents are multiplied by (net) growth less consumption. Take the case of a firm using one renewable resource. If the market price is denoted p and the cost function is linear, $h(t) - bc(t)$, then $D(t) = (p - b) * [d(t) - c(t)]$, where b is average (and marginal) cost, and $d(t)$ is net growth of the stock. This approach is often used in applications, although the approximation of using average rather than marginal cost can be very bad, as a detailed analysis of Vincent (1999) shows in the case of forests.

Finally, the Samuelson (1964) result on tax invariance goes through, as we know, in the examples studied. In the case of the mine, for example, we define net income as $\pi_t(1 - T) + TD$, where T is the tax rate. The firm faces a net lending and borrowing rate of $(1 - T)\delta$. It follows from the Hamiltonian associated with the underlying optimization problem that the firm's decisions are invariant to the uniform tax T, iff $D_t = \lambda c$.

3.1   El Serafy's Approach to Depreciation

El Serafy (1999) has proposed the so-called 'user cost method', which goes back to Hicks (1939, p. 187), who argued:

> If a person's receipts are derived from the exploitation of a wasting asset, liable to give out at some future date, we should say that his receipts are in excess of his income, the difference between them being reckoned as an allowance for depreciation. In this case, if he is to consume no more than his income, he must re-lend some parts of his receipts . . .

El Serafy (1999) picked up on this general idea and provided a simple formula. Thus, he proposed that true income (x) from an exhaustible resource with expected life n years at current extraction rate, yielding net revenues $pc - h(c)$, should be defined as:

$$x = pc - h(c) - \frac{pc - h(c)}{(1 + \delta)^{n+1}}$$

for a given choice of discount rate δ. Hence, the true income from the exhaustible resource is less than the revenues, the extent to which depend on the parameters n and δ.

El Serafy assumes, for simplicity, that net rents are constant in each period, although we shall abstract from this simplification in the sequel. It is also convenient to revert to continuous time. Thus, by the more general Hicks interpretation of 'true income', we seek to find a constant perpetual amount of money x that has the same present value as the present net value of an exhaustible resource extracted during $0 < t < T < \infty$,

$$\frac{x}{\delta} = V_t = \int_t^T [pc - h(c)]\exp[-\delta(\tau - t)]d\tau. \tag{12.13}$$

Note that x is a Fisher–Hicks–Lindahl kind of income, in the sense that income is return on wealth along the optimal path.[7] The following proposition is a consequence of the definition of x.

Proposition 2 Total Hotelling rent $(p - MC)c$ is equal to 'true income' x at time t.

Proof Differentiating (12.13) w.r.t. t gives $\partial V_t / \partial t = h(c) - pc + \delta V_t$. From Seierstad and Sydsaeter (1987, p. 213) we have the result that $\partial V_t / \partial t = H$, where $H = pc - h(c) - \lambda c$ is the Hamiltonian. Since $x = \delta V_t$ by (12.13), the result follows by using the first-order condition $p - MC = \lambda$, where $MC \equiv dh(c)/dc$. ∎

Remark 3 Since x is a constant by definition, while λc is not, the result holds only at time t.

It has been argued that El Serafy's simplifying assumptions are quite arbitrary (see, for example, Dasgupta et al. 1995), and, furthermore, that these assumptions are unlikely to hold empirically. An alternative to El Serafy's approach is the net rent method $((p - MC)c)$, although a drawback is that marginal costs must be computed. The following observation provides a potentially useful workaround. Let ε^{ATC} denote the elasticity of average total cost (ATC), and observe that $(1 + \varepsilon^{ATC})ATC = MC$. Then,

$$\lambda c = (p - MC)c = pc - h(c)(1 + \varepsilon^{ATC}) = pc - h(c) \frac{MC}{ATC}$$

where $\varepsilon^{ATC} = \{d[h(c)/c]/dc\} \times \{c/[h(c)/c]\}$ and $ATC = h(c)/c$. On certain arguments, ε^{ATC} is more amenable to empirical work than marginal costs, since average costs are directly observable.[8] A detailed investigation of this idea will be reported elsewhere. In the well-known study of Indonesia, Repetto et al. (1989) effectively assume that $MC/ATC = 1$, since they use the often used approximation $(p - ATC)c = pc - h(c)$ in their calculations. This entails disregarding $(-)x$, or, as it were, the 'true income' associated with the exhaustible resource. To see this, note that $- dV/dt = pc - h(c) - \delta V = (p - ATC)c - x$, where the last equality follows from (12.13). Hence, the claim that the net rent method disregards 'true income' x. Vincent (1999) uses a similar argument to conclude that the approach used by Repetto et al. (1989) and others to calculate depreciation for exhaustible resources is 'incorrect' (Vincent 1999, p. 253, fn. 4). As noted above, if average costs are approximately equal to marginal costs, then the approximation is defensible.

Finally, the last word in this section must go to Samuelson (1937, p. 472) who notes:

> Furthermore, the fact that the difference between net income and return on investment equals a residuum of money which could be invested in order to provide a sum of money for replacement, in no way implies that this money, even under ideal conditions, will be so used.

Indeed, when constructing measures that in one way or another reflect 'sustainability concerns', Samuelson's remark may, in the context of this chapter, be interpreted to mean that 'sustainability' is but one of many ethical norms that can be brought to bear on the discussion of long-run allocation issues.

4   CONCLUSIONS

In this chapter, I have used Hotelling's theory of depreciation to explore the concept of depreciation. While later writers have been able to generalize theories of depreciation in many directions, Hotelling provided the pivotal idea. Thus, Harold Hotelling, widely famous in the resource economics literature for his analysis of exhaustible resource and proposing the travel cost method, deserves to be known as a father of resource economics in more than two ways.

NOTES

*   I thank Olvar Bergland, Geoffrey Heal and Anni Huhtala for useful comments and Martin Weitzman for encouraging me to write down the results. I acknowledge useful discussions with Kenneth J. Arrow, Partha Dasgupta, Karl-Göran Mäler and David Starrett. The usual disclaimer applies.

1.   If the utility function is linear (or 'linearized'), the link to national product is direct. Whether or not this allows one to usefully interpret NNP as return on wealth is a subtle and controversial issue in the literature on green accounting. See Dasgupta and Mäler (2000) for a detailed discussion (with negative conclusion). See Heal and Kriström (2002) for a discussion of the connections between Fisher's, Hicks's and Lindahl's work on income.

2.   This is an average kind of utility level, the weights being given by the discount factors.

3.   Alternatively, by writing the value function as a function of the stocks and differentiating $V(s_t)$ w.r.t. t, the result follows directly, using the well-known sensitivity result that $\partial V/\partial s_i = \lambda_i$ (see, for example, Seierstad and Sydsaeter (1987, p. 212). I assume that the value function is differentiable in the stocks throughout this chapter. See Lozada (1995) for a more general treatment.

4.   The result is an abstract mathematical property of general dynamic optimization problems. The economic content of the result can be traced back at least to a famous review of A.C. Pigou by Allyn Young in 1913 in the *Economic Journal*.

5.   The World Bank has recently compiled comprehensive studies of expanded measures of

'genuine savings', which is much in the spirit of the generalized Hotelling approach to depreciation. See Dasgupta and Mäler (2000) for a discussion.
6. See also Lozada (1995, equation(1)).
7. These arguments, in effect, also follow from Proposition 2 of Lozada (1995).
8. Vincent (1999, p. 254) assumes that the marginal cost function is iso-elastic and obtains a formula that does not involve marginal costs directly. The approach suggested here entails no particular assumption about functional form.

REFERENCES

Arrow, K.J. (1987), 'Hotelling, Harold', in J. Eatwell, M. Milgate and P. Newman (eds), *The New Palgrave Dictionary of Economics*, Basingstoke: Macmillan, pp. 670–71.

Asheim, G. (2000), 'Green national accounting: why and how?', *Environment and Development Economics*, **5** (1): 25–48.

Brock, W. (1987), 'Optimal control and economic dynamics', in J. Eatwell, M. Milgate and P. Newman (eds), *The New Palgrave Dictionary of Economics*, Basingstoke: Macmillan, pp. 721–6.

Dasgupta, P., B. Kriström and K.-G. Mäler (1995), 'Current issues in resource accounting', in P.-O. Johansson, B. Kriström and K.-G. Mäler (eds), *Current Issues in Environmental Economics*, pp. 117–52.

Dasgupta, P. and K.-G. Mäler (2000), 'Net national product, wealth, and social well-being', Environment and Development Economics, **5** (1): 25–48.

El Serafy, S. (1999), 'Natural resource accounting', in J.C.J.M. van den Bergh (ed.), *Handbook of Environmental and Resource Economics*, Cheltenham, UK and Northampton, MA, USA: Edward Elgar, pp. 1191–1206.

Hartwick, J.M. (1990), 'Natural resources, national accounting, and economic depreciation', *Journal of Public Economics*, **43**: 291–304.

Heal, G. (1998), *Valuing the Future: Economic Theory and Sustainability*, New York: Columbia University Press.

Heal, G. and B. Kriström (1998), 'National income and environment', PaineWebber Working Paper, PW-98-01, Columbia University, New York.

Heal, G. and B. Kriström (2001), 'Green accounting: a survey', *forthcoming* in K.-G. Mäler and J. Vincent (eds), *Handbook of Environmental Economics*, Amsterdam North-Holland.

Hicks, J.R. (1939), *Value and Capital*, 2nd edn, New York: Oxford University Press.

Hotelling, H. (1925), 'A general mathematical theory of depreciation', *Journal of the American Statistical Association*, **20**: 340–53.

Hulten, C.R. (1995), 'Capital and wealth in the revised SNA', in J.W. Kendrick (ed.), *The New System of National Accounts*, Boston, MA: Kluwer Academic Publishers, pp. 149–81.

Lozada, G. (1995), 'Resource depletion, national income accounting, and the value of optimal dynamic programs', *Resource and Energy Economics*, August: 137–54.

Repetto, R., W. Magrath, M. Wells, C. Beer and F. Rossinni (1989), 'Wasting assets: natural resources in the national income accounts', Washington, DC: World Resources Institute.

Roos, C.F. (1928), 'The problem of depreciation in the calculus of variations', *Bulletin of the American Mathematical Society*, March–April: 218–28.

Samuelson, P.A. (1937), 'Some aspects of the pure theory of capital', *Quarterly Journal of Economics*, **51**: 469–96.

Samuelson, P.A. (1964), 'Tax deductibility of economic depreciation to insure invariant valuations', *Journal of Political Economy*, **72**: 604–6.

Seierstad, A. and K. Sydsaeter (1987), *Optimal Control Theory with Economic Applications*, New York: North-Holland.

Vincent, J.R. (1999), 'Net accumulation of timber resources', *Review of Income and Wealth*, **2**: 251–62.

Vincent, J.R., T. Panayotou and J.M. Hartwick (1997), 'Resource depletion and sustainability in small open economies', *Journal of Environmental Economics and Management*, **33**: 274–86.

Weitzman, M.L. (1976), 'On the welfare significance of net national product in a dynamic economy', *Quarterly Journal of Economics*, **90**: 156–62.

13. Real versus hypothetical willingness to accept: the Bishop and Heberlein model revisited

Chuan-Zhong Li, Karl-Gustaf Löfgren and W. Michael Hanemann

1 INTRODUCTION

Economists have long been concerned with the measurement of environmental benefits in order to make social cost–benefit analyses on which to base more informed policy decisions. Since environmental goods and services are in general not traded in any marketplace, there is no price information directly available to infer their values. This has led economists to develop techniques such as travel cost analysis (Clawson and Knetsch, 1966; Mäler et al., 1994) and hedonic pricing (Rosen, 1974) to impute their value from transactions of other goods and services. An alternative approach is to construct markets as if environmental amenities could be bought and sold, and directly ask for people's willingness to pay (WTP) or willingness to accept (WTA) for proposed changes on the environmental amenities[1] (Mitchell and Carson, 1989). Since the elicited valuation data are contingent upon the particular market scenario constructed, the approach became known as the contingent valuation (CV) method.

Compared to other approaches based on revealed preferences, the CV method has an advantage in its flexibility to construct market scenarios that can extend beyond the range of observed market behavior and, therefore, it can even capture existence values that are not intimately associated with the consumption of other goods or services. However, the method may be subject to various sources of bias depending upon the design and implementation of the survey procedure and statistical methods used for data analysis. To study the validity of the value estimates based on CV, Bishop and Heberlein (1979) performed a now famous experiment on the value of early-season goose-hunting permits for the Horicon Zone in East Central Wisconsin. Instead of asking for an exact dollar amount, they developed a discrete choice (referendum) questioning strategy, that is to ask whether or not an individual is willing to accept a pre-specified dollar amount for the permit. Using a standard logistic regression model, they found that the WTA estimate derived from a subsample with hypothetical valuation questions significantly differs from that derived from a subsample with real economic commitments.

Since the mid-1980s, the discrete choice questioning strategy has gained widespread acceptance as a preferred way to frame the valuation question,[2] and it was formally endorsed by the National Oceanic and Atmospheric Agency's (NOAA) Blue Ribbon Panel on contingent valuation in 1993 (Arrow et al., 1993). However, this approach creates a heavy demand for statistical techniques and the final value estimate may be sensitive to the assumptions made about human choice behavior. In earlier studies, it was usually assumed that people had perfect knowledge about their true preferences. If this were true, then we would expect that they would be able to specify the exact dollar value for an environmental change or to answer a discrete choice question with complete certainty on whether or not to pay any specified amount for it. However, there is evidence in the literature to suggest that this is not the case (Hanemann and Kanninen, 1996; Kriström, 1993; McFadden, 1994).

In recent years, there has been increasing interest in the issue of decision uncertainty in responses to CV questions (see Li and Mattsson, 1995; Ready et al., 1995; Wang, 1997; Alberini et al., 2000, among others). In this chapter, we attempt to shed light on whether decision uncertainty considerations can help to explain the disparity between hypothetical contingent values and real economic commitments. Specifically, we re-examine the goose-hunting data collected by Bishop and Heberlein (1979) by developing a more generalized econometric model with a decision uncertainty measure[3] taken into account. Our results indicate that the hypothetical and real WTA estimates may be derived from the same underlying model although the value information is more diffuse in the hypothetical case. We find that the disparity between the two value estimates can be considerably reduced after an adjustment for the decision uncertainty effect. As the remaining difference can be reasonably generated by economic theory, we are not inclined to attribute it to any strategic or hypothetical bias explanations.

The remaining part of the chapter is structured as follows. Section 2 reviews the original Bishop and Heberlein (1979) model and their model estimates. Section 3 develops a generalized discrete choice model with decision uncertainty taken into account, and Section 4 presents our new model estimates and compares them with the Bishop and Heberlein results. Section 5 sums up the study.

2   THE BISHOP–HEBERLEIN MODEL

In their seminal paper, Bishop and Heberlein (1979) made a double contribution to the CV literature with the introduction of the discrete choice questioning strategy[4] and the discovery of disparity between hypothetical and real WTA estimates. The sample in the experiment consists of 590 registered hunters, of which 237 were given a real cash offer for selling their hunting permit while 353 received mail questionnaires designed to develop hypothetical valuations. Each individual was asked to indicate whether or not he or she would accept a given offer as compensation to forgo hunting during the season. The offer varied from 1 to 200 dollars across the sample. To such a discrete choice question, the individual simply had to answer a 'yes' or 'no' without any need to specify the exact WTA amount. Under the assumption of a log-logistic value distribution function, Bishop and Heberlein expressed the probability for an individual to accept an offer x as:

$$F(x) = \frac{1}{1 + \exp[-\alpha - \beta \ln(x)]} \tag{13.1}$$

and estimated the regression model

$$\ln\left[\frac{F(x)}{1 - F(x)}\right] = \alpha + \beta \ln(x) + \varepsilon \tag{13.2}$$

using a generalized least squares estimator,[5] where α and β are parameters and ε is a stochastic component.

The behavioral assumption underlying this model is that the individual with a true (minimum) WTA w would accept an offer x if $w \leq x$, and reject it otherwise. With the estimated model parameters α and β, the mean WTA can be calculated by:

$$E(w) = \int_0^\infty [1 - F(x)]dx \tag{13.3}$$

provided that the WTA values are non-negative and unbounded from above (Hanemann, 1984). However, Bishop and Heberlein chose to truncate the value distribution from above at the highest dollar offer of 200 dollars and, accordingly, calculated the mean WTA by:

$$E(w \mid w \leq 200) = \int_0^{200} [1 - F(x)]dx \tag{13.4}$$

which gave a truncated mean value of 101 and 63 dollars for the subsamples with hypothetical questions and real economic commitments, respectively. This finding of disparity in value estimates has led researchers in subsequent studies to test for various sources of bias in contingent value estimates (Blackburn et al., 1994; Cummings et al., 1995).

One reason for Bishop and Heberlein to set an upper bound might be that it is a usual practice in statistics not to extrapolate outside the range of observed data, that is, the range of bids between 1 and 200 dollars in this case. Another reason might be that the survival function $S(x) = 1 - F(x)$ has a rather fat tail to the right for the subsample with hypothetical valuation questions, about 0.30 at the highest offer, and thus the integral (13.3) fails to converge, resulting in an infinitely large mean WTA. It is obvious that the disparity between the real and hypothetical mean WTA would become infinite without the truncation practice.

3   A GENERALIZED DISCRETE CHOICE MODEL WITH DECISION UNCERTAINTY

The concepts in economic theory underlying the CV method are preferences in terms of compensating and equivalent variation measures. Assuming that an individual's preferences can be represented by a utility function $u(y, q)$ where y is income and q is an indicator variable with $q = 0$ for a state without the hunting permit and $q = 1$ for a state with the permit. Then the compensating variation, that is, the minimum WTA w to forgo hunting, is defined by $u(y + w, 0) = u(y,1)$. As touched upon above, an implicit assumption underlying the Bishop and Heberlein (1979) model and many subsequent studies was that each individual perfectly knew his or her true valuation w. This implies that the individual would be able to make a perfect choice by checking 'yes' if $w \leq x$ and 'no' otherwise. If such is the case, it would not matter whether the valuation question is formulated as an open-ended one asking for the exact dollar amount or as a discrete choice one asking whether the individual would accept a given offer. However, empirical evidence indicates that this is not the case (Hanemann and Kanninen, 1996; Kriström, 1993; McFadden, 1994).

Following the line of recent research on the subject (Li and Mattsson, 1995; Ready et al., 1995; Wang, 1997; Alberini et al., 2000), we do not assume that the individual has a fixed true valuation in his or her mind so that he or she may perceive it to be within a certain interval. Thus, in making a choice between two alternatives, it is the perceived value which matters. Suppose that the true valuation is w, and the individual's perceived value $\tilde{w}$ is contained in the interval $[w - h, w + h]$, then as long as the length of this interval is non-zero (that is, $h > 0$), there will be a positive probability to observe a 'wrong' answer to the discrete choice question. By a 'wrong' answer, we mean that the individual may accept an offer for his hunting permit even if the offer is less than his true WTA and vice versa. As human beings are not designed to be super-machines for making perfect choices, such 'wrong' responses should be expected.[6] However, the appearance of such 'wrong' responses will distort the valuation distribution estimate and thereby any inference drawn from it.

Proposition 1   Let w be continuously distributed in (a, b) with $-\infty \leq a < b \leq \infty$, and $\tilde{w} = w + \eta$ conditional on w being distributed in $[w - h, w + h]$ for $h \geq 0$, where η is a random component. Then for any given dollar offer $x \in (a, b)$, the probability to observe 'wrong' responses, $\Pr(\tilde{w} > x \mid w < x)$ or $\Pr(\tilde{w} < x \mid w > x)$ is strictly positive for any $h > 0$.

Proof   Assume that $w < x$ and let $w_1 = \{w \mid w < x\}$. For any $h > 0$, there exists w close to x such that $x - w < h$ or $x < w + h$. Then, the set $w_2 = \{ (w, \tilde{w}) \mid w < x, x < \tilde{w} < w + h \}$ is non-empty. Let $\Omega_1 = \{w \mid w \in (a, b) \}$ and $\Omega_2 = \{ (w, \tilde{w}) \mid \tilde{w} \in [w - h, w + h], w \in (a, b) \}$. Then, the 'wrong' response probability is:

$$\Pr(\tilde{w} > x \mid w < x) = \frac{\Pr[w_2 \in \Omega_2]}{\Pr[w_1 \in \Omega_1]} > 0. \tag{13.5}$$

In the same spirit, the case for $w > x$ can also be proved. ∎

To operationalize the decision uncertainty concept, we assume that there is a true utility function $u(y, q)$, but that the individual himself/herself does not perfectly know about it. What he or she perceives is $\tilde{u}(y, q) = u(y, q) + \delta_q$, where δ_q is a random component, and thus the perceived WTA, $\tilde{w}$, is defined by $\tilde{u}(y, 1) = \tilde{u}(y + \tilde{w}, 0)$ or equivalently $u(y + \tilde{w}, 0) = u(y, 1) + \delta$, where $\delta = \delta_1 - \delta_0$. Let $\bar{u} = u(y, 1)$ for given y be the initial utility level with a legal hunting right, then for the given well-behaved utility function $\tilde{u}(y, q)$, we may solve for $\tilde{w}$ by $\tilde{w} = \tilde{w}(\delta \mid \bar{u})$. In most cases, the utility function is assumed to be concave in its arguments, which mimics a risk-averse behavior in decisions under uncertainty.

Proposition 2   Under the risk averse assumption, that is, the utility $u(y, q)$ is concave in income, then the perceived willingness to accept $\tilde{w} = \tilde{w}(\delta \mid \bar{u})$ is convex in δ with $\tilde{w}(0 \mid \bar{u}) = w$. As a result, the mathematical expectation of $\tilde{w}$ with respect to δ will not be below w, that is $E(\tilde{w}) \geq w$ for any given utility $\bar{u}$. If the utility function is strictly concave, then the inequality is strict, that is, $E(\tilde{w}) > w$.

Proof   Let $m(u, q)$ denote the expenditure function, that is, the minimum expenditure required to sustain a utility level u given q. Then the perceived expenditure of m for $u = \bar{u} + \delta$ and $q = 0$ becomes $\tilde{m}(\bar{u} + \delta, 0) = u^{-1}(\bar{u} + \delta, 0) = y + \tilde{w}$. By the concavity assumption, we have:

$$u[\lambda \tilde{m}_1 + (1 - \lambda)\tilde{m}_2), 0] \geq \lambda u(\tilde{m}_1, 0) + (1 - \lambda)u(\tilde{m}_2, 0), \qquad (13.6)$$

for any λ with $0 < \lambda < 1$. By taking the inverse of u on both sides, we have:

$$\lambda \tilde{m}_1 + (1 - \lambda)\tilde{m}_2 \geq \tilde{m}[\lambda u_1 + (1 - \lambda)u_2, 0], \qquad (13.7)$$

where $u_1 = u(\tilde{m}_1, 0)$ and $u_2 = u(\tilde{m}_2, 0)$. By the definition of convexity, it is evident that $\tilde{m}$ is convex in $\bar{u} + \delta$. Since $\tilde{w}(\delta \mid \bar{u}) = \tilde{m}(\bar{u} + \delta, 0) - y$ and $\bar{u}, y$ are constant, we know that $\tilde{w}$ is convex in δ. Given that $\tilde{w}$ is (strictly) convex in δ, the statement $\tilde{w}(0 \mid \bar{u}) = w$ follows directly from the definitions $u(y + w, 0) = u(y, 1)$ and $u(y + \tilde{w}, 0) = u(y, 1) + \delta$, and the stated inequalities are immediate consequences of the Jensen inequality. ∎

Proposition 2 may be interpreted as follows: under the given assumptions, an individual's *ex ante* WTA in the presence of decision uncertainty should be expected to be higher than the true value with complete certainty; and the mean WTA across a large number of identical individuals under decision uncertainty should be higher than under decision certainty.

The behavioral assumptions under decision uncertainty now become that an individual would accept the offer x if $\tilde{w} \leq x$ and reject the offer if $\tilde{w} > x$. To be comparable with Bishop and Heberlein (1979), we also assume that $\ln(w)$ is logistically distributed by distribution (13.1) with mean $\mu = -\alpha/\beta$ and standard deviation $\sigma = \pi\kappa/\sqrt{3}$ where $\kappa = 1/\beta$. Furthermore, we assume that $\ln(\tilde{w}) = \ln(w) + \eta$, where η is a random component. Thus, we have $\ln(\tilde{w}) = \mu + \eta + \epsilon$, where ϵ is logistically distributed with zero mean and constant variance σ, and η has a certain distributional form. Let the conditional distribution function of $\tilde{w}$, for a given η, be represented by $F(\tilde{w} \mid \eta) = 1/(1 + \exp\{-\alpha - \beta[\ln(\tilde{w}) - \eta]\})$, and the probability density function of η be $\phi(\eta)$, then the unconditional probability distribution of $\tilde{w}$ becomes:

$$F(\tilde{w}) = \int_a^b F(\tilde{w} \mid \eta) \cdot \phi(\eta)d\eta, \quad a \leq \eta \leq b \qquad (13.8)$$

where $[a, b]$ is the support for η. Now, suppose that η is uniformly distributed with $\phi(\eta) = 1/2h$, with $-h \leq \eta \leq h$, then it is readily shown that $\tilde{w}$ is distributed according to:

$$F(\tilde{w}) = \frac{1}{2\beta h} \ln \left[\frac{1 + \exp(\alpha + \beta\ln(\tilde{w}) + \beta h)}{1 + \exp(\alpha + \beta\ln(\tilde{w}) - \beta h)} \right] \qquad (13.9)$$

which converges to the log-logistic distribution[7] for $h \to 0$.

Now, for a number of n observations (x_i, I_i), $i = 1, 2, \ldots, n$, where I_i is an indicator variable with value 1 if the individual accepted the offer x_i and 0 otherwise, then the unknown parameters α, β, and h may be estimated by maximizing the following log-likelihood function:

$$\ln L = \sum_{i=1}^{n}\{I_i\ln[F(x_i)] + (1 - I_i) \ln [1 - F(x_i)]\}. \tag{13.10}$$

It is worth mentioning that there are methods for estimating the distribution of η using non-parametric techniques for given empirical data. Suppose that the distribution takes m discrete steps with $\phi(\eta_i) = p_i$, $i = 1, 2, \ldots, m$, with $\sum_{i=1}^{m}p_i = 1$, the unconditional distribution of $\tilde{w}$ can be written as:

$$F(\tilde{w}) = \sum_{i=1}^{m}F(\tilde{w}\,|\,\eta_i) \cdot p_i. \tag{13.11}$$

By using (13.11), we have the following log-likelihood function:

$$\ln L = \sum_{i=1}^{n}\left\{I_i\ln\left[\sum_{i=1}^{m}F(x_i\,|\,\eta_i) \cdot p_i\right] + (1 - I_i) \ln \left[1 - \sum_{i=1}^{m}F(x_i\,|\,\eta_i) \cdot p_i\right]\right\}$$
$$\tag{13.12}$$

which can be optimized with respect to the mass points η_i and the associated probabilities p_i for each given m which, in itself, can be determined by using the criteria[8] by Akaike (1973) and Lindsay (1983).

4   EMPIRICAL RESULTS AND INTERPRETATIONS

The response rates for Bishop and Heberlein's (1979) real and hypothetical market experiments were above 80 percent. For our analysis, the final sample consists of 249 and 140 observations for the hypothetical and real settings, respectively, after the elimination of observations due to various omissions. A general chi-square test for the vector of socioeconomic variables in the two subsamples does not indicate significant difference at any conventional significance level.[9] Thus, we have a fair basis for comparing the estimates of the corresponding two underlying distribution functions. By maximizing the log-likelihood function (13.10) using the LIMDEP Package (Greene, 1991), we obtain separate estimates of the parameters α, β and h, as shown in Table 13.1. For the hypothetical market data, the estimate of parameter h is positive (2.8614) and statistically significant at the 5 percent critical level, in contrast, the corresponding value for the real market data is close to 0. This may be interpreted as that the respondents in the hypothetical market experiment face higher decision uncertainty than their real counterpart. Another possibility is

Table 13.1   Parameter estimates in the valuation distribution functions (standard error in parentheses)

Experiment	New maximum likelihood			Simple log-logistic	
	α	β	h	α	β
Hypothetical	−6.7947	1.5913	2.8614	−3.3708	0.7858
	(12.71)	(2.99)	(1.43)	(0.61)	(0.14)
Real	−5.3118	1.5146	0.0042	−5.3164	1.5157
	(6.16)	(1.76)	(97.34)	(0.99)	(0.27)

that people do not search for their true preferences in a hypothetical situation as intensively as in real transactions.

As the estimate of h in the real market case is about 0, the new maximum likelihood and the simple log-logistic estimates characterize essentially the same underlying model. However, for the hypothetical case, the log-logistic one is strongly distorted by the uncertainty effect. While our new maximum likelihood method provides the mean and standard deviation estimates $\mu = -\alpha/\beta = 4.2700$ and $\sigma = \pi\kappa/\sqrt{3} = 1.1398$ ($\kappa = 0.6284$), the simple log-logistic one gives $\mu = 4.2897$ and $\sigma = 2.3082$ ($\kappa = 1.2725$). As the valuation distribution function is skewed to the right, such distortion in the distribution estimate may lead to an extremely high mean WTA estimate, which is infinite for $\kappa > 1$. By removing the uncertainty effect on the standard deviation estimate, we let $h \to 0$, and thus obtain a limit distribution as log-logistic with $\mu = 4.2700$ and $\kappa = 0.6284$, which is much closer to the distribution of the real WTA with $\mu = 5.1364/1.5157 = 3.3888$ and $\kappa = 1/1.5157 = 0.6598$. The effect is illustrated in Figure 13.1.

The truncated and overall mean WTA estimates[10] corresponding to (13.4) and (13.3) for different settings are reported in Table 13.2. While the truncated value estimate is obtained by using numerical integration, the overall value is calculated by $\exp(\mu)\Gamma(1 - \kappa)\Gamma(1 + \kappa)$ as in Cameron (1988). The dramatic effect caused by eliminating the effect of decision uncertainty on the standard deviation estimate is the reduction of the mean WTA estimate from infinity to about \$154. However, there still remains some difference between the estimates of hypothetical and real payments with the truncated mean values \$91 and \$54 and the overall mean values \$154 and \$70, respectively. An important question now is whether this difference is a result of strategic behavior and hypothetical bias as discussed in the literature. Our conclusion is that this is not necessarily the case. From Proposition 2, we know that it can be a direct consequence that the expected WTA under decision uncertainty is higher than under certainty if the utility function is (strictly) concave. Although we are not

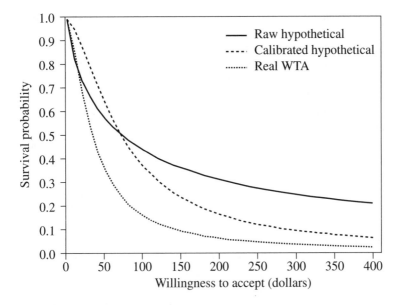

Figure 13.1 Survival functions for hypothetical and real WTA

asserting that the responses in the real market experiment indicate the absolute true preferences, it is evident from the above analysis that decision uncertainty in the hypothetical case does arise and cause problems.

The valuation estimates in the hypothetical case with decision uncertainty are distorted by at least two effects: the expected (mean) value becomes higher and the estimated distribution function becomes flattened. Even though the responses to hypothetical valuation questions contain useful information, the valuation signals may be weakened by the two distortion effects described

Table 13.2 Truncated and overal mean WTA estimates (standard error in parentheses)

	μ	κ	Truncated mean	Overall mean
Raw WTA	4.2897	1.2725	98	∞
	(0.18)	(0.23)	(6.5)	(–)
Calibrated WTA	4.2700	0.6284	91	154
	(0.19)	(0.49)	(17.5)	(234)
Real WTA	3.5072	0.6603	54	79
	(0.15)	(0.12)	(7.2)	(30)

above. Without further experimental evidence regarding the degree of individuals' decision uncertainty, the extent to which hypothetical valuation is subject to strategic and other types of bias is not settled. Thus, instead of attributing the disparity between real and hypothetical WTA estimates to some psychometric or strategic biases, the appearance of subjective decision uncertainty and risk-averse behavior may be a reasonable explanation.

To give an illustration of the effect of risk-averse behavior under decision uncertainty, suppose that there are two hunters with a utility function $u = (y + w)^{0.1}$ in the absence of the hunting access. Let the initial income be 1000 and the initial utility be 2 with access to hunting, then they both have a true WTA for the permit which is $w = 2^{10} - 1000 = 24$ with variance 0. Under decision uncertainty one perceives the new utility level as $2 - 0.05 = 1.95$ and the other perceives it as $2 + 0.05 = 2.05$. Then, their expected WTA becomes $\frac{1}{2}(1.95^{10} - 1000) + \frac{1}{2}(2.05^{10} - 1000) \approx 53$ and variance of the perceived values[11] is clearly positive.

In addition to the uniform assumption for the random term η, we have also studied the Bishop and Heberlein (1979) data using the non-parametric model variant with discrete distributions. A direct maximization of the log-likelihood function (13.12) for $m = 2$ leads to the results[12] as shown in Table 13.3. Note that the intercept α was set for 0 for the purpose of identification and thus the mass points η_1 and η_2 would be similar to match the corresponding α values. In the table, we report the probability estimate for p_1 only, since $p_2 = 1 - p_1$ for the case $m = 2$.

In effect, this amounts to an estimation of two separate log-logistic models with different intercepts, that is, η_1 and η_2. The mass points η_1 and η_2 seem to show a clearer pattern of two peaks in the hypothetical subsample than those in the real subsample where they almost collapse to a single point ($p_2 = 0.9607$). This is consistent with our earlier estimates using the uniform distribution of η. To compare the extent of the uncertainty estimate using the uniform distribution and that using the discrete distribution, we normalize the random component η by $\tilde{\eta} = (\eta - \bar{\eta})/\beta$ where $\bar{\eta}$ is the mean of η, and obtain the

Table 13.3   Model estimates using the non-parametric method (standard error in parentheses)

Parameters	Hypothetical		Real	
α	–	–	–	–
β	1.2590	(6.4230)	1.5388	(8.6820)
p_1	0.3745	(0.2730)	0.0393	(0.0455)
η_1	–3.0900	(0.9832)	–3.8603	(110.70)
η_2	–6.5598	(4.3430)	–5.4582	(55.210)

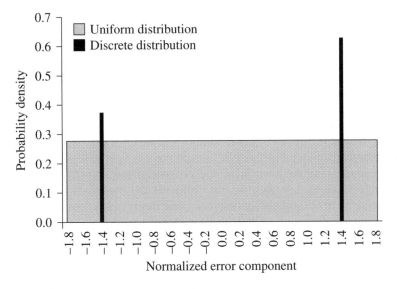

*Figure 13.2   Estimated density functions for the normalized error
            component*

distributions of $\tilde{\eta}$ as shown in Figure 13.2. Since the estimate of p_1 (p_2) is not significantly different from 0.5 for the hypothetical subsample, the empirical results here seem to support the uniform distribution assumption about the random component η.

5   CONCLUDING REMARKS

This chapter has reconsidered the famous Bishop and Heberlein model and their experimental results about the discrepancy between hypothetical and real WTA estimates. We have introduced decision uncertainty in the discrete choice response model and thus carried out separate estimates for the hypothetical and real market experiment data sets. We argue that individual respondents may not have a fixed preference ordering about alternative choices and thus may give 'wrong' responses to the discrete choice valuation question. Evidence and logic suggest that if people had a prefect preference ordering, then they would be able to figure out the exact Hicksian value for any proposed change in the state of nature. However, the fact that people usually face great difficulties when answering an open-ended question such as 'what is your minimum willingness to accept compensation if you lose this resource' does not support any perfect preference order hypothesis.

We have proved that whenever there is uncertainty regarding the true point valuation, there will be a non-zero probability to give 'wrong' responses to the discrete choice question. As a consequence, the valuation distribution estimate will become flattened, and 'fatter tails' are frequently observed for estimated survival functions. Another point is that, by risk-averse behavior, individuals who are uncertain about the welfare effects of a proposed change tend to have higher expected WTA values than under certainty. Thus, as the degree of decision uncertainty becomes lower, the expected mean WTA should also be lower. When the tidewater of uncertainty ebbs away, the true WTA value may show its face.

By introducing the concept of decision uncertainty into the referendum contingent valuation model, we may interpret the observed disparity as a consequence or rational choice from economic theory rather than attribute it to psychometric distortion or hypothetical bias. Exactly how much disparity there would be depends on both the degree of risk aversion and the degree of uncertainty in welfare evaluations. If these effects can be revealed in some way, then it should be possible to make corresponding adjustments. However, this may raise further issues concerning the design of new experiments for eliciting such uncertainties.

The Bishop and Heberlein model marked a revolution in the use of the referendum valuation method, and their finding of the disparity between hypothetical and real payments has attracted researchers to search for various sources of bias. While much research has focused on different sources of bias in contingent valuation, this chapter offers an economic explanation of the disparity problem. In fact, while the problem of state uncertainty has been studied for various decision problems, effects of preference and other decision uncertainties are largely ignored. In the search for better explanations of the disparity between real and hypothetical value estimates, this chapter provides a benchmark from an economic point of view and the propositions we have stated here may be empirically testable given suitable experimental data.

NOTES

1. The idea of using survey questions to value non-market resources was proposed by Ciriacy-Wantrup (1947), and first applied by Davis (1963) for outdoor recreation studies.
2. The reason for this was that the discrete choice question format was claimed to be more market-like and incentive compatible.
3. In making a trade off between money and the hunting permit, the individual may be uncertain about his/her preferences, prices and availability of substitutes, and the like.
4. This type of model was used in mathematical biology for dose-response data analysis in Finney (1971) and in economics by McFadden (1976) for quantal choice analysis. Hanemann (1984) offers a utility-theoretical interpretation of contingent valuation responses.

5. Since there were many observations per cell, that is, many individuals received the same offer in the experiment, the log-odd can be calculated empirically.
6. Such uncertainty in choice behavior is closely related to the stochastic preference literature (Georgescu-Roegen, 1936) and the psychological literature (Thurstone, 1927).
7. This can be easily verified by applying the L-Hospital rule.
8. Brännäs and Rosenqvist (1994) compared the properties of the different evaluation criteria for model selections.
9. The variables used in the test are age, sex, education, marital status, family income, frequency of hunting, hunting days, travel miles, travel time and so on. The reason for the elimination of the observation with omited variables is to rule out possible item non-response effects.
10. Note that the standard errors for μ and κ in the 'calibrated WTA' row are estimated by using the covariance matrix of α and β with h fixed at its estimate 2.8614.
11. Note that in this highly simplified illustration, we have not imposed the requirement that the perceived WTA be non-negative.
12. Since the log-likelihood function becomes quite flat with respect to the many parameters at the optimum, the approximate standard errors of the estimates may be rather high. Thus, we are content with $m = 2$ even though the optimum of m may be larger than 2.

REFERENCES

Akaike, H. (1973), 'Information theory and an extension of the maximum likelihood principle', in B.N. Petrov and F. Csaki (eds), *Second International Symposium on Information Theory*, Budapest: Akademia Kiado, pp. 267–81.
Alberini, A., K. Boyle and M. Welsh (2000), 'Analysis of contingent valuation data with multiple bids and response options allowing respondents to express uncertainty', Paper presented at the European Association of Environmental and Resource Economists (EAERE) 2000 Annual Conference, University of Crete, Department of Economics, Rethymnon, Greece, 30 June to 2 July.
Arrow, K., R. Solow, E. Leamer, P. Portney, R. Radner and H. Schuman (1993), 'Report of the NOAA panel on contingent valuation', *Federal Register*, **58**, 4602–14.
Bishop, R. and T. Heberlein (1979), 'Measuring values of extramarket goods: are direct measures biased?', *American Journal of Agricultural Economics*, **61**, 926–30.
Blackburn, M., G.W. Harrison and E.E. Ruström (1994), 'Statistical bias functions and informative hypothetical surveys', *American Journal of Agricultural Economics*, **76**, 1084–8.
Brännäs, K. and G. Rosenqvist (1994), 'Semiparametric estimation of heterogeneous count data models', *European Journal of Operations Research*, **76**, 247–58.
Cameron, T.A. (1988), 'A new paradigm for valuing non-market goods for "closed-ended" contingent valuation surveys', *Journal of Environmental Economics and Management*, **15**, 355–79.
Ciriacy-Wantrup, S.V. (1947), 'Capital returns from oil conversation practices', *Journal of Farm Economics*, **29**, 1188–90.
Clawson, M. and J. Knetsch (1966), *The Economics of Outdoor Recreation*, Baltimore, MD: Johns Hopkins University Press.
Cummings, R., G.W. Harrison and E.E. Ruström (1995), 'Homegrown values and hypothetical surveys: is the dichotomous choice approach incentive compatible?', *American Economic Review*, **85**, 260–66.
Davis, R. (1963), *The Value of Outdoor Recreation: An Economic Study of the Maine Woods*, Cambridge, MA: Harvard University Press.

Finney, D.J. (1971), *Probit Analysis*, Cambridge: Cambridge University Press.

Georgescu-Roegen, N. (1936), 'The pure theory of consumer's behavior', *Quarterly Journal of Economics*, **50**, 545–93.

Greene, W.H. (1991), *LIMDEP version 6.0*, Econometric Software, Inc.

Hanemann, W.M. (1984), 'Welfare evaluation in contingent valuation experiments with discrete responses', *American Journal of Agricultural Economics*, **66**, 332–41.

Hanemann, W.M. and B. Kanninen (1996), 'The statistical analysis of discrete-response CV data', Working Paper No. 798, Department of Agricultural and Resource Economics, University of California, Berkeley.

Kriström, B. (1993), 'Comparing continuous and discrete contingent valuation questions', *Environmental and Resource Economics*, **3**, 63–71.

Li, C.Z. and L. Mattsson (1995), 'Discrete choice under preference uncertainty: an improved structural model for contingent valuation', *Journal of Environmental Economics and Management*, **28**, 256–69.

Lindsay, B.G. (1983), 'The geometry of mixture likelihoods', *Annals of Statistics*, **11**, 86–94.

Mäler, K.-G., I.M. Gren and C. Folke (1994), 'Multiple use of environmental resources: a household production function approach to valuing natural capital', in A. Jansson, M. Hammer, C. Folke and R. Costanza (eds), *Investing in Natural Capital: The Ecological Economics Approach to Sustainability*, Washington, DC: Island Press, pp. 233–49.

McFadden, D. (1976), 'Quantal choice analysis: a survey', *Annals of Economic and Social Management*, **5**, 363–90.

McFadden, D. (1994), 'Contingent valuation and social choice', *American Journal of Agricultural Economics*, **76**, 689–708.

Mitchell, R.C. and R.T. Carson (1989), *Using Surveys to Value Public Goods: the Contingent Valuation Method*, Washington, DC: Resources for the Future.

Ready, R.C., J.C. Whitehead and G.C. Blomquist (1995), 'Contingent valuation when respondents are ambivalent', *Journal of Environmental Economics and Management*, **29**, 181–96.

Rosen, S. (1974), 'Hedonic prices and implicit markets: product differentiation in pure competition', *Journal of Political Economy*, **82**, 34–55.

Thurstone, L.L. (1927), 'Psychological analysis', *American Journal of Psychology*, **38**, 368–89.

Wang, H. (1997), 'Treatment of "don't know" responses in contingent valuation surveys: a random valuation model', *Journal of Environmental Economics and Management*, **32**, 219–32.

14. An economic approach to the control of invasive species in aquatic systems

Charles Perrings

1 INTRODUCTION

The economics of fisheries has been dominated by the problem of fish stock depletion. Indeed, the theory of the optimal depletion of renewable resources other than forests has largely been driven by research on fisheries. Extension of models of the harvest of single species to the multi-species case has related depletion to the relative abundance of substitute species, and has drawn attention to the fact that harvest of target species can affect the dynamics of non-target species (the problem of by-catch). To this point, however, relatively little attention has been paid to the economics of pests and pathogens in fisheries, and almost no attention to the problem posed by the introduction, establishment and spread of new species that may interact with fish stocks. This is the problem of invasive species. Most ecosystem types – terrestrial, freshwater and marine – have been impacted to a greater or lesser extent by biological invasions (Parker et al., 1999; Williamson, 1998, 2000).

By altering biodiversity, invasions have transformed ecosystems into new configurations with often surprising and severe consequences for human welfare. Ecologists define any species that establishes, naturalizes and spreads outside its home range to be invasive (Rejmanek, 1989). However, the Convention on Biological Diversity limits the term to those invasives that cause appreciable harm to the invaded system. In many cases this involves a fundamental change in the state of a system.

One of the best-known examples of a marine invasive species is in the Black Sea, where the establishment of the jellyfish, *Mnemiopsis leidii*, has transformed the ecology of the system. The zebra mussel, *Dreissena polymorpha*, has had similar effects in freshwater systems in both Europe and America. It is now thought to have invaded about one-third of all freshwater aquatic environments in the United States (Williamson, 1996). But these are only the most familiar examples of a phenomenon that is rapidly growing with the widening and deepening of international markets in goods and services. The most severe costs of invasions may be due to their impact on local and global biodiversity. Biological invasions rank second only to habitat destruction as a cause of biodiversity loss worldwide (Glowka et al., 1994; Wilcove et al., 1998; Czech and Krausman, 1997). But invasive species have other costs too. In exploited systems they can alter the relative abundance of both harvested and non-harvested species, and have the potential to change other ecological services in ways that may be irreversible.

They also impose significant costs in forgone output or defensive expenditure in a wide range of activities. Knowler (1999) and Knowler and Barbier (2000) have examined the role of *Mnemiopsis* in changing the cost of fishing effort in the Black Sea. There have also been attempts to estimate the costs imposed by the green crab, *Carcinus maenas*, on the North Pacific Ocean fisheries (Cohen at al., 1995), and by the zebra mussel on industrial plants in both Europe and the United States (Khalanski, 1997). While we may be most directly concerned with the costs imposed by human pathogens – HIV is a classical example of an invasive species – invasions turn out to be one of the most general and significant consequences of anthropogenic environmental change in both terrestrial and aquatic systems.

What makes the problem particularly interesting from an economic perspective is that it is usually an external effect of market transactions and its control is a public good of a particularly intractable sort. The wider impacts of invasive species are not taken into account by people responsible for their introduction, establishment or spread. These impacts may be localized and of relatively short duration, but they may also be widespread and have periodic, chronic or potentially irreversible effects. Ecosystems vary in their natural susceptibility to invasion. While pelagic marine systems appear to be least susceptible, mixed island systems, lake, river and near-shore marine systems are especially vulnerable (Heywood, 1995). Of course, the probability of establishment of intentionally introduced species is higher than that of unintentionally introduced species simply because intentionally introduced species have been selected for their ability to survive in the environment where they are introduced (Smith et al., 1999) and may be introduced repeatedly (Enserink, 1999). But the probability of both establishment and spread also depends on the way in which the environment is altered by human behaviour.

Marine invasions are frequently induced by changes in environmental conditions due to the effects of pollution, or are the consequences of the movement of goods and services. Among the most striking data reported by the IWCO (1998) is that 77 percent of global marine pollution is now thought to derive from land-based sources either directly or via the atmosphere. Changing patterns of land use in watersheds have had major effects on flood regimes worldwide by changing in-stream flows. In some areas, increasing surface run-off due to deforestation has boosted the frequency and severity of floods. In others, increasing rates of water abstraction have had the opposite effect. Both pollution and changes in stream flows have altered estuarine and coastal ecosystems in ways that make them more susceptible to invasion. About 90 percent of the global catch depends on coastal habitats for at least part of their life cycle. Those habitats are particularly susceptible to disruption from on-shore activities including the disposal of toxic and other waste products, devegetation that leads to increased sediment loads in rivers, and land-use change in coastal zones.

Many marine systems are characterized by multiple locally stable states, the properties and economic value of which are different. Sewage and fertilizer run-off leads to increases in algal growth which give rise to the 'toxic tides' that are causing rising mortality in fish and marine mammal populations in coastal areas. Coral reefs with high levels of fish and other aquatic diversity have been flipped into a low-value state dominated by blue green algae and otherwise low levels of aquatic diversity. Toxic algal blooms in the northern Adriatic reduce the value of the resource in tourism. It turns out that biological invasions are frequently induced by changes of this sort. Terrestrial pollution is, for example, implicated in the susceptibility of the Black Sea to invasion by *Mnemiopsis* (Knowler and Barbier, 2000).

This chapter considers the economic problem of biological invasions and their control. It identifies the factors in the control problem that determine whether a system affected by an invasion will experience a change of state. The chapter develops a model of the optimal control of biological invasions. The model specifies the dynamics of 'establishment', 'spread' and 'removal', and establishes the conditions in which it is optimal to allow establishment and spread. The chapter is in four sections. The next section develops the basic model of invasives and states the main propositions of the chapter. Section 3 then offers a discussion of these, and a final section offers some concluding remarks.

2 A MODEL OF BIOLOGICAL INVASIONS

The generic problem of biological invasions involves four phases: the introduction, establishment, naturalization and spread of a species outside of its normal range (Williamson, 1996). In what follows, these four phases are all subsumed under the spread of invasives. The process is held to be analogous to that of a virus entering and spreading within a host population (Delfino and Simmons, 2000). Indeed, the model is developed from the Kermack and McKendrick (1927) model, which underpins epidemiological theory.

Unlike epidemiological models, however, the state variables are measures of the space occupied by 'invasive' and 'native' species, rather than the population or biomass of those species. Since a biological invasion involves the occupation of habitat, it can be modelled as the growth of the space occupied by the invasive species. The problem will only be interesting if that space is otherwise occupied by species that yield a flow of goods or services. These will be referred to, for convenience, as 'native' species although in any particular situation 'native' species may actually comprise cultivated exotics. That is, 'invasive' refers to the space impacted by alien invasive species, and in the absence of control 'native' refers to the complement of that space.

The total space is assumed to be constant over the time horizon of interest, and the state variables are denominated in terms of that space. They are the proportion of the total space occupied by native and invasive species, denoted $x(t)$ and $y(t)$, respectively, and the proportion of the total space 'cleared' of invasives in the control process, denoted $u(t)$. The rate of change in the space occupied by the invasive species is taken to be proportional to the product of the space occupied by the invasive and native species. This implies that the spread of invasives is proportional to the area of contact between native and invasive species. As invasive species establish and begin to spread the rate is low. It increases up to the point where the total space is split evenly between the desired and invasive species, and decreases again as the space occupied by the invasive species approaches the total space. The invasion rate, α, is taken to be constant parameter in what follows, although I later consider the connection between the invasion rate and resource use.

In general, the control of invasives includes a number of options: exclusion, eradication, containment (control), mitigation and adaptation. Exclusion implies the uses of measures such as quarantine, blacklists or innoculation to prevent the introduction of potentially invasive species. Eradication is typically, but not always, an option only in the early stages of the spread of an invasive species. Containment implies the restriction of the space occupied by an invasive species. Mitigation and adaptation imply measures to accommodate the invasive species. In what follows these measures are collapsed into a single index of control, $\beta(t)$. Just as the area occupied by invasive species is taken to be proportional to the area of contact between native and invasive species (the product of the space occupied by natives and invasives), so the area cleared of invasives is taken to be proportional to the area of contact between invasives and the control agent (the product of the space occupied by the invasive species and the space cleared of invasives). $\beta(t)$ is a choice variable in the model, and measures the intensity of the control effort.

Finally, it is assumed that the space cleared of invasives can be returned to native species at some positive rate, the restoration rate, $\gamma(t)$. Once again, the restoration rate is assumed to be a constant parameter in this chapter, but it might easily be analysed as a second choice variable.

The equations of motion for the state variables are as follows:

$$\dot{x} = -\alpha x(t)y(t) + \gamma u(t) \tag{14.1}$$

$$\dot{y} = \alpha x(t)y(t) - \beta(t)y(t)u(t) \tag{14.2}$$

$$\dot{u} = \gamma u(t) + \beta(t)y(t)u(t), \tag{14.3}$$

in which α, the invasion rate ($-1 \leq \alpha \leq 1$) and γ, the restoration rate ($0 \leq \gamma \leq 1$), are fixed parameters, and $\beta(t)$, the control rate ($0 \leq \beta(t) \leq 1$), is a choice variable.

For most biological invasion problems α will be strictly positive, implying that invasives spread at a positive rate. However, α may also be negative. This is the case where introduced species are unable to establish, naturalize or spread.

Since $x(t)$, $y(t)$ and $u(t)$ are shares of the total space it follows that:

$$u(t) = 1 - x(t) - y(t), \forall t \geq 0 \tag{14.4}$$

hence (14.1) and (14.2) can be written in the form:

$$\dot{x} = -\alpha x(t)y(t) + [1 - x(t) - y(t)]\gamma \tag{14.5}$$

$$\dot{y} = \alpha x(t)y(t) - [1 - x(t) - y(t)]\beta y(t). \tag{14.6}$$

With these we can identify some of the dynamics of the native and invasive species. Once a potentially invasive species has been introduced, $y(t) = 0$, the condition for it to spread is that it become established. A potentially invasive species may be said to be established when it has passed the threshold for growth. This threshold is defined by the values of $x(t)$ and $y(t)$ at which $\dot{y}(t) > 0$. From (14.6) it follows that the invasive species will spread if:

$$y(t) > 1 - x(t)\left[1 + \frac{\alpha}{\beta(t)}\right]. \tag{14.7}$$

Since $0 \leq y(t) \leq 1$ and $\{1 + [\alpha/\beta(t)]\} \geq 1$ this requires that $x(t) > 0$. Moreover, the greater the control rate relative to the invasion rate, the higher will be the threshold.

The threshold level of $x(t)$ is analogous to a threshold population density in epidemiology, where a minimum population density is needed to support the spread of disease. Note that the threshold is not independent of the control,

$\beta(t)$. Since this is a function of the costs and benefits of control, the establishment threshold for invasive species is similarly a function of economic variables.

To see how, consider the social decision problem. The social objective is taken to be to maximize some index of well-being through choice of the control rate, $\beta(t)$. I assume that the index of well-being is a measure of discounted net benefit. Hence the problem is to:

$$\max_{\beta(t)}\Pi[x(t), y(t), \beta(t), t] = \int_0^\infty e^{-\delta t}\{R[x(t)] - C[y(t), \beta(t)]\}dt \quad (14.8)$$

subject to (14.5), (14.6) and

$$x(0) = x_0, \; y(0) = y_0 \quad (14.9)$$

where δ is the discount rate; $R[x(t)]$ is revenue, a function of native species; and $C[y(t), \beta(t)]$ are costs, a function of invasive species and their control.

It is assumed that biological invasions and the control of biological invasions are both costly. Indeed, this assumption is built into the definition of invasive species in the Convention on Biological Diversity. The model does apply in cases where invasive species yield net benefits to society, but that is not the problem being discussed here.

The maximum condition for this problem is:

$$C_\beta = -\mu u(t)y(t), \quad (14.10)$$

in which μ is the co-state variable/shadow price of $y(t)$. This condition requires that the marginal cost of control, C_β, is equal to the marginal benefits from the direct reduction in $y(t)$ due to the control, $\mu u(t)y(t)$. Using equation (14.10) we can accordingly define the threshold for $x(t)$ in terms of the marginal costs and benefits of control:

$$x(t) > \left[1 + \frac{\beta(t)}{\mu u(t)}\right]\left[\frac{\beta(t)}{\alpha + \beta(t)}\right]. \quad (14.11)$$

From this it is apparent that:

Proposition 1 The establishment threshold for a species subject to invasion is increasing in the marginal cost of control and decreasing in the marginal social cost of the invasive species.

Define the threshold value of $\underline{x}(t)$ to be the minimum value of $x(t)$ at which $\dot{y}(t) > 0$,

$$x(t) = \left[1 + \frac{C_\beta}{\mu u(t)} \right] \left[\frac{\beta(t)}{\alpha + \beta(t)} \right].$$

The derivatives of this with respect to the marginal cost of control and the marginal social cost of the invasive species are:

$$x(t)C_\beta = \frac{\beta(t)}{\mu u(t)[\alpha + \beta(t)]} > 0$$

and

$$x(t)_\mu = - \frac{C_\beta \beta(t)}{\mu^2 u(t)[\alpha + \beta(t)]} < 0.$$

The fact that the establishment threshold of an invasive species depends on the social cost of the invasive species and the costs of control reflects the role of the control of invasives in the dynamics of both species.

The first-order conditions for optimization of (14.8) include equations (14.5), (14.6), (14.9), (14.10) and the following conditions on the evolution of the co-state variables, the adjoint equations:

$$\dot{\lambda} - \delta\lambda = -R_x + \lambda[y(t)\alpha + \gamma] - \mu y(t)[\alpha + \beta(t)] \tag{14.12}$$

$$\dot{\mu} - \delta\mu = C_\beta + \lambda[\alpha x(t) + \gamma] - \mu\{x(t)[\alpha + \beta(t)] - \beta(t)[1 + 2y(t)]\}. \tag{14.13}$$

These imply that in the steady state, $\dot{\lambda} = \dot{\mu} = 0$, the optimal control rate is:

$$\beta^* = \left[\frac{\delta - \alpha(x^* - y^*)}{1 - x^* - y^*} \right] \left(\frac{\lambda}{\mu} - 1 \right) + \left(\frac{R_x + C_y}{C_\beta} \right) \tag{14.14}$$

Proposition 2   If the effective invasion rate is less than the rate of discount, and if the shadow price of native species is greater than the shadow price of invasive species, then the optimal level of control of invasive species is increasing in:

1. the marginal benefit of native species,
2. the marginal cost of invasive species,

and is decreasing in:

3. the marginal cost of control.

The effective invasion rate is defined to be the product of the invasion rate and the difference between the space occupied by natives and invasives at equilibrium, $\alpha(y^* - x^*)$. If $\lambda > \mu$, and if $\delta - \alpha(y^* - x^*) > 0$, the signs on the derivatives of (14.14) with respect to R_x, C_y and C_β are as stated. If $\lambda < \mu$, and if $\delta - \alpha(y^* - x^*) < 0$ and if x^* is sufficiently greater than y^* the signs on the derivatives may be the opposite.

Propositions 1 and 2 state that the control of invasive species, and therefore their establishment and spread, are sensitive to the relative costs and benefits of invasives and natives, and of the cost of invasives control. It is obvious that the level of control should be negatively related to the cost of control, and positively related to the benefits of natives and the costs of invasives. But Proposition 2 also states that the opposite relation will hold if the discount rate is less than the effective invasion rate.

Note that the location of the equilibrium corresponding to the exclusion state is independent of the level of invasion control.

3   RESILIENCE AND THE CONTROL OF INVASIVE SPECIES

Returning to the dynamics of the invasive and native species, note that the system described by (14.4) and (14.5) has up to two equilibria depending on the parameter values. For all admissible parameter values there is one equilibrium at which the invasive species is completely excluded from the system. In *xy* space this equilibrium is:

$$(x_1^*, y_1^*) = (1, 0). \tag{14.15}$$

This is the equilibrium of the exclusion state. In the case where invasives spread at a positive rate, that is, for $0 \leq \alpha \leq 1$, there is a second equilibrium at which both invasive and native species coexist. It is:

$$(x_2^*, y_2^*) = \left(\frac{\beta^* - \gamma}{\alpha + \beta^*}, \frac{\gamma}{\beta^*} \right) \tag{14.16}$$

where β^* is the optimal control rate. This is referred to as the invaded state. However, both the location of the equilibrium corresponding to the invaded state and the convergence path to this equilibrium depend on the level of control.

Now consider the stability of the system equilibria. For the equilibrium corresponding to the exclusion state:

1. if $-1 \leq \alpha < 0$ then the exclusion state is a stable equilibrium; and
2. if $0 \leq \alpha \leq 1$ then the exclusion state is an unstable equilibrium.

First take the case where an introduced species is not able to establish, naturalize and spread. This may be thought of as the general case. It covers the majority of introductions. There is only one equilibrium in these conditions – that corresponding to the exclusion state, $(x_1^*, y_1^*) = (1, 0)$. We have two cases to consider: $-1 \leq \alpha < 0$ and $0 \leq \alpha \leq 1$. The Jacobian of $F(x_1^*, y_1^*)$, $DF(x_1^*, y_1^*)$ is:

$$DF(x_1^*, y_1^*) = \begin{bmatrix} -\gamma & -(\alpha + \gamma) \\ 0 & \alpha \end{bmatrix}. \tag{14.17}$$

If $-1 \leq \alpha < 0$ the trace of $DF(x_1^*, y_1^*)$ is positive and the determinant is negative. The equilibrium (x_1^*, y_1^*) is stable. The dynamics in this case are illustrated in Figure 14.1. The optimal level of the control in this case is zero. Since the introduced species are excluded from the system by competition or predation from native species, no control is needed to keep them in check.

Now take the case where an introduced species is able to establish and spread, that is, where $0 \leq \alpha \leq 1$. In this case the system has two equilibria. The first corresponds to the exclusion state, the second to the invaded state. Since the trace of $DF(x_1^*, y_1^*)$ is negative and the determinant is positive, the equilibrium corresponding to the exclusion state is unstable. By contrast, the

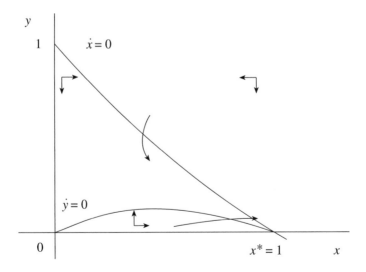

Figure 14.1 Stable exclusion state

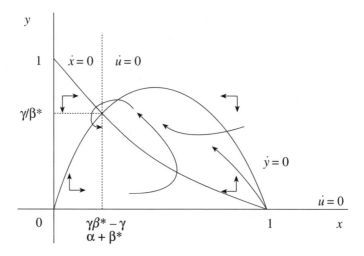

Figure 14.2   Unstable exclusion state, stable invaded state

equilibrium corresponding to the invaded state, (x_2^*, y_2^*), is stable. Both equilibria are illustrated in Figure 14.2.

The Jacobian of $F(x_2^*, y_2^*)$ (equation (14.17), $DF(x_2^*, y_2^*)$, is as follows:

$$DF(x_2^*, y_2^*) = \left\{ \begin{bmatrix} -\gamma \left(\dfrac{\alpha}{\beta^*} + 1 \right) - \left[\dfrac{\beta^* (\alpha + \gamma)}{(\alpha + \beta^*)} \right] \\ \gamma \left(\dfrac{\alpha}{\beta^*} + 1 \right) \qquad\qquad \gamma \end{bmatrix} \right\} \tag{14.18}$$

Since $0 \leq \alpha \leq 1, 0 \leq \beta(t) \leq 1$ and $0 \leq \gamma \leq \beta(t)y$ the trace of $F(x_2^*, y_2^*)$ is negative while the determinant is strictly positive for all $y > 0$. This implies that the interior equilibrium (x_2^*, y_2^*) is a stable spiral.

In the general case – if the exclusion equilibrium is stable – there is no control problem. Competition or predation will ensure that introduced species are automatically driven from the system. This is the case described in Figure 14.1. If the introduction of an alien species is interpreted as a shock to the system, the invasion rate is a measure of the system response to such a shock. A negative invasion rate implies that the response is to exclude the introduced species. No matter what proportion of the total space is occupied by an alien species at time $t = 0$, the proportion of the space occupied by natives will tend to unity as t tends to infinity. We can interpret this as a measure of the resilience, *sensu* Holling (1973) of the ecosystem indexed by $x(t)$ with respect to shocks imposed by the introduction of $y(t)$. Moreover, we have a natural measure of that resilience. It is the maximum share of the total space that the native species can lose to an introduced species and still recover. In this case, that measure is unity. It is a measure of the distance from the stable equilibrium to the boundary of the stability domain. It is apparent that there is also an analogue to the measure of resilience *sensu* Pimm (1984) in the maximum time taken for $x(t)$ to converge on the stable equilibrium (Perrings, 1998).

Although both the invasion and restoration rates have been treated parametrically in this chapter, they are in fact sensitive to the way that the host ecosystem is managed. It is often the case that species are able to invade precisely because of the pattern of resource use. A change in the pattern of resource use, perhaps associated with a change in institutional or market conditions, can change the invasion rate. It follows that if the invasion rate is not a fixed parameter of the system but a choice variable, one strategy for dealing with the risk of invasion species may be to increase the resilience of the host system to invasion shocks (to drive the invasion rate below zero). This has not been formally modelled here, but it is intuitive that where the costs of control are greater than the costs of enhancing the resilience of the host system, that will be the more cost-effective solution.

Let us return to the special case – where the invasion rate is positive and the exclusion state is an unstable equilibrium. The introduction of an invasive species to even a small proportion of the total space will lead the system to converge via a heteroclinic orbit to a stable interior equilibrium, the invaded state. In a stochastic environment this makes the invaded state the default state. But note that the location of the interior solution depends on the choice of the control rate, $\beta(t)$. The higher the control rate, the lower the proportion of the total space occupied by the invasive species at equilibrium. Like the invasion and restoration rates, $\beta(t)$ influences the resilience of the managed native system.

Once again we may begin with an extreme case: the case where the optimal control rate is zero or very small. This case is illustrated in Figure 14.3. Where the control rate reflects the relative social costs and benefits of control, this may be due either to the fact that the invasive species is benign (does not impose costs on society), or that the cost of control is prohibitive. It may also be due to the fact that there is a market failure due to the public good nature of invasive control. Indeed, a general problem with invasive species is that their costs are not adequately observed through market prices – the effects of invasives are external to the market. In Figure 14.3 it is apparent that our measure of the resilience of the ecosystem indexed by $x(t)$ with respect to shocks imposed by the introduction of $y(t)$ is close to zero. Conversely, the resilience of the invaded state is close to unity.

It is useful to interpret the dynamics of the system under different control

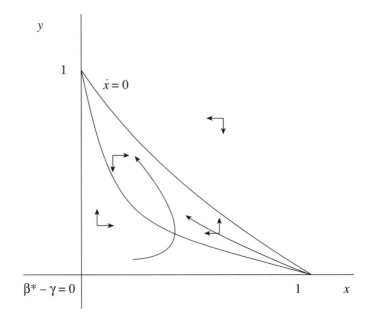

Figure 14.3   Stable invaded state

rates in terms of the resilience of the invaded state. If the optimal control rate is positive then the default state will be an interior solution to the problem. The greater the control rate, relative to the other system parameters, the higher the proportion of the total space occupied by native species at equilibrium, and the lower the resilience of the invaded state.

Figure 14.4 illustrates the case where there is a 'high' control rate and hence where the invaded state is less resilient. More precisely, since the value of $x(t)$ at equilibrium is just $(\beta^* - \gamma)/(\alpha + \beta^*)$, we have the following measure of the resilience of the invaded state:

$$\rho(\beta^*) = \frac{\alpha + \gamma}{\alpha + \beta^*}. \qquad (14.19)$$

Moreover, it is immediate that this is decreasing in β^*. Although we conventionally think of resilience as a desirable property of the system, whether it is desirable or not in any particular case depends on whether the system delivers net benefits or disbenefits. Since the invaded state is assumed to be less valuable than the exclusion state, the resilience of the invaded state is a 'bad'. Hence the effect of control is to reduce the resilience of the invaded state, or put another way, to reduce the maximum share of the total space that an invasive

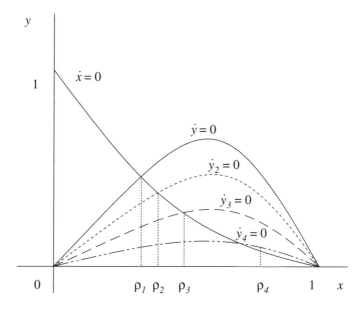

Figure 14.4   Reducing the resilience of the invaded state

species can lose to the control process and still recover. Control strategies that seek to maintain the system as close to the exclusion state as possible can be interpreted as strategies to minimize the resilience of the invaded state.

4   CONCLUDING REMARKS

The point has already been made that if a system is unobservable it will not be possible to guide it to the desired state through the application of the controls. We know, however, that even if exploited ecological systems are neither observable nor controllable, as is the case with many marine systems, they may still be 'stabilized'. This implies that exploitation of the system is restricted to levels as which the uncontrolled part (the ecological processes) can continue to function over the expected range of environmental conditions. Since the exclusion state in this case is unstable, it is not resilient with respect to environmental shocks. In the absence of accurate measures of the system it would not be possible to stabilize it in this state. It is possible to stabilize the system only in the invaded state. If the system is neither observable nor controllable, the choice of $\beta(t)$ will still fix the stable level of the invasive species.

The choice of $\beta(t)$ in these circumstances may reflect a precautionary approach. Typically, this is taken to imply action in advance of proof. The Declaration of the Third Ministerial Conference on the North Sea identified a precautionary approach to marine pollution as involving 'action to avoid potentially damaging impacts of substances that are persistent, toxic and liable to bioaccumulate even where there is no scientific evidence to prove a causal link between effects and emissions' (Haigh, 1993). The precautionary approach is also often associated with a shift in the burden of proof on to those whose decisions are the source of damage (Costanza et al., 1998). Perrings et al. (2000) have argued that in the case of invasive species this implies the adoption of control instruments, such as the environmental assurance bond. Such instruments have two functions: to provide cover against risks of biological invasions that may not be commercially insurable, and to shift the burden of proof on to those whose activities lead to the introduction of potential invaders.

Institutional and market conditions that encourage resource users to ignore the consequences of their actions increase the susceptibility of countries to invasive species. Markets generally fail to accommodate the risks posed by invasive species. While many private benefits of species introductions are captured in market prices, many of its social costs are not. In the case of biological invasions, however, there is another reason to believe that insufficient control will be exercised by the society concerned. The control of invasive species generally, like the control of communicable human diseases, is a public good with several dimensions. Invasive species threaten biodiversity, and the genetic information it contains is a global public good. Invasive species also disrupt ecosystem functions in terrestrial and aquatic systems alike. In terrestrial systems, the effect of invasive *Pinus* and the *Acacia* species on the hydrological services provided by the Fynbos in the Cape is one such example. In marine systems, the impact of pathogens spread from shrimp culture on the role of mangroves as fish nurseries is another. Although the main costs and benefits of actions to control biological invasions may be local, biological invasions almost always involve two or more countries, the actions of one affecting the welfare of another. In the absence of bilateral or multilateral agreements, there will be insufficient resources allocated to national control.

NOTE

This is a version of a paper offered at the Mote Symposium of Fisheries Research, Sarasota, FL, October 2000. That paper is forthcoming in the *Bulletin of Marine Science* under the title 'Biological Invasions in Aquatic systems: The Economic Problem'.

REFERENCES

Costanza, R., F. Andrade, P. Antunes, M. van den Belt, D. Boersma, D. Boesch, Catarino, F., S. Hanna, K. Linburg, B. Low, M. Molitor, J.G. Pereira, S. Rayner, R. Santos, J. Wilson and M. Young (1988), 'Principles for sustainable governance of the oceans', *Science*, **281**: 198–9.

Cohen, A.N., J.T. Carlton and M.C. Fountain (1995), 'Introduction, dispersal and potential impacts of the green crab carcinus maenas in San Francisco Bay, California', *Marine Biology*, **122** (2), pp. 255–237.

Czech, B. and P.R. Krausman (1997), 'Distribution and causation of species endangerment in the United States', *Science*, **277**, pp. 1116–17.

Delfino, D. and P. Simmons (2000), 'Infectious diseases as invasives in human populations', in Perrings et al. (eds), pp. 31–55.

Enserink, M. (1999), 'Biological invaders sweep in', *Science*, **285**: 1834–6.

Glowka, L., F. Burhenne-Guilmin and H. Synge (1994), *A Guide to the Convention on Biological Diversity*, Gland: IUCN.

Haigh, N. (1993), *The Precautionary Principle in British Environmental Policy*, London: Institute for European Environmental Policy.

Heywood, V. (ed.) (1995), *Global Biodiversity Assessment*, Cambridge: Cambridge University Press.

Holling, C.S. (1973), 'Resilience and stability of ecological systems', *Annual Review of Ecological Systems*, **4**: 1–24.

Independent World Commission on the Oceans (IWCO) (1998), *The Ocean, Our Future*, Cambridge: Cambridge University Press.

Kermack, W.O. and A.G. McKendrick (1927), 'Contributions to the mathematical theory of epidemics', proceedings of the Royal Statistical Society, Ser A., 115, pp. 700–721.

Khalanski, M. (1997), 'Industrial and ecological consequences of the introduction of new species in continental aquatic ecosystems: the zebra mussel and other invasive species', *Bulletin Français de la Pêche et de la Pisciculture*, **344–45**: 385–404.

Knowler, D. (1999), 'Valuing the commercial fishing benefits of joint environmental protection and fisheries management policies: a case study of the Black Sea', DPhil dissertation, University of York.

Knowler, D. and E.B. Barbier (2000), 'The economics of an invading species: a theoretical model and case study application', in Perrings et al. (eds), pp. 70–93.

Parker, I.M., D. Simberloff, W.M. Lonsdale, K. Goodell, M. Wonham, M.H. Williamson, B. von Holle, P.B. Moyle, J.E. Byers and L. Goldwasser (1999), 'Impact: toward a framework for understanding the ecological effects of invaders', *Biological Invasions* **1**: 3–19.

Perrings, C. (1998), 'Resilience in the dynamics of economy-environment systems', *Environmental and Resource Economics*, **11** (3–4): 503–20.

Perrings, C., M. Williamson and S. Dalmazzone (eds) (2000), *The Economics of Biological Invasions*, Cheltenham, UK and Northampton, MA, USA: Edward Elgar.

Pimm, S.L. (1984), 'The complexity and stability of ecosystems', *Nature*, **307**: 321–6.

Rejmanek, M. (1989), 'Invasibility of plant communities', in J.A. Drake, H.A. Mooney, F. di Castri, R.H. Groves, F.J. Kruger, M. Rejmanek and M. Williamson (eds), *Biological Invasions: A Global Perspective*, SCOPE 37, New York: John Wiley, pp. 369–83.

Smith, C.S., M.W. Lonsdale and J. Fortune (1999), 'When to ignore advice: invasion predictions and decision theory', *Biological Invasions*, **1**: 89–96.

Wilcove, D.S., D. Rothstein, J. Dubow, A. Phillips, and E. Losos (1998), 'Quantifying threats to imperiled species in the United States', *BioScience*, **48**: 607–615.

Williamson, M. (1996), *Biological Invasions*, London: Chapman & Hall.

Williamson, M. (1998), 'Measuring the impact of plant invaders in Britain', in S. Starfinger, K. Edwards, I. Kovarik and M. Williamson (eds), *Plant Invasions. Ecological Mechanisms and Human Responses*, Leiden: Backhuys, pp. 57–70.

Williamson, M. (1999), 'Invasions', *Ecography*, **22**: 5–12.

Williamson, M. (2000), *Quantifying the Ecological and Economic Risks of Invaders and GMOs'*, 'Proceedings of the Workshop on Plant Health in the New Global Trading Environment: Managing Exotic Insects, Weeds and Pathogens, Canberra: publisher.

15. Global externalities: sovereign states

Domenico Siniscalco[*]

1 GLOBAL EXTERNALITIES

'Globalization' is a new expression that does not appear in many dictionaries, even if it is increasingly used in the media and in the current debate. It obviously means 'becoming global' or, more precisely, worldwide. But what is becoming global so recently and so intensely that it needs a new word?

In the last few years we have seen increasing transnational flows of goods, services, finance, direct investment, people, culture, knowledge, information, pollution, crime and the like. Such transnational flows have been accelerated by technological, institutional and demographic changes. From an economic perspective they can be seen as the effect of a 'worldwide arbitrage' and selection process.

The global flows under review are gaining momentum and are partly new, given the nature and characteristics of modern information, communication and transportation technologies. But globalization *per se* is a historical phenomenon that comes and goes in secular waves, and usually – but not necessarily – creates convergence (see Braudel, 1997; Foreman-Peck, 1998).

Transnational and global flows imply greater interdependence among people, firms, governments, and non-governmental and international organizations. In this context, for every agent (or country), welfare depends on his or her own action as well as on the other agents' action. In general, the exchange of flows requires markets and well-defined property rights. Unfortunately, this is not always the case in the global economy. Some flows, such as pollution, knowledge, or migrations completely lack markets and prices: in this case we are in the presence of pure global externalities. Other flows, such as investment or raw materials go through markets and prices, but such markets are non-competitive: in this case we are in the presence of pecuniary global externalities. Typically, pure externalities affect welfare; in a suboptimal world, pecuniary externalities affect welfare as well, and can be discussed in the same conceptual framework (for a discussion, see Laffont, 1987).

Summing up, we live in a world of global externalities, which can be positive (namely, knowledge) or negative (pollution). In general, such externalities prevent optimality, imply market failure and need to be corrected by policies in the appropriate jurisdiction. The optimal jurisdiction, in many cases, cannot be national. This happens whenever interdependence and transnational spillovers jeopardize any unilateral effort to internalize the externality. In the latter case, given the absence of global or transnational governing bodies, the only solution left is to have voluntary agreements among sovereign states (in diplomatic language 'treatises', 'conventions', 'protocols' and, in the weakest case, 'policy coordination').

2 THE ENVIRONMENT AS A BENCHMARK CASE OF GLOBAL EXTERNALITIES

Among the transnational policy issues, environmental protection is a very interesting case. On the substantial ground, the links between the environment, demographic and economic growth give rise to one of the key challenges for the next millennium (see Hobsbawm, 1994). On institutional grounds, spillovers and the absence of property rights, in areas such as global warming, ozone layer depletion and biodiversity, create strong incentives to free ride, which undermine cooperation. On theoretical grounds, finally, global environmental issues are giving rise to a lively and fruitful literature on coalition formation theory, which is a branch of non-cooperative game theory (Barrett, 1997; Carraro and Siniscalco, 1997). Given the difficulties involved, therefore, global environmental agreements have become a prototype of 'difficult agreements' both in practice and in the theory of coalition formation. The incentives to free ride, indeed, determine the separation between the profitability and optimality of the agreements on the one hand, and their stability on the other. As a consequence, normative and positive analyses diverge and give rise to several political economy issues.

In the following sections we shall concentrate on environmental deterioration and on the policies to prevent it. But the global governance issues involved in environmental protection can be seen as a benchmark case of policy coordination and treatise design in the presence of global externalities.

The economic literature on the global environment has evolved fairly rapidly. Early contributions (see Hardin and Baden, 1977) characterized the interaction among countries as a prisoners' dilemma, inevitably leading to the so-called 'tragedy' of global common property goods. But at the same time, in the real world a large number of international environmental agreements on the global commons was signed, often involving subgroups of negotiating countries and sometimes involving transfers and other links with other policies (trade, technological cooperation and so on).

Against this background, from the 1990s, the theoretical literature began to study the logic of coalition formation in the presence of spillovers, and the possibility of increasing welfare by means of appropriate mechanisms and strategies. To this purpose, the early 1990s literature followed two main directions: (i) cooperative games; and (ii) non-cooperative games. In cooperative game theory, the focus of analysis is the coalition of countries and its characteristic function, that is, the total net benefits the coalition can share. Work by Chander and Tulkens (1997) showed that, in the case of the global commons, the core of the game is non-empty. In addition, a paper by Uzawa (1997) demonstrates that, under specific assumptions, the core of the cooperative game corresponds to Lindahl equilibrium.

Non-cooperative game theory, on the contrary, focuses on individual countries which maximize their own welfare, subject to the individual welfare-maximizing behaviour by other countries. Games can be repeated (Barrett, 1997b) as well as being on-shot (Barrett, 1994; Carraro and Siniscalco, 1993; Hoel, 1992). In both cases, the analysis focuses on coalition formation, that is, on the incentives that lead to self-enforcing international agreements and define the number of the signatory countries.

In this chapter we focus on non-cooperative games. Cooperative games are interesting in providing a benchmark, but they either assume the existence of a coalition or ignore the stability problems related to the incentives to free ride. Among non-cooperative games, we concentrate particularly on one-shot coalition formation games, as they do not need the special assumptions (on collective rationality or on discount rates) which are needed to avoid folk theorems in repeated games.

3   THE THEORETICAL FRAMEWORK

The theoretical framework which is used to analyse the feasability of international environmental agreements is the non-cooperative game theory of coalition formation. Following this approach, countries facing an international environmental problem play a two-stage game. In the first stage – the *coalition game* – they decide non-cooperatively whether or not to sign the agreement. In the second stage, they play the non-cooperative Nash *emission game*, where the countries which sign the agreement play as a single player and divide the resulting payoff according to a given burden-sharing rule (any of the rules derived from cooperative game theory).[1]

Moreover, let us assume that:

- all countries decide *simultaneously* in both stages;[2] and
- countries can sign only a *single agreement*. Hence, those that do sign cannot propose a different agreement. From a game-theoretic viewpoint this implies that only one coalition can be formed, the remaining defecting players playing as singletons.[3]

- when defecting from a coalition s, each country assumes that the other countries belonging to s *remain* in the coalition.[4]
- each country's payoff function *increases monotonically* with respect to the coalition size (the number of signatories in the symmetric case).[5]

Given these assumptions, we say that:

- a coalition s is *profitable* when each country $i \in s$ gains from joining the coalition (with respect to its position when no countries cooperate). Formally, a coalition s is profitable iff $P_i(s) \geq P_i(\Phi)$, $\forall i \in s$, where $P_i(s)$ is country i's payoff when coalition s forms.
- a coalition s is *stable* iff:
  (i)   there is no incentive to free ride, that is, $Q_i(s/i) - P_i(s) < 0$ for each country i belonging to s, where $Q_i(s/i)$ is country i's payoff when it defects from coalition s;
  (ii) there is no incentive to broaden the coalition, that is, $P_i(s \cup i) - Q_i(s) < 0$ for each country i which does not belong to s.[6]
- A profitable and stable coalition s is also *Pareto optimal* iff there exists no other profitable and stable coalition which provides all countries with a payoff larger than $P_i(s)$, $\forall i \in s$. Formally, $P_i(s) \geq P_i(s^*)$, $\forall i \in s$, $s \in S$, $\forall s^* \in S$ such that $i \in s^*$, where S is the set of all stable and profitable coalitions.

Note that a profitable and stable coalition is also Pareto optimal under the assumption that a country's payoff function increases monotonically with the coalition size.

4   SOME RESULTS

Recent work on the profitability and stability of international environmental agreements has emphasized a few important results:[7]

First, the game structure which captures countries' interactions is not a prisoners' dilemma but rather a *chicken game* in which at least two groups of players (and two roles: signatories and defectors) co-exist (Carraro and Siniscalco, 1993). More precisely, a profitable and stable, but partial, coalition emerges out of the two-stage game described in Section 2. Therefore, the equilibrium of the game is not the one in which no cooperation takes place (no countries sign the agreement) as could be expected given the characteristics of the global environment (a public good with spillovers). At the equilibrium there are instead two groups of countries, signatories and defectors, where the size of the group of signatories crucially depends on the slope of countries' reaction functions.

Second, the previously mentioned stable (and Pareto optimal if the payoff function increases monotonically) coalition is generally formed by a low number of players.[8] Hence, the research focused on ways of broadening the endogenous stable coalition by introducing appropriate policy measures which go beyond emission control. Three ideas deserve our attention.

1. *Transfers* are often proposed to tackle the profitability dimension of international negotiations, that is, to compensate those countries which, because of their asymmetries, would lose from signing the agreement. Transfers may also be an important tool to expand an originally stable, but small, environmental coalition. However, as shown in Carraro and Siniscalco (1993), countries which accept the implementation of a transfer programme to non-signatories must be *committed* to cooperation (this condition is weaker with asymmetric countries; see Botteon and Carraro, 1997a). As a consequence the international agreement becomes only partially self-enforcing.

2. *Issue linkage* As for transfer, the linkage of environmental negotiations to other economic issues (for example, trade, technological cooperation and so on) may be useful: (a) to reduce the constraints that asymmetries impose on the emergence of stable environmental agreements;[9] and (b) to increase the size of the stable coalition. This second objective can be achieved even when all countries gain from signing the agreement if issue linkage is designed to offset countries' free-riding incentives (see Carraro and Siniscalco, 1995). This is the case when the negotiation on an issue with *excludable benefits* (a club good) is linked to the environmental negotiation (which, if successful, typically provides a public good, that is, a *non-excludable benefit*). An example could be the linkage of environmental negotiations with negotiations on technological cooperation whose benefits are largely shared among the signatories whenever innovation spillovers to non-signatories are low (see Carraro and Siniscalco, 1997).[10]

3. *Threats* The number of signatories to an international environmental agreement could be increased if non-signatories were threatened with punitive measures such as adequate economic (for example, trade) sanctions (see Barrett, 1997b). However, credible threats are difficult to design. Emissions themselves are hardly a credible threat, because countries are unlikely to sustain self-damaging policies (for example, when the 'social clauses' of the General Agreement on Tariffs and Trade (GATT) are violated). Moreover, in this case, asymmetries play a double role. On the one hand, some countries may not gain from signing the environmental agreement; on the other, some countries, even when gaining from environmental cooperation, may lose from carrying out the economic

sanctions. This may reduce the effectiveness of threats in increasing the number of signatories to international environmental agreements.

The nature of the above conclusions intuitively applies to many global externalities, even if the incentives to free ride may be smaller than in the case of environmental spillovers.

5   NEW DEVELOPMENTS AND EXTENSIONS

New developments follow three directions, each originating from removing the assumptions of the standard framework described in Section 3.

5.1   Non-monotonic Payoff Function: Clubs

The literature discussed in Section 3 assumes that a country's payoff function $P_i(s)$ is monotonically increasing with the coalition size, that is, with the number of signatories when all countries are symmetric. Monotonic payoff functions may not always be appropriate, as suggested by Yi and Shin (1994). Carraro and Siniscalco (1997) provide an example showing hump-shaped payoff functions when negotiations on environmental cooperation are linked with negotiations on research and development (R&D) cooperation. The same approach can be applied to any club (say a single currency) where profitability may decrease after a certain number of members is reached.[11]

Let $L_i(s) = Q_i(s/i) - P_i(s)$ be country i's stability function. When positive, it shows that country i has no incentive to defect from coalition s. In the symmetric case, the intersection between $L_i(s)$ and the horizontal axis, where the number of countries is shown, defines the stable coalition which is formed by j^* signatories. However, j^o, the *optimal* number of countries in the joint coalition (the maximand of the payoff function), may be lower than the number of countries belonging to the *stable* group of signatories of the joint agreement. As a consequence, three groups of countries may emerge (three roles): (a) those which cooperate (j^o); (b) those which would like to cooperate but are excluded from the agreement and are therefore forced to non-cooperation ($j^* - j^o$); (c) and those which prefer not to cooperate (free riders: $n - j^*$).

5.2   Multiple Agreements: Regional Treatises

The standard stability concept of Section 2 is derived from cartel theory (D'Aspremont et al. 1983). There are several restrictive features of this stability concept: (a) only deviations by singletons are allowed; (b) players are not farsighted; (c) a single agreement is proposed and defectors cannot join to sign a different one, that is, multiple coalitions are not allowed. If the stability concept is modified, conclusions may obviously be different. In particular, when countries deciding not to sign a given agreement can propose a different one among themselves, several equilibria may emerge.

Following Bloch (1997), it can be shown that the equilibrium coalition structure depends on the equilibrium concept which is adopted. Let us consider the coalition proof Nash equilibrium concept and let us still assume that players choose simultaneously which agreement to sign, that is, which coalition to belong to. The results that can be derived from applying these theoretical refinements to a simple model of climate change negotiations are quite interesting and share some common features:

- the equilibrium coalition structure is not formed by a single coalition. In general, many coalitions form at the equilibrium;[12]
- the grand coalition, in which all countries sign the same environmental agreement, is never an equilibrium; and
- coalitions of different sizes may emerge at the equilibrium (even when countries are symmetric).[13]

These results are not enough to identify the characteristics of the likely outcome of negotiations on any given issue. In some cases coalition structures are very dispersed, while in others, coalition structures are quite concentrated. However, in general we can claim that there will be more than one coalition at the equilibrium. Therefore, the effort to achieve a single environmental agreement at the world level seems to be inconsistent with countries' incentives to sign the agreement. The goal should probably be the achievement of two or more agreements. Note that this latter claim contains an extension of previous theoretical results, derived in the case of symmetric countries, to the case of asymmetric countries. Unfortunately, there is no theoretical analysis that can support this type of extension, which can therefore be accepted only as very preliminary.[14]

5.3 Coalitional Behaviour

In the previous sections, it was assumed that a defector believes that the coalition will not collapse when he or she leaves it (this type of *Nash conjecture* is quite obvious in a simultaneous game). At the other extreme, we have already mentioned that some authors (Tulkens, 1997) assume that a defection is always followed by the defection of all other countries (this assumption is called *coalition unanimity*), which implies that stability and profitability conditions coincide. There are two other assumptions on coalitional behaviour that may be considered:

- Chew (1994), Brams (1995) and Mariotti (1997) suggest that only equilibrium strategies in which countries take into account the ultimate consequences of their decisions to join or to leave a coalition (*farsighted strategies*) should be considered. Therefore, when a country defects from a coalition s, it does not compare its coalition payoff $P_i(s)$ with its defection payoff $Q_i(s/i)$, but it rather compares $P_i(s)$ with the payoff it would get after all consequences of its defection, and therefore all possible subsequent defections and aggregations, are accounted for (see Echia and Mariotti, 1998);
- alternatively, it would be possible to apply a concept of *coalition rational conjectures* that implies that the *ex ante* conjecture on the response of the other countries to a given defection coincides with the actual *ex post* reaction of these countries.[15]

These two concepts, albeit similar, have different implications. For example, whereas the grand coalition can be an equilibrium coalition using the idea of farsighted stability, this is not the case using the idea of coalition rational conjectures.

5.4 Treatise Design

Further work in this direction in necessary, finally, in translating the implications of the above analyses into agreement design. A promising idea is to introduce coalition unanimity into the agreement (as in the case of the Maastricht Treaty). In this case, it is possible to (formally) build into the treatise, the conjectures that can make it stable.

6   POLITICAL ECONOMY

The literature on coalition formation analysed so far will develop in the next few years and interesting results are expected. In particular, the interest in global externalities (and in the related agreements) will continue, given their growing importance and their analytical characteristics. In this area, two main lines of development can be envisaged.

The first line of development is theoretical, and will lead to new equilibrium concepts and new refinements.

The second line of development will concentrate on the political economy issues which are related to the kind of results produced so far. Below, we briefly mention some scope for further work, by asking some relevant questions which are already emerging among scholars.

1. What is the relationship between international agreements and national voters, given that agreements and conventions often need to be ratified by voters or parliaments? (For a discussion, see Currarini and Tulkens, 1997.)
2. The incentive to cooperate even in the presence of free riding may lead to the emergence of new international institutions, with a coordination role, rather than a regulatory one (Compte and Jehiel, 1997 propose an international arbitrator).
3. The above political economy issues emerge both when countries are symmetric and when they are asymmetric. In the asymmetric case a further issue arises: a given country i may prefer some countries, say j and h, as partners in the cooperating group, but these countries may want to sign the agreement with country k, rather than with i. Which negotiating and voting process leads to the efficient outcome? Is it possible that linking two (or more) issues leads to no equilibrium (because there is no agreement on the members of the cooperating group) or to an equilibrium in which a small number of countries cooperate (because there is an incentive to exclude some others)?
4. From the discussion in Section 5, it is clear that the possibility of multiple agreements opens several political, institutional, and political economy issues. In particular, through which political process can we move from the negotiation on a single agreement to negotiations on multiple regional agreements. And when is it possible and optimal to bypass the national level?

The above issues are already the object of investigation by economists. Some answers will come from theory. It will be deemed a success when these answers are translated into a better global governance. The political and diplomatic experience in several areas, from the environment, to trade, to European Union construction and enlargement, to the global financial system shows that the *architecture* of agreements can be decisive and be the source of serious problems as well as of brilliant solutions.

NOTES

*   Previous versions of this work have been presented in other workshops and benefited from many comments received during the Conference on Environment and Development,

Stockholm, 8 September 2000. Special thanks to Carlo Carraro who has been working with me on these issues for several years.

1. This approach has to be contrasted with the traditional cooperative game approach (for example, Chander and Tulkens, 1993, 1997) and with a repeated game approach (Barrett, 1994, 1997b). Moreover, note that the regulatory approach often proposed in public economics is not appropriate, given the lack of a supranational authority.

2. By contrast, Barrett (1994) assumes that the group of signatories is Stackelberg leader with respect to non-signatories in the second-stage emission game. In Bloch (1997) it is assumed that countries play sequentially in the first-stage coalition game.

3. This assumption will be relaxed later on.

4. This assumption is equivalent to the assumption of 'Nash conjectures' in a simultaneous oligopoly game where a player assumes no change in the other players' decision variable when it modifies its own decision variable. However, coalition theory often uses a different assumption, 'coalition unanimity' (see Bloch, 1997), where the whole coalition is assumed to collapse when one of its members defects (see Chander and Tulkens, 1993, 1997).

5. The implications of relaxing this assumption will be discussed in Section 5.

6. This definition of stability coincides with the definition of a stable cartel provided in the oligopoly literature (D'Aspremont et al., 1983) and defines the Nash equilibrium of the first game (the one in which countries decide whether or not to sign the agreement). Note that stability coincides with profitability under coalition unanimity.

7. These results have been shown analytically for the case of symmetric countries (Carraro and Siniscalco, 1993; Barrett, 1994) but were also confirmed by numerical simulations in the case of asymmetric countries (Barrett, 1997a; Botteon and Carraro, 1997a).

8. This conclusion depends on the assumption on the returns from abatement activities and on the presence of fixed abatement costs (Barrett, 1994; Heal, 1994).

9. This point was made by Folmer et al. (1993) and Cesar and de Zeeuw (1994).

10. An extension to the case of structurally asymmetric countries is provided in Botteon and Carraro (1997b), whereas information asymmetries are accounted for in Katsoulacos (1997).

11. The reason is that R&D cooperation provides a competitive advantage to signatories which can exploit a more efficient technology and therefore produce at lower unit costs. However, the competitive advantage tends to disappear when the number of signatories increases because an increasing number of countries share the same more efficient technology. On the other hand, there are diminishing returns of R&D cooperation. This implies that it may be optimal to exclude some countries from the joint R&D and environmental cooperation (the so-called exclusive membership stability of Yi and Shin, 1994).

12. For simultaneous games, this result is shown in Yi and Shin (1994). For sequential games the proof is in Bloch (1994). A survey of different approaches to multiple coalition games is provided by Bloch (1997).

13. The specific results on the size of the coalitions depend on the model structure and in particular on the slope of countries' reaction functions. If these are orthogonal and countries are symmetric, then two main types of equilibrium coalition structures emerge. (a) A coalition structure formed by many small coalitions (three countries in each coalition) and one or two singletons if n, the total number of countries, is not a multiple of three. (b) A coalition structure defined by the Fibonacci decomposition of n. For example, if 15 countries negotiate, the coalition structure is defined by two coalitions, one of nine and one of six countries.

14. However, results contained in Barrett (1997a) and Botteon and Carraro (1997a) for the case in which a single coalition is assumed at the equilibrium, suggest that theoretical results derived for the case of symmetric countries are largely confirmed when countries' asymmetries are introduced into the model. More work on this issue would none the less be very important.

15. The idea is similar to the one of consistent conjectural variations proposed by Bresnaham (1981) in the oligopoly literature.

REFERENCES

Barrett, S. (1994), 'Self-enforcing international environmental agreements', *Oxford Economic Papers*, **46**, 878–94.

Barrett, S. (1997a), 'Heterogeneous international environmental agreements', in C. Carraro (ed.), *International Environmental Agreements: Strategic Policy Issues*, Cheltenham, UK and Northampton, MA, USA: Edward Elgar.

Barrett, S. (1997b), 'Towards a theory of international cooperation', in C. Carraro and D. Siniscalco (eds), *New Directions in the Economic Theory of the Environment*, Cambridge: Cambridge University Press.

Bloch, F. (1994), 'Sequential formation of coalitions in games with externalities and fixed payoff division', Paper presented at the CORE-FEEM Conference on 'Non-Cooperative Coalition Formation', Louvain, 27–28 February.

Bloch, F. (1997), 'Noncooperative models of coalition formation in games with spillovers', in C. Carraro and D. Siniscalco (eds), *New Directions in the Economic Theory of the Environment*, Cambridge: Cambridge University Press.

Botteon, M. and C. Carraro (1997a), 'Burden-sharing and coalition stability in environmental negotiations with asymmetric countries', in C. Carraro (ed.), *International Environmental Agreements: Strategic Policy Issues*, Cheltenham, UK and Northampton, MA, USA: Edward Elgar.

Botteon, M. and C. Carraro (1997b), 'Strategies for environmental negotiations: issue linkage with heterogeneous countries', in H. Folmer and N. Hanley (eds), *Game Theory and the Global Environment*, Cheltenham, UK and Northampton, MA, USA: Edward Elgar.

Brams, S. (1996), *Theory of Moves*, New York: Academic Press.

Braudel, F. (1997), 'Expansion Européenne et Capitalisme, 1450–1650', in R. De Ayala and P. Braudel (eds), *Les Ambitions de l'Histoire*, Paris: Fallois.

Bresnaham, T. (1981), 'Duopoly models with consistent conjectures', *American Economic Review*, **71**, 934–45.

Carraro, C. and D. Siniscalco (1993), 'Strategies for the international protection of the environment', *Journal of Public Economics*, **52**, 309–28.

Carraro, C. and D. Siniscalco (1995), 'Policy coordination for sustainability: commitments, transfers, and linked negotiations', in I. Goldin and A. Winters (eds), *The Economics of Sustainable Development*, Cambridge: Cambridge University Press.

Carraro, C. and D. Siniscalco (1997), 'R&D cooperation and the stability of international environmental agreements', in C. Carraro (ed.), *International Environmental Agreements: Strategic Policy Issues*, Cheltenham, UK and Northampton, MA, USA: Edward Elgar.

Carraro, C. and D. Siniscalco (1998), 'International environmental agreements: incentives and political economy', *European Economic Review*, **42**, 561–72.

Cesar, H. and A. de Zeeuw (1994), 'Issue linkage in global environmental problems', in A. Xepapadeas (ed.), *Economic Policy for the Environment and Natural Resources*, Cheltenham, UK and Brookfield, VT, USA: Edward Elgar.

Chander, P. and H. Tulkens (1993), 'Strategically stable cost-sharing in an economic–ecological negotiations process', in K.G. Mäler (ed.), *International Environmental Problems: An Economic Perspective*, Dordrecht: Kluwer Academic.

Chander, P. and H. Tulkens (1997), 'A core-theoretical solution for the design of cooperative agreements on trans-frontier pollution', *Game Theory and Economic Behaviour*.

Chew, M.S. (1994), 'Farsighted coalitional stability', Department of Economics, University of Chicago, *Journal of Economics Theory*.

Compte, O. and P. Jehiel (1997), 'International negotiations and dispute resolution mechanisms: the case of environmental negotiations', in C. Carraro (ed.), *International Environmental Agreements: Strategic Policy Issues*, Cheltenham, UK and Northampton, MA, USA.

Currarini, S. and H. Tulkens (1997), 'Core-theoretic and political stability of international agreements on transfrontier pollution', CORE Discussion Paper, Louvain-la-Neuve.

D'Aspremont, C.A., A. Jacquemin, J.J. Gabszewicz and J. Weymark (1983), 'On the stability of collusive price leadership', *Canadian Journal of Economics*, **16**, 17–25.

Echia, G. and M. Mariotti (1998), 'The role of institutions in international environmental agreements'.

Folmer, H., P. van Mouche and S. Ragland (1993), 'Interconnected games and international environmental problems', *Environmental Resource Economics*, **3**, 313–35.

Foreman-Peck, J. (ed) (1998), *Historical Foundations of Globalization*, Cheltenham, UK and Northampton, MA, USA: Edward Elgar.

Hardin, G. and J. Baden (1977), *Managing the Commons*, New York: Freeman & Co.

Heal, G. (1994), 'The formation of environmental coalitions', in Carraro, C. (ed.), *Trade, Innovation, Environment*, Dordrecht: Kluwer Academic.

Hobsbawm, E. (1994), *The Century of Extremes*, London.

Hoel, M. (1992), 'International environmental conventions: the case of uniform reductions of emissions', *Environmental and Resource Economics*, **2**, 141–59.

Katsoulacos, Y. (1997), 'R&D spillovers, R&D cooperation, innovation and international environmental agreements', in C. Carraro (ed.), *International Environmental Agreements: Strategic Policy Issues*, Cheltenham, UK and Northampton, MA, USA: Edward Elgar.

Laffont, J.J. (1994), 'Externalities', in *The New Palgrave Dictionary of Economics*, Cambridge: Cambridge University Press.

Mariotti, M. (1997), 'A model of agreements in strategic form games', *Journal of Economic Theory*, **73**, 128–39.

Sandler, T. and K. Sargent (1995), 'Management of transnational commons: coordination, publicness, and treaty formation', *Land Economics*, **71**, 145–62.

Tulkens, H. (1997), 'Cooperation vs. free-riding in international agreements: two approaches', CORE Discussion Paper, Louvain-la-Neuve.

Uzawa, H. (1997), 'Global warming as a cooperative game', mimeo.

Yi, S. and H. Shin (1994), 'Endogenous formation of coalitions in oligopoly: I. Theory', mimeo, Dartmouth College.

16. What if Jevons had actually liked trees?

Robert M. Solow

We usually credit W.S. Jevons with having provided a clear statement and analysis of the problem facing a producer with an intertemporal point-input–point-output production technology.

Suppose a tree is planted (costlessly, for simplicity) at time t. The real net value of its timber (after harvesting costs) is $f(a)$ if the tree is cut down at time $t+a$, that is, at age a. The producer chooses the a that maximizes $e^{-ra}f(a)$, where r is the appropriate discount rate, usually a market interest rate. The obvious necessary condition for an interior maximum at a^* is that a^* satisfy $f'(a)/f(a) = r$. This defines a local maximum if $f''(a) < 0$. (We expect an a^* to exist because the tree grows very fast when it is young, and $f(a)$ tapers off or turns down when the tree is very old. If $\ln f(a)$ is strictly concave, the maximum is unique.)

The intuition is elementary. If $f'(a) > rf(a)$, the natural growth of the tree is earning a better return than the interest rate on the proceeds from earlier harvesting, so it is better to wait.

If there is an initial planting cost c, a^* is still the best choice once the cost is sunk. Before that point, the producer would want $e^{-ra^*}f(a^*) > c$, or else it would be better to abandon the project altogether. If the land had alternative uses, we would be dealing with a quite different problem.

This solution is appropriate if tree planting is a one-time project, if nothing interesting happens after the tree is harvested. A more realistic presumption is that another tree is planted at $t+a^*$ on the land just cleared. Unless technology or the interest rate has changed, the second-generation tree will be harvested at age a^*, and so will the third-generation tree planted at $t+2a^*$, and so on. In this case the problem for the first-generation producer is to maximize $e^{-ra}f(a)$ $+ e^{-2ra}f(a) + e^{-3ra}f(a) + \ldots$ or $e^{-ra}f(a)/(1 - e^{-ra}) = f(a)/(e^{ra} - 1)$. This thought is usually attributed to the aptly named Martin Faustmann ([1849] 1968).

This new maximizing a^{**} or 'rotation period' is easily calculated to be shorter than the original a^*. The economic reason is that, although the present value of each harvest (discounted back to the date of planting) is less, the earlier harvest also makes room for the next tree. We are less tempted to prolong a pleasure if we know that it will be followed immediately by another one just as good.

One other variation on the basic model will have some usefulness when I come to the main point of this chapter. The function $f(a)$ was loosely described as the real net value achieved when a tree of age a is harvested. That is probably the right specification for a commercial enterprise. A small amateur tree farmer might be interested in the utility achievable at harvest time. Such an enterprise might wish to maximize $e^{-ra}v[f(a)]$, where $v(.)$ is a conventional utility function and r is now a rate of time preference.

In this case the equation that defines a^* is modified to $r = hf'(a)/f(a)$, where $h(a) = fv'(f)/v(f)$ is the elasticity of $v(f)$ with respect to net revenue. Since we expect h to be between zero and one, and $\ln f$ to be concave, the utility-maximizing age is less than the net-revenue-maximizing age. This is because diminishing marginal utility operates much like impatience in the context of a growing tree. The rotation-period correction can be applied straightforwardly to this version.

My old and valued friend Karl-Göran Mäler is a true man of the world but his roots (!) are Swedish. In casting about for a suitably light-hearted but relevant personal tribute to him, it occurred to me to wonder how this standard analysis would change if the decision maker were Swedish, with a deep, probably genetic, disposition to *like* trees for their own sake. (In this respect the planting and harvesting of trees is different from the other classic example of point-input–point-output technology, the aging of wine. The wine-lover wants only to drink the stuff, not to contemplate rows of stored bottles and barrels. But perhaps I am wrong about this. In that case, so much the better.) Maybe this analysis is relevant to the ongoing disputes between environmentalists and lumber companies.

So let $v(x)$ be the instantaneous utility that comes with contemplation of a live tree of age x, and let $\int_0^a e^{-sx}v(x)dx = J(a)$, where s is a utility-discount rate. This sort of tree farmer seeks to maximize $W(a) = J(a) + e^{-ra}f(a)$ by choice of a. The two terms here have to be commensurate for this formulation to make any sense. This can happen in two ways: either $f(a)$ stands for what I earlier called $v[f(a)]$ and r should be identified with s, or else $v(x)$ is measured in the same units as net revenue, say by charging admission, and s should be identified with r. Whether this can be accomplished and if so, how, is a tricky question, but not the one I want to pursue. So I shall just put $r = s$ and adopt one interpretation or the other according to circumstances. Also, I shall just deal with the one-generation Jevons model. The rotation-period case merely involves maximization of $[J(a) + e^{-ra}f(a)]/(1 - e^{-ra})$ and is only notationally more complicated.

Since $J'(a) = e^{-ra}v(a)$, the first-order condition for maximization of $W(a)$ is $r = [f'(a) + v(a)]/f(a)$. This is, naturally, very Irving Fisheresque. The return to holding the tree for another season includes both the increased value of the timber and the current pleasure that the tree gives. If this exceeds the interest on the initial value, it is better to hold the tree a while longer. Evidently, then, it will be optimal to allow trees to grow older and bigger than if they gave no current utility. Since $v(a) > 0$, this conclusion is confirmed by the first-order condition.

The second-order condition is more complicated than in the Jevons case. Straightforward calculation shows that $W''(a) < 0$ at a stationary point a^* of $W(a)$ if and only if $v'(a^*) + f''(a^*) - rf'(a^*) < 0$. One possible pattern is that $v(a)$ might be single-peaked; trees (like economists?) get nicer as they age, then reach a peak, after which branches begin to die, and the tree becomes straggly and loses its charm. So $v'(a)$ could be positive for an interval of early ages, perhaps a long interval. A tree that is not earning its keep from its growth may be worth preserving longer for the pleasure it gives.

This fact, if it is a fact, offers the possibility that $W''(a)$ might be positive at a stationary point of $W(a)$, and thus a local minimum. Indeed this line of thought offers even more extreme possibilities. Suppose we imagine $W(a)$ to be an indicator of social welfare, and the problem is to decide the best use of state-owned forest between preservation and logging. One might even quantify $J(a)$ through contingent valuation or some similar process. It is possible that $v(a)$ might increase rather sharply with age, and go on increasing effectively forever. Then $W(a)$ may have no visible maximum for as far ahead as the eye can see. Call this the 'giant sequoia syndrome' (GSS).

For several reasons, however, the GSS has to be classified as an extreme case, and therefore rare. In the first place, common sense says that $v(a)$ – the instantaneous social utility conferred by a tree of age a – must be bounded. It is true that a very large number of people can vicariously enjoy the giant sequoia. This will be reflected in a contingent-valuation exercise. But very many people also enjoy thinking about porpoises and eating ice cream. Willingness to pay, and even willingness to accept compensation, cannot be infinitely large for all of these things and others.

Second, discounting, even with a small discount rate, goes against the GSS. Even if $v(a)$ were to increase without limit, it would have to increase exponentially in order to exhibit the GSS. Of course we all know that discounting gives rise to just such paradoxes as the one that appears here. Various avoidance tactics have been proposed, including the injunction that discount rates should get lower as we look further into the future. That would make a difference, but only if $v(a)$ were to increase limitlessly with age. Of course there is more than one giant redwood. If their number started to diminish, the advantage of preservation would increase. Under those circumstances, even with a constant pure rate of time preference, the appropriate discount rate on the trees themselves could turn negative.

Remember that I am not concerned to deny the possibility of the GSS, only to suggest that it must be an extreme case. In fact, given the sheer impressiveness of the great trees, one can see how a case for permanent preservation can be made. Hardly anyone would propose cutting down a giant redwood for the timber, not even if it were used to make little redwoods for souvenirs. The moral is that the GSS can hardly be the everyday case; not every discount rate can be small, and not every sort of tree can grow for as long and as magnificently as the sequoia.

Perhaps an algebraic example will help the intuition. To this end, we shall set $v(x) = mx^p$ and $f(x) = x^q$, with both p and q between zero and one, and $p > q$. Taken literally, these choices violate the common-sense precept that both $v(.)$ and $f(.)$ should be bounded; but both functions could be truncated and made horizontal at large values of x. My purpose is only to show how the arithmetic works.

The first-order condition for a stationary point of $W(a)$ is that $e^{-ra}(ma^p + qa^{q-1} - ra^q) = 0$. Hence the stationary points are the zeroes of the expression in brackets. To see the geometry more clearly, observe that $a = 0$ is definitely not a zero, and then factor out the term a^{q-1}. This leaves the equation $g(a) = ma^{1+p-q} - ra + q = 0$. Obviously $g(a)$ takes the value $q > 0$ at $a = 0$, then decreases for small positive values of a, reaches a minimum at $a_{min} = [r/1+z)m]^{1/z}$, (in which I have temporarily written z for $p - q > 0$ to clean up notation) and then increases without bound for higher values of a. There are two, one, or no stationary points of $W(a)$ according as $g(a_{min})$ is negative, zero or positive.

The interesting case allows for two stationary points. It is easy to calculate that this situation certainly occurs whenever m is sufficiently large. This parameter measures the relative importance of the direct utility value of the tree as against its terminal timber value. That is what makes it the interesting case: significant utility value brings complications.

The pattern is now clear. $W'(0)$ is positive, so initially the social value rises with age. The smaller stationary point (the smaller root of $g(a) = 0$) is therefore a (local) maximum for $W(a)$. At still larger ages, social value is decreasing, until a local minimum is reached at the larger root of $g(a) = 0$. After that $W(a)$ increases again, forever. But now we have to take account of the exponentially falling discount factor. In the notation established earlier, $W(a) = J(a) + e^{-ra}f(a)$. With the specification in this example, the second term on the right vanishes in the limit with large a. $J(a)$, on the other hand, with $v(x) = mx^p$, is easily seen to approach $mr^{-(1+p)}\Gamma(1 + p)$, which is also the limiting value of $W(a)$ as a becomes large. The social optimum occurs either there or at the local maximum already described (where the accumulated utility value is smaller, but the present value of the timber is positive). These two values of W just have to be calculated and compared. (If $v(x)$ and $f(x)$ are truncated, as suggested earlier, the balance shifts somewhat in favour of the smaller a.) One can do routine comparative statics, but nothing surprising emerges.

The technical details are unimportant in which is obviously an oversimplified model. My purpose in going back to this ancient analysis was to bring the utility value and the commercial value onto the same page. Doing so does not solve the problem of mediating between them; but it helps to focus attention on the parameters whose magnitudes must affect the outcome in important ways. It comes as no surprise that the important parameters are the essentially contestable ones: in this case the discount rate r and the relative weight m to be given to direct as compared with commercial utility. The contribution of economic analysis has to be to find ways of discussing, if not measuring, these parameters.

There is of course a long history of thought about social discounting, and it has revived in intensity as public and professional attention has turned to policy issues with very long time horizons, such as biodiversity and climate change. The apparent paradoxes associated with constant discount rates and the very distant future still constitute an unsolved puzzle. It is not impossible that some consensus on an alternative may be found, if not axiomatically then pragmatically. (Examples of recent thinking on this topic are to be found in Portney and Weyant (1999)).

The question of commensurability of utility value and commercial value may be an even harder one to settle. One difficulty is that there exists very little by way of an established tradition of thought on this issue, hence there is no obvious place to start. The contingent valuation approach was developed with just this question in mind. It met with what struck me at the time as excessively animated opposition, but that may have occurred because there was so much financially at stake in the litigation connected with the *Exxon Valdez* spill. If hard cases made bad law, big money tends to make bad economics.

There are indeed serious difficulties with contingent valuation, both technical and philosophical. They need to be thought through carefully because, at the moment, there appears to no serious alternative approach to the commensurability question. Even minor improvements and partial validation methods would be useful. One naturally wonders if economic theory might be able to find other ways to start quantifying the appeal of those giant sequoias.

REFERENCES

Faustmann, Martin ([1849] English translation 1968), 'On the determination of the value which forest land and immature stands of timber possess for Forestry', in M. Gane (ed.) 'Martin Faustmann and the Evaluation of Discounted Cash Flow', paper no. 42, Oxford: Commonwealth Forestry Institute.

Portney, P.R. and J.P. Weyant (eds) (1999), *Discounting and Intergenerational Equity*, Washington, DC: Rosources for the Future.

17. Mobility and capitalization in local public finance: a reassessment

David A. Starrett

1 INTRODUCTION

Karl-Göran Mäler (1971), (1974) was one of the pioneers in formulating and identifying hedonic methods, by which I mean methods for learning about preferences for public goods by observing behavior on related private goods markets. These methods have been developed extensively since then and have figured prominently in the recent theories of local public finance (see Scotchmer 1985; Wildasin 1986; and Starrett 1988, who gives references to earlier literature). There, land values play the role of hedonic indicator. It is argued that improvements in amenities at home will raise land rents (thus, benefits are capitalized into land values) and local 'club' managers who own the land will have appropriate incentives to institute such improvements. Thus, in this circumstance, land values become the perfect hedonic measure of environmental improvement, satisfying conditions proposed and explored by Mäler (1971, 1974). However, as Mäler recognized and as has become clearer from subsequent work (for example, Freeman 1979 and Johansson 1987), such hedonic measures are very sensitive to the structural assumptions made.

There are two such assumptions in the local public finance literature, which taken together have very strong implications for welfare economics. These assumptions are: (i) that there is free mobility among communities and (ii) that one community is insulated from the actions taken by other communities. In their strongest versions, these two assumptions interact to guarantee that local public decision making cannot make anyone worse off and under weak behavioral assumptions must lead to a Pareto-efficient outcome. Further, with these assumptions, public amenities must indeed raise local land values since otherwise, outsiders would move in to take advantage.

Some years ago, Mäler commmissioned me to write about land-values issues in developing countries. In the resulting paper (Starrett 1997) I argued among other things that the local public finance model was inappropriate for developing countries and suggested that land values might play a completely different (and in some ways perverse) role in guiding development planning.

Since then, I have become convinced that the aforementioned assumptions are unreasonable in a much broader context. In this chapter, I shall develop this case and argue that land values may play a completely different role from that in much of local public finance; further, decentralized decision making may have quite undesirable welfare implications. In particular, unregulated decentralization may generate a systematic bias toward overdevelopment. Land values will still have a hedonic role to play, but they will be measuring costs of congestion rather than benefits of amenities.

The chapter is organized as follows. Section 2 sets out a framework for studying the local public issues of interest. The next section formalizes the two assumptions alluded to above, shows why they are closely linked to capitalization and discusses the associated welfare economics. Sections 4 and 5 explore the consequences of dropping assumptions and demonstrate that a wide range of relationships (both positive and negative) are possible between land values and public amenities (broadly defined). We argue that under quite plausible conditions, the relationship will be negative and there will be private incentives to overdevelop. In the concluding section, we discuss the implications of this analysis for applied welfare economics and, in particular, for the evaluation of development projects in advanced economies.

2   THE ECONOMIC FRAMEWORK

Location choice plays a central role in the local public goods paradigm. Here we shall think of location as a discrete choice among a finite set of alternatives (so everyone will have a single place of residence). This modeling choice forces us to treat land at each discrete location as homogeneous, but is nonetheless more palatable (at least to us) than alternative 'continuous location' models. Later in the chapter we indicate how some of the relationships will look in a continuous location formulation.

Since land plays a special role we shall have separate notation for it and write the private goods net consumption vector as (c, ℓ), where ℓ stands for land consumption and c is the consumption vector of all private goods. We shall distinguish between two types of collective goods. First, there are those directly provided through group decision making (label these g). Examples would be museums, parks and civic centers. Second are those indirectly determined as functions of economic activity (labeled G), such as congestion and pollution. Both these types are *collective* in that they are not allocated through the market and are enjoyed (or suffered) to some extent by everyone in the sharing group. Of course, use of services on such facilities (for example, museum visits) may be sold privately, in which case the associated variables are included in the consumption vector.

Local collective goods are distinguished by their limited local impact on citizens. Consequently, we model them in a way that admits local structure. The most general way to accomplish this is to allow location to enter the utility function directly. Then, localness can be captured through complementarities between location (s) and the collective provision levels (g, G).[1] A much studied special case (see, for example, Anderson and Crocker (1971) or Polinsky and Shavell (1976)) is that of pollution, where the air quality at location s is a function of ambient pollution and abatement activity at the source (say $\alpha^s(G,g)$).

It will be convenient to think of households as solving a two-stage problem. First, conditional on being in a particular location they solve the problem of choosing the continuous consumption variables. Then, they optimize over the discrete choice of location. The outcome of this process is naturally the same as if all choice variables are contemplated simultaneously, but our sequencing is mathematically convenient. We allow households to be heterogeneous both with respect to preferences and incomes; however, we do assume there are only a finite number of different types (indexed by h).

The household (type h) last-stage problem (conditional on location s) takes the form:

$$\max_{c,\ell} U^h(g, G, c, \ell, s)$$

subject to

$$p^s c + r^s \ell = y^h,$$

where p and r are the market prices of goods and land (at the specified location), and y is exogenous income (to be discussed further below). Note that we are allowing all market prices to depend potentially on location in the formulation. However, y is not so indexed, since exogenous income must be independent of location choice. This problem naturally defines an indirect utility function of the form $V^h(g, G, s, p^s, r^s, y^h)$. Frequently, we shall abbreviate this and other similar functions as V^{hs}.

When the household has a choice over a set of locations S, the first-stage problem may be represented as:

$$\max_{s \in S} V^h(g, G, s, p^s, r^s, y^h).$$

Here, the size of the choice set S determines the extent of free mobility assumed. Note that if similar individuals end up residing at different locations they must get the same level of utility at each of these locations.

Our final restriction is to consider an essentially static model. The only sequential element in our model will be of the *ex ant/ex post* type: we assume that there is an *ex ante* status quo (before projects are initiated) in which all private markets clear so that prices are determined as functions of the status quo provision levels; these functions will be represented as $r(g)$, $p(g)$. After a project is initiated a new *ex post* equilibrium is immediately established and capitalization occurs to the extent that the resulting capital gains (or losses) on land reflect the associated changes in amenity levels.

3   SUFFICIENT CONDITIONS FOR EXACT CAPITALIZATION

The two conditions discussed at the outset can be formalized as follows. Suppose that for each type h living at location s,[2] we assume that there exists a location σ (which may depend on h and s) satisfying:

Assumption 1: Isolation   For those living at location σ there is no marginal direct effect from a change in g, or G nor is there any induced marginal effect on the rental rate at σ. Stated mathematically: $\partial V^{h\sigma}/\partial g = 0$, $\partial r^{\sigma}/\partial g = 0$ (and similarly for G).

Assumption 2: Substitution   Type h lives at location σ and is freely mobile between residence locations. Mathematically, $V^{hs} = V^{h\sigma}$ for all locations s at which h is resident.

Thinking of a world in which congestion plays a significant role, the isolation assumption makes the most sense when location σ is at a considerable distance from location s, namely when the two locations are in different states or metropolitan areas. Then, the substitution assumption will hold as long as metropolitan areas are heterogeneous in types and households are freely mobile between areas. We postpone for the moment a discussion of the reasonableness of these assumptions taken together, and show how they are related to hedonics and capitalization.

3.1   Conditions for Land-Value Capitalization

Suppose a local public improvement is made in the community of region s. Then, our pair of assumptions implies that people from region σ will want to move in unless prevented from doing so by some change in market variables. If land rents are the only variables with the flexibility to serve this function, we shall find that benefits are capitalized into land values. To see, this, add the assumption:

Assumption 3: National markets[3]   Market prices (to households) for a *non-land* private goods at all locations are unaffected by the marginal project. Mathematically: $\nabla_g p^s = 0$, all s.

Capitalization can take a number of different forms and be represented in a corresponding variety of different ways.[4] Here, we shall confine ourselves to first-order analysis; namely, we shall assume that projects are sufficiently small so that a first-order approximation to the corresponding change in utility is exact. Such a first-order project change will be represented as δg, and enough smoothness will be assumed so that a sufficiently small change in g generates first-order changes in all other variables (including G).

There are several variants of capitalization depending on exactly what is measured. Here, we shall focus on *hedonic capitalization* which occurs at a set of locations when first-order change in land rent there is exactly equal to the first-order change net valuation of direct benefits from amenities and indirect costs from congestion/pollution (all measured in numeraire units). We show now that our three assumptions together imply hedonic capitalization.[5]

Since the substitution condition holds before and after the project, it can be thought of as an indentity in g. Differentiating this identity, normalizing by the marginal utility of numeraire[6] and using duality relationships yields:

$$\Omega_g^{hs}\delta g + \Omega_G^{hs}\delta G - c^{hs}\delta p^s - \ell^{hs}\delta r^s + \delta y^h = - c^{h\sigma}\delta p^\sigma + \delta y^h,$$

where Ω_x stands for the marginal rate of substitution between collective good x and numeraire, and we have omitted terms involving g and r on the right-hand side using the isolation assumption. Further, income changes (which must be independent of location choices)[7] cancel, and due to the assumption of national markets, $\delta p^s = \delta p^\sigma = 0$. Rearranging terms, and summing over all affected locations yields the hedonic capitalization formula:

$$\sum_{hs}\Omega_g^{hs}\delta g +\sum_{hs}\Omega_G^{hs}\delta G = \sum_{hs}\ell^{hs}\delta r^s.$$

Observe that to the extent that the project generates extra congestion, this will *reduce* the capital gains on land (or generate a capital loss if there were no public benefits), since the shadow value of congestion will be negative – land values reflect the correct net public incentive.

3.2   Assessing the Assumptions

The full implications of our framework for welfare economics can be best understood by thinking about the ways in which the isolation and substitution assumptions interact. Note that whenever both assumptions hold, the model takes on a competitive flavor – each agent is at all times indifferent between the 'active' community and an outside option which is affected only indirectly, if at all, by the project. In the extreme case where price and income effects in the outside world are negligible, reservation utility levels would be given, and all welfare benefits are capitalized into local land values. In this context, various authors have shown that if the local government owns local land and maximizes land values (thus internalizing the local public externality) the resulting decisions will be Pareto efficient;[8] and in any event, there is no way any agents can be 'hurt' by the public action except as their incomes might be indirectly reduced through price changes.

In addition, the capitalization part of this story relies on the presence of national markets. It is easy to see that this assumption is necessary. For example, in Starrett (1997) we show that when the developer has some discretion over the wage at the development site (so that the wage market is local in character), land-value capitalization is unlikely and 'wage capitalization' is more likely. However, regardless of what market variables do the equilibrating, the welfare economics will be much as described above.

Obviously, the two assumptions in conjunction are very powerful, but are they jointly reasonable? We think it is hard to argue that the substitution and isolation assumptions can simultaneously hold exactly – when households are constantly on the margin of moving in or out, such movements are almost certain to generate some degree of fiscal externality.[9] The most general capitalization models recognize this and introduce appropriate externality terms into the formulas; these vitiate the exact one-for-one nature of the relationship but still tend to leave a strong positive association.

However, we want to argue that the structural mobility assumption is in fact inappropriate in this context anyway, and that replacing it with something more reasonable has far-reaching consequences for the resulting welfare economics.

In particular, we want to ask what motivates the people who migrate across significant distances. Of course, this is an empirical question and one which we cannot answer definitively here. However, we think it is easy to argue that such people are not in 'infinitely elastic' supply (at a given utility level) as required by the full capitalization model. We made this case for the less-developed country context in Starrett (1997) where we argued that the numbers of people leaving peasant societies are quite limited and that those leaving were not indifferent at the margin to whether they stayed or not – once they have decided to leave, almost any available alternative would be significantly better economically, and they would take the best offer.

But even in more advanced societies (where economic alternatives are presumably more relevant) these same considerations would apply to new households, whose numbers are determined by the (mainly non-economic) decision to have children and who have no well-defined fallback option. They also apply to those who are transferred or lose jobs. We think that these groups constitute the main source of intercity migration.

4 A MODEL WITH EXOGENOUS MIGRATIONS

We consider a model now in which some subset of economic agents is always moving for some exogenous reasons. On top of this we retain some market discipline in that there will be long-run tendencies for agents to move to areas where their type enjoys higher utility. We shall show that in this circumstance, overdevelopment is a distinct possibility. In a subsequent section we shall see how incentives linked to land values can exacerbate the overdevelopment.

For this discussion, we simplify the model in a number of ways. First, we drop the spatial reference and assume that private goods prices are unaffected by project decisions. Further, we assume that congestion can be measured by the number of agents sharing the local public good(s). (The sharing group will now be referred to as a 'club'.) Finally, we assume a representative agent model where there is only one type and *equal treatment*, whereby all members of a club get the same allocation.[10] With these simplifications, the indirect utility of a representative agent effectively depends only on local public goods provision (g) and number sharing (n); we label this function $W(g, n)$.

Here we suppose that group decisions are made centrally in an optimal way (given the equal treatment restriction). We label this assumption *rational behavior* (RB):

Assumption 4 (RB): Given an *ex ante* club size (scalar n), the outcome will be determined by choosing the other club allocation variables to maximize representative utility subject to feasibility conditions.

In the next section, we shall discuss how the dynamics is modified when (RB) is dropped and decisions are made by developers acting in a decentralized way.

The outcome of the maximization process generates an indirect utility function,[11] $V(n)$. Obviously, by the definitions, $V(n) = W[g(n), n]$ where $g(n)$ stands for the choice of public facilities under (RB) as a function of population size. The analysis in this section assumes that these functions are 'sufficient statistics' for what goes on inside the club, so any generalization of the underlying model in which size is the only endogenous variable not chosen internally can be incorporated. We assume that W is differential in both arguments and quasi-concave in n for each fixed g.[12]

In all the dynamics to follow, we can think of an iterative step as starting from a status quo set of offerings $<g^i, n^i>$ which are best thought of as the communities in place when we take a snapshot of the economy.[13] It remains to specify how communities get started in the first place. Here, we take the view that they start small as 'basic service clubs'. These communities involve no scale economies or diseconomies up to a maximum feasible size $n^\#$, so that feasibility does not depend on size in that range and such offers can be made credibly without planners knowing anything about preferences. Small rural residential communities are the closest real-world counterpart to these clubs. It seems natural to assume that communities start this way, but we shall discuss later further motivation for this assumption and what happens when it is relaxed.

A service club is characterized by levels of services per person and resource tax per person and yields utility level per member of w^o. We shall maintain throughout the assumption that there are some economies of size in other types of communities. Namely, we suppose that there exists a range of sizes for which $V(n) > w^o$.

The main role played by service clubs in what follows is to prevent us from getting locked into a 'one-club' configuration; when a single club gets too big, members will prefer to opt out into a service club. Indeed, in much of the sequel we shall assume that no two-club configuration could survive such forces. To be precise, we assume the presence of *scale diseconomies* (SD):

Assumption 5 (SD): For any n^1, n^2 that sum up to total population, $\min_i(V(n^i)) < w^o$.

Verbally, if we tried to put the total population into two clubs, at least one of them would be sufficiently congested so that its members would prefer to opt out to a default service club. We let $\underline{n}$ stand for the largest 'viable' club, satisfying $V(\underline{n}) = w^0$.

Households take as given club offerings (including membership) and if making a move will seek the best available offer. As in evolutionary models, we are prevented from being stuck in configurations where memberships are badly wrong by the presence of exogenous perturbations (mutations). The role of mutations in our concept will be played by 'm-migrations'. Given an *ex ante* configuration $(n^1, \ldots, n^c)$, an m-migration occurs when m people move from an existing community (j) to another community (k), which could be an existing community or a new service community.[14]

Because of scale economies and diseconomies, allocations will necessarily change when migrations occur. In principle people might be able to predict this and use the information in deciding where to move.[15] However, here we rule this out by assuming *naive sorting* (NS):

Assumption 6 (NS): Given any status quo configuration, each household chooses (in the subsequent moving phase) a community j for which $j \in arg$ $\max_i W(g^i, n^i)$; in addition m-migrations up to size M occur from time to time among all pairs of existing communities.

Note that sorting is myopic here in that no one takes into account the impact that moving could have on sharing numbers.[16] Note further that, in the absence of M-migrations, all communities that retain members after a moving stage must have offered the same status quo utility level.

The migrations are short-term phenomena that will be permanent only if they are consistent with long-run incentives. An m-migration is termed *reversing* relative to a reference utility level $\underline{v}$ if:

$$V(n^k + m) < \underline{v} \text{ and } \underline{v} < V(n^j - m).$$

Suppose we are at a status quo of the iterative process with associated utility level $\hat{v}$. Then if an m-migration is reversing, there will be an immediate incentive (even after reoptimization) for households to leave the temporarily larger community and to join the temporarily smaller one. Conversely, if an m-migration is not reversing, then at least one of the two affected communities has 'staying power' in that it will not revert immediately toward the previous state. (Note, however, that this 'instability' interpretation does depend in a subtle way on our assumption (SD) that any viable equilibrium will involve at least three clubs; only if there are at least three clubs will the status quo utility level still be represented in the population after an m-migration.)

The current set of assumptions motivates the following definition of equilibrium: a configuration of public facility packages and associated memberships $<g^j, n^j>$ constitutes an M-stable equilibrium if there exists a number $\hat{v}$ such that:

(M1) $V(n^i) = W(g^j, n^j) = \hat{v} \geq w^o$, all j with $n^j > 0$,
(M2) For all $0 < m \leq M$, every m-migration is reversing relative to $\hat{v}$.

M-stable equilibria will constitute the rest points for dynamics of the following sort. Some household must always want to move if another club is enjoying higher utility than they are in the status quo (so that movement surely will not stop until a $\hat{v}$ of (M1) is established). Further, regardless of utility levels, there will be random m-migrations (up to size M) occurring all the time; condition (M2) requires that these moves be 'shortlived' in that as soon as they occur, they generate countervailing movements: members of the new 'larger' community will want to move out (to somewhere in the world at large) and others from the world at large will want to move to the new 'smaller' community.[17]

We characterize the set of M-stabel equilibria in a series of claims. For simplicity, we deal with the case in which there is only one local maximum to the function $V(.)$;[18] to be more precise, we assume

Assumption 7 (SQ): $V(.)$ is strictly quasi-concave and achieves an interior maximum at n^*.

It is immediate from the definitions that we can associate with an M-stable equilibrium the unique utility level that will be achieved by its 'stable' communities. Label this level $\hat{v}$.

Claim 1 Given (RB), (SD), (NS) and (SQ), no M-stable equilibrium contains service clubs.

Proof If a service club were to be included, the utility level would have to be w^o. Consequently, in any m-migration (m sufficiently small) involving the service club, the new larger club would be better off so such a migration would not be reversing. ∎

Claim 2 Under the conditions of claim 1, all communities in an M-stable equilibrium are identical.

Proof Given (RB) and (SQ), if the M-stable equilibrium contains two 'different' communities (i, j) it must be that $n^i < n^* < n^j$ (after a possible relabeling). Also, using quasi-concavity again, if m is small enough so that $n^i + m < n^* < n^j - m$, we must have:

$$V(n^i + m) > V(n^i) = \hat{v} \text{ (and also } V(n^j - m) > \hat{v}).$$

But the first of these inequalities implies that an m-migration from j to i is not reversing relative to $\hat{v}$. ∎

Next, define a community size $N(M)$ as follows:

$$N(M) = inf[n > 0 \mid V(n - M) \geq V(n)].$$

Clearly, under maintained assumptions, $N(M) - M < n^* < N(M)$ (see Figure 17.1).

Claim 3 The only candidates for M-stable equilibria are sets of identical clubs of size $n\varepsilon[N(M), \underline{n}]$. Furthermore, if the population can be divided into such a set of clubs, that set constitutes an M-stable equilibrium.

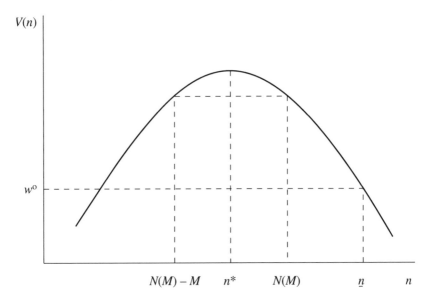

Figure 17.1   Urban welfare benefits

Proof   If $n > \underline{n}$, members would leave to join service clubs. On the other hand, when $n < N(M)$, then by the definitions, $V(n - M) < V(n)$ so that an M-migration among such clubs will not be reversing. By contrast, with $n\varepsilon[N(M), \underline{n}]$, every m-migration ($m < M$) is reversing since (then) $V(n - m) > V(n) > V(n + m)$, the last inequality following from quasi-concavity. ∎

Note that the 'window' $[N(M), \underline{n}]$ may be empty, in which case there are no equilibria. This is the case in which there are insufficient scale economies to prevent communities from dissolving into service clubs in response to out-migrations. But even if the window is not empty, equilibria still need not exist due to the aforementioned integer problem.

   Generally, however, we expect sufficient scale economies to generate a range of equilibrium club sizes. Note that all of these will be too large (and therefore too congested) relative to the utility-maximizing club size. The model is incomplete in that it does not resolve the attendant indeterminacy. This is partly because 'club managers' are completely passive with respect to choice of club size. We next relax that assumption and show that under certain behavioral assumptions, the largest sizes compatible with equilibrium will be chosen.

5   REVERSE CAPITALIZATION

In the spirit of the previous section, we assume that migrating households must choose among a limited set of options and will always take the best among these. Club managers or developers within the club will provide the options and we shall examine their incentives. Consider first an example.[19] There will be three types of agents: landlords who own all the land and rent it out, workers who rent the land and work for developers and developers who hire workers and produce the numeraire good. Developers have a choice between 'large' and 'small' operations. A particular set of households ($2n$) can be accommodated by one large or two small operations. A small operation is sufficiently compact that all workers can live next to the 'factory' and no transport costs are incurred. By contrast, in a large operation, half the workers live close, but half must live further out and incur a transport cost t. We assume that lot sizes and labor supply are fixed (normalized to one) so that a worker's net income is measured by wage minus rent minus transport paid.

Further, let the wage (w) be exogenously given and the same in all operations. Note that rental rates cannot be the same even though all marginal land still has zero value. Those living close to a large operation will have to pay a rent of t in order to deter those living further out from wanting to move in (we continue to assume free mobility *within* a community). Thus, large operations generate positive rent whereas small ones do not. All workers in large operations have net incomes of $w - t$; those outside incur the extra cost as transport while those inside pay it as a rent.

Suppose that developers make a net profit (in numeraire units) of π_1 in two small projects and π_2 in one large project (recall that these options absorb the same amount of labor). The Table 17.1 summarizes the benefits to agents from two small projects versus a single large one.

Assuming that all these benefits count equally in the welfare calculations, we see that the large project is preferable if and only if:

$$\pi_2 - nt \geq \pi_1.$$

Table 17.1   Project welfare benefits

	Workers	Developer	Landlord
Small	$2nw$	π_1	0
Large	$2n(w - t)$	π_2	nt

Since, *nt* measures the rent attributable to a large development, the capitalization argument has been turned on its head! Not only is there no net benefit attributable to rent increases, but there is actually a cost. Developers will choose the large option whenever $\pi_2 > \pi_1$, and this will be the wrong choice (from society's perspective) whenever $\pi_2 - nt < \pi_1$. And the reader should see that incentives are distorted even more if developers own the land.

Note several key features of the example. First, the welfare of newcomers depends on what is done and in fact their interests are at odds with the developer's interests, *especially* if the latter own the land; newcomers are worse off when they must pay rent (or transport) since their wages are the same in both regimes. Obviously, such a conflict cannot occur in the utility-taking model. Second, we have introduced an 'urban' spatial consideration through the presence of transport costs attributable to spatial separation. Here, transport costs are avoidable and constitute a deadweight loss to the economy as a whole. In such situations the market system, which counts transport as part of market cost, will distort the allocation of resource and ownership of land by developers worsens rather than improves this distortion. We shall see now how these features carry over in a general urban model.

5.1 Structural Characteristics of Urban Development

We examine a model with the following general features. Development activities will take place at a number of distinct 'sites' in an urban area. 'Improvements' might take the form of local public consumption goods (such as museums), local public production goods (such as roads and communication networks) or even private production goods (such as office space). Development projects will induce extra activity: new employment in connection with the improved production environment and new visits to the local public consumption facilities. We no longer assume anything about the alternatives available to these workers elsewhere and concentrate on the welfare of people assuming that the required extra workers will show up via a non-economic migration. We shall, however, generally assume a competitive labor market so that wages paid will be the same for all workers (of a type).

In the presence of urban spatial separation, increased activity will be accompanied by increased transport/congestion. Whereas we allowed such congestion to affect utility before, we now want to model it more explicitly. Improvements will increase transport costs along routes between residence and workplace or public facility; congestion at a particular location is a function of density of traffic at that location and, consequently, can be expected to increase as well. This induced congestion imposes social costs (either by increasing transport requirements and/or directly lowering utility). Note, in particular, that when people are commuting to the central place, total congestion suffered is likely to *increase* rather than decrease with distance.

Apart from the explicit modeling of transportation and congestion, the spatial model is just as in earlier sections of this chapter. However, we shall treat non-land private good prices as fixed (effectively assuming national markets). Most of the time we shall employ a non-land private good aggregate, although at certain points it will be useful to separate out labor time.

The equilibrating forces of location choice will result in land rent changes and we seek to relate these to non-market project net benefits. We work out this relationship for a bare-bones prototype that captures the essential spatial features of the previous example, and indicate later how the results will be modified in a more realistic fleshed-out version.

5.2 A Simple Prototype

A general story with many sites will generate multiple spillovers among sites. We abstract from these at first by considering a single site and its surrounding area. To keep the congestion computations simple, we think of the congestion site and surrounding area as separately homogeneous in that congestion will be thought of as uniform within each of these areas and transport distance will be thought of an uniform between any point in one of these areas and any point in the other.[20] The development site region and surrounding area are labeled s and σ respectively.

Congestion in $s(G)$ is simply a function of total employment there (L), and we choose units so that $G = L$. We suppose that the 'damage' done by congestion can be represented by an associated increase in transport costs incurred by those who must commute from the outside area;[21] $T(G)$ will stand for this cost function.

As before, a project entails a first-order change in amenity levels (δg) together with an associated incremental direct cost which is borne by the users (independently of where they choose to live in the community). The project will have further indirect effects on income and employment as it stimulates increased economic activity. We can model this effect explicitly as follows. Suppose $F(g, L)$ stands for a private production function with $\delta F / \delta g > 0$ (reflecting the role of g as a public input). Private firms will choose the employment level to maximize profits $(\pi = F(g, L) - wL)$, and assuming that g and L are complementary in production $(F_{g,l} > 0)$, both employment and indirect profits will go up with an increase in g. Finally, there will be an indirect effect on land rents as land market equilibrium is re-established.

Now we examine the problem faced by agents in the two areas. (We assume that everyone is alike, although there would be no essential differences with many types as long as they did not systematically sort themselves between the areas.) An agent in region s solves a problem of exactly the same form (absent congestion) as in previous sections since no transport costs are incurred, whereas an agent in region σ solves:

$$\max_{c,\ell} U(g, c, \ell, \sigma)$$

subject to:

$$c + r_\sigma \ell + T(G) = y(g),$$

where $y(g)$ stands for disposable income after payment of taxes to support the local public expenditures. Disposable income depends on g because of these taxes; it may have a further indirect dependence to the extent that there is local ownership of land and local firms. Optimal choice generates an indirect utility function $V(g, G, r_\sigma, y, \sigma)$.

The condition that agents are indifferent between the two locations yields the following identity in g:

$$V[g, G(g), r_\sigma, y(g), \sigma] \equiv V[g, r_s(g), y(g), s].$$

(Note that we assume that rent in the surrounding area is fixed by outside forces.) Differentiating and using the envelope theorem as before, we find:[22]

$$\ell_s \delta r_s = (\Omega^s - \Omega^\sigma)\delta g + (dT/dG)\delta G. \tag{17.1}$$

Observe that (17.1) is general enough to nest the results of Section 2. In particular, if there are no direct marginal effects at σ, and no congestion, we are back to hedonic capitalization. However, in the present urban context where everyone is commuting to the site of extra 'amenities' (the central business district or CBD), it is much more reasonable that there be no differences in direct marginal effects between the regions, in which case our formula reduces to:

$$\ell_s \delta r_s = (dT/dG)\delta G. \tag{17.2}$$

Now, increases in land rent measure increases in transport (congestion) cost much as in the previous example. Note that the incremental congestion is attributable directly to the project; in the particular story told above where congestion is proportional to employment in the CBD, we find:

$$\delta G = \delta L = (-F_{gL}/F_{LL})\delta g > 0,$$

but it should be clear that (17.2) holds more generally regardless of exactly how the extra congestion is induced.

The welfare-economic implications of our analysis are somewhat ambiguous due the presence of new agents and the accounting for absentee owners (if any). The desirability of the project depends on what alternatives (if any) there were for new households and how the owners of land and firms are counted. If there are no other alternatives for the new agents, the extra congestion may be unavoidable. However if, as in the first example, there is an uncongested alternative, this extra transport is a deadweight loss and the project involves an element of overdevelopment.

In any case, newcomers and old residents are worse off unless they own the resources whose value is enhanced. So if developers own the land, they will have an incentive to accommodate migrants in a way that increases the size of agglomerations and moves us away from the utility-maximizing club sizes. In particular, our assumption of (RB) will not be satisfied. Rather, private developers are likely to choose club allocations that are somewhat 'too large' for current membership. Consequently, sufficiently small in-migrations will always be welfare improving in the short run and these migrations will not be reversing until utility levels are reduced to the service club level. Therefore, in this situation land ownership by (absentee) developers may lead us to the worst outcome consistent with equilibrium as defined in the previous section. Even if the relationship is not exact as above, the same tendency will be present as long as there is a positive correlation between rent change and incremental congestion (see below).

5.3   Measures for the General Urban Model

It can be seen that our prototype was designed to parallel as closely as possible features of the example. Here we want to argue that similar qualitative results would emerge from a more general treatment. We consider extra complications in sequence.

Location heterogeneity
Obviously, the location framework above is very special and we may expect our extreme discreteness assumptions to have an impact on the form of results. A general treatment would recognize far more locational complexity, explicitly identifying transport routes and measuring congestion/transport costs as a function of the distribution of commuters across the various zones within the overall urban area. However, as long as congestion costs incurred are greater for those commuting from outside the immediate development area than for those inside, land rent changes (in the development area) will respond positively to congestion increases. We can get a feeling for the likely form of this relationship by considering briefly a standard model with continuous location heterogeneity.

We examine the 'linear city' model of Solow and Vickrey (1971). Commercial activity takes place in a CBD, which (for convenience) we assume takes up no space. Residents live on both sides of the CBD and we assume that residential density is constant (and normalized to one). Note that with this assumption, increased employment necessarily expands the boundary (σ) of the residential area. Indeed, normalizing so that each household supplies one unit of labor, we will have $\delta\sigma = \delta L/2$. Congestion and transport costs depend only on distance from the CBD. Furthermore, the transport cost function is assumed linear in congestion ($T(G) = T'G$).

Congestion is determined as follows. Congestion at a particular location is measured by the volume of traffic through that location. At location s this is the number of people commuting from further out: $\sigma - s$. A household residing at τ experiences congestion $G(\tau, \sigma)$ equal to the total congestion associated with all locations it passes through while commuting, namely:

$$G(\tau, \sigma) = \int_0^\tau (\sigma - s)ds = \sigma\tau - \tau^2/2.$$

Consequently, the incremental (first-order) cost suffered by such a resident (label this $\delta\Gamma(\tau)$) is given by:

$$\delta\Gamma(\tau) = T'\delta G = T'(\partial G/\partial\sigma)\delta\sigma = T'\tau\delta\sigma.$$

(Note that congestion does increase with distance, in fact proportionally under this particular set of assumptions.)

Assuming (as above) that none of the other effects of the project are local in character (at least over the distances commuted), rents must adjust so that the net total cost of all locations changes by the same amount (say Δ), namely,

$$\delta\Gamma(\tau) + \delta r(\tau) = T'\tau\delta\sigma + \delta r(\tau) = \Delta = \delta r(0), \text{ all } \tau \in (0, \sigma). \tag{17.3}$$

From this relationship it is clear that since the rent change is zero at the new boundary (where congestion is highest), it must be positive at all interior locations when congestion increases.

To obtain a neat exact relationship, define a location $v(\tau)$ by the formula:

$$\delta r(0) - \delta r(\tau) = \delta r[v(\tau)] - \delta r(\sigma), \tag{17.4}$$

and note that $v(\sigma) = 0$ and $v(0) = \sigma$. Furthermore, given the linearity in (17.3), $dv/d\tau = -1$. Now, substituting (17.4) and (17.3), integrating over all regions in the town, and using the change of variable theorem, we find:

$$\int_{\tau=0}^{\sigma} \delta\Gamma(\tau)d(\tau) = \int_{\tau=0}^{\sigma} \{\delta r[v(\tau)] - \delta r(\sigma)\}\,d\tau = \int_{v=0}^{\sigma} \delta r(v)dv - \sigma\delta r(\sigma).$$

The left-hand side of this expression represents total incremental congestion cost; we see that this quantity must fall short of total incremental rent increase (in the old community) to the extent that rent goes up at the old boundary.[23] Thus, expansionary projects that increase community employment tend to raise local rents in a way that is still closely related to the increase in congestion costs imposed.

Exact relationships such as those derived above clearly are going to depend on the particular functional form assumptions employed. However, it seems likely that any reasonable modeling of congestion in the context of commuting to a central place such as in the urban models of Arnott (1979) or Henderson (1988), will lead to positive correlations between congestion and rent changes, *ceteris paribus.*

Local effects of positive amenities
If the benefits of marginal amenities have differential spatial effects within community, then cancellation will not occur in (17.1); however, except in the aforementioned case of air quality (where living in the suburbs is likely to be more pleasant than living nearer the pollution source), it is hard to think of amenities that will be local enough in scope to matter much over the distance ranges we are considering. Consequently, it seems likely that the differential congestion effect will dominate.

Multiple sites and spillovers
The presence of multiple sites introduces spillover effects from the presence of households that work in one site, yet enjoy amenities at other sites. Such 'outside users' have an ambiguous effect on the welfare calculus above. Since outsiders are not obliged to visit the development site, and probably are not 'at the margin' of living near the site, their presence can have independent effects on rents near the site and net benefits conveyed by the site. To the extent that their use is increased, they will exacerbate congestion, raise rents near the site and reinforce 'reverse capitalization'. However, to the extent that their net utility from visits is increased (holding number of visits fixed), they will increase hedonic benefits with no corresponding effect on rents; if rents are going up due to increased congestion, this factor will generate a mitigating positive correlation between rents and hedonic benefits.

6   SUMMARY AND CONCLUSIONS

Free mobility to and from an exogenous outside option has been a central feature of most models in local public finance. These features combine to create a competitive environment in which public decision making cannot go too badly wrong and may in fact lead to first-best outcomes under certain behavioral assumptions. In this chapter, we have challenged these underlying assumptions and shown that an alternative model may lead to quite perverse incentives to overdevelop in a way that will lead to communities that are too large and congested relative to the first best.

If communities do get too large and congested in the way just suggested, it is clear that a planner could improve things by forming a new community. And if the 'surplus' from so doing can be appropriated, we should ask why it does not happen. Note that we did not allow such experimentation in Section 4, except at the level of small service communities. So at this point we should address the question of entry and why it might be restricted. The first reason involves scale economies and coordination failure. As we know, the underlying model of agglomeration involves scale economies in the provision of public services (or some other element of production). A significant and growing literature has demonstrated that decentralized decision making in the presence of private information will fail to realize social economies of scale in these circumstances.[24] This was our main motivation for restricting entry to constant-returns-to-scale communities.[25]

Further, even if the coordination failure difficulties could be circumvented, the incentives might not be there. The mere fact that a Pareto improvement is possible does not guarantee that developers will see the incentives to initiate the associated change. In the model of Section 5, part of developers' profits are derived by imposing negative externalities on third parties. The private benefit they appropriate from these externalities may well exceed any surplus they could recover from a first-best plan. They may be better off by adding on to established communities than by starting a new one even though the latter course of action would be better for the overall social good.

NOTES

1. We treat g and G as scalars for convenience. However, there is no difficulty in principle in letting them be vectors of arbitrary dimension.
2. Implicit in these definitions is the assumption that any type living as s before the project continues to live there afterwards. This stipulation can be removed at some cost in complexity in the precise statement of assumptions and conclusions.
3. This assumption can be weakened somewhat at the cost of losing some precision. As will be seen in the demonstration below, what matters here is that the effects of non-land price changes be the same in various locations, not that they be zero. However, when agents in different locations consume different amounts of such private goods we cannot expect exactly the same effects from price changes, so measures of the type derived below will not hold precisely.
4. For a compendium of such results and references to the earlier literature, see Starett (1988). For a discussion of empirical work in this area, see Yinger et al. (1988).
5. For further discussion of capitalization variants, see Starett (1988, Ch. 13).

6. Actually, even though we are comparing people who are identical in all respects, there is reason to believe that the marginal utility of income may not be the same at all residence locations. This possibility has interesting implications for welfare economics first noted by Mirrlees (1972). However, we shall assume that it does not arise here.
7. The one caveat here is that there cannot be any location-specific head taxes. If there were then, except by chance, two people of the same type (and thus, the same disposable income) could not live at different locations and the substitution assumption could never hold. Apart from this restriction, nothing need be assumed about the method of public finance.
8. There is a big hidden assumption here, namely that the decision-making process would generate an equilibrium outcome after households vote with their feet; unfortunately, such an equilibrium does not exist in many circumstances; see, for example, Bewley (1981). Also it is important to note that the free-rider problem is not 'solved' by these models but essentially assumed away by having common knowledge of preferences.
9. This literature is summarized in Starrett (1988, Chs 11, 13).
10. Again, there would be little qualitative difference in results with many types, as long as there were no 'Tiebout sorting' of types among clubs.
11. In this section we drop the type index since there is only one type.
12. Differentiability in n is naturally problematic if we think of households as integer units. As in much of the related literature, we employ an approximation in which n is treated as continuous. Clearly, this approximation will not be very good unless communities are large relative to the size of a household. For more discussion of the issues involved here, see Starrett (1988) and Berliant (1985). Quasi-concavity captures the idea that increasing membership with a fixed facility first increases representative utility (as the fixed cost is spread) and then decreases it (as congestion dominates).
13. The superscripts on g and n now index club.
14. It would be more reasonable to assume that when M people happen to leave a particular community, they tend to disperse among a variety of other communities and similarly, that when M people arrive, they come from a variety of other places. If the assumption is written in that way, similar results hold although they will not have the same level of precision.
15. See Starrett (2000) for analysis of outcomes when agents do anticipate such adjustments.
16. Of course, when numbers change, the public provision levels will generally change in the next voting phase; however, except by chance the subsequent utility level will differ from that expected.
17. The presence of at least one outside world community is assured for any configuration satisfying (M1) by our assumption (SD). It is possible to conduct a parallel analysis without assuming anything about scale diseconomies if two-community situations are handled separately.
18. For analysis of more general forms for $V(.)$, see Starrett (2000).
19. This example was first presented in Starrett (1997). We reproduce it here because we want to argue that it has much more general applicability than claimed there.
20. This is the simplest possible spatial structure, and is essentially the same as the one employed in our example earlier.
21. It would make very little qualitative difference if we allowed congestion to affect utility directly as well; however, the following expressions would be somewhat more complicated.
22. Again, assuming the marginal utility of income does not vary over locations (see note 5).
23. Note that rent cannot go down at the old boundary, since $r(\sigma) = 0$.
24. See for example, Arthur (1989), Cooper and John (1988) and Heller (1986).
25. Naturally, allowing for more aggressive entry will mitigate the severity of inefficiency in Section 4.

REFERENCES

Anderson, R. and T. Crocker (1971), 'Air pollution and residential property values', *Urban Studies*, **8**, pp. 171–80.

Arnott, R. (1979), 'Optimal city size in a spatial economy', *Journal of Urban Economics*, **6**, pp. 65–89.

Arthur, W.B. (1989), 'Competing technologies, increasing returns, and lock-in by historical events', *Economic Journal*, **99**, pp. 116–31.

Bewley, T. (1981), 'A critique of Tiebout's theory of local public expenditures', *Econometrica*, **49**, pp. 713–40.

Cooper, R. and A. John (1988), 'Coordinating coordination failures in Keynesian models', *Quarterly Journal of Economics*, **103**, pp. 441–64.

Freeman, A. (1979), *The Benefits of Environmental Improvement*, Baltimore, MD: Johns Hopkins University Press.

Heller, W. (1986), Coordination Failure in Complete Markets with Application to Effective Demand', in *Essays in Honor of Kenneth J. Arrow*, vol. II (W. Heller, R. Starr and D. Starrett (eds), Cambridge University Press.

Henderson, J.V. (1988), *Urban Development, Theory, Fact, and Illusion*, Oxford: Oxford University Press.

Johansson, P. (1987), *The Economic Theory and Measurement of Environmental Benefits*, Cambridge: Cambridge University Press.

Mäler, K. (1971), 'A method of estimating social benefits from pollution control', in P. Bohm and A. Kneese (eds), *The Economics of the Environment*, New York: Macmillan.

Mäler, K. (1974), *Environmental Economics, A Theoretical Enquiry*, Baltimore, MD: Johns Hopkins University Press.

Mirrlees, J. (1972), 'The optimum town', *Swedish Journal of Economics*, **74**, pp. 114–35.

Polinsky, A.M. and S. Shavell (1976), 'Amenities and property values in a model of an urban area', *Journal of Public Economics*, **5**, pp. 119–29.

Scotchmer, S. (1985), 'Profit maximizing clubs', *Journal of Public Economics*, **27**, pp. 25–45.

Solow, R. and W. Vickrey (1971), 'Land use in a long narrow city', *Journal of Economic Theory*, **3**, pp. 430–47.

Starrett, D. (1988), *Foundations of Public Economics*, Cambridge: Cambridge University Press.

Starrett, D. (1997), 'Public policy toward social overhead capital: the capitalization externality', in *The Environment and Emerging Development Issues*, Oxford: Clarendon Press, pp. 574–93.

Starrett, D. (2000), 'On the equilibrium size and composition of communities', unpublished MS.

Wildasin, D. (1986), *Urban Public Finance*, New York: Harwood Academic Publishers.

Yinger, J., H. Bloom, A. Borsch-Supan and H. Ladd (1988), *Property Taxes and House Values*, New York: Academic Press.

18. The core of the cooperative game associated with oligopoly firms

Hirofumo Uzawa

1 INTRODUCTION

In Uzawa (1996, 1999), we developed an analytical framework in which the structure of the n-person cooperative games associated with the economies involving public goods in the Samuelsonian sense is examined in detail. Our approach was originally formulated with the specific purpose of examining the conditions under which the core of the n-person cooperative game for global warming is non-empty, as in detail described in Uzawa (1999). The analysis may be equally applicable to the general situation where both the schedules of marginal utilities and products depend upon the aggregate quantities of private or public goods (or public bads in the case of global warming) produced in the economy.

In this chapter, we apply our approach to the analysis of the behavior of oligopoly firms engaged in the production of single or differentiated products, with a particular emphasis on the conditions under which the core of the n-person cooperative game arising out of the oligopoly market is non-empty.

As regards the analysis of the behavior of oligopoly firms, there is an extensive list of literature, beginning with the classic contribution of Cournot (1838) to the recent game-theoretic approaches. The recent game-theoretic contributions are given a well-balanced overview by the excellent survey articles of Friedman (1982) and Shapiro (1989). This chapter is largely based upon the general framework of the oligopoly theory as provided by Friedman's and Shapiro's survey articles, but also Friedman (1977, 1983), Fudenberg and Tirole (1986), and other major contributions are consulted.

Oligopoly theory primarily concerns the behavior of a number of firms that produce identical or differentiated products and sell them on the same market. The original contribution of Cournot (1838) considered the case of two firms producing the identical product on the same market and developed a prototype of duopoly theory, and it has since become the basis upon which virtually all contributions to the duopoly and oligopoly have been developed. Cournot's model concerned the behavior of duopoly firms within the single time period, but some attempts are made, particularly be Edgeworth (1925), Bowley (1924), von Stackelberg (1934), Sweezy (1939) and Cyert and de Groot (1970), among others, to examine the multi-period behavior of duopoly firms. It was Chamberlin's classic work (1956) which extended the analysis to oligopoly firms producing differentiated products and examined in detail the implications for the theory of industrial organization, followed by an extensive literature on the subject as exemplified by Bain (1949). Beginning with Cyert and de Groot (1970), a large number of contributions have been made concerning the game-theoretic approaches to the analysis of dynamic behavior of oligopoly firms, both with single and differentiated products. Particularly important was the effective application of the powerful tool of the repeated game theory to explore fully the implications of the oligopoly firms for industrial structure.

This chapter, however, is confined to the static analysis of oligopoly firms and to examining some of the more basic propositions concerning the behavior of oligopoly firms that would be useful in the dynamic analysis of such firms.

2   THE COURNOT THEORY REVIEWED

The Cournot theory of duopoly concerns the behavior of two firms producing an identical product that is sold on the same market. The technologies and the accumulation of capital, however, are different between the two firms.

Let x^v be the quantity of the product produced by firm $v(v = 1, 2)$, and X denote the total quantity produced by two firms:

$$X = x^1 + x^2. \tag{18.1}$$

The structure of the market may be characterized by the schedule of the demand price:

$$p = p(X), (X > 0)$$

which specifies the price p on the market at which the produced quantity X is in equilibrium.

We assume that the demand-price $p(X)$ is defined for all $X \geq 0$, positive valued, and continuously twice differentiable with respect to $X(X \geq 0)$. We assume also that the demand-price function $p = p(X)$ satisfies the following conditions:

$$p(X) > 0, p'(X) < 0, p''(X) < 0, \text{ for all } X > 0. \tag{18.2}$$

In the standard theory of Cournot duopoly, a slightly weaker condition is assumed:

$$2p'(X) + p''(X)X < 0, \text{ for all } 0 < X < \bar{X} \tag{18.3}$$

where $\bar{X}$ is a given positive quantity, which is sufficiently large so that all quantities X in the following discussion are smaller than $\bar{X}$.

In the following discussion, we occasionally need the stronger assumption (18.2), rather than the standard condition (18.3). Furthermore, it will be assumed that:

$$p(X) + p'(X)X > 0, \text{ for all } 0 < X < \bar{X}.$$

For each firm v, the cost function $c_v = x_v(x^v)$ specifies the minimum cost c_v required to produce the output x^v. We assume that cost function $c_v(x^v)$ is defined for all $x^v > 0$, positive valued, and continuously twice differentiable. We also assume that marginal costs are always positive and diminishing:

$$c_v(0) = 0, c_v'(x^v) > 0, c_v''(x^v) > 0, \text{ for all } x^v > 0. \tag{18.4}$$

It may be noted that:

$$c_v'(x^v) > \frac{c_v'(x^v)}{x^v}, \text{ for } x^v > 0. \tag{18.5}$$

In the Cournot theory of duopoly, it is assumed that each firm v maximizes its profit:

$$\pi_v(x^v, X) = p(X)x^v - c_v(x^v) \tag{18.6}$$

with respect to x^v, where the way total output X responds to individual output x^v is postulated in various ways. Let us first consider the case where each firm supposes that the level of the other firm's output remains at the current level. Thus the maximizing problem for firm 1 is given by the following:

Find x^{10} that maximizes (18.6), $v = 1$, subject to the constraint (18.1), with given x^2. The Lagrangian form of the maximizing problem for firm 1 is given by:

$$L(x^1, \lambda) = p(X)x^1 - c_1(x^1) + \lambda(X - x^1 - x^2).$$

The marginality conditions are the following:

$$p(X^0) - c_1'(x^{10}) \le \lambda \qquad (18.7)$$

with equality if $x^{10} > 0$;

$$-p'(X^0)x^{10} = \lambda \qquad (18.8)$$

$$X^0 = x^{10} + x^2, \text{ with given } x^2 \qquad (18.9)$$

where λ is a positive number.

It should be noted, in view of (18.7) and (18.5), that profit $\pi^1(X^0, x^{10})$ is non-negative:

$$p(X^0)x^{10} - c_1(x^{10}) \ge [p(X^0) - c_1'(x^{10})]x^{10} \ge 0.$$

In what follows, it is assumed, without loss of generality, that marginality condition (18.7) is satisfied with equality.

Then the following maximum condition is satisfied.

$$p(X^0)x^{10} - c_1(x^{10}) \ge p(X)x^1 - c_1(x^1)$$

for all $x^1 > 0$, $X = x^1 + x^2$, with strict inequality whenever $x^1 \ne x^{10}$.

Proof   This may be proved in the following manner, without recourse to the modified Kuhn–Tucker theorem on quasi-concave programming. Let (x^1, X) be any pair of the output x^1 of firm 1 and the total output X such that:

$$x^1 > 0, X = x^1 + x^2$$

and define:

$$x^1(t) = x^{10} + t(x^1 - x^{10}), X(t) = X^0 + t(X - X^0) = x^1(t) + x^2$$

$$\phi(t) = p[X(t)]x^1(t) - c^1[x^1(t)], (0 \le t \le 1).$$

Then,

$$\phi(0) = p(X^0)x^{10} - c_1(x^{10}) \qquad (18.10)$$

$$\phi'(t) = p'[X(t)]x^1(t) \frac{dX}{dt} + \{p[X(t)] - c_1'[x^1(t)]\} \frac{dx^1}{dt} \qquad (18.11)$$

where

$$\frac{dx^1}{dt} = x^1 - x^{10}, \quad \frac{dX}{dt} = X - X^0 = \frac{dx^1}{dt} \tag{18.12}$$

which are independent of t.

Then,

$$\phi'(0) = 0. \tag{18.13}$$

Differentiate both sides of (18.11) with respect to t, we obtain:

$$\phi''(t) = p''[X(t)]x^1(t)\left(\frac{dX}{dt}\right)^2 + 2p'[X(t)]\frac{dX}{dt}\frac{dx^1}{dt} - c_1''[x^1(t)]\left(\frac{dx^1}{dt}\right)^2$$

$$= \{p''[X(t)]x^1(t) + 2p'[X(t)]\}\left(\frac{dX}{dt}\right)^2 - c_1''[x^1(t)]\left(\frac{dX^1}{dt}\right)^2.$$

In view of the assumed conditions (18.3), (18.4), and relations (18.12), we obtain:

$$\phi''(t) \leq 0, \text{ for all } 0 \leq t \leq 1 \tag{18.14}$$

with strict inequality whenever $x^1 \neq x^{10}$. QED

Relations (18.10), 18.13, and (18.14) imply:

$$\phi(0) \geq \phi(1)$$

or

$$p(X^0)x^{10} - c_1(x^{10}) \geq p(X)x^1 - c_1(x^1)$$

with strict inequality whenever $x^1 \neq x^{10}$.

We have now established that, for any given level x^2 of output of firm 2, the output x^1 of firm 1 that maximizes the firm's profit:

$$\pi_1 = p(X)x^1 - c_1(x^1), \text{ with } x^1 > 0, X = x^1 + x^2$$

is uniquely determined. The maximum output x^1 of firm corresponding to the given level x^2 of output firm 2 is denoted by:

$$x^1 = \alpha(x^2)$$

to be referred to as the response function of firm 1.

The response function of firm 2 is similarly defined and is denoted by:

$$x^2 = \beta(x^1).$$

We now examine the pattern of the change in the output of firm 1 in response to the change in the output of firm 2. Differentiate both sides of equations (18.7), (18.8) and (18.9), and rearrange, to obtain:

$$\alpha'(x^2) = \frac{-[p''(X)x^1 + p'(X)]}{[p''(X)x^1 + p'(X)] + [p''(X)x^1 + c_1'(x^1)]}.$$

From the assumed conditions (18.2), (18.4), we have:

$$-1 < \alpha'(x^2) < 0. \tag{18.15}$$

Similarly for the response function of firm 2, we have:

$$\beta'(x^1) = \frac{-[p''(X)x^1 + p'(X)]}{[p''(X)x^2 + p'(X)] + [p''(X)x^2 + c_2'(x^2)]},$$

$$-1 < \beta'(x^2) < 0. \tag{18.16}$$

The Cournot equilibrium will be obtained if we find the outputs of two firms, x^1 and x^2, such that:

$$x^1 = \alpha(x^2), \; x^2 = \beta(x^1)$$

which in particular imply that the level of output X stipulated by two firms is the same.

The uniqueness of the Cournot equilibrium is easily seen if we note that the following matrix is non-singular:

$$\det \begin{bmatrix} -1 & \alpha'(x^2) \\ \beta'(x^1) & -1 \end{bmatrix} = 1 - \alpha'(x^2)\beta'(x^1) > 0.$$

The analysis we have carried out so far may be summarized as the following:

Proposition 1 Suppose there exist two firms, 1 and 2, which satisfy conditions (18.2) and (18.4). Then the Cournot equilibrium always exists and is uniquely determined.

The adjustment process defined by:

$$\begin{cases} \dot{x}^1 = k_1[\alpha(x^2) - x^1] \\ \dot{x}^2 = k_2[\beta(x_1) - x^2] \end{cases} (k_1, k_2 > 0) \qquad (18.17)$$

is globally stable.

The global stability of dynamic process (18.17) is easily seen from relations (18.15) and (18.16), and is illustrated in Figure 18.1, where the outputs of two firms are measured along the two axes and the solution paths to the system of dynamic equations (18.17) are represented by the arrowed curves.

The game-theoretic approach to the Cournot theory of duopoly, as briefly described above, is made the basis upon which the theory of duopoly in partic-ular and the more advanced theory of oligopoly in general is developed, as typically described in Friedman (1983) and Fudenberg and Tirole (1986). The concept of Cournot equilibrium in terms of the response functions of two firms involved has peculiar implications for the behavior of firms faced with the

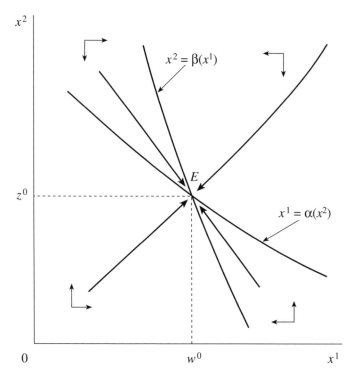

Figure 18.1 Determination of the optimum outputs (a)

market that is not perfectly competitive. We first note that the Cournot equilibrium is not admissible in the sense that both firms are able to find levels of output at which the profits of both firms are higher than those at the Cournot equilibrium.

Before we proceed with our discussion, it may be advisable to examine the structure of the profit function (18.6) regarding the concavity with respect to (x^v, X). As is easily seen, profit function (18.16) is strictly concave with respect to x^v, but it is not concave with respect to (x^v, X). However, it is strictly quasi-concave with respect to (x^v, X), whenever:

$$p(X) - c_v'(x^v) \geq 0. \tag{18.18}$$

Indeed, the bordered Hessian of profit function (18.6) is given by:

$$\begin{bmatrix} -c_v''(x^v) & p'(X) & p(X) - c_v'(x^v) \\ p'(X) & p''(X)x^v & p'(X)x^v \\ p(X) - c_v'(x^v) & p'(X)x^v & 0 \end{bmatrix}$$

whose determinant is:

$$c_v''(x^v)p'(X)^2x^{v2} + 2p'(X)^2x^v[p(X) - c_v'(x^v)] - p''(X)x^v[p(X) - c_v'(x^v)]^2 > 0$$

whenever relation (18.18) is satisfied.

Hence, in view of Fenchel's Lemma, there exists a function $u(\pi)$ such that:

$$u(\pi) > 0, \ u'(\pi) > 0, \text{ for all } \pi > 0 \tag{18.19}$$

$$u[\pi_v(x^v, X)] \text{ is strictly concave with respect to } (x^v, X). \tag{18.20}$$

A pair of outputs (x^{10}, x^{20}) of two firms 1, 2 is defined to be admissible if there exist no pairs of output (x^1, x^2) such that:

$$\pi_1(x^{10}, X^0) < \pi_1(x^1, X), \pi_2(x^{20}, X^0) < \pi_2(x^2, X)$$

where $X^0 = x^{10} + x^{20}$, $X = x^1 + x^2$.

Then, an argument again by using Fenchel's Lemma, shows that a pair of outputs (x^{10}, x^{20}) of two firms is admissible if, and only if, there exists a pair of positive number $(\beta_1, \beta_2) > (0, 0)$ such that:

$$\beta_1 u[\pi_1(x^{10}, X^0)] + \beta_2 u[\pi_2(x^{20}, X^0)] \geq \beta_1 u[\pi_1(x^1, X)] + \beta_2 u[\pi_2(x^2, X)]$$

for all $x^1, x^2 \geq 0$, and $X = x^1 + x^2$, where $X^0 = x^{10} + x^{20}$.

Let us define:

$$\alpha_1 = \beta_1 u'[\pi_1(x^{10}, X^0)], \ \alpha_2 = \beta_2 u'[\pi_2(x^{20}, X^0)].$$

Then,

$$\alpha_1, \alpha_2 > 0$$

and (x^{10}, x^{20}) satisfies the first-order conditions for the following maximum problem:

(A)   Find (x^1, x^2) that maximizes the weighted sum of the profits of two firms:

$$\alpha_1 \pi_1 + \alpha_2 \pi_2 = \alpha_1 [p(X)x^1 - c_1(x^1)] + \alpha_2 [p(X)x^2 - c_2(x^2)]$$

subjects to the constraints:

$$X = x^1 + x^2, x^1, x^2 \geq 0. \tag{18.21}$$

The following Lagrangian conditions are satisfied:

$$\alpha_v[p(X^0) - c_v'(X^{v0})] = \lambda, \ (v = 1, 2) \tag{18.22}$$

$$- [p'(X^0)(\alpha_1 x^{10} + \alpha_2 x^{20})] = \lambda \tag{18.23}$$

where $\lambda > 0$ is the Lagrange unknown associated with constraint (18.21).

However, since profit functions $\pi_1(x^1, X)$, $\pi_2(x^2, X)$ are not necessarily concave, the Lagrangian conditions (18.33) and (18.34) are necessary, but not sufficient conditions for the optimality of (x^{10}, x^{20}).

The comparison of marginality conditions (18.23) and (18.8) implies that the Cournot equilibrium is not the optimum solution for the maximum problem (A) with any pair of positive weights (α_1, α_2), and hence it is not admissible.

We may now confine ourselves to examining only those combinations of output of two firms (x^1, x^2) that are admissible. Then, it is easily shown that if two pairs of positive weights (β_1', β_2') and (β_1'', β_2'') are not proportional, then the optimum solutions $(x^{1'}, x^{2'})$ and $(x^{1''}, x^{2''})$ are necessarily distinct. Thus the set of admissible patterns of outputs of two firms is a continuum, and certain rules are required for two firms in the duopoly market to result in a uniquely determined pattern of outputs. Let us for the moment consider the situation where the two firms form a coalition so that they behave themselves in the monopolistic manner.

We consider the following maximum problem:

(B)   Find (x^{10}, x^{20}) that maximizes the combined profits:

$$\pi_1 + \pi_2 = [p(X)x^1 - c_1(x^1)] + [p(X)x^2 - c_2(x^2)]$$

subjects to the constraint (18.21).

If (x^{10}, x^{20}) is an optimum solution to maximum problem (B), then there exists a Lagrange known λ such that marginality conditions (18.22) and (18.23), with $\alpha_1 = \alpha_2 = 1$, are satisfied. The marginality conditions (18.22) and (18.23) are now sufficient conditions. In order to see this, for any (x^1, x^2) satisfying feasibility conditions (18.21), let us introduce the following function:

$$\phi(t) = \{p[X(t)]x^1(t) - c_1[x^1(t)]\} + \{p[X(t)]x^2(t) - c_2[x^2(t)]\} \quad (18.24)$$

where:

$$x^v(t) = x^0 + t(x^v - x^0), \ v = 1, 2$$

$$X(t) = \sum_v x^v(t) = X^0 + t(X - X^0), \ 0 \le t \le 1.$$

Then

$$\frac{dx^v}{dt} = x^v - x^v 0, \ v = 1, 2$$

$$\frac{dX}{dt} = (X - X^0) = \sum_v \frac{dx^v}{dt}, \ 0 \le t \le 1.$$

Differentiate both sides of (18.24) with respect to t, to obtain.

$$\phi'(t) = p'[X(t)]X(t) \frac{dX}{dt} - \sum_v c_v'(x^v(t)] \frac{dx^v}{dt}$$

$$\phi''(t) = \{p''[X(t)]X(t) + p'(X)\} \left(\frac{dX}{dt}\right)^2 - \sum_v c_v''(x^v(t)] \left(\frac{dx^v}{dt}\right)^2.$$

Hence,

$$\phi'(0) = 0$$

$$\phi''(t) = \le 0, \text{ for all } 0 \le t \le 1$$

with strict inequality if $(x^1, x^2) \neq (x^{10}, x^{20})$.

We have now:

$$\phi(0) > \phi(1), \text{ for all } (x^1, x^2) \neq (x^{10}, x^{20})$$

implying that (x^{10}, x^{20}) is the unique optimum solution to the maximum problem (B). The optimum solution (x^{10}, x^{20}) to the maximum problem (B) may be denoted by $[x^1(N), x^2(N)]$, emphasizing that it is the solution with respect to the whole coalition $N = \{1, 2\}$.

3   THE COURNOT–NASH THEORY OF OLIGOPOLY

The Cournot theory of duopoly as reviewed in the previous section may easily be extended to analysing the behavior of oligopoly firms, as in detail surveyed by Friedman (1982) and Shapiro (1989).

We consider the case of many firms each producing identical goods that are sold on the same market. The demand conditions are specified by the demand-price function:

$$p = p(X)$$

which relates the market price p with the aggregate quantity X of goods supplied:

$$X = \sum_{v \in N} x^v \tag{18.25}$$

where $N = \{1, \ldots, n\}$ is the set of the firms in question and x^v is quantity of goods produced by firm v, $(v \in N)$.

The conditions concerning the technologies and the accumulation of fixed capital for each firm v are represented by the cost function:

$$c_v = c_v(x^v), (v \in N).$$

Demand-price function $p(X)$ and cost functions $c_v(x^v)$ are assumed to satisfy the same conditions as specified for the case of duopoly firms. In particular,

$$p(X) > 0, p'(X) < 0, p''(X) < 0, \text{ for all } X > 0 \tag{18.26}$$

$$c_v(0) = 0, c_v'(x^v) > 0, c_v''(x^v) > 0, \text{ for all } x^v > 0, (v \in N). \tag{18.27}$$

The Cournot–Nash equilibrium will be obtained when each firm maximizes its profit:

$$\pi_v(x^v, X) = p(X)x^v - c_v(x^v)$$

subject to:

$$X = x^v + x^{(v)}, \text{ with given } x^{(v)} = \sum_{\mu \neq v} x^\mu \qquad (18.28)$$

and equilibrium condition (18.25) is satisfied.

Since, for each firm v, profit function $\pi_v(x^v, X)$, with the constraint (18.28), is strictly concave with respect to x^v, Cournot–Nash equilibrium will be obtained if the following marginality conditions are satisfied:

$$p(X) + p'(X)x^v = c_v{}'(x^v), \, (v \in N) \qquad (18.29)$$

together with (18.25).

We shall that Cournot–Nash equilibrium always exists and is uniquely determined. In view of the assumed conditions (18.26) and (18.27), for any given $X > 0$, the output x^v of firm satisfying (18.29) always exists and is uniquely determined. Differentiate both sides of (18.29) to obtain:

$$[p'(X) + p''(X)x^v]dX = [c_v{}''(x^v) - p'(X)]dx^v$$

which may be written as:

$$dx^v = -\frac{p'(X) + p''(X)x^v}{p'(X) - c_v{}''(x^v)} dX, \, (v \in N). \qquad (18.30)$$

Summing both sides of (18.30) over $v \in N$, we obtain:

$$\sum_{v \in N} dx^v = -\gamma dX$$

where:

$$\gamma = \sum_{v \in N} \frac{p'(X) + p''(X)x^v}{p'(X) - c_v{}''(x^v)} > 0.$$

Hence, there uniquely exists the aggregate output X that corresponds to Cournot–Nash equilibrium.

Thus we have established the following.

Proposition 2   Let the firms for the oligopoly market be denoted by $v = 1$, ..., n, and demand-price function $p = p(X)$ and cost functions $c_v(x^v)$ satisfy conditions (18.26) and (18.27). Then Cournot–Nash equilibrium always exists and is uniquely determined.

The Cournot–Nash equilibrium for the oligopoly market thus obtained is not admissible, as is easily seen from the argument exactly in the same number as for the case of the duopoly market.

A pattern of outputs of n oligopoly firms, $(x^{10}, \ldots, x^{n0})$, is defined to be admissible if there is no pattern of outputs of n firms, $(x^1, \ldots, x^n)$, such that:

$$\pi_\nu(x^\nu, X) > \pi_\nu(x^{\nu 0}, X^0), \text{ for all } \nu \in N$$

where

$$X^0 = \sum_{\nu \in N} x^{\nu 0}, \ X = \sum_{\nu \in N} x^\nu.$$

Let us denote by $u_\nu = u(\pi_\nu)$ the function such that:

$$u(\pi_\nu) > 0, \ u^{\nu\prime}(\pi_\nu) > 0, \text{ for all } \pi_\nu > 0$$

where:

$$u_\nu = u[\pi_\nu(x^\nu, X)], \ \pi_\nu(x^\nu, X) = p(X)x^\nu - c_\nu(x^\nu)$$

is strictly concave for all $(x^\nu, X) \geq (0, 0), (\nu \in N)$.

Then, a pattern of output of n firms, $(x^{10}, \ldots, x^{n0})$, is admissible if, and only if, there exists a vector of positive weights, $\beta = (\beta_1, \ldots, \beta_n), (\beta_\nu > 0, \nu \in N)$, such that:

$$\sum_{\nu \in N} \beta_\nu u[\pi_\nu(x^{\nu 0}, X^0)] \geq \sum_{\nu \in N} \beta_\nu u[\pi_\nu(x^\nu, X)] \tag{18.31}$$

for all $(x^1, \ldots, x^n), x^\nu \geq 0, (\nu \in N)$, and $X = \sum_{\nu \in N} x^\nu$.

Let us define the vector of positive weights, $\alpha = (\alpha_1, \ldots, \alpha_n)$, as follows:

$$\alpha_\nu = \beta_\nu u^\nu[\pi_\nu(x^{\nu 0}, X^0)] > 0, (\nu \in N). \tag{18.32}$$

Then, $(x^{10}, \ldots, x^{n0})$ satisfies the first-order conditions for the following maximum problem:

(A)′ Find $(x^{10}, \ldots, x^{n0})$ that maximizes the weighted sum of profits of n firms:

$$\sum_{\nu \in N} \alpha_\nu \pi_\nu = \sum_{\nu \in N} \alpha_\nu [p(X)x^\nu - \alpha_\nu(x^\nu)]$$

subject to constraint (18.25).

The following Lagrangian conditions are satisfied:

$$\alpha_v = [p(X^0) - c_v{}'(x^{v0})] = \lambda, \ (v \in N) \qquad (18.33)$$

$$-p'(X^0) \sum_{v \in N} \alpha_v x^v = \lambda \qquad (18.34)$$

where $\lambda > 0$ is the Lagrange unknown associated with constraint (18.25).

Since, for each v, profit function $\pi_v(x^v, X)$ is not concave with respect to (x^v, X), the Lagrangian conditions (18.33) and (18.34) are necessary, but not sufficient, conditions for the maximum problem (A)′. However, they become sufficient conditions for the vector of weights, $\alpha = (\alpha_1, \ldots, \alpha_n)$, defined by (18.32), for the admissible pattern of outputs, $(x^{10}, \ldots, x^{n0})$, satisfying (18.31).

We now consider the pattern of outputs corresponding to the vector of weights, $(\alpha_1, \ldots, \alpha_n) = (1, \ldots, 1)$. That is, we consider the following maximum problem:

(N) Find $(x^{10}, \ldots, x^{n0})$ that maximizes:

$$\sum_{v \in N} \pi_v = \sum_{v \in N} [p(X)x^v - c_v(x^v)]$$

subject to constraint (18.25).

The Lagrangian conditions for maximum problem (N) are given by:

$$p(X) - c_v{}'(x^v) = \lambda, \ (v \in N) \qquad (18.35)$$

$$-p'(X)X = \lambda \qquad (18.36)$$

together with constraint (18.25).

It is easily seen that Lagrangian conditions (18.35) and (18.36) are not only necessary but also sufficient for the maximum solution for problem (N) that is uniquely determined. The maximum solution for problem (N) will be denoted by $(x^1(N), \ldots, x^n(N))$ and:

$$X(N) = \sum_{v \in N} x^v(N).$$

The behavior of oligopoly firms may be clarified when it is regarded as an n-person cooperative game. In order to define the value of coalition $S \subset N$, we consider the following maximum problem:

(S) Find $(x^{v0}: v \in S)$ that maximizes:

$$\pi_S = \sum_{v \in S} [p(X)x^v - c_v(x^v)]$$

subject to:

$$X = \sum_{v \in S} x^v + x_{N-S}$$

with given

$$x_{N-S} = \sum_{v \in N-S} x^v.$$

The Lagrangian conditions for the maximum solution $(x^{v0}: v \in S)$ are given by:

$$p(X^0) - c_v{}'(x^{v0}) = \lambda, \ (v \in S) \tag{18.37}$$

$$-p'(X^0)x_S^0 = \lambda \tag{18.38}$$

where:

$$x_S^0 = \sum_{v \in S} x^{v0}, \ X^0 = x_S^0 + x_{N-S}. \tag{18.39}$$

To see that the solution $(x^{v0}: v \in S)$ satisfying Lagrangian conditions (18.37–39) is the optimum solution to the maximum problem (S), for any pattern of outputs, $(x_1, \ldots, x_n)$ satisfying (18.25), we define the following function:

$$\phi(t) = \sum_{v \in S} \{p[X(t)]x^v(t) - c_v[x^v(t)]\} \tag{18.40}$$

where:

$$x^v(t) = x^{v0} + t(x^v - x^{v0}), \ (v \in S)$$

$$X(t) = X^0 + t(X - x^0), \ (0 \le t \le 1), \ X = \sum_{v \in S} x^v + x_{N-S}.$$

Then we have:

$$\frac{dx^v}{dt} = x^v - x^{v0}, \ \frac{dX}{dt} = X - X^0 = \frac{dx_S}{dt}$$

where:

$$x_S(t) = x_S^0 + t(x_S - x_S^0), \ x_S = \sum_{v \in S} x^v.$$

Differentiate both sides of (18.40) to obtain:

$$\phi'(t) = p'[X(t)]x_S(t)\left(\frac{dX}{dt}\right) + \sum_{v \in S}[p(X) - c^v{}'(x^v)]\left(\frac{dx^v}{dt}\right)$$

and:

$$\phi''(t) = \{p''[X(t)]x_S(t) + 2p'[X(t)]\}\left(\frac{dx_S}{dt}\right)^2 - \sum_{v \in S} c''_v(x^v(t))\left(\frac{dX^v}{dt}\right)^2.$$

Hence,

$$\phi'(0) = 0$$

$$\phi''(t) \leq 0, \text{ for all } 0 \leq t \leq 1$$

with strict inequality whenever $(x^1, \ldots, x^n) \neq (x^{10}, \ldots, x^{n0})$, implying:

$$\phi(0) > \phi(1)$$

or:

$$\sum_{v \in S}[p(X^0)x^{v0} - c_v(x^{v0})] > \sum_{v \in S}[p(X)x^v - c_v(x^v)]$$

for all $(x^1, \ldots, x^n) \neq (x^{10}, \ldots, x^{n0})$.

Thus we have shown that the optimum solution to maximum problem (S) always exists and is uniquely determined. Then the sum x_S of outputs produced by the firms belonging to coalition S is uniquely determined for the given output x_{N-S}. It is denoted by:

$$x_S = \alpha(x_{N-S}). \tag{18.41}$$

Similarly, the maximum problem $(N - S)$ may be defined with respect to the complementary coalition $N - S$, with the given quantity x_S of outputs produced by the firms belonging to coalition S. The optimum quantity of outputs for complementary coalition $N - S$ is denoted by:

$$x_{N-S} = \beta(x_S). \tag{18.42}$$

Two coalitions S and $N - S$ are defined to be in equilibrium if relations (18.41) and (18.42) are simultaneously satisfied. For any coalition $S \subset N$, the value of coalition S may be defined as the sum of profits of firms belonging to coalition S when coalition S and its complementary $N - S$ are in equilibrium. For the cooperative game thus defined to be a legitimate n-person cooperative game in game theory, we must show that the pattern of outputs at which two coalitions S and $N - S$ are in equilibrium always exists and is uniquely determined.

We first see how the optimum quantity output x_S for coalition S responds to changes in the aggregate quantity of output x_{N-S} by complementary coalition $N - S$. The optimum conditions (18.37) and (18.38) may be written as follows:

$$c_v'(x^v) = p(X) + p'(X)x_s, \quad (v \in S) \tag{18.43}$$

where the optimum quantities are simply denoted by x^v and X.

Differentiate both sides of (18.43) to obtain:

$$dx^v = \frac{1}{c^{v''}(x^v)}\{[p'(X) + p''(X)x_s]dX + p'(X)dx_S\}$$

which, by summing over $v \in S$, yield:

$$[\gamma_S - p'(X)]dx_S = [p'(X) + p''(X)x_S]dX \tag{18.44}$$

where:

$$\frac{1}{\gamma_S} = \sum_{v \in S}\frac{1}{c^{v''}(x^v)} .$$

Relations (18.42) and (18.44) imply:

$$dx_S = \frac{p'(X) + p''(X)x_S}{[\gamma_S - p'(X)] - [p'(X) + p''(X)x_S]}\, dx_{N-S}.$$

Hence,

$$-1 < \alpha'(x_{N-S}) < 0, \text{ for all } x_{N-S} > 0. \tag{18.45}$$

Similarly, for the response function $\beta(x_S)$ by complementary coalition $N - S$, we have:

$$-1 < \beta'(x_S) < 0, \text{ for all } x_S > 0. \tag{18.46}$$

We now have:

$$\begin{bmatrix} 1 & -\alpha'(x_{N-S}) \\ -\beta'(x_S) & 1 \end{bmatrix}\begin{pmatrix} dx_s \\ dx_{N-S} \end{pmatrix} = \begin{pmatrix} 0 \\ 0 \end{pmatrix}. \tag{18.47}$$

The determinant of the system of linear equations (18.47) is given by:

$$1 - \alpha'(x_{N-S})\beta'(x_S) > 0.$$

Hence, the combination of (x_S, x_{N-S}) for which equilibrium conditions (18.45) and (18.46) are simultaneously satisfied is uniquely determined.

We have:

$$\lim_{x_{N-S} \to 0} \alpha(x_{N-S}) > 0, \quad \lim_{x_{N-S} \to \infty} \alpha(x_{N-S}) = 0$$

$$\lim_{x_S \to 0} \beta(x_S) > 0, \quad \lim_{x_S \to \infty} \beta(x_S) = 0$$

hence, the existence of (x_S, x_{N-S}) at which coalitions S and $N - S$ are in equilibrium is ensured.

We thus have the following:

Proposition 3 Suppose demand-price function $p(X)$ and cost functions $c_v(x^v)$, $(v \in N)$, satisfy the conditions (18.26) and (18.27).

Then, for any coalition $S \subset N$, the pair of aggregate outputs (x_S, x_{N-S}) at which coalition S and its complementary $N - S$ are in equilibrium always exists and is uniquely determined.

Furthermore, the adjustment process defined by the following system of differential equations is globally stable:

$$\begin{cases} \dot{x}_S = k_S[\alpha(x_{N-S}) - x_S] \\ \dot{x}_{N-S} = k_{N-S}[\beta(x_S) - x_{N-S}] \end{cases} \tag{18.48}$$

where k_S and k_{N-S} are positive numbers.

The global stability of the system of differential equations (18.48) is easily seen from relations (18.45) and (18.46). The existence and the uniqueness of the equilibrium (x_S, x_{N-S}) are illustrated by Figure 18.2, where x_S and x_{N-S} are measured along the abscissa and ordinate, respectively, and the solution paths to the system of differential equations (18.48) are denoted by the arrowed curves.

The behavior of oligopoly firms may now be regarded as an n-person cooperative game $G = [N, v(S)]$ with characteristic function $v(S)$ defined by:

$$v(S) = \sum_{v \in S} \{p[X(S)]x^v(S) - c_v[x^v(S)]\}, \; (S \subset N)$$

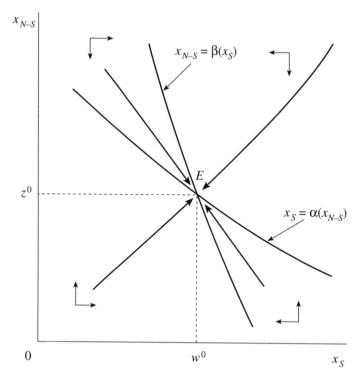

Figure 18.2   Determination of the optimum outputs (b)

where $x^v(S)$, $(v \in S)$, and $X(S)$, respectively, denote the output of firms in coalition S and the total output on the market when coalitions S and $N - S$ are in equilibrium, and:

$$X(S) = x_S(S) + x_{N-S}(S), \ x_S(S) = \sum_{v \in S} x^v(S).$$

We next address ourselves to the question of whether the core of the n-person cooperative game $G = [N, \ v(S)]$ associated with the oligopolistic behavior of n firms is non-empty. Before we proceed with our discussion, however, it may be advisable to re-examine the concept of the value of coalition $v(S)$ as formalized above. It is easily seen, as is the case with the duopoly game, that the pair of aggregate outputs, $[x_S(S), \ x_{N-S}(S)]$, at which coalitions S and $N - S$ are in equilibrium is not admissible in the sense that there always exists another pair of feasible aggregate outputs, (x_S, x_{N-S}), such that:

$$\pi_S(S) = \sum_{v \in S} \{p[X(S)]x^v(S) - c_v[x^v(S)]\} < \pi_S = \sum_{v \in S} [p(X)x^v - c_v(x^v)]$$

$$\pi_{N-S}(S) = \sum_{v \in N-S} \{p(X)x^v(S) - c_v[x^v(S)]\} < \pi_{N-S} = \sum_{v \in N-S} [p(X)x^v - c_v(x^v)]$$

where $X = \sum_{v \in N} x^v$.

To characterize the set of all pairs of aggregate outputs, (x_S, x_{N-S}), that are admissible, let us first define the following function $\pi_S = \pi_S(x_S, X)$:

$$\pi_S(x_S, X) = \max \left\{ \sum_{v \in S} [p(X)x^v - c_v(x^v)] : \sum_{v \in S} x^v = x_S, x^v \geq 0, (v \in S) \right\}.$$

The function $\pi_S(x_S, X)$ thus defined is strictly quasi-concave with respect to (x_S, X). To see this, let us consider the following function:

$$\phi_S(t) = \sum_{v \in S} \{p[X(t)]x^v(t) - c_v[x^v(t)]\}, \ (0 \leq t \leq 1) \tag{18.49}$$

where:

$$x_S(t) = x_S^0 + t(x_S^1 - x_S^0), X(t) = X^0 + t(X^1 - X^0)$$

where (x_S^0, X^0) and (x_S^1, X^1) are arbitrarily given patterns of individual outputs of firms in coalition S and total output, and $[x^v(t) : v \in S]$ is the optimum pattern of outputs of the firms in coalition S corresponding to $[x_S(t), X(t)]$, for $0 \leq t \leq 1$.

We differentiate (18.49) to obtain:

$$\phi_S'(t) = p[X(t)]x_S(t) \left(\frac{dX}{dt} \right) + \sum_{v \in S} \{p[X(t)] - c_v'[x^v(t)]\} \left(\frac{dX^v}{dt} \right) \tag{18.50}$$

where:

$$x_S(t) = \sum_{v \in S} x^v(t). \tag{18.51}$$

Since $(x^v(t) : v \in S)$ is the optimum pattern of outputs of the firms in coalition S corresponding to $[x_S(t), X(t)]$, there exists a positive number $\lambda_S(t) > 0$ such that:

$$p[X(t)] - c_v'[(x^v(t)] = \lambda_S(t) \tag{18.52}$$

where the value of $\lambda_S(t)$ is so determined that (18.51) is satisfied.

Hence, (18.50) may be written as:

$$\phi_S'(t) = p'[X(t)]x_S(t)\left(\frac{dX}{dt}\right) + \lambda_S(t)\left(\frac{dX_S}{dt}\right). \tag{18.53}$$

We now take differentials of both sides of (18.52) and rearrange to obtain:

$$c_v''[x^v(t)]dx^v = p'[X(t)]dX - d\lambda_S. \tag{18.54}$$

On the other hand, we differentiate both sides of (18.51) to obtain:

$$dx_S = \sum_{v \in S} dx^v. \tag{18.55}$$

Substitute (18.54) into (18.55) and rearrange to obtain:

$$d\lambda_S = p'[X(t)]dX - \gamma_S(t)dx_S \tag{18.56}$$

where:

$$\frac{1}{\gamma_S(t)} = \sum_{v \in S} \frac{1}{c_v''[x^v(t)]} > 0.$$

Differentiating (18.53) further with respect to t, we obtain:

$$\phi_S''(t) = p''[X(t)]x_S(t)\left(\frac{dX}{dt}\right)^2 + 2p'[X(t)]\left(\frac{dX}{dt}\right)\left(\frac{dX_S}{dt}\right) - \lambda_S(t)\left(\frac{dx_S}{dt}\right)^2. \tag{18.57}$$

Then, we can show that there exists a positive number μ such that:

$$\phi''(t) - \mu[\phi'(t)]^2 < 0, \text{ for all } 0 \le t \le 1. \tag{18.58}$$

The existence of μ satisfying relations (18.58) is easily seen from (18.26), (18.27), and from the property that the determinant of the bordered Hessian is positive:

$$\begin{vmatrix} 0 & p' & p'x_S \\ p' & 0 & \lambda_S \\ p'x_S & \lambda_S & 0 \end{vmatrix} = 2(p')^2 x_S \lambda_S > 0.$$

The relations (18.58) imply the quasi-concavity of $\pi_S(x_S, X)$.

Let us denote by $u(\pi)$ the function which satisfies the conditions (18.19) and (18.20). Then, $[\pi_S(x_S, X), \pi_{N-S}(x_{N-S}, X)]$ is admissible if, and only if, there exists a pair of positive weights, (β_S, β_{N-S}), such that it is the optimum solution to the following maximum problem:

Find (x_S, x_{N-S}) that maximizes:

$$\beta_S u[\pi_S(x_S, X)] + \beta_{N-S} u[\pi_{N-S}(x_{N-S}, X)] \tag{18.59}$$

subject to $X = x_S + x_{N-S}, x_S, x_{N-S} \geq 0$.

The necessary conditions for maximizing (18.59) are given by the first-order conditions for the following maximum problem:

Find (x_S, x_{N-S}) that maximizes:

$$\alpha_S \pi_S(x_S, X) + \alpha_{N-S} \pi_{N-S}(x_{N-S}, X)$$

subject to $X = x_S + x_{N-S}, x_S, x_{N-S} \geq 0$, where:

$$\alpha_S = \beta_S u'[\pi_S(x_S, X)], \ \alpha_{N-S} = \beta_{N-S} u'[\pi_{N-S}(x_{N-S}, X)].$$

The basic premises of the *n*-person cooperative game theory presuppose the circumstances where every player of the game is free to choose the coalition *S* to which he or she aspires to belong, with the intention of getting the maximum benefit from it. On the other hand, the Cournot–Nash solution is not necessarily admissible, so that it is possible to find another solution where each player can receive a benefit greater than he or she is getting from the Cournot–Nash solution. The Cournot–Nash solution may satisfy the behavioral criteria presumed in the standard economic theory, but it is not consistent with the behavioral characteristics of the business firms producing goods sold on the oligopoly market. The oligopoly firms are free to choose any coalition under which they may fare better. Thus, it may be reasonable to define the value of each coalition *S* as the maximum of the sum of profits of the firms belonging to coalition *S* when coalition *S* and its complementary *N – S* are in equilibrium. However, the definition of the value of coalition as suggested here, although it may make sense in terms of the behavioral characteristics on the oligopoly market actually observed, does not satisfy the conditions usually required in standard game theory, because there exists a continuum of admissible solutions, violating the basic premises of cooperative games.

We are particularly interested in the solution of the *n*-person cooperative game associated with the model of the oligopoly market, which may be termed balanced, as is precisely defined below.

Coalitions S and $N - S$ are defined balanced with respect to (x_S, x_{N-S}) if (x_S, x_{N-S}) is admissible and:

$$x_S = \theta_S X, \; x_{N-S} = \theta_{N-S} X, \; X = x_S + x_{N-S}$$

where:

$$\theta_S = \frac{x_S(N)}{X(N)}, \; \theta_{N-S} = \frac{x_{N-S}(N)}{X(N)}$$

and $X(N)$, $x_S(N)$ are the optimum values of the relevant variables for maximum problem (N).

We may now define the value of coalition for the n-person cooperative game associated with the behavior oligopoly firms as:

$$v(S) = \pi_S(x_S, X) = \sum_{v \in S} [p(X)x^v - c_v(x^v)]$$

when coalitions S and $N - S$ are balanced.

An allotment of an n-person cooperative game $G = [N, v(S)]$ is simply an n-dimensional vector $(y^1, \ldots, y^n)$ for which the following conditions, traditionally termed the efficiency conditions, are satisfied.

$$\sum_{v \in N} y^v = v(N). \tag{18.60}$$

An allotment $(y^1, \ldots, y_n)$ is defined to be in the core if, in addition to (18.60), the following conditions are satisfied:

$$\sum_{v \in S} y^v \geq v(S), \text{ for all coalitions } S \subset N.$$

The standard approach in game theory is to apply the classic Bondareva–Shapley theorem and to use the concavity property of the characteristic function $v(S)$ to show the non-emptiness of the core of an n-person cooperative game with transferable utility. In the present context of the oligopoly game, however, the profit function $\pi^v(x^v, X)$ is not concave with respect to (x^v, X), and the standard approach in game theory may not be directly applicable.

On the other hand, as discussed in detail above, the concept of Cournot–Nash equilibrium brings about the pattern of outputs of the firms in coalitions S and $N - S$ that is not admissible, implying that it is possible to find another pattern of outputs of the firms in coalitions S and $N - S$ at which all firms are better off than at the Cournot–Nash equilibrium.

If we confine ourselves to the *n*-person cooperative game $G = [N, v(S)]$ associated with oligopoly firms where the value of each coalition S is defined as the sum of profits of the firms in coalition S when two coalitions S and $N - S$ are balanced, then we can prove the following:

Proposition 4 Let $G = [N, v(S)]$ be the *n*-person cooperative game associated with oligopolistic firms $N = \{1, \ldots, n\}$ where the value $v(S)$ of each coalition S is defined as the sum of profits of the firms in coalition S when coalition S and its complementary $N - S$ are balanced. Demand-price function $p(X)$ and cost functions $c_v(x^v)$ are assumed to satisfy (18.26) and (18.27).

Then the optimum solution $(x^1(N), \ldots, x^n(N))$ to the maximum problem (N) is in the core of the *n*-person cooperative game $G = [N, v(S)]$ associated with the oligopolistic firms $N = \{1, \ldots n\}$.

Proof Let us denote by $[x^v(N) : v \in N, X(N)]$ and $[x^v(S) : v \in S, X(S)]$ the optimum solutions to maximum problems (N) and (S), respectively. As regards the value $v(S)$ of coalition S, it is assumed that two coalitions S and $N - S$ are balanced. Hence, the following relations hold:

$$p[X(N)] - c_v'[x^v(N)] = \lambda(N), (v \in N) \tag{18.61}$$

$$-p'[X(N)]X(N) = \lambda(N) \tag{18.62}$$

$$X(N) = \sum_{v \in N} x^v(N)$$

and:

$$x_S(S) = \theta_S(N)X(S) \tag{18.63}$$

where:

$$X(S) = \sum_{v \in N} x^v(S), \ x_S(S) = \sum_{v \in S} x^v(S) \tag{18.64}$$

$$\theta_S(N) = \frac{x_S(N)}{X(N)}, \ x_S(N) = \sum_{v \in S} x^v(N). \tag{18.65}$$

For each v, we define the following function:

$$\phi_v(t) = p[X(t)]x^v(t) - c_v[x^v(t)], \ (0 \le t \le 1) \tag{18.66}$$

where:

$$x^v(t) = x^v(N) + t[x^v(S) - x^v(N)]$$

$$X(t) = X(N) + t[X(S) - X(N)] = \sum_{v \in N} x^v(S, t).$$

Differentiate (18.65) with respect to t, to obtain:

$$\phi_v'(t) = p'[X(t)]x^v(t)\left(\frac{dX}{dt}\right) + p[X(t)] - c'[x^v(t)]\left(\frac{dx^v}{dt}\right) \qquad (18.67)$$

$$\phi_v''(t) = p''[X(t)]x^v(t)\left(\frac{dX}{dt}\right)^2 + 2p'[X(t)]\left(\frac{dX}{dt}\right)\left(\frac{dx^v}{dt}\right)$$

$$- c_v''[x^v(t)]\left(\frac{dx^v}{dt}\right)^2. \qquad (18.68)$$

Let us denote:

$$\phi_S(t) = \sum_{v \in S} \phi_v(t), \ x_S(t) = \sum_{v \in S} x^v(t).$$

Then, we have from (18.67), (18.68), (18.61) and (18.62) that:

$$\phi_S'(0) = p'[X(N)]x_S(N)\left(\frac{dX}{dt}\right) - X(N)\left(\frac{dx_S}{dt}\right) \qquad (18.69)$$

$$\phi_S''(t) = p''[X(t)]x_S(t)\left(\frac{dX}{dt}\right)^2 + 2p'[X(t)]\left(\frac{dX}{dt}\right)\left(\frac{dx_S}{dt}\right)$$

$$- \sum_{v \in S} c_v''[x^v(t)]\left(\frac{dx^v}{dt}\right)^2. \qquad (18.70)$$

Because the conditions (18.63) and (18.64) are balanced, we have:

$$\frac{dx_S}{dt} = \theta_S(N)\left(\frac{dX}{dt}\right), \ x_S(N) = \theta_S(N)X(N),$$

which may be substituted into (18.69) and (18.70) to obtain:

$$\phi_S'(0) = 0$$

$$\phi_S''(t) = \{p''[X(t)]x_S(t) + 2\theta_S p'[X(t)]\} \left(\frac{dX}{dt}\right)^2$$

$$- \sum_{v \in S} c_v''[x^v(t)] \left(\frac{dx^v}{dt}\right)^2 \leq 0, \text{ for all } 0 \leq t \leq 1.$$

Hence,

$$\phi_S(0) \geq \phi_S(1)$$

or:

$$\sum_{v \in S}\{p[X(N)]x^v(N) - c_v[x^v(N)]\} \geq \sum_{v \in S}\{p[X(S)]x^v(S) - c_v[x^v(S)]\}$$

which implies:

$$v_S(N) \geq v(S), \text{ for all } S \subset N$$

implying that $\pi_1[x^1(N), X(N)], \ldots, (\pi_n[x^n(N), X(N)]$ is in the core of the n-person cooperative game $G = [N, v(S)]$.   QED

4   THEORY OF OLIGOPOLY WITH DIFFERENTIATED PRODUCTS

The analysis of oligopoly firms as developed in the previous sections may be extended to the general case involving a number of distinct goods.

We now consider the case where there exist a number of goods, to be generically denoted by i, $(i = 1, \ldots, m)$. The conditions with regards to demand structure are represented by the demand-price functions:

$$p(X) = [p_1(X), \ldots, p_m(X)]$$

where $X = (X_1, \ldots, X_m)$ denotes the vector of the aggregate quantities of goods supplied to the market. Demand-price functions $X(p)$ are assumed to be defined and continuously twice differentiable with respect to $X = (X_1, \ldots, X_m) \geq 0$.

For each i, demand-price function $p_i = p_i(X)$ specifies the market price p_i at which the given quantity of X_i supplied to the market of goods i is equated to the demand for goods i, to be measured in wage-units. It is assumed that the aggregate income measured in wage-units is so adjusted that the marginal utility of income remains constant. Hence, it may be assumed that:

(P1)   For each i, demand-price function $p_i(X)$ is positive for all positive vectors X of aggregate supply:

$$p_i(X) > 0, \text{ for all } X = (X_1, \ldots, X_m) > 0, (i = 1, \ldots, m).$$

In symbols,

$$p(X) > 0, \text{ for all } X > 0.$$

(P2)   The matrix of second-order derivatives

$$\left(\frac{\partial p_i}{\partial x_j} \right)_{i,j}$$

is symmetrical:

$$\left(\frac{\partial p_i}{\partial x_j} \right) = \left(\frac{\partial p_j}{\partial p_i} \right), \text{ for all } i, j = 1, \ldots, m.$$

In symbols,

$$p_x(X)' = p_x(X).$$

(P3)   The matrix of second-order partial derivatives

$$p_x(X) = \left(\frac{\partial p_i}{\partial x_j} \right) i, j$$

is negative definite. In symbols,

$$p_x(X) \ll 0, \text{ for all } X > 0.$$

It will be furthermore assumed that

(P4)

$$p_j(X) + \sum_{j=1}^{n} \frac{\partial p_i}{\partial X_j} x_j > 0, \text{ for all } 0 < x_j \leq X_j, (j = 1, \ldots, m).$$

In symbols,

$$p(X) + p'(X)x \ll 0, \text{ for all } 0 \leq x \leq X.$$

(P5)   The symmetric matrix

$$\left(\sum_{i=1}^{m} \frac{\partial^2 p_i}{\partial X_j \partial X_k} x_i \right)_{j,k}$$

is negative-semi definite, for all $0 < x \leq X$. In symbols,

$$p_{XX}x \leq 0, \text{ for all } 0 < x \leq X.$$

It may be noted that conditions (P1–5) may be assumed to hold for all X in a certain closed convex domain Ω of the m-dimensional space R^m, where all the values of X in the following discussion are contained. In the following discussion, we do not explicitly refer to the domain in which the values of X are contained.

We assume that there are n firms which are engaged in the production of m goods in question, to be generically referred to as v, (v = 1, . . ., n). For each firm v, the production possibility set T^v describes the technologies and the accumulation of fixed capital possessed by firm v. For each firm v, production possibility set T^v is a subset of the m-dimensional space R^m consisting of all vectors of outputs $x = (x_1, \ldots, x_m)$ that it is technologically possible to produce with given fixed factors of production accumulated within firm v. It is assumed that, for each firm v,

(T1) T^v is a non-empty, closed, bounded subset of R_m consisting of non-negative vectors $x = (x_1, \ldots, x_m)$.

(T2) T^v is monotone; that is, for all $x^v \in T^v$, $0 \le x^v \le x^v$ implies $x^{v'} \in T^v$

(T3) T^v is a convex set; that is, for all $x^{v0}, x^{v1} \in T^v$, and $0 \le \theta \le 1$, $(1 - \theta) x^{v0} + \theta x^{v1} \in T^v$

(T4)   For any non-zero non-negative price, $p = (p_1, \ldots, p_m) \ge 0$, there uniquely exists a production plan $x^v(p) = [x_1^v(p), \ldots, x_m^v(p)]$ that maximizes the value of outputs px^v over $x^v \in T^v$; that is,

(i) $x^v(p) \in T^v$
(ii) $px^v(p) > px^v$, for all $x^v \in T^v$, $x^v \ne x^v(p)$

where:

$$px^v = \sum_{i=1}^{m} p_i x_i^v.$$

(T5)   The function $x^v(p)$ is continuously twice differentiable with respect to $p > 0$.

The condition (T5) implies that the matrix of second-order partial derivatives

$$x_p^v(p) = \begin{pmatrix} \dfrac{\partial x_1^v}{\partial p_1}, & \cdots, & \dfrac{\partial x_1^v}{\partial p_m} \\ & \cdots & \\ \dfrac{\partial x_m^v}{\partial p_1}, & \cdots, & \dfrac{\partial x_m^v}{\partial p_m} \end{pmatrix}$$

is symmetric and negative semi-definite for all $p \geq 0$. Because we consider the possibility of some firms being specialized in a certain number of goods, the matrix $x^v_p(p)$ is not assumed to be negative definite. It is easily seen that (T4) implies that $x^v(p^v)$ is homogeneous of order 0 with respect to p^v.

5 COURNOT–NASH EQUILIBRIUM WITH DIFFERENTIATED PRODUCTS

It is possible to extend the concept of Cournot–Nash equilibrium, as reviewed in the previous sections, to the case of oligopoly firms producing differentiated products.

The optimum output vector x^v for each firm v is obtained when the profit of firm v, to be given by:

$$\pi^v(x^v, X) = p(X)x^v, \ x^v \in T^v$$

is maximized subject to the constraint:

$$X = x^v + x^{(v)} \tag{18.71}$$

where $x^{(v)} = \sum_{v \neq \mu} x^\mu$ is given.

The maximum problem for firm v may be solved in terms of the standard Lagrangian method. Let λ^v be the Lagrange unknown associated with the constraint (18.71) and define the Lagrangian form:

$$p(X)x^v + \lambda^v(X - x^v - x^{(v)}).$$

Then the first-order conditions for the optimum output x^v are the following:

$$p(X) + p_X(X)x^v(p^v) = \lambda^v \tag{18.72}$$

$$X = x^v(p^v) + x^{(v)} \tag{18.73}$$

where p^v is the imputed price vector and $x^v = x^v(p^v)$ is the optimum output vector.

The first-order condition (18.72) simply means that firm v chooses the production plan $x^v = x^v(p^v)$ which is optimum with respect to the imputed price vector p^v, assuming that the total output vector X is adjusted in response to the output vector x^v of firm v, while the aggregate output vector of other firms, $x^{(v)}$, remains constant.

The existence of price vector p^v satisfying (18.72) may be proved in the following manner.

Proof   We consider the $(m-1)$-dimensional simplex Σ:

$$\Sigma = [p = (p_1, \ldots, p_m) : \sum_{i=1}^{m} p_i = 1, p_i \geq 0 \ (i = 1, \ldots, m)]$$

and define the following mapping on Σ:

$$\beta(p^v) = \frac{1}{\gamma(p^v)} [p(X) + p_X(X)x^v(p^v)], \ (p^v \in \Sigma)$$

where:

$$\gamma(p^v) = \sum_{j=1}^{m} p_j(X) + \sum_{i=1}^{m} \frac{\partial p_i}{\partial X_j} x_i^v(p^v) > 0$$

and X is given by (18.73).

The mapping $\beta^v(p^v)$ thus defined is a continuous mapping from Σ into itself Σ. Hence, there exists a $p^v \in \Sigma$ such that:

$$p(X) + p_X(X)x^v(p^v) = \gamma(p^v)p^v.$$

Since $x^v(p^v)$ is homogeneous of order 0, the existence of a $p^v > 0$ satisfying (18.72) and (18.73) has been proved.   QED

However, the first-order condition (18.72) is not a sufficient condition for the maximum profit for firm v, and we need a more detailed analysis to see if the output vector $x^v(p^v)$ satisfying (18.72) and (18.73) is the one at which firm v's profit π^v is maximized over the production possibility set T^v.

Let $x^{v0} = x^v(p^v)$ be the output vector satisfying (18.72) and (18.73), and let x^{v1} be an arbitrarily given vector in production possibility set T^v. We define the following function:

$$\phi(t) = p[X(t)]x^v(t), \ (0 \leq t \leq 1) \tag{18.74}$$

where:

$$x^v(t) = x^{v0} + t(x^{v1} - x^{v0}), \ X(t) = X^0 + t(X^1 - X^0)$$

$$X^0 = x^{v0} + x^{(v)}, \ X^1 = x^{v1} + x^{(v)}.$$

Hence,

$$\frac{dx^\nu(t)}{dt} = \frac{dX(t)}{dt} = x^{\nu 1} - x^{\nu 0} = \Delta x^\nu = \Delta X. \tag{18.75}$$

By differentiating (18.74) with respect to t, we obtain:

$$\phi'(t) = p_X[X(t)]x^\nu(t)\Delta X + p[X(t)]\Delta x^\nu \tag{18.76}$$

$$\phi''(t) = \Delta X\{p_{XX}[X(t)]x^\nu(t)\}\Delta X + 2\Delta X\{p_X[X(t)]\}\Delta x^\nu. \tag{18.77}$$

Then, we have:

$$\phi'(0) = p_X(X^0)x(p)\Delta X + p(X^0)\Delta x^\nu = p^\nu(x^{\nu 1} - x^{\nu 0}).$$

Hence, in view of (T4), we have:

$$\phi'(0) \le 0. \tag{18.78}$$

On the other hand, (18.75) and (18.77) imply that:

$$\phi''(t) = \Delta X\{p_{XX}[X(t)]x^\nu(t) + 2p_X[X(t)]\}\Delta x \le 0, \ (0 \le t \le 1). \tag{18.79}$$

The relations (18.78) and (18.79) imply that:

$$\phi(0) \ge \phi(1)$$

that is,

$$p(X^0)x^{\nu 0} \ge p(X)x^{\nu 1}, \text{ for all } x^{\nu 1} \in T^\nu.$$

Thus, we have shown that the output vector $x^{\nu 0}$ satisfying the first-order condition (18.72), together with feasibility condition (18.73), is optimum for firm ν.

Cournot–Nash equilibrium will be obtained if we find a pattern of output vectors $(x^1, \ldots, x^n)$ such that:

(i)   For each firm ν, x^ν maximizes profit $\pi^\nu = p(X)x^\nu$ over T^ν;
(ii) $X = \sum_{\nu \in N} x^\nu.$

Hence, $(x^1, \ldots, x^n)$ is Cournot–Nash equilibrium if, and only if, there exists an n-tuple of price vectors, $(p^1, \ldots, p^n)$, such that:

$$p(X) + p_X(X)x^\nu(p^\nu) = p^\nu, \ (\nu \in N) \tag{18.80}$$

$$X = \sum_{\nu \in N} x^\nu(p^\nu). \tag{18.81}$$

In order to establish the existence of Cournot–Nash equilibrium, let us consider the set

$$\Omega = \left\{ X = \sum_{\nu \in N} x^\nu : x^\nu \in T^\nu, \ (\nu \in N) \right\}$$

and define the mapping $X \in \Omega \rightarrow \beta(X) \in \Omega$ in the following manner:

$$\beta(X) = \sum_{\nu \in N} x^\nu(p^\nu)$$

where $(p^1, \ldots, p^n)$ is the solution to (18.73) for $X \in \Omega$.

Then $\beta(X)$ is a continuous mapping from Ω onto itself, while Ω is a compact, convex set. Hence, Brouwer's fixed-point theorem may be applied to show the existence of $(p^1, \ldots, p^n)$ which satisfies relations (18.73) and (18.74).

We have now established the following:

Proposition 5   Suppose there exist n firms for the oligopoly market, to be denoted by ν, $(\nu \in N)$, and demand functions $p(X)$ and production possibility sets T^ν, $(\nu \in N)$, satisfy conditions (P1–5) and (T1–5).

Then there always exists a Cournot–Nash equilibrium $(x^1, \ldots, x^n)$, which is characterized by marginality conditions (18.73) and feasibility condition (18.74).

It may be noted that the uniqueness of Cournot–Nash equilibrium, which has been proved for the case of a single product, may not necessarily hold for the general case of differentiated products.

6   COURNOT–NASH EQUILIBRIUM AND ADMISSIBLE PATTERNS OF OUTPUTS

As with the oligopoly firms with a single product, Cournot–Nash equilibrium for the case of differentiated products is not admissible. It is always possible to find another pattern of outputs of n firms such that each firm's profit is larger than that at the Cournot–Nash equilibrium.

A pattern of feasible outputs, $(x^{\nu 0} : \nu \in N)$ is termed admissible if there is no pattern of feasible outputs $(x^\nu : \nu \in N)$ such that:

$$\pi^{v}(x^{v}, X) = p(X)x^{v} > \pi^{v}(x^{v0}, X^{0}) = p(X^{0})x^{v0}, \text{ for all } v \in N$$

where:

$$X = \sum_{v \in N} x^{v}, \ x^{v} \in T^{v}, \ (v \in N).$$

Because the revenue function:

$$\pi^{v}(x^{v}, X) = p(X)x^{v}, \ x^{v} \in T^{v}$$

is not concave with respect to (x^{v}, X), it is not possible to apply the standard method to characterize the set of all admissible patterns of outputs of n firms for the oligopoly markets. We first show that revenue function $\pi^{v}(x^{v}, X)$ is strictly quasi-concave with respect to (x^{v}, X). This is shown as follows:

Let (x^{v0}, X^{0}) and (x^{v1}, X^{1}) be such that:

$$p(X^{0})x^{v0} = p(X^{1})x^{v1}, \ x^{v0}, x^{v1} \in T^{v}$$

and let the function $\phi(t)$ be defined by (18.74), where:

$$x^{v}(t) = x^{v0} + t\Delta x^{v}, \ \Delta x^{v} = x^{v1} - x^{v0}$$

$$X(t) = X^{0} + t\Delta X, \ \Delta X = X^{1} - X^{0}.$$

It may be noted that, unlike the discussion carried out previously, Δx^{v} and ΔX are not necessarily equal in the present circumstances.

From the relations (18.76) and (18.77), which have been obtained by differentiating (18.74) with respect to t, we have that, for any number λ,

$$\phi''(t) - \lambda[\phi'(t)]^{2} = \Delta X(p_{XX}x^{v} - \lambda x^{v}p_{X}p_{X}x^{v})\Delta X$$
$$+ 2\Delta X(p_{X} - \lambda pp_{X}x)\Delta x^{v} - \lambda\Delta x^{v}(p.p)\Delta x^{v} \qquad (18.82)$$

Proof The strict quasi-concavity of revenue function $\pi^{v}(x^{v}, X)$ with respect to (x^{v}, X) is ensured if we can show that there exists a positive number λ such that the expression on the right-hand side of (18.82) is negative for all (x^{v}, X) $\neq (0, 0)$. This amounts to showing that all the principal minors, containing the last columns and rows, of the following matrix have alternating signs:

$$\begin{pmatrix} p_{XX}x^{v} & p_{X} & p_{x}x^{v} \\ p_{X} & 0 & p \\ (p_{x}x^{v})' & p' & 0 \end{pmatrix}.$$

Thus, $\pi^v(x^v, X)$ is strictly quasi-concave if, and only if,

$$(p_X x^v, p) \begin{pmatrix} p_{XX} x^v & p_X \\ p_X & 0 \end{pmatrix}^{-1} \begin{pmatrix} p_X x^v \\ p \end{pmatrix} < 0. \qquad (18.83)$$

In order to show inequality (18.83), we may first note the following identity:

$$\begin{pmatrix} A & B \\ B & 0 \end{pmatrix}^{-1} = \begin{pmatrix} 0 & B^{-1} \\ B^{-1} & -B^{-1}AB^{-1} \end{pmatrix},$$

where A and B are symmetric matrices and B is non-singular.

Hence, the expression on the left-hand side of (18.83) may be written as follows:

$$-[2px^v - (p_X^{-1}x^v)p_{XX}x^v(p_X^{-1}x^v)]$$

which, in view of (P5), is always negative.　QED

Since revenue function $\pi^v(x^v, X)$ is strictly quasi-concave with respect to (x^v, X), there exists a function $u = u(\pi^v)$ such that:

$$u(\pi^v) > 0, \ u'(\pi^v) > 0, \text{ for all } \pi^v > 0$$

and $u[\pi^v(x^v, X)]$ is concave with respect to (x^v, X).

Indeed, such a function $u(\pi^v)$ may be obtained if we define:

$$u(\pi^v) = 1 - e^{-\lambda \pi^v}$$

with a sufficiently large number $\lambda > 0$.

It may be noted that the same function $u(\pi^v)$ may be used so that $u[\pi^v(x^v, X)]$ is a concave function of (x^v, X) for all $v \in N$.

If a pattern of outputs of the firms for the oligopoly market, $(x^1, \ldots, x^n)$, is admissible, then there exists a vector of positive weights, $(\alpha^1, \ldots, \alpha^n)$, such that $(x^1, \ldots, x^n)$ maximizes the weighted sum of the revenues of the oligopoly firms:

$$\sum_{v \in N} \alpha^v p(X) x^v$$

subject to the constraints:

$$X = \sum_{v \in N} x^v, \ x^v \in T^v, \ (v \in N). \qquad (18.84)$$

The optimum solution to the maximum problem for the oligopoly market described above may not be solved in terms of the standard Lagrangian method. Let λ be the Lagrange unknown associated with the constraint (18.84). The Lagrangian marginality conditions then are:

$$p_X(X)Z + \lambda = 0 \tag{18.85}$$

$$x^\nu = x^\nu(p) \tag{18.86}$$

where:

$$p = p(X) + p'(X)Z \tag{18.87}$$

$$Z = \sum_{\nu \in N} \alpha^\nu x^\nu. \tag{18.88}$$

Relations (18.85–88), do not imply optimality, since revenue functions $\pi^\nu(x^\nu, X)$ are not necessarily concave with respect to (x^ν, X). However, a pattern of outputs, $(x^1, \ldots, x^n)$, is admissible if, and only if, there exists a vector of positive weights, $(\beta^1, \ldots, \beta^n)$, such that $(x^1, \ldots, x^n)$ maximizes:

$$\sum_{\nu \in N} \beta^\nu u[\pi^\nu(x^\nu, X)] \tag{18.89}$$

subject to:

$$X = \sum_{\nu \in N} x^\nu, \, x^\nu \in T^\nu. \tag{18.90}$$

If we denote by λ the Lagrange unknown associated with the constraint (18.90), then the optimum conditions for the problem of maximizing (18.89) subject to (18.90) are satisfied if, and only if, relations (18.85–8) are satisfied, where:

$$\alpha^\nu = \beta^\nu u'[\pi^\nu(x^\nu, X)], \, (\nu \in N).$$

Hence, we have proved the following:

Proposition 6 Suppose there exist n firms for the oligopoly market, denoted by ν, $(\nu \in N)$, and demand-price functions $p(X)$ and production possibility sets T^ν satisfy conditions (P1–5) and (T1–5).

Then a pattern of outputs $(x^1, \ldots, x^n)$ is admissible if, and only if, there exists a vector of positive weights $(\beta^1, \ldots, \beta^n)$ such that $(x^1, \ldots, x^n)$ is the optimum solution to the following maximum problem:

Find $(x^1, \ldots, x^n)$ that maximizes:

$$\sum_{v \in N} \beta^v u[\pi^v(x^v, X)]$$

subject to the constraints:

$$X = \sum_{v \in N} x^v, \ x^v \in T^v, \ (v \in N).$$

If a pattern of outputs $(x^1, \ldots, x^n)$ is admissible, then there exists a vector of positive weights $(\alpha^1, \ldots, \alpha^n)$ such that $(x^1, \ldots, x^n)$ is the optimum solution to the following maximum problem:

Find $(x^1, \ldots, x^n)$ that maximizes:

$$\sum_{v \in N} \alpha^v \pi^v(x^v, X)$$

subject to the constraints:

$$X = \sum_{v \in N} x^v, \ x^v \in T^v, \ (v \in N).$$

7 BEHAVIOR OF OLIGOPOLY FIRMS AS A COOPERATIVE GAME

The behavior of oligopoly firms, as discussed in the previous section, may be viewed as an n-person cooperative game, and the standard approach in game theory may be applied to examine the structure of the oligopoly market with differentiated products.

We first see how the value of coalition of such a cooperative game may be determined. Let S be any non-empty subject of $N = \{1, \ldots, n\}$ and consider the following maximum problem:

(S) Find a pattern of outputs $(x^v : v \in S)$ that maximizes the sum of the values of outputs of the firms in coalition S:

$$\sum_{v \in S} p(X)x^v$$

subject to the constraints:

$$X = \sum_{v \in S} x^v + x_{N-S}, \ x^v \in T^v, \ (v \in S)$$

where the sum of outputs produced by the firms belonging to the complementary $N - S$, x_{N-S}, is given.

As was emphasized in the previous sections, for each firm v, the function:

$$\pi^v(x^v, X) = p(X)x^v, \ X > 0, \ x^v \in T^v$$

is not concave with respect to (x^v, X). However, as regards the maximum problem (S), the standard Lagrangian conditions suffice for the optimality of the pattern of outputs $(x^v : v \in S)$. Indeed, let $(x^{v0} : v \in S)$ be the pattern of outputs of the firms in coalition S that satisfies the Lagrangian first-order conditions

$$x^{v0} = x^v(p_S), \ (v \in S) \tag{18.91}$$

$$p_S = p(X^0) + p'(X^0)x_S^0, \ x_S^0 = \sum_{v \in S} x^{v0} \tag{18.92}$$

where:

$$X^0 = x_S^0 + x_{N-S}. \tag{18.93}$$

To show that the pattern of outputs of the firms in coalition S, $(x^{v0} : v \in S)$, satisfying (18.91–3) is the optimum solution to maximum problem (S), let us consider the following function:

$$\phi_S(t) = p[X(t)]x_S(t), \ (0 \le t \le 1) \tag{18.94}$$

where $(x^v : v \in S)$ is an arbitrarily given pattern of outputs of the firms in coalition S satisfying feasibility conditions (18.85),

$$x^v(t) = x^{v0} + t(x^v - x^{v0})$$

$$x_S(t) = \sum_{v \in S} x^v(t) = x_S^0 + t(x_S - x_S^0), \ x_S = \sum_{v \in S} x^v$$

$$X(t) = \sum_{v \in N} x^v(t) + x_{N-S} = X^0 + t(X - X^0).$$

Then we have:

$$\frac{dX(t)}{dt} = \frac{dx_S(t)}{dt} = \sum_{v \in S}(x^v - x^{v0}). \tag{18.95}$$

Differentiate (18.94) with respect to t and note (18.95) to obtain:

$$\phi_S'(t) = p_X[X(t)]x_S(t)\frac{dX}{dt} + p[X(t)]\frac{dx_S}{dt} = \{p_X[X(t)]x_S(t) + p[X(t)]\}(x_S - x_S^0)$$

$$\phi_S''(t) = (x_S - x_S^0)\{p_{XX}[p(t)]x_S(t) + 2p_X[X(t)]\}(x_S - x_S^0).$$

Hence, we have:

$$\phi_S'(0) = [p_X(X^0) + p(X^0)](x_S - x_S^0) = p_S(x_S - x_S^0) \leq 0 \qquad (18.96)$$

$$\phi_S''(t) \leq 0, \text{ for all } 0 \leq t \leq 1 \qquad (18.97)$$

with strict inequality whenever $(x^v : v \in S) \neq (x^{v0} : v \in S)$.
    Relations (18.96) and (18.97) imply: $\phi(0) \geq \phi(1)$, that is,

$$p(X^0)x_S^0 \geq (X)x_S, \text{ for all feasible } (x_S, X)$$

with strict inequality whenever $x_S \neq x_S^0$.
    Thus we have established the following:

Proposition 7   For any coalition $S \subset N$, the optimum solution $(x^{v0} : v \in S)$ to maximum problem (S) always exists and is uniquely determined.

The optimum solution to maximum problem (S) may be denoted by $x^v(S, x_{N-S})$
:$v \in S$ and:

$$x_S(S, x_{N-S}) = \sum_{v \in S} x^v(S, x_{N-S})$$

$$X(S, x_{N-S}) = x_S(S, x_{N-S}) + x_{N-S}.$$

We have the following relations:

$$x_S(S, x_{N-S}) = \sum_{v \in S} x^v(S, x_{N-S}), \; x^v(S, x_{N-S}) = x^v[p(S, x_{N-S})]$$

$$p(S, x_{N-S}) = p[X(S, x_{N-S})] + p_X[X(S, x_{N-S})]x_S(S, x_{N-S}))$$

$$X(S, x_{N-S}) = x_S(S, x_{N-S}) + x_{N-S}.$$

We are particularly interested in the coalition N consisting of all oligopoly firms.

(N)   Find $(x^{v0} : v \in N)$ that maximizes $p(X)X$ subject to the constraints:

$$X = \sum_{v \in N} x^v, \; x^v \in T^{\,v}, \; (v \in N).$$

The optimum solution to maximum problem (N), to be denoted by $x^1(N), \ldots, x^n(N)$, is characterized by:

$$x^v(N) = x^v[p(N)], \ (v \in N) \tag{18.98}$$

$$p(N) = p[X(N)] + p_X[X(N)]X(N) \tag{18.99}$$

$$X(N) = \sum_{v \in N} x^v[p(N)]. \tag{18.100}$$

We define the value of coalitions S when coalition S and its complementary $N - S$ are in equilibrium. That is, the value $v(S)$ of any given coalition S is defined by:

$$v(S) = p[X(S)]x_S(S),$$

where $x_S(S) = x_S(S, x_{N-S})$, $X(S) = X(S, x_{N-S})$, and

$$x_S = x_S(S, x_{N-S}), \ x_{N-S} = x_{N-S}(N - S, x_S). \tag{18.101}$$

Equilibrium conditions (18.94) are satisfied if, and only if, the following relations are satisfied:

$$p(X) + p_X(X)x_S = p_S, \ x_S = x_S(p_S) = \sum_{v \in S} x^v(p_S) \tag{18.102}$$

$$p(X) + p_X(X)x_{N-S} = p_{N-S}, \ x_{N-S} = x_{N-S}(p_{N-S}) = \sum_{v \in N-S} x^v(p_{N-S}) \tag{18.103}$$

$$X = x_S + x_{N-S} \tag{18.104}$$

Proof Let us first show that there always exists a pair of (x_S, x_{N-S}) for which relations (18.102–4) are satisfied. In order to see this, we define the following set Ω in the m-dimensional Euclid space R^m:

$$\Omega = T_S \times T_{N-S}, \ T_S = \sum_{v \in S} T^v, \ T_{N-S} = \sum_{v \in N-S} T^v.$$

The set Ω thus defined is a non-empty, compact, convex subset of R^n. We define a function $\psi(x_S, x_{N-S})$ defined on Ω in the following manner:

$$\psi(x_S, x_{N-S}) = [x_S(S, x_{N-S}), x_{N-S}(N - S, x_S)], \text{ for all } (x_S, x_{N-S}) \in \Omega.$$

The function $\psi(x_S, x_{N-S})$ is a continuous mapping from Ω onto itself, and Brouwer's fixed-point theorem may be applied to show the existence of a $(x_S, x_{N-S}) \in \Omega$ such that:

$$x_S = x_S(S, x_{N-S}), \ x_{N-S} = x_{N-S}(N - S, x_S). \quad \text{QED}$$

The definition of the value of coalition as introduced above is based upon the standard concept of Nash equilibrium in the theory of n-person cooperative games. However, when it is applied to the case of oligopoly firms with differentiated products, the uniqueness of the value of coalition may not necessarily be ensured. In addition, as with the oligopoly market with a single product, the resulting outcome is not admissible. Namely, there always exists a pattern of outputs of two coalitions, x_S and x_{N-S}, which is feasible and the following inequalities are satisfied:

$$p(X)x_S > p[X(S)]x_S(S), \; p(X)x_{N-S} > p[X(S)]x_{N-S}(S) \qquad (18.105)$$

where $X = x_S + x_{N-S}$.

The existence of a feasible pair of outputs, x_S and x_{N-S}, which satisfy (18.105), may be shown if we note the following property.

We define

$$\pi s(x_S, X) = \max \left\{ \sum_{v \in S} p(X)x^v : x^v \in T^v, (v \in S) \right\}.$$

An argument similar to those leading to Proposition 6 may be applied to show the existence of a function $u(\pi)$ satisfying:

$$u(\pi) > 0, \; u'(\pi) > 0, \text{ for all } \pi > 0$$

such that $u[\pi_S(x_S, X)]$ is a strictly concave function of (x_S, X).

Then, a pair of feasible outputs, x_S^0 and x_{N-S}^0, of two coalitions, S and $N - S$, is admissible if, and only if, there exists a pair of positive numbers (β_S, β_{N-S}) such that:

$$\beta_S u[S(x_S^0, X^0)] + \beta_{N-S} u\{S[N - S(x_{N-S}^0, X^0)]\}$$

$$\geq \beta_S u[\pi_S(x_S, X)] + \beta_{N-S} u[\pi_{N-S}(x_{N-S})]$$

for all feasible pairs of outputs (x_S, x_{N-S}), where:

$$X^0 = x_S^0 + x_{N-S}^0, \; X = x_S + x_{N-S}.$$

Hence, there exists a positive number λ such that:

$$\alpha_S \frac{\partial \pi_S}{\partial x_S} = \alpha_{N-S} \frac{\partial \pi_{N-S}}{\partial x_{N-S}} = \lambda \qquad (18.106)$$

$$-\alpha_S \frac{\partial \pi_S}{\partial X} - \alpha_{N-S} \frac{\partial \pi_{N-S}}{\partial X} = \lambda \tag{18.107}$$

$$X = x_S + x_{N-S} \tag{18.108}$$

where:

$$\alpha_S = \beta_S u'[\pi_S(x_S, X)], \ \alpha_{N-S} = \beta_{N-S} u'[\pi_{N-S}(x_{N-S}, X)].$$

As was the case with the oligopoly market with a single product, the conditions (18.106–8) are necessary conditions for the optimum solution to the following maximum problem:

Find (x_S, x_{N-S}) that maximizes:

$$\alpha_S \pi_S(x_S, X) + \alpha_{N-S} \pi_{N-S}(x_{N-S}, X)$$

subject to the constraint (18.108).

The marginality conditions (18.106–8), however, are not sufficient to the optimality of (x_S, x_{N-S}).

We define that coalition S and its complementary $N - S$ are balanced if:

$$x_S(S) = \theta_S(N)X(S), \ x_{N-S}(S) = \theta_{N-S}(N)X(S) \tag{18.109}$$

where:

$$\theta_S(N) = \frac{x_S(N)}{X(N)}, \ \theta_{N-S}(N) = \frac{x_{N-S}(N)}{\partial X(N)}$$

$$x_S(N) = \sum_{v \in S} x^v(N), \ x_{N-S}(N) = \sum_{v \in N-S} x^v(N)$$

and $x^v(N)$, $X(N)$ are the value of relevant variables at the optimum for maximum problem (N).

The existence of a pair of positive weights (α_S, α_{N-S}) for which condition (18.107) is satisfied is easily established in the manner similar to those for the case of a single product.

The value of coalition S may now be defined as v(S) when coalition S and its complementary $N - S$ are balanced.

The following proposition may be established.

Proposition 8 Let there be n firms, $v = 1, \ldots, n$ with differentiated products, $i = 1, \ldots, m$. The demand-price function and production possibility set for each firm v are given by $p(X)$ and T^v, respectively, where conditions (P1–5) and (T1–5) are satisfied.

The value of the n-person cooperative game $G = [N, v(S)]$ associated with the oligopoly market with differentiated products is defined as the value $v(S)$ of coalition S when coalition S and its complementary $N - S$ are balanced in the sense that equilibrium conditions (18.101), together with the balance conditions (18.109), are satisfied.

Then the optimum solution $(x^1(N), \ldots, x^n(N))$ to maximum problem (N) is in the core of the cooperative game $G = [N, v(S)]$ associated with the oligopoly market.

Proof Proposition 8 is proved exactly in the same manner as for Proposition 4. We consider any coalition $S \subset N$ and denote by $(x^1(S), \ldots, x^n(S))$ the pattern of outputs of n firms on the oligopoly market when coalition S and its complementary $N - S$ are balanced. Then,

$$v(S) = p[X(S)]x_S(S) = \sum_{v \in S} p[X(S)]x^v(S)$$

and relations (18.109) are satisfied.

Let $(x^1(N), \ldots, x^n(N))$ be the optimum solution to maximum problem (N). It may be recalled that relations (18.98–100) hold at $(x^1(N), \ldots, x^n(N))$.

Let us define the following function:

$$\phi_S(t) = p[X(t)]x_S(t),\ 0 \le t \le 1 \tag{18.110}$$

where:

$$x_S(t) = x_S(N) + t[x_S(S) - x_S(N)],\ X(t) = X(N) + t[X(S) - X(N)].$$

Hence:

$$\frac{dx_S(t)}{dt} = x_S(S) - x_S(N),\ \frac{dX(t)}{dt} = X(S) - X(N) \tag{18.111}$$

while the balanced conditions (18.109) imply:

$$x_S(S) - x_S(N) = \theta_S(N)[X(S) - X(N)]. \tag{18.112}$$

Differentiate both sides of (18.112) and note (18.110), to obtain:

$$\phi_S'(t) = p_X[X(t)]x_S(t)[X(S) - X(N)] + p[X(t)][x_S(S) - x_S(N)] \quad (18.113)$$

$$\phi_S''(t) = [X(S) - X(N)]\{p_X[X(t)] + p_{XX}[X(t)]x_S(t)\}[X(S) - X(N)]$$
$$+ [X(t) - X(N)]p_X[X(t)][x_S(N) - x_S(N)]. \quad (18.114)$$

We have, from (18.113) and (18.114), that:

$$\phi_S'(0) = \{p_X[X(N)]X(N) + p[X(N)]\}[x_S(S) - x_S(N)]$$
$$= p(N)[x_S(S) - x_S(N)]. \quad (18.115)$$

Since $x_S(N)$ maximizes of $p(N)x_S$ over all feasible x_S, we have, from (18.115), that:

$$\phi_S'(0) \leq 0. \quad (18.116)$$

On the other hand, equality (18.114), in view of (P3) and (P4), together with (18.112), implies:

$$\phi_S''(t) \leq 0, \text{ for all } 0 \leq t \leq 1. \quad (18.117)$$

Two inequalities (18.116) and (18.117) imply:

$$\phi_S(0) \geq \phi_S(1);$$

that is,

$$p[X(N)]x_S(N) \geq p[X(S)]x_S(S)$$

which may be written as:

$$\sum_{v \in S} \pi^v[x^v(N), X(N)] \geq v(S), \text{ for all coalitions } S \subset N. \quad (18.118)$$

By definition, relations (18.118) mean that the pattern of outputs $(x^1(N), \ldots, x^n(N))$ is in the core of the n-person cooperative game associated with the oligopoly market.   QED

REFERENCES

Bain, J.S. (1949), 'A note on pricing in monopoly and oligopoly', *American Economic Review* **39**, 448–64.

Bowley, A.L. (1924), *The Mathematical Groundwork of Economics*, Oxford: Oxford University Press.

Chamberlin, E.H. (1956), *The Theory of Monopolistic Competition*, Cambridge, MA: Harvard University Press.

Cournot, A.A. (1838), *Recherches sur les Principes Mathématiques de la Théorie des Richesses*, Paris: Hachette. Translated by N.T. Bacon, as *Researches into the Mathematical Principles of the Theory of Wealth*, New York: Macmillan, 1929.

Cyert, R.M. and M. de Groot (1970), 'Multiperiod decision models with alternating choice as a solution to the duopoly problem', *Quarterly Journal of Economics*, **84**, 410–29.

Edgeworth, F.Y. (1925), 'The pure theory of monopoly', in *Papers Relating to Political Economy*, **1**, London: Macmillan, 111–42.

Friedman, J.W. (1977), *Oligopoly and the Theory of Games*, New York: North-Holland.

Friedman, J.W. (1982), 'Oligopoly theory', in K.J. Arrow and M.D. Intriligator (eds), *Handbook of Mathematical Economics*, **II**, Amsterdam: Elsevier Science B.V., 491–534.

Friedman, J.W. (1983), *Oligopoly Theory*, New York: Cambridge University Press.

Fudenberg, D. and J. Tirole (1986), *Dynamic Models of Oligopoly*, Chur, Switzerland: Harwood Academic Publishers.

Shapiro, C. (1989), 'Theories of oligopoly behavior', in R. Schmalensee and R.D. Willig (eds), *Handbook of Industrial Organization*, **I**, Amsterdam: Elsevier Science B.V., 329–414.

Sweezy, P.M. (1939), 'Demand under conditions of oligopoly', *Journal of Political Economy*, **47**, 568–73.

Uzawa, H. (1996), 'Lindahl equilibrium and the core of an economy involving public goods', Beijer Institute Discussion Paper Series.

Uzawa, H. (1999), 'Global warming as a cooperative game', *Environmental Economics and Policy Studies*, vol. 2, pp. 1–37.

von Stackelberg, H. (1934), *Marktform und Gleichgewicht (Market Structure and Equality)*, Vienna: Springer.

19. Highlighting the acid rain game

Aart de Zeeuw

1 INTRODUCTION

It was to be expected that Karl-Göran Mäler would start up the research on the acid rain game. As a Swedish professor, he would be aware of Scandinavia's difficult situation. On the one hand, the northern countries still have one of the largest forest densities in Europe but the forests were dying and knowledge was developing that this may be caused by the deposition and by the ambient concentration of sulphur dioxide and nitrogen oxides. On the other hand, Scandinavia could do little about the problem by itself since most of the emissions were generated outside this area. In particular, Scandinavia's downwind position with respect to the United Kingdom and its polluting industry has been very problematic. Mäler's strong motivation for environmental problems is one reason why he was attracted to the acid rain game. In 'The acid rain game II' (1993) he writes that 'it is *imperative* that we can find solutions to the problems of international cooperation in the environmental field in order to secure continued welfare for the European people' (p. 1; italics added). He was also already far beyond the limited view that this is an environmental problem and not an economic problem. The 'substantial reduction in timber supply . . . will affect not only nature conservationists but also everyday man because of the economic consequences in a conventional sense' (p. 1). The other reason why Mäler was attracted to the acid rain game was the intellectual challenge. In 'The acid rain game' (both I, 1989 and II, 1993) he writes:

> [I]t offers a fascinating multitude of intellectual challenges, one being that the information on causes and effects is very uncertain, another being that it concerns the use of a common property resource in a very asymmetric way, a third being that it is about a game with incomplete information and with many players so that problems with incentives compatibility will be at the heart, and finally the parties involved are different nations with no agreed rules of the game. In addition to these challenges, there are of course a multitude of equally challenging empirical problems. ('The Acid Rain Game' p. 231, and 'The Acid Rain Game II' p. 1.)

It was the time of the great leap forward for game theory, and Mäler was convinced that this was a very important development in economic theory.

The purpose of this chapter is to review some of Mäler's work on the acid rain game and to comment on one of the issues that kept bothering him in the course of his thinking about the problem. It will be clear by now what the acid rain game is. Countries are playing a game in the sense that they are emitting sulphur dioxide and nitrogen oxides which are damaging not only the emitting country but also other countries, because winds carry these oxides across borders. The focus is on European countries for two reasons. First, these countries are in close proximity so they inevitably affect one another, although recent studies have shown that pollution is also taken, for example, across the Atlantic. Second, data on the patterns of transboundary pollution are available from the European Monitoring and Evaluation Programme (EMEP) in Oslo and Moscow. The objective of each country is to minimize the costs of both reducing emissions and damage. The valuation of these costs has always been a tough issue. Regarding costs to reduce emissions, studies can make use of the RAINS model of acidification, developed at the International Institute for Applied Systems Analysis (IIASA) in Laxenburg, but there are no estimated damage costs for acid depositions for the whole of Europe. Mäler introduced what he often called 'the heroic assumption' that the current situation is a Nash equilibrium, so that he could equate marginal cost and marginal damage, which in the case of a linear damage function solves the problem.

The papers written by Mäler on the acid rain game have three major strands. First, the game was formulated as a static game. This allowed him to investigate the gains of cooperation, the corresponding allocation of the emission reductions and the institutional set-up to achieve this. Because of imperfect information, mechanisms may also be needed to induce countries to provide reliable and accurate information concerning their valuation of costs. The literature provides these mechanisms in the form of a transfer scheme. Transfers or side-payments are also needed to make the outcomes individually rational for all countries so that they will participate in the cooperation. The first major problem encountered by Mäler was that there was no simultaneous solution for these two mechanisms. The second strand considers two dynamical aspects of the game. It is in fact more accurate to relate the damage to the accumulated depositions of acidifying compounds, which turns the game into a differential (Mäler and de Zeeuw, 1998). Another dynamical aspect game is that decisions at one point in time may affect decisions of other countries later. This aspect is essential in formulating equilibria that support the cooperative outcome when the static game is repeated. Mäler remarks that the folk theorem in the strict sense is not useful for the repeated acid rain game because the minmax solution is minus infinity, but it is useful to refer to trigger strategies that support the cooperative outcome if the discount factor is high enough. Since differential games are also dynamic games, he always wondered whether a similar result could be formulated in that context. This chapter will try to shed some light on that. Finally, the third strand originated from one of the other sources of inspiration for Mäler: the debates between ecologists and economists (Mäler, 1992). Many ecologists argue that there is no scope for economics in the acid rain problem because the analysis must be driven by the concept of critical loads. A critical load is defined as the maximal exposure to a pollutant that an ecological system can adjust to without suffering long-term damage. Management then simply means that acid depositions have to be reduced below the critical load and issues such as cooperation and non-cooperation disappear. Mäler, however, argues that everything remains a trade-off and even if it is best to reduce depositions below the critical load in the long run, cooperation helps in speeding up the adjustment process. Analysing this in the context of a simple differential game implicitly assumes that in the steady state there is a vector of non-negative emission levels in Europe that exactly meets the critical loads but this proves not to be true. However, the differential game with non-negativity constraints is very hard to solve analytically, so it would appear that only advanced numerical techniques, like the ones developed for dynamical industrial organization, can give a solution here.

This chapter reviews some of the highlights in the papers on the acid rain game and tries to shed some light on the scope for trigger strategies in the difference game (which is a differential game in discrete time). Section 2 formulates the acid rain game and Section 3 reviews the main results. Section 4 shows that a general type of folk theorem with trigger strategies in a difference game is not to be expected and Section 5 concludes the chapter.

2   FORMULATIONS OF THE ACID RAIN GAME

The basic model is simply:

$$d = Ae, \tag{19.1}$$

where d is the vector of depositions, e is the vector of emissions and A is the transport matrix. The acid rain game considers only sulfur, but the analysis for nitrogen is, of course, the same. The EMEP model is based on a grid by which Europe is divided into about 700 squares, but for the purpose of the acid rain game this matrix is aggregated into a country-by-country matrix, so that an element a_{ij} of the matrix A denotes the fraction of country j's emissions that is deposited in country i. At the time of the analysis, the Soviet Union and Czechoslovakia still existed and West and East Germany were still separated; Iceland and Luxemburg were left out of the analysis, as their contribution to the acid rain game can be ignored, leaving a dimension of 25 countries.

In the acid rain differential game, the idea is that equation (19.1) describes the steady state and that the depositions should respect the critical load in the steady state. Furthermore, the critical loads are interpreted as the natural assimilation so that the accumulation of pollution is described by:

$$\dot{d}(t) = Ae(t) - c, \; d(0) = d_0, \tag{19.2}$$

where c denotes the vector of critical loads. Equation (19.2) can also be interpreted as the depletion of the buffer stocks against acidification. If the depositions Ae are below the critical loads, then equation (19.2) implies that the buffer stocks are replenished, which is a reasonable assumption as long as no irreversible damage is done, but when the buffer stocks are so far depleted that heavy metals start to be released, this assumption no longer holds. However, equation (19.2) is not intended to model soil acidification precisely but will merely be used as a vehicle to show that if a decision is made to adjust to critical loads, then cooperation still matters. Critical loads are given as grams of sulfur or nitrogen oxide per year per square metre and can differ substantially between regions. For the acid rain game a measure is needed for a country's critical load, which is calculated as the area of the country times the average regional critical load. Note that some of the emissions leave Europe and some of the depositions enter Europe from outside, so that the critical loads have to be adjusted for the net background depositions.

The next step is to formulate the objectives of the countries. One idea, which is employed in the acid rain differential game, is to take simple quadratic functional forms:

$$C_i(e_i) = \tfrac{1}{2}\gamma_i(e_i - \bar{e}_i)^2, \; D_i(d_i) = \tfrac{1}{2}\delta_i d_i^2, \; \gamma_i > 0, \; \delta_i > 0, \tag{19.3}$$

where C denotes the costs of emission reductions and D the damage related to the depositions. The second parameter in the cost function C has to be chosen high enough so that the function is decreasing in the range of analysis. Furthermore, these values are chosen such that countries with lower per capita sulfur emissions have higher marginal emission reduction costs. Note that the parameters γ and δ are effectively one parameter, and that δ/γ also reflects how green the preferences are in that country. In the analysis this parameter is guessed and then varied in order to check the robustness of the results.

Another idea that is employed in the static acid rain game is to guesstimate the quadratic cost functions C on the basis of results from the RAINS project (Amann and Kornai, 1987), although these cost functions have the drawback that they do not include fuel substitution or a switch to fuels with lower sulfur content, and that they assume exogenously given energy demand. The initial situation is assumed to be a Nash equilibrium which yields:

$$-\frac{dC_i}{de_i} = a_{ii}\frac{dD_i}{dd_i}.$$ (19.4)

If the damage functions D are assumed to be linear, so that the marginal damage is constant and independent of the deposition d, then equation (19.4) yields this constant marginal damage as marginal cost of emission reduction divided by a_{ii}. This is in fact revealed preference under the assumption that the current situation is a Nash equilibrium. It also implies that if countries are high on the cost curve C with high marginal cost of emission reduction, then these countries have a high valuation of damage. Note that if the true damage function is convex, the damage will be underestimated. Note also that with constant marginal damage, the choice in one country is independent of what all the other countries choose, so that the Nash equilibrium becomes an equilibrium in dominant strategies.

The static acid rain game is now simply:

$$\min [C_i(e_i) + D_i(d_i)], i = 1, \ldots, n,$$ (19.5)

subject to equation (19.1) with n the number of countries, where C is guesstimated with the help of RAINS, and where D is assumed to be linear and is determined by equation (19.4), characterizing the Nash equilibrium of this game.

The acid rain differential game is now simply:

$$\min \int_0^\infty e^{-rt}\{C_i[e_i(t)] + D_i[d_i(t)]\}dt, i = 1, \ldots n,$$ (19.6)

subject to equation (19.2) with n the number of countries and r the interest rate, where C and D are given by equation (19.3).

The transport matrix A, as we stated above, resulted from aggregation of the EMEP data. In the static acid rain game the EMEP Report 1/86 by Lehmhaus et al. (1986) was used, and in the acid rain differential game, the later EMEP Report 1/92. The critical loads were transformed (as we described above) from regional to national ones, based on the data in the RIVM report by Downing et al. (1993).

3   RESULTS FROM THE ACID RAIN GAME

The first thing Mäler investigated was the gains of cooperation in the static acid rain game, by comparing the Nash equilibrium (by assumption the current situation: 1984) with the full-cooperative solution, which results from minimizing the sum of the objectives (19.5) subject to equation (19.1). The calculations show that total emissions in Europe would be reduced by about 40 percent, as compared with the current situation, with a total net benefit of 6248 million D-marks. Almost all countries would gain from the full-cooperative solution except, in order of total loss, for the United Kingdom (substantial), Italy (moderate), Spain (small) and Finland (negligible). It is clear that the United Kingdom, in particular, would have no incentive to cooperate in reducing sulfur emissions in Europe, unless side-payments were possible in some form and were made to the UK. This is in line with what is observed in practice. These transfers are not necessarily financial but can be in the form of different services such as access to resources, trade privileges or military concessions. The results are not very sensitive to changes in the cost functions C (which is to be expected since, due to the revealed preference approach, the damage functions D change too), but the transport matrix A is essential for the results.

Another interesting result was that the average reduction would be about 40 percent and the allocation of reductions would be very uneven, ranging rom 2 to 86 percent. This was in sharp contrast with the '30% club', the first international agreement on the reduction of acid rain that proposed even reductions of 30 percent. Mäler showed that the total net benefit of a uniform reduction of 30 percent in all countries is only about one-third of what could be the case in the full-cooperative solution, and that a uniform reduction of 40 percent in all countries is even worse. It is clear that asymmetries are at the heart of the problem and that efficiency requires that efforts must be spread unevenly. Whether this is considered fair or not is another matter and must be treated in another way. Similarly, the conclusion above that side-payments must be made to countries like the United Kingdom in order to induce them to participate in cooperation can also be questioned from principles of fairness. The victim pays principle is at work rather than the polluter pays principle (PPP) and most people would favour the latter on ethical grounds. However, the PPP cannot be enforced in the international context and in that case it is important to investigate which institutions can help to create economically efficient solutions. One reason for uneven allocation of emission reductions is that cost and damages differ in the European countries: some soils are more vulnerable than others; some countries have made more effort in the past than others, resulting in higher marginal reduction costs because they moved higher up the cost curve C. Other reasons are related to the location of the countries: some are more downwind and others are more upwind; some are more central and others are more at the periphery of Europe.

Mäler was the first one to stress that the numbers should not be taken too seriously but that their main purpose is to illustrate and motivate the theoretical concepts of game theory. However, the general picture is quite clear and it is useful to think about institutions which can generate the full-cooperative solution. Three kind of schemes suggest themselves: agreements on emission reductions and financial transfers, a tax on the export of sulfur and a European market for emission permits. In the case of a tax, Mäler suggested the following institutional set-up: (i) establish a European Acidification Fund that would manage the agreement, redistribute the tax revenues and monitor the emissions; (ii) agree on a transport model for sulfur; (iii) decide on a scheme for the redistribution of proceeds from the tax; and (iv) negotiate the tax rate. The advantage is that steps (ii) and (iii) have to be negotiated only once. If new information comes in or if aspirations change, only step (iv) has to be renegotiated. The ideal tax would have to be equal to the marginal damage a country creates in other countries, but this would be very difficult to implement. Mäler, therefore, tried a second-best approach with the same tax on the export of sulfur for all countries. This also increases the chance of being accepted because it incorporates an idea of fairness. Note that this does not imply a uniform tax on emissions, because the fraction of total emissions that a country exports, varies. In the static acid rain game, Mäler tried a tax of 4 D-marks per kg of sulfur and he reached the surprising result that this tax gives a solution which is very close to the full-cooperative solution. The total net benefit of 6213 million D-marks is almost the same and the total emission reduction is only about 3 percent lower. The distribution of emission reductions and net benefits is also approximately the same. It seems that it is possible to design an institution which is not very complicated but almost yields the full-cooperative solution and in addition to that, has dynamic efficiency properties in the sense of stimulating the development of cleaner technology.

In 'The acid rain game II' (Mäler, 1993), many results in game theory were reviewed to see if they could be relevant for the acid rain game. The fact that, in principle, each country can be damaged by the other countries as much as they want by increasing their emissions, makes many of the results in cooperative game theory less relevant. This also applies to the folk theorem in the strict sense when the static acid rain game is repeated, because the minmax solution is minus infinity, but it is useful to note that the discounted net benefits in the full-cooperative solution can be supported by a non-cooperative equilibrium in trigger strategies, if the discount factor is high enough. It is shown in Friedman (1986) that such an equilibrium in trigger strategies exists if and only if:

$$\alpha \geq \frac{NB_i^{ch} - NB_i^{co}}{NB_i^{ch} - NB_i^{na}}, \text{ for all } i = 1, \ldots n, \tag{19.7}$$

where α is the discount factor and NB denotes net benefits, *ch* denotes cheating, *co* denotes the full-cooperative solution and *na* denotes Nash equilibrium in the static game. The proof is simply that it does not pay to cheat on the full-cooperative solution for any country, because the trigger strategies prescribe that the other countries will switch to their Nash equilibrium emissions in all the following games (so that the country under consideration is also best off by switching to its Nash equilibrium emission), and rewriting inequality (19.7) yields:

$$NB_i^{ch} + \frac{\alpha}{1-\alpha} NB_i^{na} \le \frac{1}{1-\alpha} NB_i^{co}. \tag{19.8}$$

The discount factor has to be high enough in order to at least offset the gains of cheating by the future losses of switching from the full-cooperative solution to the Nash equilibrium. This idea can be extended to more sophisticated punishment strategies, shorter periods of punishment, and finite horizons with bounded rationality or incomplete information. The important conclusion is that, by including the time dimension, the incentive problems of the static acid rain game will to a large extent disappear. The last issue is the availability of information. The Nash equilibrium concept is built on the idea that the countries have full information and can calculate the strategies of the other countries, but this is a very strong assumption. However, the analysis of the static acid rain game above does not have this requirement because of the assumption that marginal damage is constant, which turns the Nash equilibrium into an equilibrium in dominant strategies. A more serious problem may be that the calculation of the full-cooperative solution requires information on the cost and damage functions that have to be provided by the countries themselves, but the countries have strong incentives to overstate this information. The literature (for example, Green and Laffont, 1979) provides revelation mechanisms, such as the Groves mechanism, where transfer functions are designed which make truth-telling an optimal strategy for a country. Remember, however, that transfers were also needed to induce some countries to participate in the cooperation or, to put it differently, to make the full-cooperative solution individually rational for all countries. If the European Acidification Fund has full control over the emission vector e, it can design a scheme which makes it beneficial for the countries to reveal their true valuations, and if the European Acidification Fund has perfect information on the costs and damages, it can design an incentive and transfer scheme which makes it profitable for the countries to follow the full-cooperative solution. However, it is more complicated to solve the problems in one scheme.

The analysis of the acid rain differential game stemmed from the discussion on the critical loads. A critical load can be defined as the level of pollution below which no physical damage occurs, but this does not mean that depositions have